"Monumental."—*Choice*

"Truly amazing."—*Musical Traditions*

"A stunning work of curation and scholarship. . . . Whether you're a music-maker or just a listener, reader, and thinker, there's a surprise on every track and every page."
—*Huffington Post*

"So comprehensively detailed and thoroughly vetted that it would be hard to see where one would have a complaint about this magnificent volume. . . . It should serve as a standard text for understanding folklore in this region." —*ARSC Journal*, Association for Recorded Sound Collections

"A treasure. . . . Leary's deep knowledge of the subject matter is demonstrated by thought-provoking facts placing the dance tunes, ballads, lyrics songs, hymns, political anthems, and more in historical context." —*Library Journal*

"A priceless compendium, a fascinating work for anyone interested in the deeper streams of Americana, American ethnic culture and the history of the Upper Midwest."
—*Milwaukee Shepherd Express*

"Attains the highest standards of folklore studies. . . . A landmark presentation of traditional music of the Upper Midwest." —*Journal of Folklore Research*

"Groundbreaking. . . . Renders accessible and familiar the varied music traditions of the region's multiple ethnic groups, presented in prose both luminous and graceful." —*Journal of American Folklore*

"The cultural gifts of immigrants are amply demonstrated. . . . An exceptional achievement that demonstrates for the first time the full worth and cultural wealth of the Upper Midwest for music listeners." —*Deutschlandradio Kultur*

"[A] landmark project. . . . Leary challenges the ways that scholarship in folk music often neglects the depth and breadth of music in the Midwest." —*Western Folklore*

"Tremendously valuable to students of ethnicity, labor, and local and regional history. . . . A rich and complex portrait of a region." —*Michigan Historical Review*

"The United States just got bigger. . . . This set, so astounding in its exhumation of sounds many of us were only distantly aware of, is like nothing else on this earth." —*Old Time Herald*

"Breathtaking. . . . Demonstrates research and scholarship of the highest quality that paints a complex and evocative picture of racial and ethnic elements too long disregarded in the study of American music." —*Minnesota History*

"A priceless soundscape experience of another America." —*Blogfoolk: Storie e Visioni sulle Strade del Folk*

"A staggering set of diasporic folklore. . . . Constructed so that as you listen, there's a continual unveiling: each disc moves across continents, as with the Sidney Robertson recordings, which leap from French Canadian songs to Finnish melodies. But the crux is the Helene Stratman-Thomas recordings that make up the final two discs, where moving, disarmed performances like Martha Steinbach's 'An einem Fluss daraus an Schuss,' rub against gorgeous Dutch melodies, dirty lumberjack songs, and wild Welsh melancholy." —*Uncut*

"An important history and ethnography . . . vividly brings to life a full picture of the musical traditions of the Upper Midwest." —*Notes: Quarterly Journal of the Music Library Association*

"The modest title doesn't really prepare you for the wonders to be found once you open this amazing work of scholarship. . . . An abundant and intriguing American melting pot, whose diversity has remained largely unknown to the rest of the nation—and the world." —*Songlines*

"A significant achievement in the rich story of American folk song and tune collection. . . . A multimedia scholarly production of prodigious breadth and monumental significance to ethnic and folkloric studies." —*Journal of Finnish Studies*

"Encyclopedic and thoroughly exhaustive and astonishing. . . . These are songs sung by lumberjacks, performed at country dances, sung out in the fields; songs sung in twenty-five languages, capturing the diversity of Wisconsin culture." —*On Wisconsin*

"Wisconsin, Minnesota, Michigan, and parts of Canada comprised an informal laboratory for . . . musical cross-pollination. . . . Emphasizes the dizzying diversity of the region, where immigrants from all over the world settled." —*The Bluegrass Situation*

"Un document extraordinaire." —*Metamkine*

"A colossus of a book." —*Folkemusikk*

FOLKSONGS OF ANOTHER AMERICA

Languages and Folklore of the Upper Midwest

Joseph Salmons and James P. Leary, Series Editors

Published in collaboration with the Center for the Study of Upper
Midwestern Cultures at the University of Wisconsin–Madison

Folksongs of Another America:
Field Recordings from the Upper Midwest, 1937–1946
James P. Leary

The Tamburitza Tradition:
From the Balkans to the American Midwest
Richard March

Wisconsin Talk:
Linguistic Diversity in the Badger State
Edited by Thomas Purnell, Eric Raimy, and Joseph Salmons

Yooper Talk: Dialect as Identity in Michigan's Upper Peninsula
Kathryn A. Remlinger

Pinery Boys: Songs and Songcatching in the Lumberjack Era
Edited by Franz Rickaby with Gretchen Dykstra and James P. Leary

FOLKSONGS OF ANOTHER AMERICA

FIELD RECORDINGS FROM THE UPPER MIDWEST, 1937 1946

JAMES P. LEARY

The University of Wisconsin Press

The audio and video files that accompanied the hardcover edition are now accessible and downloadable through the University of Wisconsin Digital Collections website (http://digital.library.wisc.edu/1711.dl/fsoaa)

Originally published in collaboration with the American Folklife Center at the Library of Congress and the Association for Cultural Equity/Alan Lomax Archive

The hardcover edition was published with generous support from the Brittingham
Trust, the University of Wisconsin–Graduate School with funding from the
Wisconsin Alumni Research Foundation, the University of Wisconsin–Madison
Department of Scandinavian Studies' Birgit Baldwin professorship, the Finlandia
Foundation, and the National Endowment for the Humanities.

The University of Wisconsin Press

1930 Monroe Street, 3rd Floor
Madison, Wisconsin 53711-2059
uwpress.wisc.edu

3 Henrietta Street, Covent Garden
London WC2E 8LU, United Kingdom
eurospanbookstore.com

Printed in the United States of America

Names: Leary, James P., 1950–, author.
Title: Folksongs of another America: field recordings from the Upper Midwest, 1937–1946 / James P.
    Leary.
Other titles: Languages and folklore of the Upper Midwest
Description: First paperback edition. | Madison, Wisconsin: The University of Wisconsin Press, [2018] |
    Series: Languages and folklore of the Upper Midwest | "Originally published in collaboration with the
    American Folklife Center at the Library of Congress and the Association for Cultural Equity/Alan
    Lomax Archive."
Identifiers: LCCN 2018002646 | ISBN 9780299301545 (pbk. alk. paper)
Subjects: LCSH: Cowell, Sidney Robertson, 1903–1995. | Lomax, Alan, 1915–2002. | Stratman-
    Thomas, Helene, 1896–1973. | Archive of American Folk Song. | Folk songs—Middle West—History
    and criticism. | Folk music—Middle West—History and criticism.
Classification: LCC ML3551 .L35 2018 | DDC 782.4216200977—dc23
LC record available at https://lccn.loc.gov/2018002646

In memory of my parents,
Patricia Berigan Leary (1925–1992)
and Warren Leary Jr. (1922–2009)

And for Janet, Bella, and Finn,
who endured and sometimes even encouraged
my mania to see this whole unruly thing through

CONTENTS

TRACK LIST

CD1
PIGTOWN FLING
THE SIDNEY ROBERTSON
RECORDINGS

French Canadian

1   Leizime Brusoe *Fisher's Hornpipe*

2   Leizime Brusoe *Pigtown Fling*

3   Leizime Brusoe *Lancer's in Five Parts*

Lumberjacks and Farmers

4   Robert Walker *Lost Jimmie Whalen*

5   Warde Ford *Little Brown Bulls*

6   Warde Ford *Crandon*

7   Warde Ford and Art Ford
    I'd Rather Be a Nigger than a Poor White Man

8   Charles Spencer
    Mighty Adley-ca-budley-fatley-ca-ham-shaw

9   Charles Spencer *Locks and Bolts*

10 Clyde Spencer and Harry Fannin
    The Sinking of the Titanic

Scots Gaelic

11 John H. Matheson
    A Mhàiri bhàn òg / O Fair Mary

12 John H. Matheson
    *Stocainnean daoimean /
    Diamond-Patterned Socks*

13 John H. Matheson
    Eilean Leòdhais / Isle of Lewis

14 John H. Matheson
    *Gabhaidh sinn a' rathad mòr /
    We Will Take the High Road*

Serbian

15 The Balkan Troubadours (Dan
    Radakovich, Nick Mitrovich, Lubo
    Mitrovich, Bob Rajacich, and
    George Rajacich)
    Alaj Gigi

16 The Balkan Troubadours (Dan
    Radakovich, Nick Mitrovich, Lubo
    Mitrovich, Bob Rajacich, and
    George Rajacich)
    *Angelina vodu lije / Angelina
    Is Pouring Water*

Finnish

17 Cecilia Kuitunen *Charm for Hiccups*

18 Anna Leino *Charm for Toothache*

19 Olga Simi and Sue Simi *Pium, paum*

20 Matti Simi and Sue Simi
    Vilho ja Pertta / Vilho and Bertta

21 Matti Perala
    Heramäen pukki / Old Man's Goat

22 Josefiina Perala *Kataja / The Juniper*

23 Otto Sarkipato
    *Lähtetään pojat nyt soutelemaan /
    Boys, Let's Go Rowing*

24 Otto Sarkipato
    Keskellä lahtea / In the Middle of the Bay

25 Maria Heino
    *Laurilan Aleksin harmoonipeli /
    Laurila Aleksi's Accordion*

26 Maria Heino
    *Ei kukaan puhu puolestani /
    No One Speaks on My Behalf*

27 Maria Heino
    *Eikä ne haavan lehdet lakkaa /
    Never Cease the Aspen Leaves*

28 Maria Heino *Istuta, tyttö / Plant, O Girl*

CD2
THE RIVER IN THE PINES
THE WISCONSIN LUMBERJACKS
RECORDINGS

1   Earl Schwartztrauber and Ray Calkins
    Fred Sargent's Shanty Song

These files are now available at http://digital.library.wisc.edu/1711.dl/fsoaa

These files are now available at http://digital.library.wisc.edu/1711.dl/fsoaa

Lumberjacks

11 Bill McBride *No Sir*

12 Bert Graham *Joe Williams*

13 Unidentified man *Torch Lake*

14 Lester Wells *Traverse City*

15 Nils Larsen *Yulia and Olaf*

16 Lester Wells *Long Barney*

17 Adolphus Delmas *Hayfoot, Strawfoot*

18 Ed Thrasher *Shoot the Cat*

Lithuanian

19 Charles Ketvirtis *Russian Gigue*

20 Charles Ketvirtis *Buffalo Gals*

21 Charles Ketvirtis *Mother Song*

German

22 Herman Meyers
*Was war an diesem Baum? /
What's on This Tree?*

Polish

23 Edwina Lewandowski and
Stephanie Lewandowski
Chodźcie gąski moje / Come My Little Geese

24 Felix Kania *Wedding March*

25 Tony Strzelecki and possibly Tony Wasylk
Irish Washerwoman

26 Tony Strzelecki *Polish Polka*

27 Adolph Romel and Sylvester Romel
W żelaznej fabryce / In the Steel Mill

28 Tony Strzelecki and possibly Tony Wasylk
Turkey in the Straw

29 Felix Kania
*Czerwono posiadło, a zielono
zniszło / Red When It Was Planted,
Green When It Bloomed*

30 Edwina Lewandowski and Stephanie
Lewandowski
Goldmine in the Sky

Finnish

31 Yalmer Forster
Kulkurin valssi / Vagabond Waltz

32 Amanda Härkönen
*Kaurapellon pientareella kasvoi
kaunis kukka / On the Side of an Oat
Field Grew a Beautiful Flower*

33 Aapo Juhani *Juliana*

34 Henry Mahoski *Kauhavan Polka*

35 Selma Elona Halinen
*Pikkulintu erämaassa lauleleepi suruissana /
A Little Bird in the Desert Sings Sadly*

36 Frank Maki
Meripojan laulu / Sailor's Song

37 Amanda Härkönen
*Oli mulla ennen punaset posket /
I Used to Have Red Cheeks*

38 Kalle Kallio
*Kuule sinä Hiltu kun laulelen /
Listen Hiltu When I Am Singing*

39 Wäinö Hirvelä *Kylläpä kai / I Guess So*

40 Kusti Similä
*Yli kymmenen vuotta Korpiinissa oli jo
asuttu / Ten Years We've Lived in Corbin*

41 Lillian Aho
*Oi Herra, jos mä matkamies maan /
Oh Lord, if I, a Wanderer of the Earth*

42 Pekka Aho and Lillian Aho
*Mun kanteleeni kauniimmin / My
Kantele Will Sound More Beautiful*

43 Emil Maki
*Suun kloorin kloorin halleluuja! /
Oh Glory, Glory Hallelujah!*

DVD
ALAN LOMAX GOES NORTH
"THE MOST FERTILE SOURCE"

The Wisconsin Lumberjacks: From Rice Lake
and Ladysmith

In August and September 1938, Folklorist
Alan Lomax Traveled Michigan Recording "a
Thousand Songs" for the Library of Congress

Serbs: Detroit Area

Croatians: Copper Country (The Floriani
Tamburitza Group)

These files are now available at http://digital.library.wisc.edu/1711.dl/fsoaa

French Canadians: Baraga

Finns: Upper Peninsula

"Enough Material for Years of Work"

CD4
WHEN THE DANCE IS OVER
THE HELENE STRATMAN-THOMAS
RECORDINGS, PART ONE

Ho-Chunk
1   Stella Stacy and Henry
    Thunder *Flute Song*

2   Winslow White Eagle *War Dance*

Oneida
3   Wallace Smith and Albert Webster
    Tsyatkatho

Pan-Indian
4   Margaret "Laughing Eyes" Edaakie
    (Eagle) and Phyllis Lewis
    49 Song

French Canadian
5   Leizime Brusoe, Robert McClain,
    Walter Wyss, and Emery Olsen
    Good for the Tongue

6   Ernest Joseph Belisle
    *Je ne veux pas d'un avocat /
    I Do Not Want a Lawyer*

7   Charles Cardinal
    *How They Sang the Marseillaise
    in Chippytown Falls*

8   Mary Agnes Starr *Michaud*

9   Marie Donalda Lagrandeur
    Bonsoir, mes amis / Good Night, My Friends

Belgian (Walloon)
10 Alfred Vandertie *I Went to Market*

11 Alfred Vandertie
    *C'est l'café / It's the Coffee
    [the Kermiss Song]*

12 Emile Boulanger *Dance Tune*

Cornish
13 John Persons *Cornish Story*

Welsh
14 William Reese and Selina Phillips
    Cawn esgyn o'r / Paradise

15 Dr. Daniel W. Wickham *My Welsh Relation*

16 Hugh P. Jones *Y mochyn du / The Black Pig*

17 John Williams and chorus
    Siani bach / Dearest Sian

African American
18 Lillie Greene Richmond *Hide Thou Me*

19 Lillie Greene Richmond
    Little Old Log Cabin in the Lane

20 Lillie Greene Richmond *One More River*

Anglo-American
21 Preston Willis *Chase the Buffalo*

22 Hamilton Lobdell *Barker's Call*

23 Pearl Jacobs Borusky
    My Old Hen's a Good Old Hen

24 Pearl Jacobs Borusky
    Last Saturday Night I Entered a House

25 Charles Dietz *Did You Ever See the Devil?*

26 Charles Dietz
    Three Dishes and Six Questions

Lumberjack and Irish American
27 Emery DeNoyer *Snow Deer*

28 Emery DeNoyer *Shantyman's Life*

29 Emery DeNoyer *Irish Jubilee*

30 John Muench with Ralph Weide
    Irish Washerwoman

31 Noble Brown
    *Oh, It's Nine Years Ago I Was
    Diggin' in the Land*

32 Robert Walker
    McNamar' from County Clare

33 Charles Robinson *Fond du Lac Jail*

34 Lewis Winfield Moody *Alphabet Song*

35 Bill Neupert *Red Light Saloon*

Polish

Lithuanian

Finnish

Swedish

Danish

Norwegian

Icelandic

BUCKHORN BEGINNINGS

A PREFACE

It all began for me in the early 1950s in the Buckhorn, in Rice Lake, Wisconsin. It was summer, and Art McGrath—my dad's best man, college pal, fellow combat veteran—had come north from Indiana to see Warren Leary in his hometown. The two set out for a drive, a hike in the woods, and a beer. Rather than leave my mom at home with four mischievous kids under age six, Dad took my older brother and me along. Our final destination was—as touted in its promotional brochure—"The Friendly Buckhorn," a bar and café on Rice Lake's Main Street famed for its Display of Curios. While Art and Dad secured barstools, sipped Breunig's Lager, and swapped stories, Mike and I, clutching bottles of pop, roamed the checkered floor and gaped.

Mounted heads of moose, bear, and deer, whole wild cats, weasels, birds of prey, and fish festooned the walls, mingled with fantastic mutant creatures: the owl-eyed ripple skipper, the fur fish, the dingbat, the shovel-tailed snow snake. There was a slot machine, a thick pockmarked, bulletproof windshield from Al Capone's car, and best of all, occupying an entire wall, "the world's largest assortment of odd lumberjack musical instruments": guitars, mandolins, and fiddles fashioned from cheese and cigar boxes, an elongated tin trumpet, a steel triangle, a bowed saw, a single-string bass fiddle cobbled from a shovel handle and a flour bin, a pitchfork fitted-out similarly, and more. "Otto Rindlisbacher and some of those old lumberjacks made 'em," Dad explained, sweeping his hand toward the bald proprietor and a handful of wool-clad old-timers along the bar.

My visits thereafter were few and fleeting until the mid-1960s when, employed by the weekly *Rice Lake Chronotype*, I delivered bundled newspapers to a throng of Buckhorn patrons. The instruments were still there, and I learned from my dad's sister— Katherine Leary Antenne, "Aunt Kay"—that Otto played them all and had even made records for the Library of Congress in Washington, D.C. What's more, while attending that city's Trinity College, she had seen him perform with the Wisconsin Lumberjacks at the National Folk Festival of 1938. Too young and shy to approach Otto and ask

TOP: A dingbat on display at the Buckhorn, Rice Lake, Wisconsin, ca. 1950. (postcard, author's collection)
BOTTOM: Otto Rindlisbacher with the "World's Largest Collection of 'Odd Lumberjack Musical Instruments,' at Rice Lake, Wisconsin," ca. 1950. (postcard, author's collection, courtesy of Lois Rindlisbacher Albrecht)

him to play, I finally heard his music around 1968 when, prowling Rice Lake's Carnegie Library in search of folksong records, I came across a plainly packaged LP produced by the Recording Laboratory of the Library of Congress, Music Division: *Folk Music from Wisconsin*. Inside were four tunes from Otto, a fifth from his wife, Iva, and rich notes cheaply offered in a stapled typescript. From it I learned that someone named Helene Stratman-Thomas had traveled Wisconsin in the 1940s recording performers for the Library of Congress.

As a young folklorist in the mid-1970s, I was lucky to work for the Smithsonian Institution's summer-long bicentennial Festival of American Folklife. The Library of Congress beckoned. On a day off, I visited its Archive of Folk Song for the first of many times. Aided by archivist Joe Hickerson, I discovered the broad scope of Stratman-Thomas's Wisconsin recordings, that Rindlisbacher had not only recorded for her but also for Sidney Robertson and Alan Lomax, and that the Upper Midwestern work of all three—from 1937 to 1946—was interconnected.

From the 1980s through the mid-1990s, as a folklorist working in my home region, I happened onto the fieldwork trails of Robertson, Lomax, and Stratman-Thomas with increasing regularity. In 1981 an octogenarian retired streetcar conductor and piano accordionist in Ironwood, Michigan, John Shawbitz, remembered "some guy from Washington" recording Slovenian tunes from him in the 1930s. Elsewhere in Michigan, the daughters of Exilia and Mose Bellaire recalled their teenage excitement when good-looking Alan Lomax recorded mother, dad, and assorted French neighbors in their Baraga home. In 1989 Ed Kania and the brothers Jake and Joe Strzelecki had similar recollections of their fathers recording for Lomax in Posen, where Sylvester Romel, the lone survivor of a singing family, wept as he listened to and sang along with a duet performed fifty-one years earlier with his late brother. In Wisconsin, Lois Rindlisbacher Albrecht told me about her parents' preparation for the 1937 National Folk Festival, where Sidney Robertson recorded them. She and Al Mueller described how, three years later, Stratman-Thomas captured Swiss tunes from them, while Ken Funmaker Sr. and Olwen Morgan Welk offered childhood recollections of their respective Ho-Chunk and Welsh elders being recorded by Stratman-Thomas in the 1940s. And Al Vandertie was still singing Walloon songs when I met him at a Belgian Days parade in 1990. Bit by bit, I began to wonder about the lives, experiences, songs, and tunes of other Upper Midwesterners documented on discs in the 1930s and 1940s.

Mr. Lumberjack Goes to Washington

A BANGALO, made from a washtub and a lumberjack's peavey, an Irish bull fiddle and a squeeze box will be among the 40 musical instruments dating from the logging camp days which will be taken to Washington, D. C., by four northern Wisconsin men when they leave for the national folk festival Apr. 21. The men, billed as The Lumberjacks, are (left to right) Otto Rindlisbacher, Rice Lake; Frank Uchytil, Haugen, and Earl Schwartztrauber and Ray Calkins, Ladysmith.

"Mr. Lumberjack Goes to Washington," photograph and caption regarding the Wisconsin Lumberjacks, *Rice Lake Chronotype*, May 1938. (author's collection)

My curiosity concerning bygone regional field recordings was shared. In the 1970s, seeking source materials, playwright Dave Peterson, director of the Wisconsin Idea Theater at the UW–Madison, allied with the UW's Mills Music Library to secure reel-to-reel copies of Upper Midwestern field recordings from the Library of Congress. In the early 1980s, Judy Woodward (now Judy Rose) of Wisconsin Public Radio's *Simply Folk* set to work on a thirteen-part series, *The Wisconsin Patchwork*, highlighting selections

John Shawbitz (with piano accordion and two-tone shoes) shares the stage with Bill Koskela, North Country Folk Festival, Ironwood, Michigan, 1981. (photo by author)

from the Stratman-Thomas recordings. Having consulted on that project, I was hired by Peterson to write commentaries on each installment, resulting in a booklet published in combination with cassette reissues of the radio series (Leary 1987). Gradually, foolishly, I began to imagine the current project, still only dimly aware of the challenges of restoring sound on deteriorating discs, deciphering songs in more than two dozen languages, tracking down biographies of hundreds of scarcely documented performers, and determining the often murky provenance of as many songs and tunes. Rather than tediously recount the twisty path from there to here, I salute the many institutions and individuals without whose support and expertise *Folksongs of Another America* would never have emerged.

Incremental research happened along the way amid contract work for many organizations and with their particular staff members, including the Michigan Traditional Arts Program (Kurt Dewhurst, Marsha MacDowell, Luanne Kozma, Yvonne Lockwood, and especially Laurie Sommers), Northland College (Marina Herman), the Smithsonian Institution (Tom Vennum), the Wisconsin Arts Board (Richard March), and the Wisconsin Folk Museum (Phil Martin). This project was supported specifically by grants from the Finlandia Foundation, the National Endowment for the Humanities, and the Graduate School of the University of Wisconsin. My home department, Scandinavian Studies, generously provided a research assistant, as well as research funds through a two-year Birgit Baldwin Professorship.

Since the 1980s the extraordinary librarians of University of Wisconsin's Mills Music Library (Matt Appleby, Arne Arneson, Jeanette Casey, Tom Caw, Geri Laudati, Mary Prochniak, John Solon, and Steve Sundell) have offered steadfast support in countless ways, especially with access to correspondence, field notes, and song and tune notes in the Helene Stratman-Thomas Collection. The staff of the American Folklife Center at the Library of Congress has been equally remarkable, especially Judith Gray, Nancy Groce, Todd Harvey, Joe Hickerson, Cathy Kerst, Nicki Saylor, Guha Shankar, and Stephen Winick. Pioneering work by Kerst and Saylor contributed immeasurably to the Sidney Robertson sections, as did access to correspondence and field notes in the Resettlement Administration section of the Sidney Robertson Cowell Collection; as curator of the library's Alan Lomax Collection, Harvey kindly shared countless essential, otherwise inaccessible documents, including correspondence and field notes; and Shankar masterfully restored Lomax's 1938 color silent-film footage, then edited and coproduced the finished film included here. Brad McCoy, stellar audio engineer for the Library of Congress's Motion Picture, Broadcasting, and Recorded Sound Division (in the Recorded Sound Reference Center), transferred the library's original disc recordings, many of them deteriorating, into digital format. Jim Miksche undertook basic sound restoration and equalization of the resulting digital files, while Nathan Salsburg and Michael Graves completed final sound editing for the CD masters.

Nathan Salsburg, Don Fleming, and Anna Lomax Wood of the Association for Cultural Equity, which oversees the dissemination of Alan Lomax's astonishing field recordings, persuaded me at the start to think about this project as an ambitious multimedia production. The University of Wisconsin Press has been terrific in every phase, including the acquisition process, fund-raising, editing, design, production, and marketing. Special thanks to Andrea Christofferson, Matthew Cosby, Terry Emmrich, Raphael Kadushin, Sheila Leary, and Adam Mehring. Kip Lornell and Hank Sapoznik provided the press with helpful outside evaluations when this project was in proposal stage. Joyce Hakala painstakingly proofread the manuscript before it went to the press, and eagle-eyed copyeditors Gail Schmitt and Adam Mehring eliminated further errors and inconsistencies. Lance and April Ledbetter of Dust-to-Digital invested the final production with their visionary design skills and entrepreneurial savvy. Bill Malone read the field notes of fellow Texan Alan Lomax to accompany the film footage. And Bella Leary drew upon images and titles for the CDs and film to create a series of striking prints and accompanying lettering in the style of nineteenth-century broadsides.

Hilary Virtanen helped track down elusive biographies and descendants for Finnish performers in Michigan, while Joyce Hakala generously permitted me to draw on her extensive research into Finnish performers in Minnesota. David Natvig tirelessly

Lillian Aho Aukee's daughters, Maria Brunet and Carol Bocskay, with David Brunet, Finn Fest, Hancock, Michigan, June 2013. (photo by author)

sought contact information for next of kin. Scores of descendants provided biographical information, reminiscences, photographs, permissions, and more. They include Lois Rindlisbacher Albrecht, Janet Albosta, Colleen Birt, Carol Bocskay, Maria Brunet, John Cadeau, Virginia Cloud Carrington, Gail Cywinski, Helen Davis, Jim Floriani, Corey Fredrickson, Judy Grumstrup, William Hirvela, Leo Holmberg, Ron Jestila, Doug Karttunen, Patti Ketvirtis, Karen McBride King, George King, Bill Larson, Henry Mahoski Jr., April Miller, Evelyn Palosaari, Stevan Raicevich, Hanna Raskin, Donald St. Angelo, Charlie Spencer, Jake Strzelecki, Joe Strzelecki, Priscilla Bellaire Tahtinen, and Jim Uchytil. I ask forgiveness of any whose names I have unintentionally neglected.

Paul Gifford, LeRoy Larson, and Paul Tyler each drew upon their unmatched familiarity with the Upper Midwest's traditional tunes to identify melodies that were otherwise mysterious. Most of all, I am grateful to the linguistically gifted transcribers, translators, and annotators of songs in so many languages: Austrian (Rudi Pietsch), Belgian/Walloon French (Francoise Lempereur), Croatian (Richard March,

Vedran Mehinovic), Czech (Joe Grim Feinberg, Tereza Smejkalová), French Canadian (Anjili Babbar, Sylvain Gaillard, Florence Théroud), Danish (William Banks), Dutch (Jolanda Vanderwal Taylor), Finnish (Pertti Antonen, Tom DuBois, Tim Frandy, Joyce Hakala, Jaana Isohätälä, Jukka Karjalainen, Susanna Linna Moliski, Juha Niemela, Lotte Tarka, Arttu Tolonen, Hilary Virtanen, Simo Westerholm), German (Antje Petty), Icelandic (Dick Ringler), Italian (Luisa Del Giudice), Irish (Brian Ó Broin, Kevin Conroy, Dineen Grow), Lithuanian (Tom DuBois, Vita Ivanauskaite-Šeibutiene, Debra Raver, Guntis Smidchens, Aurelija Tamosiunaite), Norwegian (Odd Lovoll, Anna Rue), Polish (Tim Cooley, Marcin Gąsienica-Byrcyn, Lina Michalewicz, Robert Rothstein, Max Statkiewicz), Scots Gaelic (Tom McKean), Serbian (Stephanie Vuljanic-Lemke, Richard March), Swedish (Paul F. Anderson, Susan Brantly), and Welsh (Maria Teresa Agozzino, Gwenan Puw, Stephen Williams).

Janet Gilmore, my wife and fellow folklorist, cheerfully, patiently tolerated my never-ending folksong obsessions, as did our far-flung children, Bella and Finn. I beg their continued indulgence, because I'm getting older and am unlikely to change.

PREFACE TO THE PAPERBACK EDITION

The original publication of *Folksongs of Another America* (FSOAA) ambitiously combined a hardbound book, five compact discs, and a DVD in an elegant yet bulky single package weighing nearly four pounds. The years of research, writing, sound and film restoration, and overall production underlying its existence were matched by hard-won one-time subsidies bringing retail costs within an average buyer's reach. The response was exhilarating: stellar reviews from far and wide, awards that included a Grammy nomination, events in Minnesota and Wisconsin featuring new performances of old songs culled from FSOAA, and a sold-out press run before a year elapsed. But with neither copies in the warehouse nor sufficient funds in the coffers, we faced the sad prospect of FSOAA's disappearance just as interest was building.

This paperback edition is our best solution. Far trimmer in heft and price than its predecessor, it swaps the costly inclusion of discs for their free online access. Thanks to a partnership between the University of Wisconsin Press and the University of Wisconsin Libraries, sound files for each of the five original CDs—as well as the film *Alan Lomax Goes North*, coproduced with the American Folklife Center at the Library of Congress—are now accessible and downloadable through the University of Wisconsin Digital Collections (http://digital.library.wisc.edu/1711.dl/fsoaa).

This parallel website overlaps with and complements related sites further revealing the complexity and diversity of the Upper Midwest's folk/vernacular musical traditions. FSOAA necessarily focused on a small yet representative set of songs, tunes, and recitations. Selected tracks were sonically restored, accompanied by transcribed lyrics along with English translations when warranted, and augmented by new contextual, biographical, and comparative background. Yet the raw sound and spare documentation for hundreds of additional field recordings made by Sidney Robertson, Alan Lomax, and Helene Stratman-Thomas from 1937 to 1946 offer still more to discover, ponder, and pursue.

The Wisconsin Folksong Collection, 1937–1946 (http://digital.library.wisc. edu/1711.dl/WiscFolkSong), produced by the University of Wisconsin's Mills Music Library and Digital Collections Center, combines field recordings made by Robertson and Stratman-Thomas. The Library of Congress's *Alan Lomax Collection of Michigan and Wisconsin Recordings* (https://www.loc.gov/collections/alan-lomax-in-michigan /about-this-collection/) offers sound recordings from 1938 "in their raw form, as full disc sides without speed correction or other digital processing." In addition, the University of Wisconsin's Mills Music Library, Center for the Study of Upper Midwestern Cultures, and Digital Collections Center, with support from the National Endowment for the Humanities, have launched *Local Centers/Global Sounds: Historic Recordings and Midwestern Musical Vernaculars* (http://digital.library.wisc.edu/1711.dl/LocalCenters), a site combining post–World War II home and field recordings featuring diverse Upper Midwestern folk/vernacular musicians with early twentieth century 78 rpm recordings performed by or influencing regional musicians.

We encourage readers to roam these sites. In the realm of 78s especially, many will be familiar with widely available classic recordings made in the 1920s by performers in the "Race" and "Hillbilly" series of American record labels. Yet we cannot fully grasp the richness of American roots music without experiencing, for example, such stellar Upper Midwestern Germanic, Nordic, and Slavic "Foreign" series performers as the Swedish comic vaudevillian Olle i Skratthult, the Norwegian Hardanger fiddler Gunleik Smedal, the Finnish accordion virtuoso Viola Turpeinen, the singing Polish mountaineer Karol Stoch, the trumpet-playing Bohemian bandleader Romy Gosz, or the German concertinist Hans "Whoopee John" Wilfahrt.

Beyond making connections with online resources, this new edition presents a chance to make corrections. The daunting task of publishing lyrics and translations for songs in more than two dozen languages resulted in a few errors. Vedran Mehinovic and Robert A. Rothstein kindly provided corrections for Croatian and Polish songs, respectively, and appropriate changes have been made. Stephen Winick of the American Folklife Center gently informed me that, despite Joseph Carriere's claim to composing "the biggest part," his rendition of "Pretty Polly" (pages 119–121) was actually a standard version of "The Cruel Ship's Carpenter," a British ballad widely sung throughout North America.

My relentless fascination with "Scandihoovian" dialect humor also revealed that "Yulia and Olaf" (pages 130–133), for which I previously lacked an original source, was a version of "Gude Faller," composed by William F. Kirk (1877–1927) and published in his *The Norsk Nightingale* (1905), a "little volume of Scandinavian dialect verses" dedicated to "the residents of Northern Wisconsin and Minnesota, where the 'lumberyack' lives and thrives." Born in Mankato, Minnesota, Kirk grew up in Chippewa Falls, Wisconsin, a logging town with Norwegian lumberjacks aplenty—and several of his verses entered oral tradition.

Finally, hats off to Dennis Lloyd, director of the University of Wisconsin Press, and Ed Van Gemert, vice provost for libraries and university librarian, for supporting side-by-side Press paperback and Library website.

The songs and tunes figuring in *Folksongs of Another America* had been hidden for too long to let them vanish once again. May their persistence spur new understandings and performances, along with ongoing recognition and appreciation of the many peoples, tongues, and sounds that—whether past or present, from mainstream or from margin, deservedly acknowledged or unjustly ignored—have always made America great.

Print by Isabella Leary

FOLKSONGS OF ANOTHER AMERICA

AN INTRODUCTION

Particularly in the Lake Superior area of northern Michigan, Wisconsin, and Minnesota
. . . traditions are so mixed that no narrow specialist approach can hope to reveal their
breadth. (Dorson 1947: 48)

Folklorist Richard Dorson's astute observation—as true in the twenty-first century as it
was in the mid-twentieth—has proven prophetic regarding the full range of the Upper
Midwest's folksongs. Trained at Harvard University in American Civilization and con-
versant with folk traditions in the East, the South, and the West, Dorson was nonetheless ill-prepared, astonished, and inspired upon venturing into the Upper Midwest in
1946. During extended fieldwork in Michigan's Upper Peninsula, he documented the
oral traditions of "Ojibwa, Potawatomi, and Sioux Indians"; of "Finns, Swedes, Poles,
Germans, Italians"; of Irish, French, and English; and of "Luxemburgers, Slovenians,
and Lithuanians," all toiling variously as "farmers, lumberjacks, copper and iron miners,
fishermen, sailors, railroaders, bartenders," maids, cooks, and more. In the aftermath, he
proclaimed "the abundance and diversity of the oral traditions I found still stagger me"
([1952] 2008: 1). Having thoroughly traversed Michigan's U.P., Dorson ranged briefly
into Wisconsin and learned enough about northern Minnesota to recognize their kindred polyglot, egalitarian, working-class frontier ferment.

The Upper Midwest was not the America of New England villages, New York ten-
ements, Pennsylvania Dutch farms, Appalachian hollows, Southern cotton plantations,
or Western plains celebrated by folklorists and familiar to the nation. Here was a territory of deep woods, inland seas, mines, mills, and hardscrabble farms; a place wherein
Native peoples, native-born, and newcomers jostled, jangled, and intermingled to forge
Another America.

Toiling in a pre-tape-recorder era and fluent only in English, Dorson relied on interpreters, his own good ear, and a nimble pencil to set down stories while neglecting folksongs and tunes altogether. Fortuitously, unbeknown to Dorson, a trio of like-minded folklorists had already been roaming the Upper Midwest for a decade—each equipped with a heavy disc-cutting machine, spare needles, scores of blank records, and a bulky microphone—to capture the region's full span of folksongs in English and otherwise. From 1937 to 1946, Sidney Robertson, Alan Lomax, and Helene Stratman-Thomas, with federal support from the Archive of American Folk Song at the Library of Congress, recorded nearly two thousand traditional performances in more than twenty-five languages from representative musicians and singers in Michigan, Minnesota, and Wisconsin.

Recorded in kitchens and parlors, churches and dance halls, the discs made by Robertson, Lomax, and Stratman-Thomas spanned dance tunes, ballads, lyric songs, hymns, laments, political anthems, street cries, recitations, and more. Many were sonic fragments of lost worlds: a Missouri-born ex-slave's comic commemoration of Noah's ark; an Icelandic mother-daughter duet concerning a Christian knight enticed by cliff-dwelling elves; an exuberant calling of the clans by a Scots Gaelic émigré. Others featured dramatic adaptations of esoteric indigenous and Old World repertoires for then contemporary public events: a Ho-Chunk warrior song repurposed for summer tourists; a Finnish lullaby arranged for the stage of a workers cooperative hall; a Norwegian one-stringed solo church instrument cast into a quartet to offer secular tunes for multiethnic culture shows. Some were well-known nineteenth-century patriotic songs reinvigorated from afar with twentieth-century despair and rage as invading fascists occupied Lithuania, the Netherlands, and Norway. Still others addressed new circumstances through witty or poignant makeovers of familiar genres: an Italian sojourner's paean to America's grandeur; an impoverished Polish immigrant's lament for a family whose passage to America he can never pay; a former Czech soldier's song transposed to Prairie du Chien, Wisconsin. A handful included scurrilous or bawdy ditties previously ignored or censored by genteel folklorists: a Finn's versified lashing of cheating merchants; a lumberjack's rasty condemnation of biscuits that "would make an ox fart"; an alphabet song commencing with "Oh A is for asshole." And there were startling mash-ups of languages, genres, and cultures: Ojibwe hand-drum songs rendered on fiddle; a Finnish sailor's homesick lyric sharing its tune with the cowboy song "When the Work's All Done This Fall"; "The Irish Washerwoman" played on accordion by Germans chanting square-dance calls in English; a Quebecois mixed-language ditty about a bumpkin's misadventures in Michigan. Songbooks, radio, and 78 rpm recordings in many languages likewise circulated throughout the region, with lyrics and melodies added to those learned from oral tradition alone: a ballad sung verbatim from a Danish folk-school songbook; a version of "Gambler's Blues" acquired from a Paramount 78 cut in Grafton, Wisconsin; Gene Autry's "Gold Mine in the Sky" harmonized by Polish sisters who had heard his broadcasts over Chicago's WLS *National Barn Dance*.

America's Upper Midwest emerges from these field recordings as a distinctive American region wherein, from the nineteenth century through the 1940s, a remarkable array of American Indian, Anglo-American, African American, and especially non-Anglo-European peoples maintained, modified, borrowed, merged, and composed songs and tunes from their respective and frequently shared folksong traditions. Critically, these performances were captured in all their variety and complexity at a significant historical moment: when America was in the throes of the Great Depression, World War II was erupting, media- and market-driven mass culture was developing as a national force, and concerns with who and what was "American" were rife.

Yet despite the efforts of Sidney Robertson, Alan Lomax, and Helene Stratman-Thomas—none of whom were the "narrow specialists" of Dorson's admonition—the depth and breadth of the Upper Midwest's folksong traditions, so complex and "so mixed," have remained elusive and almost forgotten. The numerous linguistic and cultural traditions documented through field recordings defied their individual and collective reach. More regrettably, because of reservations regarding cultural pluralism that, until recently, have dominated America's government, academy, and popular culture, the trio's subsequent books and record albums emphasized English-language performances exclusively—as if the majority of the songs they recorded simply did not exist. No Upper Midwestern indigenous or "foreign" language songs figure, for example, in Alan Lomax's *Our Singing Country* (1941) or in his still-in-print *The Folk Songs of North America* (1960), which is considered canonical. Only English-language songs appear in the documentary recordings produced, respectively, by Robertson and Stratman-Thomas: *Wolf River Songs* (1955) and *Folk Music from Wisconsin* (1960 [2001]). Stratman-Thomas tried but failed to find a publisher for her manuscript representing the full span of Wisconsin's folk musical traditions. Yet her anthology that focused exclusively on English-language material, *Folksongs Out of Wisconsin* (1977), was published posthumously. As the curator of the Archive of American Folk Song, Joseph Hickerson, pointed out in a 1976 symposium, *Ethnic Recordings in America: A Neglected Heritage*: "On the federal level, there was some reluctance at first to publicize the recordings of foreign language singers in the United States. Congressional philosophy was not strongly pluralistic, and the melting-pot persuasion was prevalent" (1982: 77).

Hence *Folksongs of Another America* is a redemptive countercultural project recalling and honoring the efforts of Robertson, Lomax, and Stratman-Thomas while illuminating the nearly but not quite lost singers and dancers, songs and tunes, individuals and communities characterizing America's Upper Midwest in the mid-twentieth century. Looking at and listening to the full extent of this region's vibrant songs and tunes effectively challenges and considerably broadens our understanding of folk music in American culture.

THREE SONGCATCHERS' STORIES

Sidney Robertson, Alan Lomax, and Helene Stratman-Thomas—despite quite different backgrounds—were each fortuitously qualified and positioned for field recording in the culturally diverse rural, industrialized backwoods, and working-class urban communities characterizing the Upper Midwest.

Sidney Robertson, as she was known in 1937, was born Sidney William Hawkins in San Francisco in 1903, the daughter of Charles Albert Hawkins and Mabel Morrison Hawkins. The family was well-to-do, and as a youngster Sidney had "piano, violin, dancing, and elocution lessons," as well as "French tutors, riding and polo lessons, children's cooking classes, and more" (Kerst 2007). She spent summers in Europe from age ten through fourteen, earned a degree in romance languages from Stanford in 1924, and that year married a philosophy student, Kenneth Robertson. The couple lived subsequently in France and Switzerland, where Sidney studied with the composer-pianist Alfred Cortot at the École Normale du Musique in Paris, then assisted her husband with translations in Zurich as the psychiatrist Carl Jung held forth. Upon their return to California in 1926, Robertson taught at the Peninsula School for Creative Education in Menlo Park until 1932. During that period she also studied at the San Francisco Conservatory of Music, acquiring an introduction to "the music of non-European cultures" from the avant-garde composer Henry Cowell, whom she would later marry in 1941 (Kerst 2007; see also Stone 2009).

Sidney Robertson Cowell copying recordings for the Library of Congress, Berkeley, California, 1939. (courtesy of the Archive of Folk Culture/American Folklife Center, Library of Congress)

While a student at Berkeley, Cowell had been influenced by Charles Seeger, a founder of the field of ethnomusicology and the patriarch of a prominent family dedicated to American folk music. Similarly compelled, Robertson incorporated transcriptions of cowboy songs collected by John Lomax into Peninsula School classes, delighting her students. Her pedagogical shift from classical to folk music at the onset of the Great Depression contributed to her growing dissatisfaction with a life of privilege. Divorcing her husband in 1934, she moved to the Lower East Side of New York City, where Lillian Wald—a nurse, suffragette, peace activist, and founding member of the NAACP—had established the Henry Street Settlement School, which catered to immigrant and working-class youngsters. Robertson became the director of the school's Social Music Program in 1935, the very year that Charles Seeger was appointed head of the Music Unit within the Resettlement Administration's Special Skills Division. Based in Washington, D.C., as part of President Franklin Roosevelt's New Deal, the Resettlement Administration was concerned with the well-being of displaced farmers and migratory workers, and it was Seeger's firm conviction that musical traditions sustained the human spirit. In 1936 Robertson's attraction to folk music led her to visit the fledgling Archive of American Folk Song at the Library of Congress, whereupon she was referred to Seeger, who immediately recruited her. That summer she gained valuable experience with newly developed portable sound-recording equipment that used acetate discs with an aluminum base. Seeking out traditional performers in Arkansas, Tennessee, and Virginia, she also assisted veteran songcatchers Frank C. Brown and John Lomax on a field recording trip through North Carolina.

Dismayed by what she regarded as Lomax's patronizing attitude toward singers and Brown's antiquarian disregard for any but the oldest songs, Robertson combined an outgoing egalitarianism with a commitment to recording—as her like-minded boss Charles Seeger put it—"EVERYthing. . . . Don't select, don't omit, don't concentrate on any single style. We know so little! Record everything!" (Filene 2000: 142). Having proven her mettle, Robertson became the Special Skills Division's Midwest representative in 1937, while also assisting the Farm Security Administration with resettled communities in Michigan, Wisconsin, and Minnesota. In April 1937 she ranged across northern Wisconsin and Minnesota laying the groundwork for summer field recordings. In May, during the National Folk Festival in Chicago, she went considerably beyond the prior Anglo- and African American preoccupations of American folksong collectors by recording those groups along with Finnish, Lithuanian, Polish, Swedish, and Winnebago (Ho-Chunk) performers, as well as the Wisconsin Lumberjacks, whose repertoire intermingled French Canadian, Scandinavian, and Swiss traditions. Thereafter Robertson followed up on spring contacts by recording many more lumber camp performers in northern Wisconsin, while focusing on Finnish, Scots Gaelic, and Serbian singers in Minnesota.

Robertson's correspondence from the era—housed in the Resettlement Administration sections of her papers at the Library of Congress—illuminates an adept, witty, and daring fieldworker at a time when single women seldom ventured through the hinterlands unaccompanied. In a report to her Washington superiors regarding April 25–28 activities, she observed: "This is a rough country, three saloons ('taverns') to every block on each side of the street, and at small cross-roads villages there is usually a store, a gas station, two houses and two taverns. I went into three taverns on the main street in Rhinelander, in the morning, at Mr. Sorden's suggestion, looking for a miniature carved logging-camp some tavern-keeper owned; and I swear, I was a marked character the rest of the day—I've never been so stared at, nor so suggestively appraised, anywhere in the world—wherever I went—and by the toughest-looking characters—I swear my Lower East Side gang couldn't touch 'em. I wouldn't have been so surprised if these men had actually just emerged from a winter's work in the deep forests, but the woods are logged out now, the few small camps aren't remote at all—and Rhinelander is a town of 8 or 9 thousand, with a complete assortment of the female of the species parading up and down the street" (Robertson 1936–1938).

Her 1937 letters, brimming with savvy comments about performers, likewise reveal her debt to an established network of folksong-finding veterans. A newcomer to the region, with limited time and resources, she relied heavily on the advice and contacts of Sarah Gertrude Knott, Marjorie Edgar, and L. G. Sorden. Her profiles of performers— as well as her relationships with Knott, the founder of the National Folk Festival, with Edgar, an authority on immigrant folksongs in Minnesota, and with Sorden, a northern Wisconsin county agent steeped in lumberjack lore—inform and adorn the track notes for the Robertson and Wisconsin Lumberjacks CDs.

Robertson's job with the Resettlement Administration ended in late summer 1937. Thanks to her accomplishments for and contacts in the federal government, she then headed the California Folk Music Project in her home territory for the Works Progress Administration in 1938, resulting in recordings from 185 performers in twelve languages. This remarkable work became part of the Library of Congress's online American Memory project in 1997: *California Gold: Northern California Folk Music from the Thirties* (http://memory.loc.gov/ammem/afcchtml/cowhome.html, accessed January 10, 2014). In summer 1938, however, at the outset of her California fieldwork, Robertson wrote to Alan Lomax—assistant in charge of the Archive of American Folk Song since June 1937—championing the Upper Midwest's rich folksong field recording possibilities, listing scholars who might assist, and sketching the worth and whereabouts of key performers. Yet her generosity ("go to Michigan, Wis., and Minn. with my blessing") was tempered with wistfulness in a letter from San Francisco on July 14, 1938: "I had rather in the back of my mind a scheme for abandoning California after six months or a year and repeating the set-up as a state project in Wisconsin. . . . I'm green with envy, you must know! I love the Iron Range country in Minn., but Wis. simply has my heart."

By the time of Robertson's letter, as we know thanks to the Alan Lomax Collection at the American Folklife Center, Lomax had secured $965 through the efforts of Harold

Spivacke—the chief of the Division of Music at the Library of Congress—for a trip "to the Lake States—Michigan, Wisconsin, and Minnesota—for a period of two months to record folk songs for the Archive" (A. Lomax 1938: Memorandum, Spivacke to the Librarian of Congress, June 9, 1938). Heeding Robertson's counsel, Lomax dispatched letters to the region's few folksong scholars, commencing with a standard opening: "The Archive of American Folk Song is planning for this summer a rapid recording survey of folk music in Michigan, Wisconsin, and Minnesota. This work is to be done by a modern field recording machine, with the idea of getting down in the most accurate fashion the folk tunes and the folk styles of the region, for preservation and scholarly study." Tailoring each message to the recipient's specific expertise, Lomax offered a larger vision for the archive to Theodore Blegen, the director of the Minnesota Historical Society: "Someday we hope to be able to supply the needs in terms of records to any student of American folk song and to exchange our collections with the great archives of Europe" (A. Lomax 1938: June 29, 1938).

Although only twenty-three, Alan Lomax (1915–2002) was on his way to becoming an award-winning writer, radio producer, and filmmaker, as well as the most able and famous folksong collector of the twentieth century. Lauded appropriately as *The Man Who Recorded the World* by his biographer, John Szwed (2010), Lomax "discovered" or popularized such icons of American roots music as Lead Belly, Jelly Roll Morton, Aunt Molly Jackson, Woody Guthrie, and Muddy Waters. His astonishing field recordings from the United States, the Caribbean, and Europe have been issued on hundreds of LPs and CDs, form a distinct collection at the Library of Congress, and are nowadays increasingly accessible to all through a visionary organization he founded, the Association for Cultural Equity (http://www.culturalequity.org, accessed January 10, 2014).

Raised in Texas, the son of John Lomax—a renowned ballad scholar whose classic study, *Cowboy Songs and Other Frontier Ballads*, had been published in 1910 with a foreword by President Theodore Roosevelt—Alan had been educated, like his father, at the University of Texas and at Harvard. In contrast to the elder Lomax's social conservatism, however, seventeen-year-old Alan—already exposed to, fascinated with, and moved by the songs and plight of Southern blacks and Appalachian miners—was very much a free-thinking radical when he set out on his first folksong recording trip in summer 1933. John Lomax had acquired modest funds from the Library of Congress, and

> Alan Lomax, ca. 1940. (courtesy of the Association for Cultural Equity)

that June father and son embarked on a song quest for the fledgling Archive of American Folk Song that extended from Texas through Louisiana, Mississippi, Tennessee, and Kentucky. Acquiring an Ediphone cylinder recorder and "a Model A Ford with its back-seat removed," the Lomaxes "traveled light: nothing but a few changes of clothes, two army cots, bedding, and camping gear" (Szwed 2010: 35).

By the time Alan Lomax entered Michigan on July 31, 1938, intent on trekking through the "Lake States," he was a seasoned veteran of field recording trips throughout the American South, in New York City, along the Ohio River valley, and in Haiti (Averill 2011; Cohen 2011; Szwed 2010). Aided by Sidney Robertson's advice and apprised of prior folksong work, he had prepared for his jaunt by reading the available sources on the region's ethnic communities, pinpointing their whereabouts on a road map, and—as he explained in an August 11 letter from Detroit to Harold Spivacke at the Library of Congress—contacting potential helpers: "Professor I. H. Walton of the University of Michigan has made a very important collection of Lake Ballads and Lake chanteys. He has agreed to work with me in the field. I have letters of introduction to various collectors of Lumberjack material all over the state and a number of Cornish, Polish, Bohemian, Finnish and French Canadian mining and frontier communities upstate" (Cohen 2011: 96). Thanks to Ivan Walton and Earl C. Beck, a professor at Central Michigan whose fieldwork would eventually result in *Songs of the Michigan Lumberjacks* (1942), Lomax had little trouble recording superb English-language singers from Lower Michigan, especially on Beaver Island, where Walton had worked extensively, and from old-timers who formed the Michigan Lumberjacks troupe organized by Beck for the National Folk Festival (Harvey 2013; Sommers 1996). His successes in the Upper Peninsula and with performers in languages other than English, however, testify to his own resourceful energy coupled with an unfettered commitment to the region's many voices.

Those voices and Lomax's keen observations enliven notes accompanying the Lomax CD and film. Although hardly systematic at chronicling either fieldwork experiences or the biographies of performers, he adeptly interjected pithy comments or prompted pointed conversations amid recording, while occasionally elaborating on a singer, a song, or a situation in letters, in his field notebooks, or even on the paper sleeves of recorded discs. His 1938 Michigan field notebooks especially reveal a relentless field researcher jotting phrases, names, and networks, especially when roaming the Upper Peninsula on his own. Some names resulted in recording sessions, others proved elusive, and there were always more singers than even the most tireless fieldworker could meet.

Among them:

Nuppo [?] Erickson, Swede—mouth organ

The Bosley's, Sault St. Marie—a musical family—Frank, Sr. (violin) + Frank, Jr. (guitar)

Camp Marquette—turn off the rd from Newberry to Sault near Emerson [?] North—
Government CCC camp—known as the Indian camp [fiddlers and step dancers]

Harve Dillett, Tower, MI, great lumberjack singer, ref. Charles Thayer

Bert Letz, Negro (gone South/barroom singer) Munising, MI

Charley Kitchelmeyer [Kitchelsmeyer?], in the Jungle, Munising (has to be drunk to
sing—off of drinking because out of a job)

Esther something at the radio station with guitar and singing Finnish songs

old Finn dances—Sulo's Schoolhouse—also at Worker's Hall in Hancock—Edna Raudier
runs the rowdiest place in town for the lumberjacks on 5th street—she's very agree-
able—Karl Pohjala—upstairs over the Vienna Bakery, guitar + songs

French Contacts

George Denn, Ishpeming

Mrs. Monville, Baraga + Ont. [Ontanogan?] Rd

By October 14, after seventy-six consecutive days of fieldwork, some of them prolonged
by his discovery that "songs in Mich. absolutely require beer," Lomax was low on funds,
beset with car problems, and short on blank discs. What's more, as he confided in a
postcard from Ironwood, Michigan, to his Library of Congress boss, "I'm tired as hell
and ready to come home" (A. Lomax 1938: postcards to Harold Spivacke, September 7
and October 15, 1938). Except for a brief session across the border in Wisconsin, where

he recorded the Ojibwe fiddler Joe Cloud on the Bad River Reservation, Alan Lomax's tristate "rapid recording survey" was over. And although it came up short geographically, it exponentially expanded the cultural territory of the Archive of American Folk Song.

In the late summer and fall of 1938, as he later reported to the Librarian of Congress, Lomax recorded "about a thousand songs, lumberjack, lake sailor, Irish, Southern Negro, Finnish, Serbian, Polish, Canadian French, German, Hungarian, and Croatian" in Michigan, while acknowledging that there was "more material than I had time to record" (A. Lomax 1939: 220–221). Exclaiming in a 1938 letter to his superiors in Washington, D.C., that the Upper Midwest might be "the most interesting country I have ever traveled in," Lomax requested that he be sent there again the following summer (Cohen 2011: 100). Once back at the Archive of American Folk Song, however, Lomax became increasingly involved with radio productions related to federal programs and America's growing involvement in World War II. Yet the Upper Midwest's unrecorded folksong riches remained on his mind.

On July 18, 1940, Lomax wrote to Leland Coon, chair of the School of Music at the University of Wisconsin, echoing Sidney Robertson to urge folksong fieldwork throughout the state. Recommending the advice of Robertson, along with Beck and Walton, his Michigan lumberjack and lake songs specialists, Lomax also invoked Charles E. Brown, an archeologist and folklore aficionado at the State Historical Society of Wisconsin who had assisted the National Folk Festival, and Frances Densmore, an ethnomusicologist who had made cylinder recordings of Menominee, Ojibwe, and Winnebago (Ho-Chunk) singers in Wisconsin for the Smithsonian Institution's Bureau of American Ethnology: "My suggestion is that you obtain from Dr. Brown, Frances Densmore, Dr. E. C. Beck of Mt. Pleasant, Michigan, Dr. Ivan Walton of the University of Michigan and others, a highly selected list of folk music informers in Wisconsin" (Leary 1998: 18, 26–27).

Offering to "send the recording machine and the discs" on "two weeks' notice," Lomax continued with precise advice regarding travel, recording techniques, and potential public programs.

Map out an itinerary of two thousand miles (5 cents a mile) of twenty days duration at $5.00 a day and send your technician over this carefully planned route. Informants should be notified and prepared in advance so that the recorder may record already rehearsed performances in the briefest time possible. The material should be selected,

1. From the point of authenticity of the performers, and 2. Upon the point of view of the greatest variety. At the end of twenty days, if you have a good field worker, you should have at least fifty or perhaps a hundred fine records of Wisconsin Folk Music—a sampling of the rich variety to be found in your state. This body of records can, more than anything else, make a case for the necessity of Folk Song work in the states. Lectures, demonstrations, and radio transcriptions can be based on this group of records and I should think that such a program of demonstration propaganda should guarantee the continuance of work under more favorable circumstances next year. (Cohen 2011: 171–172)

Confessing "I have very few contacts in the state of Wisconsin," Lomax was only able to recommend performers previously recorded by Sidney Robertson, but he ventured that "a group of fifty records from Wisconsin should include, (a) Lumberjack songs, (b) Lake sailor songs, (c) Anglo-American songs and ballads, (d) Fiddle tunes and game songs, (e) Vulgar ballads and songs, (f) Finnish songs, (g) French-Canadian songs, (h) Norwegian songs, (i) Swedish songs, (j) Icelandic songs from Washington Island" (Cohen 2011: 172).

Provided with instruction, incentive, and the promise of equipment, but no money, Leland Coon secured sufficient funding from the UW Graduate School's Research Committee to send two people on a summer field trip. One was Robert F. Draves, a graduate-student tympanist from Oconomowoc who had begun an electrical engineering major before switching to music and becoming the School of Music's recording technician. The other was Helene Stratman-Thomas, an instructor in voice and music theory who also directed the Women's Chorus and managed the Pro Arte Quartet (*Wisconsin State Journal*, July 13, 1941). With Stratman-Thomas managing the overall effort and Draves tending the equipment, the pair traveled throughout Wisconsin in the summers of 1940 and 1941. Draves left for the military at the onset of World War II, and further constrained by wartime gasoline and tire restrictions, Stratman-Thomas postponed a final field trip until summer 1946, when she was assisted by another student-technician, Aubrey Snyder. Altogether the Stratman-Thomas-led trips captured more than seven hundred performances, including all of the groups prescribed by Lomax, as well as African Americans, Austrians, Belgians, Cornish, Croatians, Czechs, Danes, Dutch, Germans, Ho-Chunks, Irish, Italians, Lithuanians, Luxemburgers, Norwegians, Oneidas, Poles, Swiss, Welsh, and more.

Helene Stratman-Thomas (1896–1973) was born in Dodgeville, a mining and farming community in southwest Wisconsin. Her mother, Helena Emma Stratman (b. 1862), was the daughter of Frederick and Anna Stratman, natives of Cronenberg in the Rhineland-Palatinate district. The elder Stratmans immigrated with a wave of fellow Germans in 1853, traveling down the Ohio River, then up the Mississippi to Galena, Illinois, before becoming permanent residents of Dodgeville, where they raised a large family and Frederick, a blacksmith, established a carriage- and wagon-making business. Stratman-Thomas's father, Warren H. Thomas (1854–1930), was raised on a farm in McHenry, Illinois, just south of the Wisconsin border, by parents of Cornish heritage. Perhaps the abundant presence of Cornish lead miners in southwestern Wisconsin drew him to Dodgeville, where he ran a grocery store. The Stratman-Thomas extended family was fond of music, and young Helene, an able singer and pianist, heard songs aplenty from German and Cornish relatives and neighbors while growing up, as well as Welsh hymns from the area's Primitive Methodist congregations. After high school, she earned teaching credentials from Platteville Normal School, taught in several small Wisconsin towns, including the heavily Swiss community of Monticello, earned a business degree from the University of Wisconsin in 1919, and worked eight years for a Minneapolis investment firm. Yearning for a change, she returned to the University of Wisconsin to complete her BA in music as well as MA degrees in music and education. Hired as an instructor by the School of Music in 1930, she also served as the director of music for the campus area Methodist and Presbyterian churches and was a soprano soloist for the University and Madison Civic Choruses (*Capital Times*, January 12, 1973).

Far more a folk-music novice than Lomax or Robertson, the energetic and efficient Stratman-Thomas had the decided advantage of living where she did her fieldwork. Over the course of three summers, she ably combined hometown experiences, familiarity with Wisconsin, networks of acquaintances, and organizational skills with frequent talks, radio appearances, and newspaper features to discover hundreds of performers. Beginning with her own contacts—singing Welsh neighbors from Dodgeville and a Swiss zither player from just north of Monticello—she dutifully heeded Lomax's instructions to follow up on Robertson's contacts, seek out Icelandic singers, and record songs aplenty from lumberjacks. In summer 1940, equally mindful of Lomax's admonition that a twenty-day trip of two thousand miles should yield "at least fifty or perhaps a hundred fine records," Stratman-Thomas and Draves took only a fortnight to cover 2,300 miles and produce 105 records.

Helene Stratman-Thomas with traditional singer Harry Dyer, a former logger and Mississippi riverboat hand, University of Wisconsin campus, Madison, 1941. (Wisconsin Historical Society, WHi-25183)

The duo's impressive pace was attributable in part to Stratman-Thomas's breakneck careening on country roads. When interviewed by Judy Woodward for Wisconsin Public Radio in 1983, Draves estimated that "the average speed was seventy miles an hour" (June 27). Like Lomax, Stratman-Thomas pushed herself and her vehicle, as she revealed in her journal at the end of summer 1941: "Throughout the summer we were working against time as Bob was leaving for military service. We had hope that the little one-seated Ford in which we had traveled would hold out until the end of the trip. Bravely it did so until a short distance from Spring Green where, weary with traveling Wisconsin highways and byways, a back tire blew out and fell off, and we found ourselves finishing the trip on the rim" (Stratman-Thomas 1940–1960). Yet even the most daring and wily road racer could hardly have managed what Stratman-Thomas did without a deeply affectionate understanding of songs and singers. As Draves attested forty years later: "She was a very loveable person; a warm person who could become very interested in you."

In May 1941, as Stratman-Thomas was planning for her second summer foray, Alan Lomax sent Leland Coon this equivocal assessment of the first 105 discs shipped to the Archive of American Folk Song.

I've just finished listening to the Wisconsin records for the first time. Some I like very much and others seem to be wasted acetate. The lumberjack material is uniformly interesting and certainly folky, even if the people are old. Mrs. Borousky [Borusky] is very fine. Mr. Rousseau [Brusoe] is one of the best country fiddlers I've ever heard. A repeat visit should result in more records. Why don't you try to get at this sometime. French-Canadian tradition at the north of the state is pretty sure to be oral in character. Out of all the foreign records, I felt that only the Icelandic and possibly the Swiss-zither records were worth making from the folklorist's point of view. Singing to the accompaniment of the piano and from a book and written source by cultured voices is not the subject of study for which the Archive was started or set up. It's almost always possible to find persons in any sizable community no matter how prosperous who have received their songs by word of mouth and without interference from learned sources, from traditional folk song informants. These people almost universally sing in the folk fashion and therefore have interesting and important musical ideas to contribute to the record.

He closed with a request followed by words of apology, praise, and encouragement: "There is one item in the collection that I'd particularly like to have and that is the full version of 'Red Light Saloon' which I'd heard only in part. Please do not feel that this letter is in any wise cantankerous or captious. Your trip may be regarded as very fruitful and you have a rich future of collecting before you" (Cohen 2011: 220).

We do not know what Stratman-Thomas thought of these comments. Jalmar Nukala of Superior certainly did deliver a high-toned transformation of a Finnish lullaby while his wife played piano (Stratman-Thomas CD part 2, track 34). Yet Robertson, in tune with Charles Seeger's instruction to "record everything," would have sympathized. Likewise it's hard to dispute the "folk fashion" or style of "foreign records" made in summer 1940 featuring the Belgian tavern keeper Alfred Vandertie (part 1, track 11), the Welsh song leader John Williams (part 1, track 17), the Elias Tamburitzans (part 2, track 21), or the Czech brass players' vocal chorus for "Švestková alej" (part 2, track 22). Whatever her reaction, she forged ahead, recording a spate of French singers in northern Wisconsin, avoiding "foreign records" fraught with pianists, and delivering not one, but three versions of the foulmouthed "The Red Light Saloon" (two are included in part 1, tracks 35 and 36).

On the strength of three summers' fieldwork, Stratman-Thomas was promoted to assistant professor in 1946, a position she held until retiring in 1961. In 1948 she married a hometown friend, A. J. "Pat" Blotz. Although thwarted in her efforts to publish and promote the full extent of her recordings, her vivid field notes, extensive correspondence with performers, and research into particular songs contributed mightily to the commentary on each of eighty-one Stratman-Thomas recordings in this collection. Her 1973 obituary in Madison's *Capital Times* rightly emphasized a prolonged dedication to Wisconsin folksong through a fitting epitaph from her field notes: "We went directly to the people and recorded songs in their homes, occasionally in churches, once in a barn, and several times in dance halls" (January 12, 1973).

A REPRESENTATIVE FOLKSONG SELECTION

The selected 186 songs and tunes herein—174 on five CDs, 12 exclusively accompanying the film—encompass the Upper Midwest's cultures, performers, languages, genres, and contexts encountered by Robertson, Lomax, and Stratman-Thomas in their full range and complexity. Distilled from a corpus of roughly two thousand recordings, they were chosen to span relatively well-recorded, representative, and remarkable songs, tunes, singers, and musicians from all of the documented languages and cultural groups. The chapters to come, which are focused on the five CDs and the film, are fundamentally "liner notes" that correspond sequentially with the audio and film tracks. Each track begins with basic information: track number, title, performer/speaker, instrumentation, recording location and date, recordist/collector, transcriber/translator/annotator, and disc number in the Archive of American Folk Song (now the Archive of Folk Culture), part of the American Folklife Center at the Library of Congress. For example:

7   Non que j'aime donc que la boisson / No, So I Don't Love Anything but the Drink

Sung by John Cadeau, lead vocal, with Ed Cadeau, Adelore Vizina, and probably Joe Miron, Mose Bellaire, and Edward King, Baraga, Michigan, October 12, 1938. Recorded by Alan Lomax. Transcription, translation, and annotation by Anjili Babbar, 2010.

2440

Those seeking more about a performer's recorded repertoire, recordings made in a specific place or on a certain date, other recorded instances of a certain song or tune, and more may consult the web-accessible *Traditional Music and Spoken Word Catalog* of the Library of Congress, which is derived from an original card catalog listing thirty-four thousand ethnographic sound recordings made mostly between 1933 and 1950 (http://memory.loc.gov/diglib/ihas/html/afccards/afccards-home.html, accessed January 10, 2014). Basic track information is supplemented, to the extent possible, with lyrics in the original languages and English translations, the background of songs and tunes, performers' biographies, commentaries on cultural communities, the circumstances of recording, and photographs.

The first two CDs feature Sidney Robertson's 1937 Minnesota and Wisconsin recordings, including a CD devoted to the Wisconsin Lumberjacks commencing with a few tunes Alan Lomax captured from them in May 1938 when the National Folk Festival was held in Washington, D.C. The following chapter covers Lomax's 1938 Michigan recordings, with an emphasis on northern Lower Michigan and, especially, the Upper Peninsula. Commentary on Lomax's 1938 film follows, with the 1940s recordings by Helene Stratman-Thomas occupying the final two installments.

May the words, images, and sounds herein move you and make an era, a region, its chroniclers, and its singing people come alive. May the Upper Midwest, Another America long neglected, be received into the nation's folksong fold.

Print by Isabella Leary

PIGTOWN FLING
THE SIDNEY ROBERTSON RECORDINGS

FRENCH CANADIAN

French Canadians, mainly from Quebec, have been a continuous presence in what is now the American Upper Midwest since the seventeenth and eighteenth centuries, when the fur trade attracted many young men, some of whom intermarried with Native peoples. French Canadian immigrant families also established farms and settled in small towns throughout the nineteenth century, with men often working all winter in lumber camps where music flourished.

1   Fisher's Hornpipe

Spoken by Sidney Robertson; played on fiddle by Leizime Brusoe, Rhinelander, Wisconsin, July 1937. Recorded by Sidney Robertson.
3278 A1

We're going to have a series of old fiddle tunes played by Mr. Leizime Brusoe of Rhinelander, Wisconsin, in July 1937. Mr. Brusoe was champion fiddler of the contest held in Chicago by the *Herald and Examiner*—in Chicago in 1926. He holds the title as champion fiddler of the Midwest. The first thing he's going to play is "Fisher's Hornpipe."

Leizime Brusoe (1870–1949) was born in Canada where he learned to fiddle from an older brother. He came to the United States around 1890, and in 1895 he married a fellow French Canadian, Sophia Hibbard (1871–1964), in Ironwood, Michigan. Soon after, the couple settled permanently in Rhinelander. A dedicated hunter and fisherman who operated a dray line, Brusoe was above all an extraordinary fiddler. His regional champion's title, the culmination of local contests sponsored by Henry Ford in 1926, led to wider fame, as Brusoe performed on the vaudeville circuit and over Chicago's WLS radio as part of the *National Barn Dance*. From 1932 to 1934 he was a regular with Rube Tronson and His Texas Cowboys, barnstorming throughout the Midwest. Invariably decked out in cowboy boots and enormous Stetsons, this deceptively named group was led by a third-generation Norwegian farm boy from Amherst, Wisconsin, who had previously fiddled on WLS with Tommy Dandurand and also had toured with Otto Gray and His Oklahoma Cowboys. Other Tronson bandmates included Wisconsinites Donald "Red" Blanchard, the erstwhile "Texas Yodeler," and Lester Polsfuss, best known later as the guitar wizard Les Paul. Three seasons on tour were enough for Brusoe, however, and he returned to Rhinelander where he played on his own or in a small orchestra until shortly before his death.

Robertson learned of Brusoe thanks to L. G. Sorden (1898–1981). Born in Iowa, Sorden earned a BS degree from Iowa State, did graduate work at the University of Wisconsin, and in 1928 became an agricultural extension agent for northern Wisconsin, with his headquarters in Rhinelander. An expert on soil conservation and instrumental in establishing rural zoning ordinances, Sorden was also an amateur folklorist focused on lumber-camp culture. In 1932 he was the driving force in creating Rhinelander's Logging Museum, for which Brusoe served as a volunteer attendant (*Rhinelander Daily News*, November 1, 1939; D. Taylor 1976). Although Sorden left Rhinelander in 1939 to join the faculty in the University of Wisconsin's College of Agriculture, he maintained his lumber-camp interest, eventually publishing *Wisconsin Lore* (1962), with Robert Gard, and his own compilation, *Lumberjack Lingo* (1969).

Required to report periodically to Adrian J. Dornbush, the overall head of the Special Skills Division of the Resettlement Administration, Sidney Robertson wrote at length about Brusoe in her characteristically vivid, learned, and cheeky style.

> In Rhinelander I found a self-educated musician and piano-tuner, who makes violins also, and has piano he made himself; and plays the accordion; Emery Olsen. He had an 8-stringed fiddle which he'd made himself. . . . The tone was exquisite, light and fine. His friend, Lorenzo [Leizime] Brusoe, was a fine-looking old boy who played over the famous Prairie Farmer station in Chicago [WLS] for several years, and at one time won the title of best fiddler in the U.S. from among several hundred (he said) competitors.

Leizime Brusoe with Rube Tronson and His Texas Cowboys: (*from left to right*) Leizime Brusoe, Rube Tronson, Wally Van Trees, Al Mee, Ted Simons, Tom Johnson, and "Red" Blanchard, WLS *National Barn Dance*, 1933. (courtesy of Mills Music Library, University of Wisconsin–Madison)

At any rate the cup he won is large and fancy enough to support the contention! Mr. Brusoe used to play for formal dancing schools in Canadian towns 40 years ago, and he knows endless quadrilles and schottisches, etc. He has also played, and still plays now and then, when he considers his elevated reputation will allow of the condescension, for barn dances and such, around Rhinelander—to the accordion accompaniment of Mr. Olsen. He knows many jigs and reels—indeed, he must have played nearly 40 different tunes for me between 9 p.m., when we routed Mr. Olsen out of bed to receive us, and 1:30 a.m., when Mr. Olsen finished lecturing to me on the history of the violin. . . . Mr. Brusoe can't read a note, though he can play any tune after hearing it once or twice; Mr. Olsen reads a little, badly. They insisted I play with them, which I did—everybody making the most noise he could.

Mr. Brusoe belongs to the same "school" of fiddling as Frank Hendrick, my Irish friend in Springfield [Illinois]—his bowing is very smooth and skillful, and he uses the positions a little. When he takes a reel tune and plays what he calls a medley on it, actually he plays a variation on it with additions in the form of elaborate ornamentation. I kept thinking of the Allemandes and rapid bourrees and gigues of Bach's suites—it was dance music at the stage at which Bach took possession of it, probably. Mr. Brusoe told

me firmly that there *is* no such thing as a square dance!!—seemed to think they were
quadrilles gone wrong. (Robertson 1936–1938: April 25–28, 1937)

Sidney Robertson recorded eleven solo tunes from Brusoe, some of which he reprised for
Helene Stratman-Thomas in 1940 and 1941.

Alan Jabbour, who included four tunes by Brusoe—"French Four" (Soldier's Joy),
a quadrille, "Two-Step Schottische," and a "Highland Fling"—in the authoritative documentary recording, *American Fiddle Tunes*, noted in reference to Brusoe's version of
"Fisher's Hornpipe" that only "a few fiddlers such as Leizime Brusoe have cultivated
their left hand technique to the extent that they can execute complicated hornpipes at
a dazzling pace." Hornpipes emerged as a solo British dance form in the late eighteenth
century, and "Fisher's Hornpipe" is among the earliest and best-known instances. First
published in J. Fishar's *Sixteen Cotillions, Twelve Allemands and Twelve Hornpipes*
(London, ca. 1780), the tune was first recorded commercially in the mid-1920s by Al
Hopkins and His Buckle Busters (Vocalion 5017), while ten fiddlers besides Brusoe—
from Texas to Nova Scotia, from North Carolina to Iowa—recorded it for the Library
of Congress between 1937 and 1946 (Jabbour 1971: 8).

2   Pigtown Fling

Spoken and played on fiddle by Leizime Brusoe, Rhinelander, Wisconsin,
July 1937. Recorded by Sidney Robertson.

3278 B3

I'm going to play "Pigtown Fling," better known as the "Long-Eared Mule."

This reel has been widely reported from the west of Ireland, throughout the American
South, New England, Pennsylvania, the Midwest, and westward to the Rocky Mountains.
Known by several names—including "Big Town Fling," "Pigtown Hoedown," and
"Pigtown"—it has been called "Pigtown Fling" most commonly by "northern fiddlers"
in the United States, but their southern counterparts know it by such names as "Old
Dad," "Wild Horse," and "Stony Point" (Jabbour 1971: 18–20). Although Brusoe also
heard it called "Long-Eared Mule," his tune is quite different than the one sometimes
known by this name but usually called "Flop-Eared Mule" (Kuntz 2012).

3 Lancer's in Five Parts

Spoken and played on fiddle by Leizime Brusoe, Rhinelander, Wisconsin, July 1937. Recorded by Sidney Robertson.

3279 A1

I will play the "Lancer's." It's five numbers.

The quadrille emerged in eighteenth-century France as an elegant dance involving sets of four couples engaged in a series of figures: salutes, swings, promenades, chains, and more. By the early nineteenth century, it had become popular in England and North America, contributing to the American square dance. The "Lancers Quadrille," with its five distinctive parts, was created in Paris in the 1820s and associated with military balls featuring cavalry lancers. Subsequent renditions of this five-part quadrille featured various dance movements and tunes. According to Robertson's field notes, Brusoe "used to play the lancers like this for dancing classes in Quebec in the 1880s. He was taught to play by his older brother, who was well known as a fiddler in Canada . . . and his playing is unusually true, clean and clear, for all his thickened fingers." Steeped in the grace and precision of Quebec's ballroom traditions, Brusoe offered Robertson his low opinion of American square dances: "They ain't no sech thing as a square dance, I seen them in Chicago but they was just quadrilles—they didn't know how to do them."

Elsewhere in the Upper Midwest, Paul Gifford reported that Bill Bigford (1898–1986), a fiddling farmer and laborer from north-central Lower Michigan was "the only Michigan fiddler I ever met who played a Lancers or a tune by that name. . . . This tune, however, was called 'Pacific Quadrille' by others, and was credited to O. F. ('Cub') Berdan, music publisher of Detroit active in the 1870s–1880s." Gifford speculates that Bigford probably learned the tune from his father, William Bigford, a lumberjack, and that "in Michigan at least the Lancers was out of fashion by about 1910" (Gifford 2010). Well-known in the Quebec of Brusoe's youth, the "Lancers Quadrille" had all but disappeared from that area by the mid-twentieth century. Yet in the early 1970s, the ethnologist Jean Trudel was able to reconstruct a set of tunes and steps in collaboration with the traditional fiddler Jules Verret, as described and elaborately illustrated in a booklet accompanying an LP record (Verret 1975: 4, 23–25, 35–37).

LUMBERJACKS AND FARMERS

Large camps for workers cutting conifers over a winter's season no longer flourished by the 1930s, nor did the springtime river drives that floated buoyant pine to mills. Yet logging persisted in northern Wisconsin. Roads and rail lines laced the landscape, with lumberjacks and mill hands harvesting and processing hardwood and pulpwood. Many of these latter-day workers were also small farmers lured to northern Wisconsin by unscrupulous lumber companies. Seeking to rid themselves, as Asher Treat astutely put it, of "worthless and tax-encumbered wastes," they exaggerated the fertility of the stump-covered, thin, rocky soil hampered by severe winters and a short growing season. "Some of the victims were Polish and Bohemian peasants; some were native Americans in more or less distant parts of the country. Ten or twelve years before the turn of the century a stream of migrants began to flow northward from eastern Kentucky" (Treat 1939: 1). Logging and hardscrabble farming communities like Crandon in Forest County included many singers and song makers steeped in older English, Irish, and occupational traditions. Sidney Robertson's efforts to document Crandon's varied singers—selectively treated below—are presented more fully in a website created by Nicole Saylor, *Folk Music of Wisconsin 1937*.

4   Lost Jimmie Whalen

Sung by Robert Walker, Crandon, Wisconsin, July 1937.
Recorded by Sidney Robertson.

3287 A1

As slowly and sadly I strayed by the river,
A-watching the sunbeams as evening drew nigh,
As onward I rambled I spied a fair damsel,
She was weeping and wailing with many a sigh.

Sighing for one who is now lying lonely,
Sighing for one whom no mortal can save,
For the dark rolling waters roll sadly around him,
As onward it rolls o'er young Jimmy's grave.

"Jimmy," said she, "won't you come to my arrums,
And give me sweet kisses as oft-time you've done?

You promised you'd meet me this evening, my darling,
O come dearest Jimmy, love, come from your grave."

Slowly there rose from the depths of the river
A vision of beauty far brighter than sun,
While red robes of crimson encircled around him,
Unto this fair maiden to speak he'd begun.

"Why did you call me from the rellums of glory
Back to this cold earth that I'll soon have to leave,
To clasp you once more in my fond loving arrums?
To see you once more I have came from my grave."

"Jimmy," said she, "won't you stay on earth with me?
Do not leave me here for to weep and to rave.
But if you cannot stay on this cold earth with me,
Oh Jimmy, take me to your cold silent grave."

"Darling to me you are asking a favor
That no earthly mortal could grant unto thee.
For death is the dagger that holds us asunder,
And wide is the gulf, love, between you and me.

"One fond embrace, love, and then I must leave you,
One loving kiss, pet, and then we must part."
And cold were the arms he encircled around her,
While cold was the bosom she pressed to her heart.

Then straightway he vanished before her,
Straight to the clouds he appeared for to go,
Leaving his loved one distracted and lonely,
Weeping and wailing with anguish and woe.

Throwing herself on the banks of the river,
A-weeping and wailing as though she would rave,
Sighing, "My loved one, my lost Jimmy Whalen,
[Spoken:] I will sigh 'til I die by the side of your grave."

Robert William Walker was born in Crandon in 1883. His father, Henry Walker (1850–1912), who was of Scotch Irish descent, hailed from New York State, as did his mother, Leila Harris Walker (1850–1907), whose family was English. Part of the logging industry's westward migration, the elder Walkers arrived independently in central Wisconsin's Waupaca County, where they married in 1873 prior to settling further north

in Forest County near Crandon. In a posthumously published reminiscence, *Crandon Is My Hometown*, C. Harry Poppy recalled the Walkers in the late 1890s: "About a mile from Stone Lake (today Lake Lucerne) . . . was Schlitz Brewing Company's clubhouse. This is where the owners and head men came to spend their vacations. To the north and some distance (about twenty yards) was a large clearing with a large two story log house and a large log two story barn. These were the only buildings on the lake. Here is where the Walker family lived and worked the farm and took care of the vacationers. They kept several horses and cows. One team of draft horses and saddle and driving horses. When any of the Milwaukee people came for an outing, Mr. Walker or one of the boys would meet them at Pelican. The Walkers were considered one of the town's pioneers. Mr. Walker, 50, six feet, 200 pounds; Mrs. Walker, five feet six inches, 160 pounds; Charles, 18, six feet, 170 pounds; Robert, 14; and Clayton, 10." Henry Walker also worked in the woods, with his sons Charles and Robert following suit in their teens. An active logger until his retirement in 1955, Robert Walker experienced the heyday of the winter lumber camps, the transition to hardwood logging, and the development of pulpwood harvesting for the region's paper mills. He died in 1961.

Walker was a fine traditional singer throughout his long life. Sidney Robertson recorded nine songs from him in 1937, then after her marriage to Henry Cowell in 1941 she captured more between 1952 and 1955, releasing six on a documentary recording, *Wolf River Songs*, accompanied by a booklet of detailed notes and photographs (Cowell 1956). Hence we learn that Walker's parents, Henry and Leila, "knew a power o' songs and sang 'em everyday of the world." Robert Walker's sister, Elizabeth, was likewise a formidable singer, as were her husband, Jerome Ford, their sons Arthur and Warde, and other members of the extended family. By Robertson's estimation, "The Ford-Walker family repertory (about 140 titles) includes some comparatively rare Child ballads, lumber camp ballads and songs of the sea, along with many love songs (most of them not long from Ireland), ditties made up to suit special occasions, and stage and minstrel songs. None of the family ever sings these particular songs with an accompaniment. . . . There is a strong Celtic imprint on most of the tunes sung by the Walkers and Fords, evident in the general melodic style as well as in actual transplanted Irish and Scottish tunes and texts. . . . Several newly-arrived Irishmen whom Walker met in the woods reinforced this element in the family with a number of Anglo-Irish ballads" (Cowell 1956).

< Robert Walker, Crandon, Wisconsin, 1941. (Wisconsin Historical Society, WHi-25189)

According to Robertson, Walker's rendition of "Lost Jimmie Whalen" may have been "learned from a family friend named Mike Brennan who worked with the Walker brothers in the woods before World War I" (Cowell 1956). Born in Crandon in 1890, Michael J. Brennan was the son of an Irish Canadian logger. In the 1870s James Phelan (locally pronounced as "Whelan") drowned when he was pinned by a jam during a log drive near Perth, Ontario, thus inspiring two songs that circulated widely in the oral tradition of Canadian and American lumber camps (Rickaby 1926: 20–24, 194–196; Laws 1964: 150–151; Fowke 1970: 111–116). In her notes to *Wolf River Songs*, Robertson cited Samuel Bayard's contention that "the tune belongs to the Gaelic *Fainne Geal an Lae* family," while noting distinctly Irish mannerisms in Walker's performance: the spoken ending and "the pronunciation of arms as 'arrums' and realms as 'rellums.'"

5   Little Brown Bulls

Sung by Warde Ford, Crandon, Wisconsin, July 30, 1937.
Recorded by Sidney Robertson.
3281 B2

Not a man on the river had McCluskey to fear,
As he swung his gored stick[1] o'er the big spotted steers,
Young, strong, quick, and handsome, girded eight foot and three,
Said McCluskey, the Scotsman, "They're the laddies for me."

Then up came Bull Gordon when the rollway[2] was full,
And shouted, "Wha, hush!" to the little brown bulls.
Short-legged and shaggy, girded six foot and nine.
"Too light," said McCluskey, "to handle our pine."

Now it's three to the thousand[3] our contract did call.
The skidding[4] was good and the timber was tall.
Said Sandy to Gordon, "To make the day full,
I'll skid two-to-one of your little brown bulls."

"Ah no," said Bull Gordon, "that you cannot do,
Although your big steers are the pets of the crew.
I'll tell you, my boy, you'll have your hands full
If you skid one more log than my little brown bulls."

Now a day was appointed and soon it drew nigh,
For twenty-five dollars their fortune to try.

All eager and anxious when the morning came round
And the boss and the scaler[5] appeared on the ground.

With a whoop and a holler McCluskey came in view
With the big spotted steers, the pets of the crew,
Saying "Chew your cud well, boys, and keep your mouths full,
And today we will conquer those little brown bulls."

Then up came Bull Gordon with his pipe in his jaw,
And the little brown bulls with a cud in each jaw.
And little did we think when they swung them around,
'Twas a hundred and forty he'd skid at sundown.

Now at sundown that evening our foreman did say,
"Turn in, boys, turn in—you've enough for the day."
All numbered and scaled, each man and his team,
And we thought that we knew which had knocked down the beam.

When supper was over, McCluskey did appear,
With a belt he had made for the big spotted steers.
And to make it he'd torn up his best mackinaw,[6]
As he was conducted according to the law.

Then up jumped the scaler, said, "Hold on your while,
Your big spotted steers are behind by a mile.
You've skidded a hundred and ten and no more,
While Gordon has beat you by ten and a score."

How all the boys shouted, and McCluskey did swear
As he pulled out in handfuls his long curly hair.
Now fill up your glasses and fill them up full,
And we'll drink to the health of the little brown bulls.

———

1. A goad stick or prod used by a teamster.
2. An area alongside a river bank or adjacent to a train track where logs could be temporarily "decked,"
   or piled, and then when the time was right, "rolled" into a river or onto a flatbed rail car.
3. Big logs, three of which would yield one thousand board feet.
4. The process of hauling logs out of the woods with chains and a team.
5. A worker who used a special ruler and a mathematical table to calculate how many board feet a
   given log would render.
6. A heavy woolen coat in a plaid pattern.

Warde Hollis Ford (1906–1979) was born in Crandon. His parents, Jerome "Rome"
Ford (1873–1932) and Elizabeth Walker Ford (1879–1970), sister of the woods singer

Robert Walker, were both born in Waupaca County, Wisconsin, and each came north to Crandon sometime before marrying there in 1899. Like his father and maternal uncle, Warde Ford went into the woods as a teenager and was an active logger through the mid-1930s. In 1938 he headed to northern California where he toiled, along with an uncle and a brother, in the construction of Shasta Dam, a massive federal project employing thousands from 1937 to 1945. Thereafter Ford enlisted in the army and served in Germany.

Ford was a remarkable traditional singer from whom Sidney Robertson recorded scores of songs over a seventeen-year period: in Wisconsin in 1937, in California in 1938, and in Munich in 1954 and 1955. Yet as Nicole Saylor explains, Robertson happened on Ford and the entire Ford–Walker extended family quite by accident:

> She first met Ford in the county welfare office, where she had gone to find leads on out-of-work Kentucky loggers. She explained to Ford, a temporary clerk in the office, that she was on the hunt for old songs. He said he knew some and would gather them that evening. It was only after two or three trips to Crandon that Robertson discovered that Ford was a singer himself. He had been too shy to reveal his abilities, as he explained to her, she hadn't asked him directly.
>
> Robertson spent so much time collecting songs from Ford that she was known around Crandon as his "girlfriend." He had different jobs around town, including one looking after horses owned by the wife of the local undertaker. A few times Robertson would join Ford in the barn, with her typewriter on a coffin, so that he could dictate texts while polishing the saddles. One of their most vivid collaborations occurred during a long car trip where the singer sang almost the entire trip without repeating the same song twice. (Saylor 2004)

"Little Brown Bulls" commemorates a log-hauling, or "skidding," contest between a boastful Scots Canadian and a determined Maine Yankee. In 1946 the folklorist Richard Dorson heard a similar account from Bernard McTiver (1893–1978) of Newberry, Michigan, regarding his father. Born in Maine, Silas McTiver "lumbered from Alpena to Cheboygan in the Lower Peninsula, came up here [to the Upper Peninsula] in 1911, and then went west to cruise for Weyerhaeuser in Minnesota" (Dorson [1952] 2008: 205). When the elder McTiver ran a pine and hemlock camp on the Sucker River near Perry's Landing on Lake Superior, teamsters' names were posted on a bulletin, along with "the number of board feet hauled that day." The teamster who skidded the most logs in a month won "a mackinaw, worth about fifteen or twenty dollars" (Dorson [1952] 2008: 100). Well-known throughout Upper Midwestern lumber camps, and also in Ontario, the "Little Brown Bulls" was likely composed in northern Wisconsin in the early 1870s (Rickaby 1926: 65–68, 206–207; Laws 1964: 154; Fowke 1970: 168–170). The Wisconsin-woods singer Emery DeNoyer (Stratman-Thomas CD part 1, tracks 27–29) confirmed this assertion, because he knew one of the contestants: "DeNoyer once sang the song in a camp where McCloskey was working. McCloskey told him that several versions were being sung to several different tunes. He was glad to hear DeNoyer sing it as it was first recorded and as he, himself, thought it should be sung. McCloskey was a big Scotchman and very popular wherever he worked. His head was almost entirely bald. He claimed to have lost his hair when he was only eighteen years old" (Ebert [1940s] 1998: 211). This may have been the Alexander McCluskey (also McCloskey and McClusky in census records) who was born in Canada in 1850, worked in northern Wisconsin prior to 1870, and lived in a Langlade County boardinghouse in 1900.

6 Crandon

Sung by Warde Ford, Crandon, Wisconsin, July 30, 1937.
Recorded by Sidney Robertson.

3285 A3

There's a town in old Wisconsin and it isn't much for fame,
But the boys and girls there love her, and Crandon is her name.
All the people of our village are always sociable and gay,
And they find that that's the only way, there is no other way.

CHORUS:
Because that's the way we have of doing things in Crandon.
We don't get our styles from Paris or from London.
But we're jolly just the same and you bet we know the game,
'Cause that's the way we have of doing things in Crandon.

Now can you blame the girls of Crandon for staying out late on Sunday night
With a bunch of happy fellers who can entertain them right?
Down by the shores of Lake Metonga we go to take a walk,
And we don't care if we don't get back 'til three or four o'clock.

Now it's early in the morning and the old man will arise
And walk into the parlor, and there to his surprise
Sits a young man with his daughter, been there since the night before,
Then he'll politely show this ardent lover to the door.

Now perchance some gay young couple are out late upon the street,
'N' run across old Happy O'Brien just a-strollin' on his beat,
Right to the jail he'll have to take them and a fine they'll have to pay,
'Cause he says, "It's my sworn duty and there is no other way."

'Cause that's the way we have of doing things in Crandon.
We don't get our styles from Paris or from London.
But we're not jolly anymore, like we used to be before,
O'Brien stopped the way we had of doing things in Crandon.

This local song appears to protest a curfew. Robertson's field notes reveal that O'Brien was the chief of police and that the song was "composed by Ed King of Crandon about 1935." An Edward Joseph King (1892–1952) of Crandon was the father of ten children, four of whom were teenagers in the mid-1930s.

7 I'd Rather Be a Nigger than a Poor White Man

Sung by Warde Ford and Art Ford, Crandon, Wisconsin, July 1937.
Recorded by Sidney Robertson.

3285 B1

There's potatoes in the oven,
They are turning nice and brown.
There's a watermelon growing
When the season comes around.

There's a chicken on the burner,
In the smokehouse there's a ham,
So I'd rather be a nigger
Than a poor white man.

Arthur Jerome Ford (1903–1973), the firstborn child of Jerome Ford and Elizabeth Walker, and Warde Ford's brother, also worked in the woods and was an accomplished traditional singer. He recorded for Sidney Robertson a trio of songs he had learned in the lumber camps: "The Mermaid," number 289 in Francis James Child's canonical collection, a sailor's song with wide circulation in the British Isles and along the

American-Canadian border; "Lather and Shave," a comic Irish song well known in North America; and another comic Irish ballad, "The Twenty Pound Dog," also recorded by his uncle, Robert Walker.

The phrase "I'd rather be a nigger than a poor white man" dates at least to the 1860s and perhaps earlier, especially among African Americans. In 1938 Waters McIntosh, born in slavery, told an interviewer for the Federal Writers Project: "When I was a boy we used to sing, 'Rather be a nigger than a poor white man.' Even in slavery they used to sing that" (McIntosh 1938). In 1922 the African American folklorist Thomas Talley included a song with this phrase in his *Negro Folk Rhymes*, while Karl Knortz called it part of a plantation song (Schamschula 1996: 152–153) and Newman Ivey White associated it with reconstruction in their respective 1902 and 1928 collections. The Ford brothers' version, however, comes from an 1894 composition by the white songwriter Harry Earle, whose "I'd Rather Be a Nigger than a Poor White Man" shares only its title with the southern black folksong. A contribution to the era's "coon song" genre, it was popularized on the New York City stage by Maud Huth who, with her husband Billy S. Clifford, specialized in blackface performances.

Such minstrel shows were common forms of entertainment in Upper Midwestern communities, introduced by traveling performers in the post–Civil War era but sustained through "home talent" versions well into the twentieth century. The Fords' rendition, delivered with minstrelsy's harmonized sentimentality, includes only the song's chorus while departing considerably from Earle's original:

> For dar's taters in de cellar
> With short cake good and brown.
> And sweet old watermelon
> When de season rolls around.
>
> Dar's flour in de kitchen,
> In de cupboard's dar's a ham,
> And I'd rather be a nigger
> Den a poor white man.
> (Earle 1894)

8   Mighty Adley-ca-budley-fatley-ca-ham-shaw

Spoken by Charles Spencer, Crandon, Wisconsin, July 1937.
Recorded by Sidney Robertson.

3293 A2

M-i-g-h-t-y, mighty.
A-d-l-e-y, Adley. Mighty Adley.
C-a, ca. Adley-ca. Mighty Adley-ca.
B-u-d-l-e-y, budley. Ca-budley. Adley-ca-budley. Mighty Adley-ca-budley.
F-a-t-l-e-y, fatley. Ca-budley-fatley. Adley-ca-budley-fatley. Mighty Adley-ca-budley-fatley-ca.
H-a-m, ham. Ca-ham. Fatley-ca-ham. Budley-fatley-ca-ham. Adley-ca-
    budley-fatley-ca-ham. Mighty Adley-ca-budley-fatley-ca-ham.
S-h-a-w, shaw. Mighty Adley-ca-budley-fatley-ca-ham-shaw.
The prognostical [?] force [?] that gives us the [?] and makes it sound as [?].

Charles Spencer was born in eastern Kentucky in 1874 where he farmed, worked in the woods, and learned many old-time songs. As he told Helene Stratman-Thomas and her engineer, Robert Draves, on July 28, 1941: "I was a music teacher in the mountains of Kentucky . . . before I was nineteen years old. . . . I could sing at one time with figures [shape notes]. . . . I can well remember the old-time songs. . . . They became a part of my mind when I was a boy." Sometime before 1910, Spencer, his wife Rosa, and their son Clyde joined the exodus of "Kentucks" seeking small farms and woods work in Forest County, Wisconsin.

Spencer had vivid memories of attending a country school, "when I was a bare-footed boy—a clapboard roof, no loft, a big open fireplace—the seats . . . was made out of split logs with the rounded side down. . . . They left so many splinters on them benches that a little fellow like me had to sit quietly." Memorization, recitations, and spelling contests were common country-school activities in Kentucky and Wisconsin alike, as were parodies of them. Spencer characterized "Mighty Adley" as "funning for children" by spelling an absurdly long name supposedly belonging to an ancient Greek king. In 1928 Ernest Stoneman and His Blue Ridge Corn Shuckers recorded a comic skit, "Possum Trot School Exhibition," on a double-sided 78 (Victor 41933) that included a competition between the school's "best spellers." Battling to a draw, "Rufus Jones" and "Cyrus Riggins" used the same old-fashioned incremental, repetitive, syllabic method to spell their respective words: "incomprehensibility" and the nonexistent "inconcessibility." Since at least the 1940s a similar, albeit raunchy, parody of it has circulated in oral

Charles Spencer and an unidentified young woman, Crandon, Wisconsin, 1941. (Wisconsin Historical Society, WHi-25182)

tradition and, nowadays, on the Internet regarding an improbably named youngster, Archibald Barasol (or a variation thereof), who is required by an insistent teacher to spell his name accordingly:

> You got your A-R-C-H, got your Arch. Got your I, got your Arch-eye. Got your B-A-L-D, got your bald, got your eye-bald, got your Arch-eye-bald. Got your B-A-R, got your bare, got your bald bare, got your eye-bald-bare, got your Arch-eye-bald-bare. You got your A-S, got your ass. Got your bare ass. Got your bald bare ass. Got your eye-bald-bare-ass, got your arch-eye-bald-bare-ass. You got your O-L, got your ole. Got your ass-ole. Got your bare-ass-ole. Got your bald, bare ass-ole. Got your eye-bald-bare-ass-ole, you got your Arch-eye-bald Bare-ass-ole.

9   Locks and Bolts

Sung by Charles Spencer, Crandon, Wisconsin, July 1937.
Recorded by Sidney Robertson.

3283 A1

Last night I dreamed of my true love,
My arms were all around her.
When I awoke she was not there,
And I had to lie without her.

Those yellow locks like chains of gold
Come, dazzling, down my pillow.
That pretty girl that I loved so well.
They called her name Bo-ellow.

I went unto her uncle's house,
Inquiring for my true lover.
They answered me, "There is none such here,"
Which set my heart to aching.

She heard my welcoming [?] voice.
She answered me through the window,
"I would be with you this lonely night
If locks and bolts don't hinder."

I stood one moment all amazed,
A-viewing her from a fissure.
My passion flew, my sword I drew.
That room I swore I would enter.

The locks and bolts did scatter,
The doors and [?] did shatter.
That pretty girl that I loved so well,
So soon did I come at her.

Her uncle and some other men
Soon after me did follow.
They swore before they would part with her,
In my own heart's blood they would wallow.

Blood was shed on every side.
I got my true love from amongst them,
And the brave boys that get such brides
Will have to fight some for them.

One of many "Ballads of Family Opposition to Lovers" within the standard ballad classification scheme of G. Malcolm Laws, this song is well known in England, Ireland, Scotland, and throughout North America, where it has circulated in oral tradition and through printed broadsides since the seventeenth century (Laws 1957: 186–187). Cecil Sharp, the English folksong scholar, found it flourishing in the southern Appalachians during his fieldwork from 1916 to 1918 (Sharp 1932), while in the 1930s Asher Treat set down a fragment from the Jacobs family, "Kentucks" from Carter County, who had settled on a farm in 1906 near Bryant in Langlade County, Wisconsin (Treat 1939: 13).

10 The Sinking of the Titanic

Spoken introduction by an unknown male, possibly Warde Ford;
sung by Clyde Spencer and Harry Fannin, Crandon, Wisconsin,
July 1937. Recorded by Sidney Robertson.
3283 B

We'll hear "The Sinking of the Titanic" by Clyde Spencer, soprano, and Harry Fannin, tenor. Both of Crandon.

Titanic was a ship, just on her maiden trip,
Sailed across Atlantic Ocean wide.
This was a pleasure trip,
Millionaires aboard the ship,
But they never lived to reach the other side.

CHORUS:
Titanic was her name,
Sailing Atlantic was her fame.
Oh she sank about 500 miles from home.
Sixteen hundred were unsaved,
Went down in the angry waves,
Down in the angry waves to rise no more.

'Twas a dark and moonless night
And there was not a gleam of light
To light them from the darkness o'er the sea.
It was a solemn sound,
Just as the ship went down,
To hear the band play "Nearer My God to Thee."

Mrs. Isadora Strauss,
The wife and husband lost.
They were to each other noble, true and brave.
As they sang the evening hymn,
She prepared to die with him.
So they both went down beneath the angry waves.

There was an awful crowd,
Who had gathered like a cloud
To watch the ocean steamer as she came.
But the captain and the crew
Went down in the ocean blue,
And they never, never heard them call their names.

Warde Ford (tracks 5–7) organized an evening session of "Kentuck" and other local singers for Sidney Robertson and is probably the one who introduces this song. Clyde Spencer (1900–1967) was born in Kentucky and had come to northern Wisconsin with his parents, Charles and Rosa Spencer, as a young boy. The local milkman at the time, Clyde Spencer eventually served as the chair of the Forest County board. He also played guitar and banjo in the style of the era's "hillbilly" performers, recording a banjo solo, "Sourwood Mountain," for Robertson, as well as a trio of sentimental songs: "The Boys in Blue," a Spanish Civil War ballad that shares a verse with "The Texas Rangers"; "Lindbergh," one of the scores of musical tributes to the Minnesota aviator's 1927 trans-Atlantic solo flight; and "Jack and Joe," also known as "Give My Love to Nell," recorded by Asa Martin, Bradley Kincaid, Ernest Stoneman, Riley Puckett, and others. Spencer's fellow singer, Harry Fannin (1900–1966), was born in Sandy Hook, Kentucky, and came to Wisconsin with his parents in 1907. Fannin worked for the Crandon Distilling Company, which had been established for whisky production by a branch of Kentucky's Beam family, and was also sheriff of Forest County from 1942 to 1946 (*Forest Republican*, October 5, 1966).

The sinking of the Titanic on its maiden voyage in 1912 inspired many songs. This lesser-known instance, which was performed by Spencer and Fannin, came from Kentucky. Originally entitled "The Lost Ship," it was probably composed, and certainly published, by Richard D. "Dick" Burnett (1888–1977) in *Songs Sung by R. D. Burnett, the Blind Man* (ca. 1913). A fine songwriter from Monticello, Kentucky, whose credits include "Man of Constant Sorrow," Burnett was also a banjo and guitar player who teamed with fiddler Leonard Rutherford. Their records on the Columbia label, however, did not include this song.

SCOTS GAELIC

Situated on Lake Superior, and Minnesota's major port for shipping grain and iron ore, Duluth attracted Scots in the post–Civil War era. There they founded a St. Andrew's Society in 1870, established Presbyterian churches, and were active in commerce and organized labor (Rubinstein 1981: 124–125). Duluth's immigrants from the Isle of Lewis, the largest and most northerly of the Outer Hebrides archipelago, were especially prominent, arriving in the 1860s and forming a Lewis Society in 1911 that conducted its meetings in Scots Gaelic until its demise in 1955. Donald M. Morrison (1862–1951), who arrived in 1886, was celebrated as the Bard of Duluth (Bakk-Hansen 2012). Two of his songs—"Bailig an Iasgich" and especially "Eilean Beag Donn a 'Chuain"—became more widely known and are remembered by traditional musicians in present-day Scotland (MacKenzie 2012).

In the 1920s Marjorie Edgar (1889–1960)—a force in the Girl Scout movement, a folksong interpreter, and an internationalist from a prominent Minneapolis family—became especially interested in the folksongs of Minnesota's Finns and Gaelic-speaking Scots. Her papers include an unpublished manuscript focused on Duluth's Lewis Society and its other acclaimed singer, John Matheson (Edgar ca. 1940).

11 A Mhàiri bhàn òg / O Fair Mary

Sung by John H. Matheson, Duluth, Minnesota, September 18, 1937.
Recorded by Sidney Robertson. Transcription and translation by
Thomas McKean, 2011.

3301 A1

A Mhàiri bhàn òg, gur h-òg a bha mis' agus tu.	O Fair Mary, how young we were.

Nan shnaiminn an clò's gum
    pògainn fèin thu gu dlùth.
	I would tie the knot and kiss
	    you passionately.

Do ghruaidh mar na ròsan, is bòidheach
    leam sealladh do ghnùis.
	Your cheeks like the roses,
	    your face so beautiful.

Chan fhad bhios mi beò ma phòsas fear eil' agus tu.	I shan't live long if you marry another.
CHORUS: Air fal-al-al ò horò air fal-al-al è Air fal-al-al ò horò air fal-al-al è	*CHORUS:* Air fal-al-al ò horò air fal-al-al è Air fal-al-al ò horò air fal-al-al è

Air fal-al-al ò horò air fal-al-al è
Fal ì fal ò horò air fal-al-al è.

Nuair rachainn air sràid, a ghràidh,
    bhiodh gini nam phòc'
'S gun òlainn do shlàint 's gach àit'
    an suidhinn mun bhòrd.
An cridhe geal fialaidh aotrom
    aighearach òg,
Bu mhilis leam fèin am beul
    on tigeadh an ceòl.

Nan robh mis' is tu am beinn no
    'm monadh no'n t-sliabh
No air an tràigh bhàin an t-àit'
    nach robh duine riamh
Seachd oidhche, seachd là, gun
    tàmh, gun chadal, gun bhiadh
Ach thusa bhi ghràidh 's do làmh
    gheal tharam gu fial.

Air fal-al-al ò horò air fal-al-al è
Fal ì fal ò horò air fal-al-al è.

When I go out, love, I'd have a
    guinea in my pocket
And I would drink your health
    whenever I'm at table.
The pure, generous, light and
    ebullient young heart,
So sweet to me is the mouth
    the music comes from.

If I were in the mountains, hills, or moors

Or on the white deserted beach

Seven days, seven nights without
    rest, sleep or food
Except you, love, and your fair,
    gentle hand on me.

John Matheson (1875–1952) was born in Bhaltos (Valtos), a village in the Uig parish on the west coast of the Isle of Lewis. He fought with the Cameron Highlanders in South Africa during the Second Boer War, thereafter immigrating in 1903 to Duluth, where he worked as a bookkeeper for a tailor. He married Camille McLeod in 1913 and the couple lived for a time in Canada, where John worked for the Canadian National Railway, but by 1917 they had returned to Duluth, where Matheson was a timekeeper for the Duluth, Missabe, and Iron Range Railway.

Matheson grew up immersed in traditional song during a time when Scots Gaelic speakers had organized to preserve their linguistic and cultural traditions, as exemplified by An Comunn Gàidhealach (The Gaelic Association), founded in 1891. In 1894 Matheson entered a *Mod*, or dancing and singing competition, at Dundee, winning first prize there and, subsequently, at Inverness. Once in North America, he performed at Scottish festivals in Winnipeg, Vancouver, and Saskatoon and also served for a time as president of Duluth's Lewis Society (Hakala 2007: 257).

Sidney Robertson recorded John Matheson thanks to the efforts of Marjorie Edgar, who had known him for some time and had attended Scots Gaelic events in Duluth. She was particularly struck by the persistent yet repurposed presence of "waulking songs"—originally performed collectively by groups of women in Scotland as they rhythmically softened newly woven tweed by beating it, but which became part of reminiscent pageantry in America.

> An interesting feature of the Lewis Society program was the enactment of an island *Luadh*, the gathering for work and singing where the cloth is shrunk for the looms, to the accompaniment of songs with strange rhythm and fascinating airs. Like many Americans, I had heard the waulking songs which were collected in the Hebrides in 1905 and 1907–8 and later published with English words and musical arrangements. I rather expected to renew my acquaintance with the waulking songs called by Madam Kennedy Fraser [Marjory Kennedy-Fraser (1857–1930)] . . . but the songs I did hear were peculiar to the island of Lewis and some, I understand, had not been published at that time. . . . Of the four waulking songs, the most striking was the fascinating air whose title comes from the chorus, "Air-fal-al-al-o" a refrain with no meaning. A characteristic of these waulking songs is their wild sea quality and the absence of words concerning the work at hand. As in many northern folk-songs, the words are apt to tell of departures, voyages, unlucky love affairs: in the rousing "Air-fal-al-al-lo," the words are thoughtful and end sadly. (Edgar ca. 1940)

This song shares its opening phrase but is not to be confused with "A Mhàiri bhàn òg," composed by the poet Duncan Ban MacIntyre (1724–1812) in honor of his young wife; nor is it the same, despite sharing a chorus, as "Air Fa La La Lo," written by the Glasgow choirmaster Hugh S. Robertson and popularized in the 1960s by the Dubliners. Rather it is an old traditional song, known in both Scots Gaelic and Irish: "A' bhuachaille bhàin" (O Fair-Haired Cowherd).

12 Stocainnean daoimean / Diamond-Patterned Socks

Sung by John H. Matheson, Duluth, Minnesota, September 18, 1937. Recorded by Sidney Robertson. Transcription, translation, and annotation by Thomas McKean, 2011.

3300 B1

Hò hai-rum chunna mis' a-raoir thu	Hò hai-rum I saw you last night
Hò hai-rum chunna mis' a-raoir thu	Hò hai-rum I saw you last night
Hò hai-rum chunna mis' a-raoir thu	Hò hai-rum I saw you last night
A' dìreadh an staidhir as a' "Royal."	Climbing the stairs at the Royal [Hotel].

CHORUS: *CHORUS:*
Hò hai-rum hidl adl ai rum   Hò hai-rum hidl adl ai rum
Hò hai-rum hidl adl ai rum   Hò hai-rum hidl adl ai rum
Hò hai-rum hidl adl ai rum   Hò hai-rum hidl adl ai rum
Hidl hadl ai hadl ò-rum.   Hidl hadl ai hadl ò-rum.

Hò hai-rum stocainnean daoimean[1]   Hò hai-rum, diamond-patterned socks
Hò hai-rum stocainnean daoimean   Hò hai-rum, diamond-patterned socks
Hò hai-rum stocainnean daoimean   Hò hai-rum, diamond-patterned socks
'S iad bhiodh grinn ann a' "Lòrnes."[2]   Wouldn't they be elegant in the dress shoes.

O hù ach cha ghabhainn an t-Ùigeach   O hù I won't take the Uig man
O hù ach cha ghabhainn an t-Ùigeach   O hù I won't take the Uig man
O hù ach cha ghabhainn an t-Ùigeach   O hù I won't take the Uig man
Cha dèan e càil ach rùthadh na mònadh.   He's no good for anything but stacking peat.[3]

O hioram cha ghabhainn a' Siarach   O hioram I won't take the west coaster
O hioram cha ghabhainn a' Siarach   O hioram I won't take the west coaster
O hioram cha ghabhainn a' Siarach   O hioram I won't take the west coaster
Cha dèan e càil ach biathadh nan òisgean.   He's no good for anything but feeding sheep.

O hù ach cha ghabhainn an t-Ùigeach   O hù I won't take the Uig man
O hù ach cha ghabhainn an t-Ùigeach   O hù I won't take the Uig man
O hù ach cha ghabhainn an t-Ùigeach   O hù I won't take the Uig man
Cha dèan e càil ach rùthadh na mònadh.   He's no good for anything but stacking peat.

-----

1. Socks or hose with diamond-shaped patterns; e.g., Argyle socks.
2. *Lòrnes* was a common way of referring to dress shoes, brogues, or shoes for Sunday best, so named for the Lorne Macintyre mail-order catalog from which they were ordered.
3. After peat is cut from the bank it is stacked to dry in small stooks of three or four peats.

This lively song conveyed good-natured self-deprecation for Matheson since *Uig*—derived from the Old Norse *vik*, meaning "bay" or "cove"—is also the parish on the Isle of Lewis's west coast, where he was raised. In her unpublished manuscript, Marjorie Edgar offered astute remarks about "two gay dance-songs sung by Mr. Matheson and recorded by Mrs. Robertson," with names from the refrains, "Ho, ho, hiram" and "A-lu-a-lu-a-loram": "They are reel-tunes and belong to the *port-a-beul* or mouth tunes of tradition, for in some parts of Scotland, as in Brittany, it was the old custom for people to sing while others danced. When John Matheson and his cousin went back to their old home on the island of Lewis they found the old form of dancing still popular, and were asked to help sing for the dancers, who danced all night in the reels. Of course this kind of dancing has not been transplanted to this country, although you may still see sword dances in Duluth, as in St. Paul and Minneapolis surviving with the enduring popular-ity of bag-pipe playing" (Edgar ca. 1940).

13 Eilean Leòdhais / Isle of Lewis

Sung by John H. Matheson, Duluth, Minnesota, September 18, 1937.
Recorded by Sidney Robertson. Transcription, translation, and
annotations by Thomas McKean, 2011.

3299 B

Ochain a Rìgh gur mi tha cianail.
Tha còrr is bliadhna bho rinn mi seòladh.
Ma tha e 'n dàin dhomh gun till mi sàbhailt'
Gu faic mi Chàbag, gach bàt' is òb ann.

CHORUS:
O 's e mo dhùrachd 's e siud a' lùiginn
A bhith tighinn dlùth 's ann ri
   fearann Leòdhais.
Ma nì mi tìr, dheth ged b'ann a' Lìte,
Gun tèid mi dìreach a dh'eilean Leòdhais.

Nuair a thèid mi gu na cuibhle
Air meadhan oidhche nuair a bhios i reòite,

O, 's mòr gum b'fheàrr leam a bhi le pailt'
Ann an leabaidh àrd an eilean
   bàn 's mi Leòdhas.

Thug mi cuairt dhomh Buenos Aires,
Far robh na h-eulagan dheth gach seòrsa,
O 's ann tha m' fharmadsa ris an iasgair
Tha cur a' lion an ear 's an iar air Rònaigh.

O, nach mise bha aig a' bhaile
Am measg nam balach 's a' mealadh òighean
O 's mi gu siùbhladh 's gu falbhainn aotrom
Air bhàrr an fhraoich, 's mi
   air tìr 's mi Leòdhas.

Oh Lord, I am pining.
It's more than a year since I sailed.
If it is my destiny, I will return safely
Till I see Càbag, every boat and bay.

CHORUS:
It is my wish and my desire
To be nearing the land of Lewis.

If I make land, though it be in Leith,
I will go straight to the isle of Lewis.

When I go to the wheel
In the middle of the night when
   it's freezing cold,
Oh, how I would prefer to be replete[1]
In the master bed[2] in the fair isle of Lewis.

I took a voyage to Buenos Aires,
Where there were diversions of every kind,
But I am envious of the fishermen
Casting nets round Rònaigh east and west.

Oh, would that I were at home
Among the lads and teasing the girls
Strolling and skipping
Upon the heather, and me ashore in Lewis.

---

1. Literally, "with plenty" (*pailteas*).

2. Literally, the "high bed," the fancier box bed in the kitchen, where normally the parents or the young
couple would sleep.

Perhaps Marjorie Edgar was thinking of Matheson's performance of "Eilean Leòdhais" where she observed: "In marked contrast to the vigorous, almost stormy group songs, the solo songs at the Lewis gathering were quiet, gravely beautiful, often sad" (Edgar ca. 1940). The homesick sailor of this plaintive song pines for familiar territory: "Chàbag," or Cabag Head, a cape on the northeastern side of Lewis, as well as "Rònaigh," or North Rona, a remote island forty miles to the north. Even Leith, the port city serving Edinburgh on the Scottish "mainland," seems appealing. There are many such exile's paeans to the Isle of Lewis. In 1939 Sidney Robertson recorded a quite different "Eilean Leòdhais" from Donald Macinnes in Oakland, California.

14 Gabhaidh sinn a' rathad mòr / We Will Take the High Road

Sung by John H. Matheson, Duluth, Minnesota, September 18, 1937. Recorded by Sidney Robertson. Transcription and translation by Thomas McKean, 2011.

3302 A2

CHORUS:	*CHORUS:*
Gabhaidh sinn a' rathad mòr	We will take the high road
Gabhaidh sinn a' rathad mòr	We will take the high road
Gabhaidh sinn a' rathad mòr	We will take the high road
Olc air mhath le càch e.	Whatever the rest think.
Olc air mhath le Clann an-t-Saoir	Whatever Clan MacIntyre thinks
Olc air mhath le Clann an-t-Saoir	Whatever Clan MacIntyre thinks
Olc air mhath le Clann an-t-Saoir	Whatever Clan MacIntyre thinks
'S bodaich maola Làghainn.	And the naïve old men of Laggan.
Gu mac Mhic Alasdair 's Lochiall,	To MacAlasdair's son and Lochiel,
Bidh iad leinn mar bha iad riamh	They'll be with us as they ever were
'S fear na Ceapaich mar ar miann	And the Keppoch chief, as it should be
Olc air mhath le càch e.	Whatever the rest think.
Thig Clann Ghriogair, feachd nam buadh.	Clan Gregor, able host, will come.
'S thig Clann Choinnich bho'n Taobh-tuath,	Clan MacKenzie from the North,
'S mairg an dream do'n nochd iad fuath	Pity the band that they despise
Nuair dh'èireas fuaim nam blàr orr'.	When the sound of battle rises.
Thig Clann Ghriogair garg san strì,	Clan Gregor will come, ferocious in battle,
Stiùbhartaich 's iad sluagh a' Rìgh	The Stewarts, the royal host

Mèarrsaibh uallach, suas a' phìob—
Olc air mhath le càch e.

[Matheson sings the next three
verses in English]

Gabhaidh sinn a' rathad mòr
Gabhaidh sinn a' rathad mòr
Gabhaidh sinn a' rathad mòr
Olc air mhath le càch e.

March proudly, sound the pipe—
Whatever the rest think.

We will up and march away,
We don't mind what anybody says.
We will up and march away,
We will never mind them.

Bold MacGregors will come forth
With MacKenzies from the north.
Woe be they who try their worst
In battle strives before them.

We will up and march away,
We don't mind what anybody says.
We will up and march away,
And we'll never mind them.

We will take the high road
We will take the high road
We will take the high road
Whatever the rest think.

This old Scottish tune, dating at least to the seventeenth century and possibly earlier, is the melodic source for "London Bridge Is Falling Down" and nowadays is most often performed, sans lyrics, as a pipe march. Claimed historically by rival clans, the MacIntyres and the Stewarts, it is, in John Matheson's bilingual rendition, an aggressive calling of Highland clans opposed to Lowlander ties with England. The readily identifiable Highland clans—Gregor (MacGregor), MacKenzie, Stewart—are swelled through esoteric clan references: "Lochiel" (Cameron) and "Keppoch" (MacDonald). The particulars of Matheson's lyrics relate to the Battle of Inverlochy in 1645 when the Highlander forces of Montrose, aided by Irish allies, defeated the Lowlanders led by Argyll. In this context "the naïve old men of Laggan" may not refer to the eponymous village and loch in the Highlands, but rather to the "Laggan Army" of Lowland Scots settlers who put down an Irish rebellion in Ulster in 1641. Perhaps Matheson acquired this martial song as a soldier in the Cameron Highlanders.

SERBIAN

Between 1890 and 1910 significant numbers of South Slavs—Croatians, Montenegrins, Serbs, and Slovenians—settled in South St. Paul's meat-packing district and especially in the iron-mining region of northeastern Minnesota. Initially these immigrants were mainly sojourning males who resided in boardinghouses with workers from their respective ethnic group. Families arrived or were formed increasingly by the onset of World War I, as South Slavic immigrants established churches, saloons, and fraternal organizations. Music was a regular feature for church picnics, weddings, tavern entertainment, and in ethnic halls (Holmquist et al. 1981). Slovenians were known for accordion music, whereas Croatians and Serbs fostered string ensembles built around the tamburitza, a lutelike instrument brought into the Balkans by Turks. Chisholm, Minnesota, featured a tamburitza group as early as 1908, with active ensembles soon performing in such Iron Range communities as Ely, Eveleth, Hibbing, Keewatin, and Virginia (Opacich 2005: 127–131).

15 Alaj Gigi
Played and sung by the Balkan Troubadours (Dan Radakovich, Nick Mitrovich, Lubo Mitrovich, Bob Rajacich, and George Rajacich), Eveleth, Minnesota, July 28, 1937. Recorded by Sidney Robertson.
3281 A

Born in Yugoslavia, Dan Radakovich (1908–1991), the leader and eldest of the Balkan Troubadours, founded the group in 1933 (Opacich 2005: 130–131). As Sidney Robertson wrote to Alan Lomax, he ran "the first gas station on the right as you come into Eveleth from Virginia" (June 14, 1938). Nick Mitrovich (1911–1983) sold insurance, while his brother Lubo (1913–2007) worked in an iron ore mine. Like their sister Mary (b. 1915), who was also Dan Radakovich's wife, the Mitroviches were born in Portland, Oregon, to immigrant parents and arrived on the Minnesota Iron Range in the 1920s. Bob Rajacich (1915–2006) and his brother George (1916–1983) were both born in Lucknow, Minnesota, a now-deserted mining location that was also an ore-shipping station on the Great Northern Railroad. In the 1930s the family started the Rajacich Market in Eveleth.

Robertson learned about the group from Ruby Hagie, whose husband Clarence was superintendent of schools in Aurora, on the Iron Range. More than three months prior to recording the Balkan Troubadours, Robertson wrote to her Resettlement Administration supervisor, Adrian J. Dornbush: "I asked Mrs. Hagie whether people played guitars and banjos in the Iron Range country, and she said: 'My goodness, no; but practically everybody has a squeeze-box (an accordion) and plays it badly with great vigor!' No harmonicas to speak of either, she says; but tambouritzas [*sic*] in large numbers, costing up in the hundreds of dollars for the fine big ones. . . . There is a good group there that plays tambouritzas of all sizes and registers. . . . It has played over Duluth radio stations once or twice. This is the music played for wedding dances and parties at the homes of the Austrians [i.e., from the former empire of Austria-Hungary]" (Robertson 1936–1938: April 20, 1937).

Not quite knowing what she was hearing, Robertson recorded only parts of songs from the group. The following summer, after encountering other such bands amid field-work in northern California, she expressed second thoughts in a letter to Alan Lomax, hoping he might capture full versions: "Please get in touch with my swell tambouritza orchestra at Eveleth, Minn. . . . If you tell him you've come to finish the recording of his orchestra's repertoire 'for the government' I'm sure he'll cooperate. He is a swell guy, and the boys he's trained are nice kids. After hearing tambouritza records out here and the local tambouritza orchestras, I realize how exceptionally good his little band of five is. Serbs out here simply rave over his records that I made. Unfortunately I didn't make a whole record of the playing of one tune so that it can be used for dancing" (June 14, 1938).

Robertson's notes reveal, according to Dan Radakovich, that this fragment of "Alaj Gigi" asserts that "a man what could drive a horse in the old days was much more a man than it takes to drive a car these days." This well-known Serbian traditional song has been performed by many groups, including the Balkan Mountain Men, featuring tamburitza stars Milan Verni and Ivan Vidak, who were regulars on NBC broadcasts in the early 1930s. In March 1931 Verni's Troubadours recorded "Alaj Gigi" in New York City for Columbia (1197-F).

FOLLOWING PAGE: The Balkan Troubadours, Eveleth, Minnesota, ca. 1936. (author's collection)

16 Angelina vodu lije / Angelina Is Pouring Water

Played and sung by the Balkan Troubadours (Dan Radakovich, Nick Mitrovich, Lubo Mitrovich, Bob Rajacich, and George Rajacich), Eveleth, Minnesota, July 28, 1937. Recorded by Sidney Robertson. Transcription and translation by Stephanie Vuljanic-Lemke, July 2010.

3280 B2

Angelina vodu lije,	Angelina is pouring water,
Na vodu se omijela.	At the water she washes herself.
Sama sebi govorila:	She says to herself:
"Mili Bože, mili Bože,	"Dear God, dear God,
Bijelo lice, lepo lice."	What a white face, what a beautiful face."

This is an Old World song that reminded its translator, Stephanie Vuljanic-Lemke, of her village girlhood where, lacking mirrors, young women relied on reflections in the water to see what they looked like. The Serbian immigrant Mitar Bulatović recorded a post–World War II version of this song on a 78 rpm record for Chicago's Serbian Record Company. A popular radio announcer and a member of the Windy City's Serbian Radio Orchestra, Bulatović also recorded on the Balkan label (Opacich 2005: 203).

FINNISH

In the 1930s, Minnesota trailed only Michigan as the home to Finnish Americans, with the vast majority concentrated in two northeastern counties, Carlton and St. Louis. The former was heavily timbered, fostering lumber camps and the development of Cloquet as a sawmill town. The latter included the Vermilion and Mesabi Iron Ranges and the port city of Duluth on Lake Superior. Woods workers, mill hands, and domestics dwelling in Cloquet's "Finntown" established public saunas, a "Finn Hall" featuring regular performances, and what was, in the 1930s, the largest retail cooperative in the United States. On the iron ranges, Finns joined Italians and South Slavs in the mines, while also forming cooperative stores, Lutheran churches, workers' halls, and chapters of the Kaleva Lodge, a fraternal and cultural organization (Riippa 1981: 296, 303–304).

In the 1920s immigrant members of the Ladies of Kaleva led Girl Scout troops on the Vermilion Range. When they incorporated Finnish songs into a 1928 statewide founder's day program held in Ely, the audience included Marjorie Edgar. A folksong

FOLKSONG RECITALS
of
MARJORIE EDGAR

Marjorie Edgar poses in Finnish traditional dress against a backdrop of birches for the cover of her "Folksong Recitals" brochure, 1934. (Joyce Hakala collection)

enthusiast instrumental in launching Minnesota's first Girl Scout troop in 1915, Edgar soon befriended scout leaders in Ely and nearby Winton, began to learn the Finnish language, and embarked upon the documentation of Finnish American folklore. By the mid-1930s she had published a trio of pioneering essays: "Finnish Charms from Minnesota" (1934), "Finnish Folksongs in Minnesota" (1935), and "Finnish Charms and Folksongs in Minnesota" (1936). In May 1937 Edgar attended the National Folk

Festival in Chicago where, fortuitously, she met Sidney Robertson—already a seasoned folksong collector for the federal government's Resettlement Administration—and the two made plans resulting in a field recording trip, August 16–19, 1937, capturing thirty-six performances from thirteen Finnish Americans (Leary 2001a: 479–482).

The notes for selected recordings from this trip, including the transcribed and translated lyrics, rely heavily on Joyce Hakala's superb book *The Rowan Tree* (2007), which not only chronicles the life and work of Marjorie Edgar but also includes both biographical profiles of the singers recorded through Edgar's collaboration with Robertson and an annotated edition of Edgar's unpublished Finnish folksong anthology, "Songs from Metsola" (ca. 1950)—a mythical forest kingdom figuring in the Finnish national epic, the *Kalevala*.

17 Charm for Hiccups

Spoken by Cecilia Kuitunen, Winton, Minnesota, August 17, 1937.
Recorded by Sidney Roberston.

3270 B2

This charm was used to cure hiccoughs, both in Finland and America, and is to be said in one breath.

Nikko niineen,	Go to the loom,
Toinen tuoheen,	The second to the bark,
Kolmas koivun,	The third to the birch,
Neljäs neulaan,	The fourth to the needle,
Viides viittaan,	The fifth to the thicket,
Kuudes kuuseen,	The sixth to the spruce,
Seitsemäs seipääseen,	The seventh to the post,
Kahdeksas kyllää,	Eighth to the neighbor,
Yhdeksäs yllää!	And the ninth up!

Cecilia Kuitunen (1895–1984) was born in St. Petersburg, Russia, where her Finnish-born parents, Oscar and Silja Laitinen, worked respectively in a steel mill and as a cook for the Russian army. Laid off in the late 1890s, Oscar Laitinen departed in 1900 for Minnesota, where he had Finnish friends in Ely. Working in turn cutting timbers for mine supports, in an underground mine, and in a planing mill in Winton, he saved enough to send for his wife and daughter in 1901 (Kuitunen 1974). Cecilia completed eighth grade in Winton, where she became especially active in the local temperance

Jack Stark, Hans Koski, and Cecilia Kuitunen in Moliere's *The Miser*, Finn Hall, Winton, Minnesota, 1916. (Joyce Hakala collection)

society and in Finnish hall activities, helping to organize a library with six hundred Finnish books, acting in and directing a range of plays, and even translating plays from English into Finnish with help from her husband, Toivo Kuitunen (1885–1952). Cecilia and Toivo also operated a public sauna in Winton. A charter member of the Minnesota Finnish American Historical Society, founded in 1943, she "broadcast the news in Finnish from radio stations in Ely, Hibbing, and Duluth and, in later years, moved to Duluth to work for the daily newspaper" (Hakala 2007: 252).

In 1934 Marjorie Edgar published a variant of this charm, without attribution but undoubtedly from Kuitunen.

> A practical charm to cure hiccough, from Kangasniemi, eastern Finland, was recorded in Winton, Minnesota; it must be said without taking a second breath. It has a good many dialect words, and the alliteration popular in Finnish folk-poetry.

Nikko niineen	Hiccough to the heddle (of the loom)
Toinen tuoheen	Second to the bark
Kolmas koivun	Third to the birch
Neljäs neulaan	Fourth to the needle
Viides viittaan	Fifth to the thicket
Kuudes kuuseen	Sixth to the spruce
Seitsemäs seipääseen	Seventh to the pole
Kahdeksas kantoon	Eighth to the stump
Yhdeksäs yllää!	Ninth up!
Kymenes kyllää.	Tenth to the neighbor (villager).

(Edgar 1934: 382)

Magical charms or incantations (*loitsut*) were common in rural Finland (Virtanen and DuBois 2000: 179–186). Perhaps Kuitunen's mother, Silja Laitinen, whom she described as "old fashioned" in a 1974 interview, was the source and an active user of this charm.

18 Charm for Toothache

Spoken by Anna Leino, Ely, Minnesota, August 17, 1937.
Recorded by Sidney Roberston.

3270 B1

This *loitsu* or healing charm was used on my mother, first to cure a severe toothache and then another time to allay the pain of a severe burn. The sorceress who used the charm was a tall, imposing woman, an aristocrat in appearance and, supposedly, by birth. In using the charm, she took a basin of water, stirred it with a *puukko* or Finnish knife, and had mother take a sip of the water and spit it into the fire, repeating the charm at the same time. In the case of the burn, she bathed the leg with the water, repeating the words:

Your pains to the wind,
Your aches to the fire,
Your sufferings to the kettles of hell!

And in the Finnish, these words are:

Tuulehen tuskas'
Valkehan vaivas'
Kipus' helvetin kattilaan!

Anna Leino, Ely, Minnesota, 1926.
(Joyce Hakala collection)

Anna Leino (1884–1955) was born in Tornio, in Finnish Lapland, to August and Maria Hario, with whom she immigrated to Minnesota in 1889. She completed coursework at Duluth Business in 1900, then from 1903 to 1904 taught school in Ely and White Iron Lake, the first Finn to hold such a position for the state of Minnesota. After marrying fellow immigrant Emil Leino (1874–1949), Anna worked as a bookkeeper for Ely businesses that included the Finnish Stock Company. Active with the United Finnish Temperance Council and as a singing teacher for Kaleva Lodge youth camps in the 1930s, she was a charter member of the Ely Girl Scout Council and one of Marjorie Edgar's main contacts regarding Finnish American culture and songs.

In 1934 Edgar published this anonymously attributed charm, identifying only its place of origin. The Finnish words were exactly those Leino recited in 1937, but the English translation differed slightly.

From the northwest of Finland, near Tornio comes a charm for a scalded foot. The child, whose foot had been scalded very badly, was told by the wise woman to put her foot in a bowl of water, which the *loihtija* [wise woman] had stirred with a knife. She then threw the water on the fire, calling out in a strange deep voice:

Your torment to the winds,
Your ache to the fire,
Your pain to the kettles of hell!

(Edgar 1934: 383)

19 Pium, paum

Sung by Olga Simi and Sue Simi; played on kantele by Sue Simi, Cloquet, Minnesota, August 16, 1937. Recorded by Sidney Robertson.

3268 A2

Pium, paum! Kehto heilahtaa,	Pium, paum! The cradle rocks,
Ja lapsi viatonna uinahtaa.	And the innocent child is sleeping.
Pium, paum! Äiti laulahtaa,	Pium, paum! The mother sings,
Kun sydänkäpyänsä tuudittaa.	While she rocks the little one-of-her-heart.
Pium, paum! Viulu vingahtaa,	Pium, paum! The sound of the violin is heard,
Ja nuoret karkelohon kiiruhtaa.	And young folks hurry off to games.
Pium, paum! Onni häilyää.	Pium, paum! Fortune is fickle.
Se tuopi varjoa ja pimeää.	Life has its shadows and sunshine.
Pium, paum! Kerran kajahtaa,	Pium, paum! Death soon,
Tuo kylmä kirkonkello ilmoittaa;	For you will toll the cold church bells;
Pois, pois, henki vaeltaa,	Away, away, your spirit will go,
Ja ruumis mullan alla kajan saa.	Your body in the earth, a shelter find.

Suoma "Sue" Simi (1912–1966) and her sister, Olga (1914–1997), the daughters of Hilda Kääntä and Matt Simi, were born on a farm near Kalajoki, on the Gulf of Bothnia in the Finnish province of Oulu. In 1923 Matt Simi, twice a sojourner in the United States, brought his family to settle in Cloquet. The Simi sisters were performing for plays and musical events in Cloquet's Finn Hall almost immediately, with Sue sometimes playing

LEFT: Suoma "Sue" Simi, Minneapolis, Minnesota, 1940. (Joyce Hakala collection)
RIGHT: Olga Simi, 1935. (Joyce Hakala collection)

the kantele. In 1928 she had the lead role in *Haihtuvia Pilviä* (Fading Clouds), a musi-cal by Lauri Lemberg (1887–1965), a Duluth-based journalist, novelist, playwright, and booking agent for Finnish language plays. Sue Simi earned a BA in art education from the University of Minnesota in 1940, then taught art in several elementary and high schools until her premature death from tuberculosis. Olga Simi attended Duluth State Teacher's College prior to earning a degree in home economics from the University of Minnesota in 1940. She married Fred Broders in 1949 and worked variously at govern-ment jobs and as an educational therapist in a psychiatric hospital before spending her final years in California (Hakala 2007: 265–266).

"Pium, paum," learned in childhood by the Simi sisters, was also among the first Finnish songs Marjorie Edgar heard in 1928. An old traditional lullaby, the opening words of which onomatopoeically invoke a rocking cradle, this song acquired its sec-ond and third verses from Kustaa Killinen (1849–1922), a Finnish poet and educator (Hakala 2007: 135, 289–290). Shifting succinctly from cradle to grave, these verses were aptly identified in Sidney Robertson's notes as "often sung at children's and young peo-ple's funerals." A year later, Alan Lomax would record two different versions of "Pium, paum" from the Michigan singers Selma Elona Halinen and Kusti Similä.

20 Vilho ja Pertta / Vilho and Bertta

Sung by Matti Simi; played on kantele by Sue Simi, Cloquet, Minnesota,
August 16, 1937. Recorded by Sidney Roberston.

3268 A1

Yksi talo, rikas talo Keski-Suomessa,

Ja Vilho siellä pojan nimi, vilkas luontonsa.

Vilho nautti opetusta kansakoulussa,
Siellä hän tuli tuntemaan, se Pertan ihanan.

Yhdessä he leikkivät, kun kouluun kulkivat,

Ja tietämättä sydämensä yhteen sulivaat.

Vilho yliopistossa jatkoi oppiaan,

Vain Pertta sitä vastoin kävi
    työssä tehtaassaan.

Vilkas se oli kirjeenvaihto heidän välillään,

Iloiset aina olivat kun toisensa näkivät.

Vain halpa se oli tehtaan tyttö
    hänen mielestään;
Kun arvonimi lääkäri oli hänellä istellään.

Vilho palas koulusta herrana suurena,

Niin ei hän enään tuntenut
    rakasta Perttaansa.

Sunnuntai aamuna levisi tieto niin kamala,
Että yhden naisen ruumis oli
    löydetty koskesta.

In central Finland there was once
    a wealthy manor-farm,
And there a boy named Vilho
    lived, a lively boy and gay.

Vilho liked his lessons at the village school,
And there he came to know the
    girl, his Bertta, his fair one.

Often together they played games
    and walked the path to school,
And as they grew, unconsciously,
    their hearts together grew.

Grown older, Vilho went away to
    college, more to learn,
But Bertta had to go to work in a factory.

Now letters briskly came and went
    between the boy and girl,
And happy they would always be
    when they could meet again.

But mean, to Vilho, seemed Bertta's work;

When he had finished college with
    a doctor's honored name.

When Vilho returned from college
    as a great gentleman,
He no longer he felt anything for
    once-beloved Bertta.

One Sunday morning came the awful news,
That a girl's body had been found
    below the waterfall.

< Olga Simi and her father, Matti Simi, Cloquet, Minnesota, 1928. (Joyce Hakala collection)

Vilho se oli käskyn saanut ruumiin avata,	Vilho ordered them to bring her body to discover
Jos olis syytä itse murhaan voinut havaita.	What might have caused her death, if it were suicide.
Vilho tunsi Pertan kasvot niin heti vaaleni,	Vilho beheld his Bertta's face and, seeing it, turned pale,
Hän muisti kuin hän sydämens' Perttale lupasi.	Remembering when his heart had been promised to this same girl.

Matti "Matt" Simi (1881–1955) was born in Kalajoki, Finland. In 1904 he traveled to Mass City, Michigan, joining a brother to work successively in copper, lead, and silver mines in Michigan, Montana, and Idaho. Blacklisted for union activities, he returned to Finland, where he married Hilda Kääntä in 1909. A few years later, Simi sojourned again to earn money in America but came back to Finland with the onset of World War I to purchase a small farm near Kalajoki in 1917. In 1923, however, Simi, a Social Democrat, was arrested during the Finnish Civil War as a "Red sympathizer," prompting him to emigrate for good with his wife and three daughters, Vieno, Suoma (Sue), and Olga. Bringing with them a thirty-two-string kantele, the Simis settled in Cloquet, where Matti found work successively in a sawmill and a paper mill (Hakala 2007: 264).

"Vilho ja Pertta," a tragic ballad dramatizing class differences in an urbanizing Finland, was recalled by Matti Simi as sometimes including a final verse "in which Vilho kills himself when he discovers that the dead girl is Bertta" (Hakala 2007: 123). Indeed that is how Anneli Asplund—who calls this ballad "The Revenge of the Factory Girl" in a concordance of Finnish narrative folksongs—concludes her plot summary: "Vilho is told to perform an autopsy and recognizes Bertta as his former beloved. Vilho dies of shock." Circulating through oral tradition and broadsheet publications dating to 1897, the song expresses "values and attitudes . . . typical of Finnish society at the turn of the century" (Asplund 1994: 842–843).

21 Heramäen pukki / Old Man's Goat

Played on kantele by Matti Perala, Mountain Iron, Minnesota,
September 19, 1937. Recorded by Sidney Robertson.

3274 B3

Matti Perala (1885–1983) was born in Alavus, a farming and logging community in Finland's Southern Ostrobothnia. His extended family was musical and included an eminent Finnish composer, Toivo Kuula (1883–1917), who drew inspiration from regional folksongs. As a young boy, Perala learned to play kantele in the Säärijarvi style, relying on "the damp-and-strum method using a matchstick." Adventurous, he immigrated at seventeen, settling in Mountain Iron, Minnesota, where he worked as a miner and, later, for the town's Water and Light Department. In 1908 he sent for his sweetheart, Josefiina Tääli, and they were married in Eveleth in 1908. Perala performed frequently at home but not in public, despite being an accomplished kantele musician who also played organ, button accordion, and harmonica.

Perala's daughter Elsa (1913–1994), however, donned Finnish folk dress to play the kantele at various events in the 1930s and early 1940s. A sometime assistant in Marjorie Edgar's Finnish folksong quest, she subsequently performed at the National Folk Festival in Washington, D.C. (Hakala 1997: 196–205; Hakala 2005: 69–71, 258–259).

"Heramäen pukki" (Old Man's Goat) is an old traditional kantele tune that persisted in the repertoires of Arvi Pokela, a performer from central Finland who won the master's competition at the 1983 Kaustinen Folk Music Festival, and of Tallari, a Finnish folk music "super group" associated with the Kaustinen Folk Arts Center since 1986. Like the old man invoked in the song title, Matti Perala raised goats for a time in Minnesota. He learned this tune prior to emigrating in 1902 and used a slower tempo than more recent performers (Hakala 2007: 70).

Wedding of Matti Perala and Josefiina Tääli, Mountain Iron, Minnesota, 1908.
(Joyce Hakala collection)

22 Kataja / The Juniper

Sung by Josefiina Perala, Mountain Iron, Minnesota, September 19, 1937.
Recorded by Sidney Robertson.

3275 A3

Kataja se marjoja kasvaa,	The juniper, its berries, grows,
Kataja se marjoja kasvaa,	The juniper, its berries, grows,
Ilman kukkimata,	Although it never blossoms,
Ja ilman kukkimata.	Although it never blossoms.
Kataja on matalas ojas';	The juniper is in a shallow trench;
Sen marjat on karvahia.	Its berries are bitter.
Poikan sorjat mamman poijat	Boys, graceful mother's boys
On tyttöjen armahia.	Are darlings of the girls.

Josefiina Perala (1888–1976), the daughter of Maria Kahra and John Jarvenpaa Tääli, was born in Alavus, Finland, like her husband, Matti Perala (track 21), whom she married in 1908. The couple had six children. In a 2004 letter to Joyce Hakala, granddaughter Lois Sands remembered Josefiina as "very soft spoken, a great hostess and cook. . . . I remember her endless conversations in Finnish when her friends came over for coffee and her homemade sweet bread." Perala was also renowned as a seamstress (she sewed garments for the family) and for her crocheted doilies and table runners (Hakala 2007: 258–259, 273).

In 1935 Marjorie Edgar set down the first verse of "Kataja" in her songbook, attributing it to "Mrs. M. J. Perala and her daughter [Elsa]." This Old World metaphorical song relies on Finland's ubiquitous junipers to warn that beauty may come with bitterness. Edgar documented, but Robertson did not record, a second juniper song, "Kataja se matala" (The Juniper Is Low-Growing) from John Huhtala (1886–1969), an immigrant to Hibbing who was a blacksmith for the Oliver Mining Company (Hakala 2007: 284, 295). Kuuno Sevander recorded this song in 1930 for Columbia (93168-F).

23 Lähtetään pojat nyt soutelemaan / Boys, Let's Go Rowing

Sung by Otto Sarkipato, Ely, Minnesota, August 17, 1937.
Recorded by Sidney Roberston.

3271 B4

Lähtetään pois pojat soutelemaan,	Boys, let's go, let's go rowing now,
Koska järvi se on noin klaari ja klaari.	When the lake is calm, so calm.
Lähtetään pois pojat soutelemaan,	Boys, let's go, let's go rowing now,
Koska järvi se on noin klaari.	While the lake is calm.
Joka taloss' ja harvassa kylässä	In every village and almost every house
On pojalla appi vaari, ja vaari.	The boy has a father-in-law, in-law.
Joka taloss' ja harvassa kyläs	In every village and almost every house
On pojalla appi vaari.	The boy has a father-in-law.
Mitäs minä muuta kun juon ja rallaan	I do nothing but drink and sing
Mun akkani tavaralla, ja ralla.	On my old woman's money, money.
Mitäs minä muuta kun juon ja rallaan	I do nothing but drink and sing
Mun akkani tavaralla.	On my old woman's money.
Juomaripojan ei sovi olla	It doesn't suit a drinking boy
Akkavallan alla, ja alla.	To be bossed by the old woman, old woman.
Juomaripojan ei sovi olla	It doesn't suit a drinking boy
Akkavallan alla.	To be bossed by the old woman.

Otto Sarkipato (1882–1962) was born in Lahti, Finland, and sailed to New York City by way of Liverpool in 1903. He settled initially near a sister in Fitchburg, Massachusetts, where he met and married fellow immigrant Ida Koivu (1890–1978) in January 1910. The couple moved to Minneapolis in the fall of 1910, then in 1912 to Ely, where Otto worked as a machinist for the local school system and as an engineer for the Ely Water and Light Plant. The family also operated Sarkipato's Tourist Haven on Shagawa Lake, part of Minnesota's Boundary Waters area, with Otto using his skills as a woodworker and mechanic to build a launch, the *White Beauty of Shagawa*. From 1942 until 1959 the Sarkipatos lived in Washington, D.C., where Otto was a machinist for a Navy munitions plant. The Sarkipatos spent their final years in Ely. Unlike his wife, who had classical training on the violin, Otto was a traditional musician who played kantele, zither, valve trombone, piano, and violin by ear (Hakala 2007: 262–263).

Ida and Otto Sarkipato, early 1940s. (Joyce Hakala collection)

For this song, Sarkipato uses a well-known Old Country melody, yet the lyrics have not been reported from Finland. In her "Songs from Metsola" Marjorie Edgar suggests it was a locally composed song: "The verses of this boat song were made up by various singers, each trying to be funnier or tougher than the other" (Edgar ca. 1950). Sarkipato's hometown, Lahti, is situated at the southern end of a chain of lakes, a watery highway extending more than two hundred kilometers. Traders, churchgoers, relatives, and friends all depended on boats, and Sarkipato was necessarily familiar with rowing and singing. His rowdy, rebellious, "drinking boy" lyrics contrast markedly with the serious, sedate performances of the Finnish temperance activists typically recorded by Edgar and Robertson.

24 Keskellä lahtea / In the Middle of the Bay

Sung by Otto Sarkipato, Ely, Minnesota, August 17, 1937.
Recorded by Sidney Roberston.

3271 B3

Keskellä lahtea laineet käy,	In the middle of the bay, the waves go high,
Vaan rannalla on kuin peili.	But by the shore it's like a mirror.
Silkin mä ostan mun sievälleni	I'll buy my sweetheart a silken scarf
Kuin linjalaivan seili.	Like the sail of an ocean ship.

Marjorie Edgar's notes for "Songs from Metsola" reveal that Otto Sarkipato had sung this song for her in 1931 and 1933, prior to its recording in 1937: "This old air, in the Aeolian mode, was sung for me, very slowly and with an almost southern laziness, by a boatman [evidently Otto Sarkipato] who had heard it sung on the rivers and lakes of central Finland. It is obviously an occupational song and had changed its surroundings very little by coming to the border lakes of Minnesota" (Edgar ca. 1950). Variations of Sarkipato's Old World lyrics have been used with another melody as a ring-dance song (Hakala 2007: 296).

25 Laurilan Aleksin harmoonipeli / Laurila Aleksi's Accordion

Sung by Maria Heino, Virginia, Minnesota, August 17, 1937.
Recorded by Sidney Roberston.

3269 .A3

Laurilan Aleksin harmoonipeli,	Laurila's Aleksi has an accordion,
Se hopialta hohtaa.	It shines just like silver.
Kun maaherra passin kirjootaa,	When the governor writes out an order,
Niin lähtiä täytyy kohta.	Then you must leave at once.

Maria Nummelin (1882–1951) was born near Härmä, an inland Finnish village east of Tampere. In 1901 she settled on the Iron Range, where she married fellow immigrant Herman Heino (1881–1948) the following year. The couple lived successively in the Minnesota mining communities of Eveleth, Aurora, and Virginia, where both worked as tailors and were active members of the Finnish Temperance Union (Hakala 2007: 245).

Temperance halls were sites for community programs, with more than thirty active Finnish poets and public readers of poetry in Minnesota during the 1930s, including Adolph Lundquist (1887–1948). A Finnish immigrant to Duluth as a child in 1894, Lundquist was a poet and journalist who cofounded *Minnesotan Uutiset* (Minnesota's News) in New York Mills in 1932. He was praised after death by the Duluth playwright Lauri Lemberg (in whose musical, *Haihtuvia Pilviä*, Sue Simi [see track 19] performed) for writing poems that were conciliatory, uniting, and opposed to discord (Wasastjerna 1957: 151, 307). Similarly remembered by her daughter, Leila Heino Akola, as "very open, good natured" with "a humorous streak," Maria Heino was known for reading special "festival" poems composed by Lundquist at midsummer celebrations in Virginia in 1930 and 1937; she also gave comic readings at festivals in Bovey in 1939 and Cloquet in 1941. Heino also sang with the local Finnish American Mixed Choir in Virginia and Duluth, as well as at the 1933 Chicago World's Fair. And she hosted a Finnish radio program in Virginia from the late 1930s through the early 1940s (Hakala 2007: 245–246, 270).

Marjorie Edgar had this to say about "Laurilan Aleksin harmoonipeli" in "Songs from Metsola": "This song has a typical northern Finnish air, odd and fascinating. The words make little sense to the average Finnish American but had an inner meaning when the Russian provincial governors were all-powerful in Finland. To 'write out an order' often meant to send a man to prison in Siberia. These songs, in which the first part seems to have little relation to the second, are made up with a real idea in mind, not accidentally, as it would appear at first. . . . Aapo Similä [1891–1972, author of a popular Finnish songbook series] has written some interesting things about 'Laurila Aleksin' in *Suomalaiset kansanlaulut* [Finnish Folksongs, 1923]. . . . Not common in Minnesota" (Edgar ca. 1950).

26 Ei kukaan puhu puolestani / No One Speaks on My Behalf

Sung by Maria Heino, Virginia, Minnesota, August 17, 1937.
Recorded by Sidney Roberston.

3269 A4

Ei kukaan puhu puolestani,	No one speaks on my behalf,
Vaan jokahinen kaataa,	But everyone ill treats me,
Ne pansivat, jos taisivat,	They would put me, if they could,
Mun alemmaksi maata.	Even lower than the ground.

Maria Heino, Eveleth, Minnesota, 1941. (Joyce Hakala collection)

Asserting that this song was "very rare" in Minnesota, Marjorie Edgar set down an additional Old World verse from Aapo Similä's 1923 popular anthology of Finnish folksongs, *Suomalaiset kansanlaulut*.

Voi, jos saisin takasin	Alas, if I were only back again,
Sen ajan, jonka elin,	As in former days,
Ja saisin nähdä sen vanhan kullan,	And if I could but see my old love,
Jota minä rakastelin.	That I loved well.

Presumably quoting Maria Heino, Sidney Robertson's notes declared that "Mrs. Heino's songs are all from Vaasa land, 'the southern part of the north part' of Finland" (Robertson 1936–1938). In her annotations of Edgar's "Songs from Metsola," Joyce Hakala adds that "Ei kukaan puhu puolestani" is "representative of a typical two-line repeated structure and melody [that] follows a longstanding tradition from south Ostrobothnia. Anneli Asplund (Sibelius Academy Folk Music Department) credits the structure to Sweden, but Ilkka Kolehmainen (Kaustinen Folk Music Institute) maintains that it developed from runic melodies" (Hakala 2007: 293).

27 Eikä ne haavan lehdet lakkaa / Never Cease the Aspen Leaves

Sung by Maria Heino, Virginia, Minnesota, August 17, 1937.
Recorded by Sidney Robertson.

3296 B3

Eikä ne haavan lehdet lakkaa	Never cease the aspen leaves
Tuulella huiskumasta;	From quivering in the wind;
Eikä se lakkaa vanha kulta	Never cease the memories
Mielehen muistumasta.	Of the old love in my mind.
Sinä pidät musta ja minä pidin susta,	You cared for me, and I cared for you,
Ja ero piti tulla meistä,	And it happened that we were parted,
Eikä mun silmäni kesken kuivu	Nor shall my eyes soon be dry
Surun kyyneleistä.	From weeping for my sorrow.

Marjorie Edgar found "Eikä ne haavan lehdet lakkaa" to be "rare" in Minnesota, but in accord with "a sort of sound pattern traditional in old Finnish folk songs" (Edgar 1936). As Joyce Hakala points out, the song is a *reki laulu*, or "sleigh song," a genre of secular songs associated with youngsters' wintry sleigh rides that emerged in seventeenth-century Finland and were sustained by Finnish American singers and folk poets (Hakala 2007: 295). Familiar trees in the forests of Finland and the Upper Midwest figure in many *reki laulat*, including the "quaking aspen" or "white poplar," with its quivering leaves, along with "juniper, birch, spruce, pine, and alder," as Edgar observed. In the 1930s the red-berried mountain ash was "growing in many a Finnish yard in the streets of mining towns, and planted beside the house doors of farmhouses, to bring good luck" (Edgar 1936: 410).

28 Istuta, tyttö / Plant, O Girl

Sung by Maria Heino, Virginia, Minnesota, August 17, 1937.
Recorded by Sidney Roberston.

3269 B2

Istuta, tyttö, sun ikkunas alle	Plant, O girl, beneath your window
Haapa se harallinen;	An aspen many-branching;
Mutt' ällä riijaa muita kun yhtä,	But take no more than one to love,
Se on niin vaarallinen.	For dangerous are many.

Marjorie Edgar characterized this song, which she first heard Maria Heino sing in 1936, as "rare in Minnesota, possibly in Finland," an assertion partially confirmed by Joyce Hakala, who identifies it as a "ring dance song" while citing several "songs of similar character" in Finnish folksong anthologies (Edgar ca. 1950; Hakala 2007: 57). The ring-dance song, or *rinkkitanssi laulu*, was typically performed by young people in rural Finland who sang, held hands, and danced in a circle. Like the sleigh song in the previous example, "Istuta, tyttö" uses the familiar aspen tree metaphorically while dispensing advice about lovers in proverbial fashion (another ring-dance song is on the Lomax CD, track 32).

Print by Isabella Leary

THE RIVER IN THE PINES
THE WISCONSIN LUMBERJACKS RECORDINGS

The Wisconsin Lumberjacks hailed from northern Wisconsin's timber-rich Chippewa Valley: Rice Lake in Barron County and Ladysmith in Rusk County—mill towns situated, respectively, on the Red Cedar and Flambeau Rivers, surrounded by forests where once-flourishing lumber camps had diminished by the 1930s. Formed in response to a request from the National Folk Festival, the troupe created nostalgic yet vital representations of bygone lumber camp music, dance, and song for May events in Chicago in 1937 and Washington, D.C., in 1938.

Launched in 1934, the National Folk Festival was "the first folk festival to present the cultural expressions of several ethnic and regional groups on the same stage," the first to include an array of occupational groups (cowboys, miners, sailors, and woods workers), and "the first to utilize the skills of persons trained in folklore and related disciplines" (Wilson 1988: 6). Its founder, Sarah Gertrude Knott (1895–1984), had studied with and worked for Frederick Koch and the Carolina Playmakers at the University of North Carolina. The Playmakers, in turn, drew inspiration from Irish romantic literary nationalists like Lady Gregory, John Millington Synge, and W. B. Yeats, who used peasant folklore as the raw material for their own politically informed artistic creations (Ellis-Fermor 1939). Knott was also influenced by the reform-minded Settlement House movement, notably exemplified by Jane Addams's Hull House in Chicago, wherein newly urbanized immigrants and rural Americans were provided with practical skills for adapting to modern life and encouraged to retain their expressive cultural traditions through festive displays, pageants, and performances (Lloyd 1997; M. Williams 2006).

From 1934 to 1936 Knott had featured the Michigan Lumberjacks, a group organized by folklorist Earl C. Beck, at the National Folk Festivals held successively in St. Louis, Chattanooga, and Dallas (Kozma 1991). In spring 1937, Sarah Gertrude Knott began a flurry of correspondence in hopes of discovering a Wisconsin parallel to the Michigan contingent: "This year, since our Festival is to be held in Chicago, next door to Wisconsin, we are tremendously interested in having the best possible representation from the lumberjacks of Wisconsin" (Federal Writers Project of the Works Progress Administration of Wisconsin 1935–1937: April 15, 1937). The chief recipient of Knott's initial correspondence was Charles E. Brown, the director of the State Historical Society of Wisconsin's museum, who also headed the federal Works Progress Administration's Wisconsin Folklore project. An archeologist, Brown's interest in folklore combined nineteenth-century scattershot antiquarianism with a genteel educator's penchant for dramatic retellings and charming rewritings of "raw" folk texts (Leary 1998: 26–28). Brown initially recommended "Chris Crosshaul," whose logging act was in demand at outdoor expositions and whose pseudonym stemmed from a character created by W. B. Laughead, the Minnesota ad man who popularized Paul Bunyan through circulars for the Red River Lumber Company. When Crosshaul proved elusive, Knott sent desperate form letters to Bayfield's Mystic Knights of the Blue Ox, to county agents, and to chambers of commerce. Fortuitously, word reached Otto Rindlisbacher.

Rindlisbacher's life epitomized the cultural ferment of America's Upper Midwest in the early twentieth century. Of immigrant working-class origins, he was by turn a cheesemaker, lumberjack, sawmill hand, café and tavern operator, and taxidermist. A versatile musician in an ethnically diverse area, he had played and recorded Swiss tunes for the Helvetia label, toured regional opera houses with a Norwegian troupe, organized Henry Ford–inspired Old Time Fiddlers Contests, been a regular attraction for a quintessential Wisconsin festival, Cheese Days, and performed on Minneapolis radio with a Hawaiian group (Leary and March 1996). Rindlisbacher likewise had a long-standing involvement with lumber-camp music. As northern Wisconsin's logging economy declined, he opened a café and billiard parlor with his brothers John and Louis. Given Otto's reputation as a musician and his habit of playing, making, and repairing instruments on site, the Buckhorn became a hangout for traditional musicians and woods workers.

Franz Rickaby, who provided the first rich glimpse of Upper Midwestern lumber-camp folksongs, found his way to the Buckhorn in the early 1920s, where he was enlightened concerning the area's Anglo-Celtic and French Indian fiddling. Rickaby accordingly acknowledged his "good friend Otto Rindlisbacher of Rice Lake, Wisconsin,"

Old Time Fiddling contestants pose in front of Rindlisbacher's billiard parlor and café, Rice Lake, Wisconsin, 1926. (author's collection, courtesy of the *Rice Lake Chronotype*)

whom he quoted in *Ballads and Songs of the Shanty-Boy* regarding the style of the lumber camp fiddler: "He gets the swing of the tune and then plays it to suit himself" (Rickaby 1926: xli). Upon learning of the National Folk Festival's eleventh-hour need, Rindlisbacher and his wife Iva proposed an ambitious, culturally diverse program, *An Evening in a Bunkhouse*, to Sarah Gertrude Knott in a letter of April 9, 1937 (Federal Writers Project of the Works Progress Administration of Wisconsin 1935–1937). Besides "lumberjack fiddlers and old style jiggers" of the Anglo-Celtic sort comprising the Michigan Lumberjacks, Rindlisbacher urged the inclusion of Swiss, Scandinavian, and French Canadian performers.

Mingling studied authenticity in repertoire and regalia, romantic nostalgia for a fading era, and a liberal embrace of cultural pluralism acknowledging the diversity of woods workers, the Wisconsin Lumberjacks' program mixed the entrepreneurial moxie of small-town boosters with the show business savvy of ethnic vaudeville veterans. Since participants in the National Folk Festival had to pay their own way, Rindlisbacher

The Wisconsin Lumberjacks: *(back row, left to right)* Earl Schwartztrauber, Frank "Frenchy" Uchytil, J. H. Wallis, mayor of Rice Lake; *(front row, left to right)* Otto Rindlisbacher, Iva Kundert Rindlisbacher, Ray Calkins, Rice Lake, Wisconsin, 1938. (author's collection, courtesy of Lois Rindlisbacher Albrecht)

secured sponsorship from the chamber of commerce of northwestern Wisconsin's multicounty Indian Head Country in 1937, then won financial support from the German-born state governor, Julius P. Heil, in 1938. Performing that year in Washington, D.C., at a time when Hitler's armies were ravaging Europe, the Lumberjacks emblazoned their Viking cello with a Star of David.

Sidney Robertson recorded the group's 1937 stage performances in Chicago, necessarily placing her microphone at a distance to capture an airy yet vital "live" sound, complete with an audience's claps and whoops. Alan Lomax's 1938 recordings, in contrast, were made in studio conditions at the Library of Congress, away from the hurly-burly of the National Folk Festival's Washington site.

1 Fred Sargent's Shanty Song

Sung by Earl Schwartztrauber; percussion by Ray Calkins using a cant
hook and stick, National Folk Festival, Washington, D.C., May 9, 1938.
Recorded by Alan Lomax.

1622 B2

In eighteen hundred and seventy-one,
To swamp for a go-devil we begun.
'Twas on the banks of the Eau Claire,
We landed there when the ground was bare.

CHORUS:
Yoooooo!
Tra-la-la, tru-da-le-la, la-le-li-lo,
Tra-la-la, le-li-lo,
Tra-la-la-la, la-le-li-lo.

Early in the morning we arose.
It was not day till the horn did blow.
Manfully put on our clothes.
Tra-la-la, la-la-la-la.

Now to conclude and end my song,
My shanty story won't be long
Here's to the health of men so strong,
To Fred Sargent and his gang.

Yoooooo!

Earl Schwartztrauber and Ray Calkins, both of Ladysmith, joined the Wisconsin
Lumberjacks in 1937. Recruited by Otto Rindlisbacher, they persisted with the group
long after he withdrew in 1939. In the 1950s they were regulars—along with Milwaukee's
Mazur Polish Dancers and the ballad singer Pearl Jacobs Borusky (Stratman-Thomas
CD part 1, tracks 23 and 24)—for a folk festival at the Wisconsin State Fair patterned
after the National Folk Festival; and in 1964 Schwartztrauber and Calkins were the
lone original Wisconsin Lumberjacks to entertain at the twenty-seventh National Folk
Festival, which was held in Covington, Kentucky (*Waukesha Daily Freeman*, August
27, 1952; *Janesville Daily Gazette*, August 18, 1953, and August 19, 1955; *Milwaukee
Sentinel*, May 11, 1964).

Ray Calkins plays the Viking cello, Chetek, Wisconsin, 1988. (photo by author)

Yet unlike Ray Calkins (track 3), Earl Schwartztrauber remains an elusive fig-
ure. Only an Earl Schwartzstrauber—born in 1900 near Ellsworth in Pierce County,
Wisconsin—turns up in census records. "Our" Earl, sans the extra *s*, lived in the
Ladysmith area from the mid-1930s until at least the mid-1960s, was married to Anna
Schrader, the daughter of a German immigrant farmer in Clark County, and presumably worked in the woods where, among other things, he learned to dance the "Peg-Leg
Jig" from a wooden-legged lumberjack. Schwartztrauber regularly played the "bangola,"
described by Iva Rindlisbacher for the 1940 National Folk Festival Program as "a crude
instrument, made from a washtub and a peavey," strung with hay wire "from the bottom of the tub upward and fastened to the peavey," and played "by plucking the string
and tipping the peavey at various angles." Schwartztrauber sings instead on this performance, with Calkins using a stick to tap out rhythm on a lumberjack's cant hook.

Although Schwartztrauber's singing is very much in woods style, the song itself was
learned from Rindlisbacher's copy of Rickaby's *Ballads and Songs of the Shanty-Boy*. The
opening phrase "to swamp" refers to the process of cutting limbs from felled trees then
chaining the resulting logs to a "go-devil," a forked log or travois, so they could be hauled
to a "tote road" and loaded onto a sled. The published version adds "And in to breakfast

we did go" in the second verse, while substituting "Here's to the health of whisky strong" in the penultimate line (Rickaby 1926: 92–93, 211). Rickaby attributes the song to Emmet Horen of Eau Claire, Wisconsin, while an undated newspaper clipping from Rickaby's papers at the Wisconsin Historical Society adds that "Fred Sargent was a big logger in his day."

Rickaby's "Emmet Horen" was undoubtedly Emmet Horan (1849–1928). Born in Ontario, Horan settled on an Eau Claire–area farm in 1863 with his Irish immigrant parents. In the late 1860s, he "entered the employ of the Eau Claire Lumber Company. His ability to handle men and the faculty he exhibited in attending to the details of the business secured for him the position of foreman of the logging camps of the company." Subsequently a local businessman, politician, and civil servant, Horan was appointed in 1913 as a regent for the state Normal School System and "was a leading factor in securing the location for the Normal School at Eau Claire" (Bailey 1914: 734–735). He was undoubtedly present in 1923 when, as the *Eau Claire Leader* (July 13) proclaimed, "Ballads of Old Days Delight Normal School" thanks to a performance by Franz Rickaby during which he also solicited information on lumber-camp folksongs.

2   Hounds in the Woods

Played on the cigar-box fiddle by Otto Rindlisbacher, with spoken afterword by Alan Lomax, National Folk Festival, Washington, D.C., May 9, 1938. Recorded by Alan Lomax.

1622 A1

Lomax: Now this fiddle tune, "Hounds in the Woods," was played on the cigar-box fiddle of his own make by Otis [*sic*] Rindlisbacher of Rice Lake, Wisconsin. This record was made in the Library of Congress, May 9, 1938. Will you pluck the strings, Mr. Rindlisbacher, so we can hear the tuning? [Rindlisbacher complies.] The tuning is the same as the violin tuning.

Otto Rindlisbacher (1895–1975) was the only musician to be recorded by Sidney Robertson, Alan Lomax, and Helene Stratman-Thomas (for more on his Swiss and Norwegian repertoire, see Stratman-Thomas CD part 2, tracks 9 and 39). Four of his lumber-camp fiddle tunes were included on the Library of Congress LP (1960) and subsequent Rounder Records CD (2001), *Folk Music from Wisconsin*: "Swamper's Revenge

Otto Rindlisbacher with cigar-box fiddle, Rice Lake, Wisconsin, 1950s. (author's collection, courtesy of Lois Rindlisbacher Albrecht)

on the Windfall," "The Couderay Jig," "Lumberjack Dance Tune," and "Pig Schottische." Rindlisbacher had a deep interest in fiddle tunes of all kinds, even publishing a collection—*20 Original Jigs, Reels, and Hornpipes* (1931)—largely memorializing the participants in Rice Lake's 1926 Old Time Fiddlers Contest.

Rindlisbacher was also an avid hunter who belonged to the local One-Shot Gang, whose marksman's motto was "We grease the pot with just one shot." This particular tune invokes both the woods and baying hounds. Just weeks before its May 1938 recording, on March 31, Alan and Elizabeth Lomax recorded a tune of the same name from Henry Davis, a fiddler from Hamilton, Ohio. In the 1970s, the Michigan fiddling scholar Paul Gifford recorded a pair of "tunes in C"—one nameless piece from Helen Goss of Saline and one from Gail McAfee of Manton called "Jumpin' Toothache"—that share features with Rindlisbacher's "Hounds in the Woods" (http://www.giffordmusic. net/TwoFour%20in%20C.html, accessed July 29, 2013).

3 Shantyboy Tune (Kväsarvalsen)

Played on the Paul Bunyan harp, with spoken afterword, by Ray
Calkins, with unknown percussion player, National Folk Festival,
Washington, D.C., May 9, 1938. Recorded by Alan Lomax.

1622 A2

This instrument was called a Paul Bunyan harp, made out of a piece of birch tree,
made by an old-time logger, lumberjack, from Ladysmith, Wisconsin. His name is Dave
Mathers, a direct descendant of Cotton Mathers [*sic*]. It is tuned ADGC as a tenor
banjo. Used in the northern Wisconsin lumber camps.

Ray D. Calkins (1894–1990), the son of Reuben Calkins and Jenny Clark, grew up on
a Barron County farm east of Chetek (Aim 1983). Reuben was born in Iowa in 1866
to parents who came, respectively, from New York and Vermont and then settled on
a farm in Chippewa County, Wisconsin, in the early 1870s. Like his father, Albert,
Reuben Calkins farmed from spring until fall, worked in the woods through the winter,
and practiced carpentry and cabinetmaking on the side. In 1905 the family moved to
Ladysmith, where eleven-year-old Ray followed his dad into the woods. While Reuben
was a skilled sawyer and loader, young Ray was in turn a cook's assistant, or cookee, a
swamper, and finally a sawyer, first with a crosscut saw and years later with a chain saw.
A World War I combat veteran, Calkins married Angeline Holland. They raised four
children in the Ladysmith area, where Calkins hauled gasoline, worked on the highway,
made cabinets, tools, and musical instruments, and played in bands. There was always
music in the camps: accordions, concertinas, fiddles. Although he sometimes played
drums in town, tenor banjo and mandolin sufficed during stints in the woods. "Lots
of guys couldn't buy instruments, so they made them" (Calkins 1988). Calkins's Paul
Bunyan harp was a homemade guitar named for the legendary giant logger associated
with romance and tourism in the 1930s.

Calkins's title, "Shantyboy Tune," refers to a lumberjack whose dwelling is a rough
log shanty during winters spent toiling with fellow woods workers. The tune originated
in Sweden, however, and was widely known there and in Scandinavian America as
"Kväsarvalsen." It may have been acquired from Hank Thompson, a Norwegian fiddler
from Rice Lake with whom Calkins began playing in 1934, or it may have been known
to Otto Rindlisbacher, since he too played this tune (track 12). The earliest extant report

of the tune came from Charles Artur Högstedt (1877–1942), who first heard it as an unnamed melody at a dance in the rural Swedish district of Hälsingland. In 1898 he created the title and lyrics, publishing "Kväsarvalsen" in the Swedish humor magazine *Strix*, which had been founded the year before by the artist and illustrator Albert Engström. In 1899 Emil Norlander, Stockholm's "revue king," incorporated the song in his first production, *Den Stora Strejken* (The Big Strike), regarding the Sundsvall sawmill strike of 1879, Sweden's first major strike by industrial workers. As the Swedish literature scholar Susan Brantly points out, *kväsa* means "'to quell' as in, 'to quell a revolt.'" An 1899 edition of *Strix* further declared that *kväsare* and *kväsarjänta*, respectively, were derogatory terms for a man and a woman from the working class (Brantly 2014). The song features a flashy worker swaggering into a dance hall in search of a pretty girl. Brantly provided and translated this description from *Strix* (1899): "Först den oundvikliga vegamössan med ett veck fram vid kullen och en snodd tvärsöfver, kavajkostym, kulört skjorta, en i ögonen lysande sidenhalsduk, vårdslöst knuten i rosett. Hans gång liknar en vaggande ankas, händerna nedstuckna i byxfickorna, kutar med axlarne samt hufvudet något framsträckt, ungefär som en tjur färdig att stångas, samt till slut en Dukehars [cigarrett]" (First the unavoidable cap with a fold near the top and a cord across it, a suit, colored shirt, a silk scarf that catches your eye, casually tied in a rosette. His gait resembles a waddling duck's, his hands stuck into his pants pockets, hunches his shoulders and stretches his head forward somewhat, about like a bull about to be stuck, and then finally a Dukehars [cigarette]).

The tune and, to a lesser extent, the song were well known to Swedish and Norwegian immigrants alike by 1900. The Swedish immigrant baritone Joel Mossberg recorded a version for Victor in 1906 (3423), while accordionist John Lager, who toured the Upper Midwest in the early twentieth century, cut several instrumental renditions in the 1920s (e.g., Victor 77661 in 1924). Mossberg's lyrics correspond with descriptions from *Strix* seven years earlier: a school-of-hard-knocks woods worker comes to the dance hall. The Swedish kväsare was much the same as the American shanty boy at play; indeed, many a Scandinavian kväsare later became Upper Midwestern shanty boys. Lumberjacks in northern Wisconsin were not alone in appreciating "Kväsarvalsen." In the 1930s, the folksong collector William A. Owens heard a version from singing Swedish cowboys on the Texas plains (Owens 1983: 233).

4 The River in the Pines

Played on the Viking cello, with spoken afterword, by Iva Kundert
Rindlisbacher, National Folk Festival, Washington, D.C., May 9, 1938.
Recorded by Alan Lomax.

1622 A3

Iva Kundert Rindlisbacher (1899–1981), like her husband Otto, was of Swiss German
heritage. The Kunderts were drawn to Monroe, a Swiss community in Green County,
as Wisconsin's post–Civil War dairy industry created demand for experienced cheesemakers. Born in Mazomanie, Iva also lived in the southwestern Wisconsin communities
of Reedsburg and Platteville before moving north with her family to Rice Lake sometime prior to 1920. She was a gifted and versatile musician. After marrying in 1921,
Iva and her husband, Otto, were billed as "The Rindlisbachers, Famous Swiss-Italian
Alp Players" for performances with a troupe led by the Norwegian immigrant accordion
virtuoso Thorstein Skarning (*Rice Lake Chronotype*, September 3, 1924). Capable on
piano, organ, piano accordion, banjo, mandolin, guitar, and Hawaiian guitar, she played
in dance bands with her husband, for church services, and to accompany silent films in
Rice Lake's Majestic Theater. A music teacher as well for the Barron County Normal
School and an affiliate of the Conservatory of Music in Superior, she used her organizational skills to produce a basic script and preside over rehearsals for the Wisconsin
Lumberjacks' *An Evening in the Bunkhouse* (Albrecht 1990).

Iva's daughter Lois Rindlisbacher Albrecht (1926–1998) recalled those practices
vividly in 1990, especially "my mother playing the Viking cello. . . . It was beautiful."
In her program notes for the National Folk Festival, Iva Rindlisbacher wrote: "The
Viking Cello was also known as the Psalmodikon. . . . The tone chamber is made from
an old Norwegian chest dated 1722." The psalmodikon—a one-stringed, bowed, fretless
instrument—was developed in Scandinavia in the early nineteenth century as an aid
to hymn singing in rural churches. Immigrants to Wisconsin made and used psalmodikons, initially for church but also for their own entertainment or for concerts that
might often include secular tunes (see Stratman-Thomas CD part 2, track 43).

A few miles northwest of Rice Lake, for example, Emma Stevenson, born in 1874
"in a peasant home in southern Sweden," settled in Shell Lake in 1884, where her dad
worked in a mill: "We had no musical instrument, but my father, who had a wonderful
voice, once made a kind of one-string affair. He attached a cigar box to a long stick. Then

he stretched a cat-gut string to it and had places marked off, something like they do on a banjo. Then he bought a fiddle bow. He'd lay this instrument on the table and play and sing for dear life" (Winton 1976: 211–212).

Further south, in Vernon County, a Norwegian immigrant farm boy, Orben Sime (1903–1975), grew up in a psalmodikon-playing family. An adept player of numerous stringed instruments, Sime left home at sixteen, following a call of faith, and spent the rest of his life traversing the region to give concerts to religious and community groups in return for "free will" offerings (Humphrey 2010). An account of a 1959 concert in La Crosse reveals that he made a one-string bowed instrument from a pitchfork around 1914:

> Another unusual instrument Mr. Sime played was the pitchfork cello which he had made 45 years ago when he was but 11 years old. Should you like to make one in your spare time, it is really very simple. Take an ordinary pitchfork, add a small wooden box about half-way between the handle of the fork and the tines, attach a single string. A leather loop suspended from the tines holds the "instrument" steady, and now you're ready to sit down and play. We'll wager it's harder to play than to make! The instrument bears no resemblance to anything musical. At first glance, it is simply a long, narrow box, each of the four sides about four inches wide, and possibly four feet long. It is made of crude pine boards, now darkened by time. There is one single string which runs nearly the length of the box. The player puts the instrument in a vertical position, one end resting on the floor, and sits down to play it with a bow. (http://murphylibrary. uwlax.edu/digital/lacrosse/AroundCoulees/text/01310121.txt, accessed July 31, 2013)

By the end of his life, Sime owned three such "cellos," including one commissioned in 1929 from Knute Reindahl (1857–1936). A Norwegian immigrant from Telemark who settled with his parents in Dane County's town of Burke in 1867, Reindahl drew on his youthful woodworking skills to become an accomplished luthier. By 1900, having been featured at Chicago's Columbian Exhibition of 1893, he was the Upper Midwest's most celebrated violin maker. It was Reindahl who coined the playfully patriotic term "Viking cello" for the erstwhile pitchfork cello.

In the late 1940s and early 1950s, Grant and Bernice Haium of Clayton, which is southwest of Rice Lake, exploited the instrument's comic possibilities by performing as rustic rubes for the *Sunset Valley Barn Dance* on St. Paul's KSTP station: "Father,

Grant, affixed a sound box and an oversized violin bridge to a pitchfork which he held upwards from the floor near an over-turned washtub. As he bowed a string attached fiddle-fashion to the fork, he thumped the tub with his foot while his daughter, Bernice, accompanying on guitar, sang with him" (Barfuss 1983: 64–65).

Iva Rindlisbacher's repertoire on the Viking cello was limited to a pair of mournful ballads concerning drowned lumberjacks and distraught sweethearts. Both drawn from Rickaby's *Ballads and Songs of the Shanty-Boy* (1926), "The Pinery Boy" was issued by the Library of Congress—*Folk Music from Wisconsin* (1960, 2001)—and "The River in the Pines" is included here. Acquired by Rickaby from William Bartlett (1861–1933), a prominent Eau Claire local historian with particular interests in logging, the song recounts an occurrence on the Chippewa River and was attributed by Bartlett to "Ruth F. G." (Rickaby 1926: 119–121, 217). Performed by Iva Rindlisbacher as an instrumental solo without vocals, "The River in the Pines" was also sung by the Wisconsin Lumberjacks' Frank Uchytil (track 7).

5   Dinner Horn Solo

Played on the lumber-camp dinner horn, with spoken introduction, by Sven "Shantyman" Svenson (Otto Rindlisbacher), National Folk Festival, Chicago, May 27, 1937. Recorded by Sidney Robertson.
3252 B5

Here we go. That's the best music that we hear when we hear it call us home for dinner with the dinner horn.

Sven "Shantyman" Svenson is undoubtedly Otto Rindlisbacher. No such person resided in either Rice Lake or Ladysmith in the 1930s, nor is anyone with that name evident in the numerous published stories and photographs concerning the Wisconsin Lumberjacks' performances, excepting brief reference to "Sven Svenson with his birch bark flute" in a clipping from an unidentified Wisconsin newspaper. Likewise, neither Ray Calkins nor Lois Rindlisbacher Albrecht mentioned such a person when interviewed in 1988 and 1990. Lois did, however, recall her parents working "a Swedish cook" into "a skit of a lumber camp, the things that took place there." Comic "Scandihoovian" character types—typically with such redundant patronymic names as Yon Yonson, Ole Olson, and Sven Svenson—were common figures in regional folk and popular culture.

Indeed the Minneapolis-based Swedish performer Olle i Skratthult recorded "Sven Svenson's Sven" in 1917 (Columbia E3494), as did another Swedish American comic singer, Charles Widden in 1921 (Victor 73048). Although the person who performed on a piece of birch bark at the 1937 National Folk Festival introduced himself as "Sven Svenson" (tracks 11 and 12), Lois Albrecht not only provided a preliminary program typed by her mother listing "Mr. Rindlisbacher" as the performer of a birch-bark solo, but also distinctly recalled her father making and playing birch bark, as well as blowing both the dinner horn included here and the cow horn (track 10).

The Buckhorn's curiosities also included the display The World's Largest Collection of Odd Lumberjack Musical Instruments, among them a long conical tin trumpet used by a lumber camp's cookee to summon the men to meals. Commonly called a dinner horn, it was also referred to as a Gabriel, in reference to the archangel's apocalyptic trumpeting.

6 Soldier's Joy

Played by Otto Rindlisbacher, cigar-box fiddle, and Ray Calkins,
Paul Bunyan harp, National Folk Festival, Chicago, May 27, 1937.
Recorded by Sidney Robertson.
3252 A2

Otto Rindlisbacher made the fiddle heard on this track from a cigar box and a broom handle. Thanks to his skilled construction and fine musicianship, the tune sounds as if played on a less humble instrument. Evident in Scotland as early as 1779, "Soldier's Joy" is arguably "the fiddle tune most widely known and played in Great Britain and North America" (Jabbour 1971: 3; Bayard 1945: No. 21). Leizime Brusoe, the French Canadian fiddler from Rhinelander, Wisconsin, also recorded a stellar version for the Library of Congress that leads off Alan Jabbour's authoritative anthology, *American Fiddle Tunes*.

7 The River in the Pines

Sung by Frank Uchytil; played by Otto Rindlisbacher, piano accordion, and Iva Kundert Rindlisbacher, Viking cello, National Folk Festival, Chicago, May 27, 1937. Recorded by Sidney Robertson.

3253 B

Oh Mary was a maiden when the birds began to sing.
She was fairer than the blooming rose so early in the spring.
Her thoughts were gay and happy and the morning gay and fine,
For her lover was a river boy from the River in the Pines.

'Twas early in the morning in Wisconsin's dreary clime
That he rode the fatal rapids for that last and fatal time.
They found his body lying on the rocky shores below
Where the silent rippling waters and the whispering cedars blow.

Now every raft of lumber that comes down the Chippeway,
There's a lonely grave that's visited by drivers on their way.
They plant wild flowers upon it in the morning gay and fine.
Tis the grave of Charlie Williams from the River in the Pines.

Frank J. Uchytil (1910–1971) was the son of Ruzena (Rose) Skola (1892–1969) and Frank Uchytil (1886–1945). Rose was raised in a Czech neighborhood in Omaha, and her husband was an immigrant from Czechoslovakia. Nebraska and South Dakota had been destinations for Czech, or "Bohemian," immigrants since the 1880s, and the couple tried their hand at dryland farming in southern South Dakota, where Frank J. was born. The presence of relatives, the promise of better land, and according to family tradition, the profusion of mushrooms—essential to Czech cuisine—that sprang from abundant maple stumps drew the Uchytils to the burgeoning Bohemian settlement of Haugen, Wisconsin, six miles north of Rice Lake, sometime before 1920 (Uchytil 2013). Frank J. did not stay on the farm, however, and lived most of his life in the port city of Superior.

Described by Ray Calkins as a "professional singer," Uchtyil was more a crooner than a typical woods singer. As a newspaper clipping from April 1940 put it, "the sweet-voiced individuals who could render the tear-jerking songs . . . were called 'wailers.' . . . Mr. Uchytil is the 'wailer' of the Rindlisbacher group." Seizing upon his nickname, "Frenchy"—derived from an old-time acknowledgment of "Francis" or "Frank" as originally signifying the Franks or French—Sidney Robertson mistakenly asserted on this recording's dust jacket that "Frenchy was a real Fr-Canadian lumberjack." She rightly noted, however, that "he was taught this song by Mrs. Rindlisbacher, a small-town music teacher and choir leader." More than a year later, she elaborated in a letter to Alan Lomax as he prepared for his Upper Midwestern field trip: "The Rindlisbachers in Rice Lake are a kind of fake—that is to say, Mrs. R.—taught her Fr. Canadian boy the song he sang at Chicago out of Rickaby's book" (Robertson 1936–1938: June 14, 1938). Frank Uchytil's version of "The River in the Pines," shortened to ensure a crisp stage show, replicates verses 1, 3, and 8 of the eight-verse rendition published by Rickaby (1926: 119–121). In 1959 and 1966 Edith Fowke recorded versions, with varying lyrics, in Ontario and in Quebec (1970: 131–135).

8   Woods Holler; Hoot Owl Holler
Played on Schweizer hand-orgeli (Swiss button accordion) by Otto Rindlisbacher, with yodeling by John Giezendanner, National Folk Festival, Chicago, May 27, 1937. Recorded by Sidney Robertson.
3252 B1

John "Gits" Giezendanner (1893–1975) was a Swiss immigrant who had lived for a time in southern Wisconsin before moving north to Barron County, where he became an established Guernsey breeder (for more biographical information, see the notes for Stratman-Thomas CD part 2, track 8). A button accordionist and an accomplished yodeler, Giezendanner and his fellow Swiss performer, Otto Rindlisbacher, kept close ties with kindred musicians and singers in Wisconsin's core Swiss communities, New Glarus and Monroe. In the mid-1930s the Monroe Yodel club traveled to Rice Lake to put on a program, and in 1937, just a few weeks after performing at the National Folk Festival, Otto and Iva Rindlisbacher, their daughters Laurel and Lois, and John Giezendanner were featured Swiss musicians in the Cheese Days parade in Monroe, Wisconsin (Leary 1991: 27–30).

Traveling performers from Switzerland also included Rice Lake on their tours, as evident from this May 1926 edition of the *Rice Lake Chronotype*: "Moser Bros. of Berne, Switzerland, Swiss yodelers, will give a musical concert at the armory in Rice Lake, on Tuesday, May 11. They come here by special arrangement of John Mani, who years ago came from the same canton in Switzerland. . . . Nearly 1000 people turned out to hear them in Monroe, Wis. It will be a rare treat to hear the Moser Bros. Some of their best selections have been recorded by the Victor company and may be purchased in this city." Giezendanner's "Woods Holler" is loosely patterned after the Moser Brothers 1926 recording "Jodler Ländler" (Victor 78502).

9   Medley: Die lustigen Holzhackerbuab'n / The Jolly Lumberjack; Fred Sargent's Shanty Song; Schuhplattler

Played by Otto Rindlisbacher, piano accordion; Iva Kundert Rindlisbacher, Viking cello; Ray Calkins, Paul Bunyan harp; Frank Uchytil, cigar-box mandolin; Earl Schwartztrauber, percussion and lead vocals; and John Giezendanner, yodeling; National Folk Festival, Chicago, May 27, 1937. Recorded by Sidney Robertson.
3247 B1

This medley, which was performed live on a Chicago stage, commences with "Die lustigen Holzhackerbuab'n," a lively alpine march featuring yodeling and associated with Old World woodcutters paralleling Wisconsin's lumberjacks. Composed by Josef Franz Wagner (1856–1908), the Austrian March King, also famed for creating "Unter dem Doppeladler" ("Under the Double Eagle"), this tune, sometimes known by its translated title, "The Jolly Lumberjack," is a standard in the repertoires of Upper Midwestern polka bands. The second part of the medley, "Fred Sargent's Shanty Song" (see also track 1), sustains the woods theme, augmented by Giezendanner's yodeling and a full band. The third piece, a "Schuplattler," is the Lumberjacks' version of an ancient alpine social dance that is associated with Austria and Bavaria and involves young men showing off by clapping their hands, stomping their feet, and rhythmically slapping their thighs, knees, and the soles (*platteln*) of their shoes.

In 1932 Jack Bundy (1913–1973) assumed the stage name Heinie to perform with his band, Heinie and His Grenadiers, on an enormously popular program over Milwaukee's WTMJ radio. The six songs the band recorded in Chicago in 1935 included both "Schuhplattler" (Decca 5120) and "Tiroler Holzhackerbuab'n" (the original title of Wagner's "Jolly Lumberjack" composition, Decca 5146).

10 Cow Horn Solo

Played on cow horn by Sven "Shantyman" Svenson (Otto Rindlisbacher),
National Folk Festival, Chicago, May 27, 1937.
Recorded by Sidney Robertson.
3247 B2

This short blast by Otto Rindlisbacher in the guise of Sven Svenson was blown on a
cow's horn. Such horns were blown by herders throughout Europe, including in Sweden,
Norway, and Switzerland. In Nordic countries women tending cattle in summer pastures
used cow horns to call one another, as well as to scare marauding animals (Krogsæter
1968: 29–30; Nupen 1999: 16–17, 74–77). In Switzerland cow and goat horns cleaned
in boiling water have been made and blown by children especially in connection with
St. Nicholas Day and with carnival bonfires (Geiser ca. 1970: 48; Bachmann-Geiser
1996: 45).

11 Lumberjack Story; Swedish Dialect Story

Spoken by Sven "Shantyman" Svenson (Otto Rindlisbacher), National
Folk Festival, Chicago, May 27, 1937. Recorded by Sidney Robertson.
3252 B4

My name is Sven Svenson from Wisconsin. I used to drive all over, on the drive, in
Wisconsin and all the rivers there is. And when we come to a big jam in the river, and
the boss he told me to go on one side and blow this birch bark for him—and he'll break
the jam so much quicker. But then, when the boss come around, he get mad and he told
me he can't keep one—"I can't keep one man here, for to lay off three hundred men. So
you'd better go down the river," he said. Well, all the boys hear that. They says, "We'll
all go if you send him down the river." That's all.

Dialect humor requiring the mastery of another lingo or brogue, and Scandihoovian dialect especially, were hallmarks of playful banter and joke telling in the region where Otto
Rindlisbacher was raised, as was the art of fooling outsiders (Dorson 1948; Leary 2001b:
63–81). A skilled taxidermist whose restorations of local fauna were mounted on the
walls of the Rindlisbacher brothers' Buckhorn Tavern, Otto also hoodwinked gullible

visitors and entertained savvy locals by interspersing such imaginative creations as the shovel-tailed snow snake, the owl-eyed ripple-skipper, the dingbat, and the fur herring.

12 Kväsarvalsen / Swagger Waltz

Played by Sven "Shantyman" Svenson (Otto Rindlisbacher), birch bark; Iva Kundert Rindlisbacher, piano accordion; Ray Calkins, Paul Bunyan harp; and Frank Uchytil, bangola, National Folk Festival, Chicago, May 27, 1937. Recorded by Sidney Robertson.

3247 B3

Otto Rindlisbacher's alter ego, Sven Svenson, was sometimes mistakenly identified as "Swan Swanson" or "Swen Swenson." Sidney Robertson wrote on the disc sleeve for this recording, "Kvsar [*sic*]—Norwegian tune played by Mr. Swen Swenson on a piece of birch bark, acc. by Rindlisbacher group—like playing on a blade of grass." Lois Rindlisbacher Albrecht remembered that "Otto used to make them. He would fold and bend birch bark between his lips and blow it like a whistle" (1990). Perhaps Rindlisbacher learned this through his musical extended family since blades of grass, leaves, dandelion stems, acorn cups, and bark tubes have all been used as rudimentary reed instruments in Switzerland (Geiser ca. 1970: 36, 42, 44–45; Bachmann-Geiser 1996: 37–39). (Regarding "Kväsarvalsen," see the notes for track 3.)

13 Rippling Brook

Played on Hardanger fiddle by Otto Rindlisbacher, National Folk Festival, Chicago, May 27, 1937. Recorded by Sidney Robertson.

3255 A1

Norwegians were the most numerous of Rice Lake's many ethnic groups and the skilled, versatile, open-minded Swiss American Otto Rindlisbacher learned instruments and tunes aplenty from his various neighbors. When he was a boy, the Helland Brothers, immigrants from Telemark, lived just to the south in the village of Cameron. Accomplished makers of Norway's national instrument, the eight-string Hardanger fiddle, the Hellands were at the center of an Upper Midwestern Hardanger fiddling network in the early twentieth century. This tune simulates the roiling waters of a mountain stream.

14 Saeterjenten's sontag / Herdsgirl's Sunday

Played by Iva Kundert Rindlisbacher, Viking cello; Otto Rindlisbacher, piano accordion; and unknown pianist, National Folk Festival, Chicago, May 27, 1937. Recorded by Sidney Robertson.

3254 B1

The *saetter* is a mountain cottage adjacent to summer pastures where young women tended cow herds in Norway. This tune, along with "Saetterliv"(Life at the Saetter), comes from a larger composition, "Et Saetersbesog"(A Visit to the Saetter), by Norway's premier violinist and romantic nationalist composer, Ole Bull (1810–1870). Bull lived for a time in Madison, Wisconsin, where he performed in local Norwegian settlements. "Saeterjenten's sontag," the most popular tune from his larger composition, was recorded commercially at least six times by Norwegian American musicians from 1907 to 1929.

15 Styrmans vals / Pilot's Waltz

Played on Paul Bunyan harp by Ray Calkins, National Folk Festival, Chicago, May 27, 1937. Recorded by Sidney Robertson.

3255 A2

The Wisconsin Lumberjacks left this waltz unnamed in their program, but LeRoy Larson, the leader of the Minnesota Scandinavian Ensemble, identified it immediately as "Styrmans vals," invoking a pilot or helmsman who steers a seagoing vessel. Well-known in Sweden and throughout the Upper Midwest's Scandinavian and Finnish communities, it was first recorded with lyrics in 1915 by the Swedish-immigrant comic singer Charles Widden (Columbia E 2613). A year later the influential accordion duet of John Lager and Eric Olsen, who toured throughout Minnesota and Wisconsin, recorded an instrumental version (Victor 69133).

16 Rolling the Logs; French Dialect Story

Spoken by Peter H. Plante, National Folk Festival, Chicago,
May 27, 1937. Recorded by Sidney Robertson.

3252 B3

Why Joe, I's laughed today.
The boss, he was coming down the road this way.
I was coming down the road this way [i.e., the other way].
Well, when he come to me, he say, "Where youse go, Joe?"
Well, Slim, he was laid on the log. He jumped quick. He grabbed
    his peavy, you know, he tried to roll that log.
"Well, four men can't roll that log I tell you!"
Well, the boss, he say to me, "You, where youse go?"
I say, "Well, you know, some load of logs is stuck down here. I's go get some team for help pull."
He say, "Well, you hurry up."
I start run. I get some team after while. I get back. And Red,
    he was there. He was try to roll that log yet.
And I say, "Well, Red. Let's go home. You can't roll that, eh."

The broken English syntax and stress patterns suffusing this brief story of an impatient foreman and a Sisyphean worker were characteristic of the "Frenchyman" dialect once commonly heard throughout northern Wisconsin's French Canadian settlements. Although this speaker is called "unidentified" in the records of Library of Congress's Archive of American Folk Song, it is very likely Buck Plante. A 1937 newspaper clipping in Lois Rindlisbacher Albrecht's possession mentioned "Ray Calkins and Buck Plante of Ladysmith with their playing and talks." When interviewed in 1988, Calkins recalled "Buck Plante, a Frenchman from Ladysmith, a jigger and mandolin player." In 1892 Antoine Plante purchased land along the Flambeau River just north of Ladysmith, alongside other French Canadian newcomers: Bessette, King (Roi), and Vinette. Plantes also settled downriver in Chippewa Falls. Since "Buck" is a common nickname, we do not know this performer's identity for certain, but it is likely Peter H. Plante (1884–1966), who lived variously in Chippewa Falls and Ladysmith, turning up in the 1940 census as living in the latter community's Second Ward.

17 Marie Patin

Sung by Frank Uchytil, National Folk Festival, Chicago, May 27, 1937.
Recorded by Sidney Robertson. Transcribed, translated, and annotated
by Anjili Babbar, 2010.

3252 B2

Oh Marie Patin, ce soir [tonight], tonight, along the Flambeau,[1]
Oh comment ça va [how are you], Marie Patin, you see.
Oh tu (ne) commences plus [you do not start again],[2] Marie Patin,
Ce soir, tonight, along the Chippeway River
On the banks of the Flambeau, Marie Patin!

———

1. The Flambeau River, a tributary of the Chippewa River, was a "driving" stream for transporting
    logs in the heart of northern Wisconsin's pinery. Like the Turtle Flambeau Flowage from which it
    emerged, as well as the nearby Lac Du Flambeau, the river's French name refers to the torches used
    by Ojibwes to illuminate springtime waters as they paddled canoes to spear walleyes.
2. When Uchytil—of Bohemian or Czech, not Quebecois heritage—sings "Oh tu commences plus,"
    he may in fact be trying (feebly) to say "Oh comment ça se peut" (How is it possible? or How can it
    be?), which would make abundantly more sense.

This mixed-language plea to a French Canadian woman, invoking noted log-driving rivers in northwestern Wisconsin, was likely composed in the lumber camps. Its tune and
some of its language, however, are drawn from "On the Banks of the Wabash," which
was composed by Paul Dresser in commemoration of his childhood home alongside
Indiana's Wabash River. Published in 1897, and one of the best-selling songs of the nineteenth century, it became a popular music standard and was adopted as Indiana's state
song in 1913.

18 Turkey in the Hay

Played by Otto Rindlisbacher, cigar-box fiddle, and Ray Calkins,
Paul Bunyan harp, National Folk Festival, Chicago, May 27, 1937.
Recorded by Sidney Robertson.

3252 A3

Although set down in the Library of Congress catalog as "Turkey in the Hay," this tune is
the well-known "Turkey in the Straw." Arguably the best-known American fiddle tune,
"Turkey in the Straw" emerged on the minstrel stage in the late 1820s. A century later,
in 1928, Walt Disney used it throughout the first Mickey Mouse cartoon, "Steamboat

Willie." The Lumberjacks' version ends with the classic "shave and a haircut—two bits" closing formula. Polish fiddlers in Michigan also performed this tune for Alan Lomax in 1938 (Lomax CD, track 28).

19 Woodchopper's Jig
Played by Otto Rindlisbacher, cigar-box fiddle, and Ray Calkins,
Paul Bunyan harp, National Folk Festival, Chicago, May 27, 1937.
Recorded by Sidney Robertson.
3254 A2

Despite its lumberjack title, this tune is actually "Chicken Reel," an intentionally archaic-sounding 1910 composition by Joseph M. Daley that emulates the minstrel show style and fowl name of "Turkey in the Straw." Figuring as the sonic backdrop for cavorting barnyard beasts in early cartoons, "Chicken Reel" entered the repertoires of hillbilly and polka bands alike. In 1951 Wisconsin's Lester Polsfuss (1915–2009), better known as Les Paul, repopularized the tune through a guitar instrumental featuring mock chicken clucks (Capitol 1373).

20 Gamle reinlander / Old Reinlander
Played on Hardanger fiddle by Otto Rindlisbacher to accompany folk
dancers, National Folk Festival, Chicago, May 27, 1937.
Recorded by Sidney Robertson.
3255 B1

Hardanger fiddles in Norway, and for the most part in America's Upper Midwest, have been used for regional dance forms, or *bygdedans*, especially the *springar*, a running-couple dance in irregular 3/4 time, and the *halling*, an energetic male solo dance featuring high kicks. Requisite at weddings and sharing common features from one district to another, these dance forms and their accompanying tunes were nonetheless distinguished by peculiarities in steps, tempos, and tunings. In the mid-nineteenth century new couple dance forms entered Nordic countries from continental Europe, with the waltz, the polka, and the schottische transcending national and regional barriers. Dubbed *gammaldans* (old dance or old-time dance), these tunes were typically played by brass bands, accordions, and conventional four-string fiddles (Goertzen 1997: 16). In the

Upper Midwest, however, some Hardanger fiddle players departed from an exclusively bygdedans repertoire to perform gammaldans tunes on their eight-string instrument.

Reinlander is a common Scandinavian term for what is otherwise known as a schottische, a German-derived couple dance emulating Scottish court dances and featuring step-hop promenades alternating with twirls. The decidedly generic title "Gammel reinlander" has been attached to several tunes persisting in the twenty-first century. Part of Otto Rindlisbacher's rendition matches musical phrases in two Norwegian American performances uploaded to YouTube that featured the Adult Recreational Dance Group at the Scandinavian Festival in Junction City, Oregon (2009) and the Fjell og Fjord dancers at the Sons of Norway lodge in Battle Lake, Minnesota (2010).

21 Yodeling

Played on Swiss button accordion by Otto Rindlisbacher, with yodeling by John Giezendanner, National Folk Festival, Chicago, May 27, 1937. Recorded by Sidney Robertson.
3246 B2

Brief breakneck yodeling in the style of the touring Swiss recording artists, the Moser Brothers.

22 Sørland springar'n

Played by on Hardanger fiddle by Otto Rindlisbacher to accompany folk dancers, National Folk Festival, Chicago, May 27, 1937. Recorded by Sidney Robertson.
3255 B2

This *springar*, or running couple dance, invokes Sørland, a fishing village and the administrative center of Værøy, located on the southern coast of an island of the same name in the Norwegian district of Nordland.

Print by Isabella Leary

HARPS AND ACCORDIONS
THE ALAN LOMAX RECORDINGS

OJIBWE

The Ojibwe, or Anishinaabe, once commonly called Chippewa, are an Algonquian-speaking people who, since the eighteenth century, have occupied the American and Canadian hinterlands surrounding Lake Superior and extending west from northern Ontario into Manitoba, and from northern Minnesota into the Turtle Mountains of North Dakota. Hand drums, end-blown wooden flutes, and various rattles have been their traditional instruments, and they have used the big drum prominent in powwows since the end of the nineteenth century. Native and mixed-blood, or métis, peoples acquired fiddles during the fur-trade era, and "Indian fiddlers" flourished especially in Upper Midwestern lumber camps.

1   Introduction to Joe Cloud
Spoken by Alan Lomax, Odanah, Wisconsin, October 16, 1938.
Recorded by Alan Lomax.
2469 B1

These fiddle tunes are being recorded by Joe Cloud in Odanah, Wisconsin, on October 16, 1938, for the Archive of American Folk Song in the Library of Congress. Mr. Cloud is fifty-three and has the blood of the Chippewa Indians flowing in his veins. He has played the fiddle since he was fifteen years old and learned to play from his father, who was also a fiddler. He plays entirely by ear.

In 1938 Odanah, Wisconsin, in the heart of the Bad River Ojibwe reservation, was a logging village just east of Ashland, a sawmill city and Lake Superior port attracting Slavic and Nordic immigrant workers. Joe Cloud was born in Hollow Lake, Wisconsin, in 1885, one of seventeen children, several of whom fiddled and worked in the woods in the manner of their father, Menogwaniosh Anakwad, or George Cloud (1849–1911). Joe married a Swedish immigrant, Anna Anderson (1886–1981), and the couple had three children: George, Harriet, and Clarence. Clarence Cloud (1908–1969), who accompanied his father on the four-string banjo, married Theresa Soulier, a piano player. Joe, Clarence, and Theresa performed as a trio for weddings and community dances at Odanah-area halls and taverns until a few years before Joe Cloud's death in 1965.

Verbally situating Joe Cloud as recording commenced, Alan Lomax also wrote "Joe is married to a slim handsome Swede and Clarence to an Ind. French" on the first disc's dust jacket. This session marked his only foray into Wisconsin and only recording of Woodland Indians. Perhaps because the music of American Indians had been recorded by fieldworkers for the Smithsonian Institution's Bureau of American Ethnology since the 1890s, and because indigenous music of Native peoples was at the time regarded as "tribal" rather than "folk," Lomax made no attempts to capture the traditional songs of Michigan's Odawa, Ojibwe, and Potawatomi peoples. Yet clearly fascinated by the Euro-Native fusions of Indian fiddlers, he set down several leads in his field notebooks: "Alex Mashka, Indian fiddler, near Suttons Bay, MI"; "Billy Nolan, the Shad Road, fiddler, Sugar Island"; "Camp Marquette . . . Government CCC [Civilian Conservation Corps] Camp—known as the Indian Camp." More than fifty years later, Oliver "Duke" Sebastian (1915–1993) recalled Camp Marquette: "Back in the '30s there were 300 Indians from all over at that Marquette logging camp near Eckerman, and about 150 of them were fiddlers. Some played American style, some played Canadian style. But they all had their own way of playing. You could hear fiddle music every night and somebody might be jigging—step dancing—over in a corner" (Sebastian 1987; Leary 1992: 30).

On September 12, 1938, evidently thwarted, Lomax wrote to Harold Spivacke, his boss in the Music Division of the Library of Congress, that some "want pay and are suspicious and elusive in that way that the French Indian mixtures so often are. . . . This is the region that I want to return to for my next summer's field trip. . . . I'm leaving the Indian and mixed blood problem until that time." Lomax's eventually successful

> Joe Cloud and Anna Anderson Cloud with their children: (left to right) Harriet, George, and Clarence, Odanah, Wisconsin, ca. 1916. (author's collection, courtesy of Virginia Cloud Carrington)

recording of an Indian fiddler on Wisconsin's Bad River Ojibwe reservation nearly a month later is hardly surprising.

The situation was much the same as in Michigan. More than a few fiddling French Canadian fur traders, like Joseph Toussaint Guibord (ca. 1840–1912), married Ojibwes. In 1926 his grandson, Ernest "Pea Soup" Guibord (1903–2003)—born in the town of Oak Grove, northeast of Rice Lake, and an enrolled member of the Lac Court Oreilles Ojibwe—won third place in one of the Old Time Fiddlers Contests organized in Rice Lake by Otto Rindlisbacher.

2   Red River Jig

Played by Joe Cloud on fiddle, Odanah, Wisconsin, October 16, 1938.
Recorded by Alan Lomax.
2469 B1

Named for the Red River of the north that flows along the Minnesota–North Dakota border into Manitoba, and thence to Hudson's Bay, and also associated with jigging, or step dancing, brought to the region by French and Celtic peoples, the "Red River Jig" has been a revered, vigorously performed traditional dance for the Canadian métis and North Dakota's Turtle Mountain Ojibwe since the late nineteenth century. Lomax's field materials do not reveal a source, but Joe Cloud acquired other tunes—and perhaps this one too—while in the Dakotas.

3   Squaw Dance

Played by Joe Cloud on fiddle, Odanah, Wisconsin, October 16, 1938.
Recorded by Alan Lomax.
2469 A2

Lomax: What's the name of that tune?
Cloud: What do you mean?
Lomax: What kind of song is that?
Cloud: Squaw dance. Squaw dance.

Despite its now pejorative name, the long-used term "squaw dance" described a women's dance that was performed to the accompaniment of a drum, which nowadays is most evident in the stately procession of "women traditional dancers" at powwows as they proceed circularly around a dance ground without losing contact with "Mother Earth." Indeed, the tune Cloud rendered on fiddle remains recognizable to Ojibwe powwow drum groups as a women's dance.

4 White River Two-Step

Played by Joe Cloud, fiddle, and Clarence Cloud, four-string banjo, Odanah, Wisconsin, October 16, 1938. Recorded by Alan Lomax.
2470 B2

Lomax: Did you make that up?
Cloud: Well, we call it the "White River Two-Step."

This lively fiddle-banjo duet is indebted partially to Southern black-white blues-inflected fusions proliferating on records and radio in the 1930s. Old-time fiddling authority Paul Gifford (2010) recognizes elements of the Clouds' performance as resonating with "Florida Blues" (Bluebird 6844), recorded in 1937 by Tennessean Fiddling Arthur Smith (1898–1971) and also performed by the Virginia-born fiddler Burk Barbour (1910–1991). Barbour's Southern Serenaders played on Chicago's WJJD radio in the mid-1930s where, as the Hired Hands, they recorded "transcription" discs that were syndicated to other stations. Yet the Clouds favor straightforward drive over bluesy swing, while their asymmetrical four-time iteration of a phrase at the outset departs from the standard AABB fiddle-tune structure to assert a musical pattern prominent with the big drum songs of powwows and aligned with the significance of the number four in Woodland Indian culture.

FRENCH CANADIAN

Immigrants mostly from Quebec swelled the Upper Peninsula of Michigan's French Canadian population in the 1870s. Unlike the fur-trade era's male sojourners, these newcomers were mainly families who established farms, with the men working in lumber camps and sawmills. Developers in the L'Anse and Baraga area, hoping to make it "the Chicago of the North," attracted Bellaires, Cadeaus, Kings, and others from

Quebec to settle in Section 12 of Baraga County where, despite hard times and little money, they "loved to get together, laugh and talk and sing and dance to a fast fiddle" (Maier 1982: 18).

5   Le Jour de l'an / New Year's Day

Sung by Edward King, Baraga, Michigan, October 12, 1938. Recorded by Alan Lomax. Transcription, translation, and annotation by Anjili Babbar, with assistance from Sylvain Gaillard and David Boulanger, 2012.

2446 B1

This song, improvised on the spot amid a party and to the accompaniment of Quebecois *podorhythmie* (foot percussion), includes repetitive exclamations typical of composition in performance, as well as some passages that, thus far, defy transcription and translation. The words in parenthesis in the French version were difficult to transcribe with certainty. At times they offer similar-sounding possibilities that might both fit. Question marks indicate unintelligible passages.

. . . reposer,[1] et je regarde ton cœur	. . . to rest, and I look at your heart
En y voyant ton portrait.	While seeing your portrait.
Et j'ai pendu mon pantalonnes.[2]	And I hung up my pants.
Et à chaque fois qu'elle y frissonne,	And every time that she shivers,
Nous voyons mais dans l'hiver	For goodness sake,[3] but in winter
Y fait frette et en calvaire.	It's damn freezing.[4]
Oh voyons-les [?] et voyons ce temps!	Oh goodness, the [?] and goodness, the weather!
J'ai quand même [?] contre une petite bière de coté.	Just the same I have something to trade for a little beer on the side.
Et j'ai perdu le jour de l'an.	And I lost (missed) New Year's Day.
J'suis cassé comme un cadran.	I'm like a clock with a broken dial.
J'ai pu une maudite cenne d'in poches.[5]	I don't have a damn cent in my pockets.
Et moi voyons toute là cette neige!	And goodness, all of this snow!
[Second voice:] Ah oui!	[Second voice:] Ah yes!
Je (partirai/partirais) pour les chantiers	I will leave (would leave) for the work site
Travailler jusqu'au bout de la semaine.	To work until the end of the week.
Chaque fois que je [?] son cœur voit le Bon Dieu!	Every time that I [?] see her heart, Good Lord!
Oh je regarde le lit de ma femme.	Oh I look at my wife's bed.

Qui m'y [?] et voyons,

Who [?] me and, my goodness,

Et a chaque fois qui reposera

And each time that (you) will rest[6]

Ton petit coeur transporta.

Your little heart carries you away.

Les petits [?]

The little (ones) [?]

A chaque fois qu'il ira

Every time he will come

Il porte des petits yeux qu'il te [?] (mourra).

He brings little eyes[7] that [?] kill you.

Je prends mon violon sur mes bras,

I take my violin in my arms,

Je m'y marcher jusqu'au bois.

I walk to the forest.

J'y prends ma petite [?]

I take my little [?]

[?] est tombé la [?]

[?] fell there [?]

J'ai mis de trente jours

It has been thirty days

Depuis que je me suis pas lavé.

Since I last washed myself.

Je regarde dans mon figure,

Look at my face,

Je ne suis pas crotté.

I am not dirty.

Et je prends une autre bière

And I have another beer

A chaque fois qu'une jeune (trinquette)[8]

Every time a young (sailor)

M'emportent leur Canada

Comes to me from Canada

Pour leur manger de la trempette.

To eat a crust of bread.

Je prends mon violon sur mes bras

I take my violin in my arms

Et j'y voilà que ton cœur est transporté

And I behold that your heart is carried away

Mes petits voyageurs [?] (porta)

My little travelers [?] carry

Je prends le grand champ de
   ma vie, Joe, Maggie,

I take the great field of my life, Joe, Maggie,

Et a chaque fois que la petite [?]

And every time the little one [?]

Voyons les transportés

Look, transported people

Mets ton cœur [?]

Put your heart [?]

Voyons mes chers amis

Look, my dear friends

Ce que ton cœur y (voit là / voilà)

What your heart (sees there / behold!)

J'ai ce que [?] le regard d'un enfant

I have that which (is) [?] the look of a child

Et qui mit à s'endormir

And who goes to sleep

Et la trouvé (dans ta [?] donc
   tranquillement).

And found it, thus, peacefully.

A chaque fois qu'elle les garda

Every time she (my wife) takes care of them

Elle m'a dit qu'y a (un trou dedans).

She told me that there is (a hole inside).

Oh le temps nous est bien long.

Oh the time is long for us.

Je regarde ma femme couchée
   dans un lit blanc.

I look at my wife lying on a white bed.[9]

Pas une [?] (miroir) je prend mes pantalons

Not one [?] (mirror) I take my pants

Et en voyant dans toute une vie

And seeing in a whole life

Et a chaque fois que je souris

And every time I smile

Et a chaque fois qu'elle [?]
On dirait qu'elle fait comme ça.

And every time she [?]
One would say that she does it like that.

Et je mets ma petite chemise
   dans un bouragan.
Dans le Canada m'en alla faire
   comme les petits gars.
Ah elle dit qu'on va prendre un petit coup.
On s'en va dans l'Amérique
On va transporter ça chez nous [?]

And I put on my little shirt of rough wool.[10]

I'm going to Canada as the little boys do.

Ah she says we will have a little drink.
We're going to America
We will bring that to our home [?]

Et je [?] jusqu'au [?]
[?]
Chaque fois qu'elle me regarde avec
   ses petits yeux d'amoureux,
Et voyant on est le jour de l'an,
On regarde par chez nous.
Et a chaque fois [?] à journée de l'an [?]
Ce composé par un fou—Edward King!

And I [?] until [?]
[?]
Every time she looks at me with
   her loving little eyes,
And seeing that it is New Year's Day,
We will look from our home.
And every time [?] on New Year's Day.
This was composed by a crazy
   man—Edward King!

Lomax: When did you make this up?

King: Right now! A song made up by Edward King right now!

------

1. The beginning of the first phrase of the song has been cut off in the recording. The character in the song, however, commences an end-of-the-day reverie inspired by an image of his wife.
2. *Pantalonnes* = *pantalons*, changed to force a rhyme with *frissonne*; hanging up one's pants implies quitting work and preparing to sleep.
3. *Voyons* is technically the first person plural present indicative form of *voir* (to see) but is frequently used as an interjection, as in *Nous voyons*, *Voyons donc*, or just *Voyons*—meaning, essentially "My goodness," "For goodness sake," or "Would you look at that!" King uses it frequently to connect phrases in these spontaneous lyrics since he is composing while performing.
4. *En calvaire* is a mild Québécois blasphemy, referring to Calvary and used for emphasis.
5. *J'ai pu* = *Je n'ai plus*; *cenne* = *cent*; *d'in poches* = *dans les poches*. These are all typical of Québécois dialect.
6. Here the "you" is self-referential, and the "he" that follows in the next verse is a child at home.
7. "Little eyes" is an expression that implies an irresistible look, as when a child gives a sweet, pouty face; here the lumberjack remembering his child's look feels like dying from the sorrow of separation.
8. *Trinquette* is actually a sailor's term for a staysail, but in this context it seems to refer to Canadians who have traveled by water to the Upper Peninsula of Michigan.
9. The "white bed" where the character imagines his wife implies clean sheets that contrast with a lumber camp's bedding.

10. Putting on one's shirt, the opposite of hanging up one's pants, signals going to work.

Note additionally that, in Québécois dialect, *y* is often used to replace *il*, as in *y fait frette* in this song. Elsewhere, it is used as a filler or as a verbal liaison to tie words together and does not necessarily imply a preposition.

Born in rural Quebec, Edward King (1908–1988) had anglicized his surname from Roi by 1936 when amid the Depression he sought work in Baraga, where a paternal uncle had settled. A relatively young man when recorded by Lomax, King was an energetic and boisterous performer, improvising songs and pounding out a rhythm with his feet. He was also a fiddler who, like his father Albert, had worked and played in Canadian lumber camps. A World War II veteran of the United States Army, King, like several of his French Canadian neighbors, married a Finnish American woman, Esther Maki (1925–2005), in 1945. Years later she recalled: "I (Mrs. Ed. King) remember him telling me about Alan Lommax [*sic*] recording the singing. I was younger so never attended the parties. He told me about the French speaking families (they lived in the country—most were farmers or woodsmen). The singing group were older than Ed, and came from Canada also, so when they heard a French Canadian was in the area they had a real party." As a performer, King was best recalled by his family for entertaining with "mostly the harmonica, which he played until his passing away in 1988" (King 1991).

King's improvised song draws its tune and invocation of the New Year from "Le Jour de l'an" composed and recorded in November 1930 by Mary Rose Anna Travers (1894–1941), the era's Queen of Canadian Folksingers, otherwise known as Madame Bolduc or Le Bolduc. Born into a poor family in Newport, Quebec, a French-speaking village on the Gaspé Peninsula, Travers met her husband, Edouard Bolduc, while working as a maid in Montreal. A singer and multi-instrumentalist, she composed earthy comic songs set to Irish and Quebecois folk tunes that were wildly popular with the French Canadian working class. She joined Conrad Gauthier's old-time music troupe in 1928 (see Stratman-Thomas CD part 1, track 6), formed her own company in 1932, performed widely in halls and over the radio, and made nearly eighty 78 rpm records.

The lyrics for La Bolduc's rendition of "Le Jour de l'an" celebrates New Year's Day as a time for working people to relax, kiss, dance, drink, eat pies, and enjoy family festivities that come but once a year. La Bolduc's performances and recordings typically included the use of "nonsense" syllables simulating an instrument, what the Irish call "mouth music" and the French Canadians call *turlutage*. Perhaps King's more inexplicable lyrics serve the same purpose as La Bolduc's turlutage? His free-associating improvisation is otherwise an immigrant's lament that loved ones are so far away. Anjili Babbar, who transcribed and translated King's lyrics, suggests that he may have been thinking of "La Chasse-Galerie," a well-known French Canadian legend involving homesick lumberjacks on New Year's Day who make a pact with the devil enabling them to paddle home briskly in an airborne canoe. In 1946 folklorist Richard Dorson found this legend flourishing in the Upper Peninsula of Michigan (Dorson [1952] 2008: 80–81).

6 Ida Goyette, no. 1

Played by Edward King on fiddle, Baraga, Michigan, October 12, 1938.
Recorded by Alan Lomax.

2446 A2

Lomax: Where did you learn that?

King: Albert King, my dad.

Lomax: Where did he learn it?

King: Oh, he learned it in a lumber camp. . . . He learned it by himself. . . . He made it up. Just playing the violin, thinking up things.

The Ida Goyette commemorated in this Albert King composition has a surname common in Quebec. Played with intermittent double-stops that lend a droning effect characteristic of French Canadian fiddling, the melody, as Paul Gifford notes, resonates in part with the well-known tune "Buffalo Gals."

7 Non que j'aime donc que la boisson / No, So I Don't Love Anything but the Drink

Sung by John Cadeau, lead vocal, with Ed Cadeau, Adelore Vizina, and probably Joe Miron, Mose Bellaire, and Edward King, Baraga, Michigan, October 12, 1938. Recorded by Alan Lomax. Transcription, translation, and annotation by Anjili Babbar, 2010.

2440

Oui on s'en va voir les filles,	Yes we are going to see the girls,
Tout enivré de boisson (bis).	All intoxicated with drink.

CHORUS:	*CHORUS:*
Non que j'aime donc que la	No, so I don't love anything but
boisson, sans cesse.	the drink, incessantly.
Non que j'aime donc que la boisson.	No, so I don't love anything but the drink.
Ils ont faites mettre la table,	They set the table,
Ils ont faites mettre tout du long.	They set the whole length of it.
Ils l'ont faites mettre sur la table	They put on the table
Du bon lait et du jambon.	Good milk and ham.
Du bon lait et du jambon.	Good milk and ham.
Ils ont faites mettre sur la table	They put on the table
Cinq ou six verres et flacons.	Five or six glasses and flasks.
Ils ont faites mettre à la table	They put at the table
Cinq ou six filles et garçons.	Five or six girls and boys.
Les jeunes gens se sont mis à rire,	The young people started laughing,
À rire de ces vieux garçons.	Laughing at these old boys.
Les jeunes gens se sont mis à dire	The young people started saying
Vient donc voir ces vieux garçons.	Come see these old boys.
Buvons cinq ou six belle terres,	Let's drink to five or six beautiful lands,
Cinq ou six belles maisons.	Five or six beautiful houses.

Lomax's notes mention John Cadeau as the lead singer, joined by "five men." Besides John Cadeau, the session included his brother Ed Cadeau, Edward King, Adelore Vizina, Joe Miron, and Mose Bellaire. All but King were established settlers in Baraga County's heavily French Canadian Section 12, and perhaps King is the singer who is hesitant and a little behind the others at the song's outset.

John Cadeau (1879–1948) was born in Baraga, the descendant of Amans Cadeau, who came from France to Three Rivers in Canada, on the St. Lawrence River, in 1620. He married a Huron woman, then moved west to Quebec, and later to Montreal. The Cadeaus came to Laurium, Michigan, in the 1850s and some of them, including John's parents, Jean Baptiste and Delima Cadeau, came to Baraga in the 1870s. John was a farmer and sometime logger who spoke only French and enjoyed singing and festivities. His mother, Delima, was well remembered for baking prior to New Year's celebrations and for her maple-sugar houses and dandelion wine. In the 1930s, when John had a

Mathilda, Adolphus, and John Cadeau, Baraga, Michigan, 1940s. (author's collection, courtesy of the Cadeau family)

Joe Miron, in lumberjack boots, with one of his eight children, Baraga, Michigan, 1930s.
(author's collection, courtesy of the Miron family)

new barn built, barn dances were held every other Saturday, with John's brother, Ed Cadeau Sr., fiddling. In later years John was kicked in the head by a horse and couldn't do much work.

Ed Cadeau Sr. (1894–1981), nicknamed Sned, was a great one for maple-syrup boiling. Once he had seven hundred pails out and gathered seventeen fifty-gallon barrels of sap. He sometimes dressed up in a sheet to scare kids at the sugar bush with his ghostly disguise. He was a noted fiddler and, according to Ed Jr., when he played the fiddle his "feet were going all the time." Ed Jr. recalled that his brother Gabe, also a fiddler, was "great for jigging."

Adelore Vizina (1885–1981), a farmer and logger, was born in Michigamme, Michigan. In his younger days he called for square dances, usually in English but with an occasional French phrase. Remembered as "always jolly," he liked to garden and to get visitors "shined up" on brandy—he regularly took a shot in the morning "to get his blood going" and one at night to relax. His end at ninety-six came a few days after he insisted on dancing every number at his great-granddaughter's wedding (Cadeau, Cadeau, and Jestila 1991).

Joe Miron (1888–1942) was born in Canada and arrived in Baraga in 1892 with his parents, August and Christine. He married Alma Anderson (1893–1932) in 1912, and the couple had eight children. A farmer known for his strawberries, Miron was remembered by his children as singing "to them all the time when they were little" (Pelto 1991). Besides joining this chorus, he performed one solo song for Lomax.

Mose Bellaire (1883–1955) was born in Baraga where his Canadian-born parents, Joseph Bellaire and Malvine Sirard Bellaire, were among the first French settlers. Mose farmed, worked in lumber camps, and in his later years was a caretaker for a local estate. He and his wife, Exilia Sylvester Bellaire (see track 9 below), raised thirteen children in a big eleven-room house that had been built by Mose's father in 1900. Both active singers with large repertoires, the Bellaires had a reputation for being friendly and neighborly. Their spacious kitchen was a place for house parties, with fiddling and French singing that regularly included Finnish neighbors.

The vigorous chorus and assured lead vocal for the exuberant drinking song by John Cadeau and company suggest that it was a staple at house parties.

8   La fille du roi / The King's Daughter; Le mariage anglaise / The English Marriage

Spoken and sung by Fred Carrière, Champion, Michigan, October 10, 1938. Recorded by Alan Lomax. Transcription, translation, and annotation by Anjili Babbar, 2010.

2430 A1

Chanson composée en Canada, chantée par Fred Carrière [This song was composed in Canada and is sung by Fred Carrière].[1]

La fille du roi[2] s'est mariée,
La fille du roi s'est mariée
La fille du roi s'est mariée,
La fille du roi s'est mariée.

Toutes les dames du village
(Ne) faisaient que pleurer
De voir ce(tte) belle princesse
Mariée avec un anglais.

Quand c'est venu pour traverser,
Quand c'est venu pour traverser,
L'anglais voulait lui bander les yeux,
L'anglais voulait lui bander les yeux.

"Band les toi (tiens), et laisse-moi
   (les miens), maudit anglais.
Car si jamais (je) m'suis offense
   (offensée), Je veux la voir.
Band les toi (tiens), et laisse-moi
   (les miens), maudit anglais.
Car si jamais (je) m'suis offense
   (offensée), Je veux la voir."

Quand c'est venu pour le souper,
Quand c'est venu pour le souper,
L'anglais voulait lui porter le manger,
L'anglais voulait lui porter le manger.

"Porte le toi (tien) et laisse moi
   (le mien), maudit anglais,

The king's daughter married,
The king's daughter married,
The king's daughter married,
The king's daughter married.

All the women of the village
Did nothing but cry
To see this beautiful princess
Married with an Englishman.

When it was time to cross,
When it was time to cross,
The Englishman wanted to blindfold her,
The Englishman wanted to blindfold her.

"Cover your own (eyes) and leave mine
   alone, damned Englishman.
For if ever I am offended, I want to see it.

Cover your own (eyes) and leave mine
   alone, damned Englishman.
For if ever I am offended, I want to see it."

When it was time for supper,
When it was time for supper,
The Englishman wanted to bring her food,
The Englishman wanted to bring her food.

"Bring your own and leave mine
   alone, damned Englishman,

Car j'ai des gens de mon
    pays pour m'y servir.
Porte le toi (tien) et laisse moi
    (le mien), maudit anglais,
Car j'ai des gens de mon pays
    pour m'y servir."

For I have people from my country
    to help me with that.
Bring your own and leave mine
    alone, damned Englishman,
For I have people from my country
    to help me with that."[3]

Quand c'est venu pour se coucher,
Quand c'est venu pour se coucher,
L'anglais voulait la déchausser,
L'anglais voulait la déchausser.

When it was time to go to bed,
When it was time to go to bed,
The Englishman wanted to take off her shoes,
The Englishman wanted to take off her shoes.

"Déchausse-toi et laisse-
    moi, maudit anglais,
Car j'ai des gens de mon
    pays pour m'y servir.
Déchausse-toi et laisse-
    moi, maudit anglais,
Car j'ai des gens de mon pays
    pour m'y servir."

"Take off your shoes and leave me
    alone, damned Englishman,
For I have people from my country
    to help me with that.
Take off your shoes and leave me
    alone, damned Englishman,
For I have people from my country
    to help me with that."

Quand c'est venu vers le minuit,
Quand c'est venu vers le minuit,
L'anglais (ne) faisait (rien) que pleurer,
L'anglais (ne) faisait (rien) que pleurer.

When it was near midnight
When it was near midnight,
The Englishman did nothing but cry,
The Englishman did nothing but cry.

"Oh devise-toi, mon cher
    amant, embrasse-moi,
Puisque c'est Dieu qui nous a
    marié, il faut s'aimer.
Oh devise-toi, mon cher
    amant, embrasse-moi,
Puisque c'est Dieu qui nous a
    marié, il faut s'aimer."

"Oh compose yourself,[4] my dear lover, kiss me,

Since it is God who has married us,
    we must love each other.
Oh compose yourself, my dear lover, kiss me,

Since it is God who has married us,
    we must love each other."

Lomax: This song was composed in Canada and is sung by Fred Carrière. What kind of a song do you call that? It's not a complaint is it?

Carrière: No, that's a wedding song. You see, she married an Irishman and everybody in town was against them. And, at first, she thought it was a kind of a dishonor to marry— some years ago—a man of an odd language. Like today the French will get married with Finns and everything. They say it's a disgrace. But when she saw that she was married, she said we might just as well love each other now we're married. See.

1. This song was not, in fact, composed in Canada but in France. It is the story of a French princess forced to marry an English king. Even in this version, there are remnants of these original roots—she is referred to as a *princesse*, is used to people serving her food and taking off her shoes, has to cross water to reach her new husband's home, and has enough clout in the community to cause all of the village women to cry at her marriage to a *maudit anglais*. Carrière quite interestingly assumes that the Quebecois social "translation" of the song (wherein the young lady marries an Irishman) is the original intent of the song, even while he suggests a means by which the song might also "translate" into the culture of the Upper Peninsula (wherein French Canadians and Finns intermarry).
2. *La fille du roi* literally means "the king's daughter," which was the original intent of the song. However, in New France, *une fille du roi* was a young woman of limited means sent to the colony with a dowry provided by Louis XIV to promote marriage and procreation of French inhabitants. The marriage of such a woman to an Irish sailor would likely have been frowned upon.
3. *M'y server* is translated as "help me with that" because the *y* implies a preposition and because "serve" seems a strong word to use in comparison to the husband's attempts to help her.
4. *Devise-toi*, literally "unscrew yourself," is an old idiomatic expression similar to "get your shit together," and translated here as "compose yourself."

Wilfred "Fred" Carrière (1875–1954) was born in Champion, Michigan, where French and Irish Canadian immigrants alike were part of the same Catholic parish, Sacred Heart. His parents—Jean Baptiste Carrière (1828–1907) and Margaret Hewitt (1840–1885)—were both born in Quebec and had come to Champion in the early 1870s with others from Quebec to work on the Mackinac Railroad, to log, and to farm. While Carrière's father was a Catholic French Canadian, his mother was an Irish Protestant. Carrière worked in the woods for many years—in both the Upper Peninsula of Michigan and Ontario—where he learned and composed songs. In 1919, at age forty-one, Carrière married Louise Armitage (1891–1975), with whom he had twelve children.

Fred Carrière recorded two hours of material for Lomax, mostly long ballads interspersed with conversation, eight in English and the rest in French. "Le mariage anglais" is an old French folksong that has been recorded by and was the title of an album by the leading French folk rock group of the 1970s, Malicorne (Hexagone 883 004). Carrière told Lomax that he learned this song from Daniel Durand in Baraga, Michigan, perhaps when visiting his nephew Dolph (Dolphis) Carrière, who was born in Champion but had married a woman from Baraga, Rosanna LaCasse, and lived in the French settlement there. A field journal entry, "French Contacts," mentions Fred Carrière and Mose Bellaire, suggesting that Lomax may have learned of Carrière on October 4 when recording the lumber-camp fiddler, Fred Foucault, in Baraga. He subsequently recorded Carrière on October 10, before traveling to Baraga, where he recorded and filmed from October 11 to 15.

9   I Went to Marquette

Sung by Exilia Bellaire, Baraga, Michigan, October 12, 1938.
Recorded by Alan Lomax. Transcription, translation, and annotation
by Anjili Babbar, 2010.

2442 B1

I went to Marquette, mon panier desous mon bras [my basket under my arm].
On my way j'ai rencontré la fille de l'avocat [I met the lawyer's daughter].

CHORUS:
"And I love you."
"Oh non il (ne) m'aimait guère" [Oh no he hardly loved me at all].
"And I love you."
"Oh non il (ne) m'aimait pas" [Oh no he didn't love me].

I bought some apples, puis toi tu n'auras pas [and you, you'll not have them].
I bought a dozen, oh Pa vous les paieras [oh Pa will pay you for them].

I bought some apples, puis toi tu n'auras pas[1] [and you, you'll not have them].
I bought a dozen, oh Pa vous les paieras [oh Pa will pay you for them].

I went upstairs, le bonhomme (n)était pas là [the gentleman wasn't there],
I went downstairs, le bonhomme il (n') est pas là [the gentleman isn't there].

I went downstairs, le bonhomme il était là [the gentleman was there].
I asked for some money, le bonhomme il n'(en) avait pas [the gentleman didn't have any].
[Spoken:] So I took my basket and I went back to Marquette.

Lomax: What's your name?

Bellaire: Mrs. Mose Bellaire.

Lomax: Where did you learn that song?

Bellaire: When I was a little girl, grasshopper-high, about forty-eight, no forty-five years
ago [i.e., ca. 1892].

Lomax: Where was that?

Bellaire: Ewen, Michigan, in Ontonagon County.

Lomax: And what was your maiden name?

Bellaire: Exilia Sylvester.

———

1. The singer likely means to repeat this phrase here but she hesitates and sings nonsense
   words instead.

Exilia Sylvester Bellaire (1889–1965) was born in Baraga and lived for a time in Ewen prior to marrying Mose Bellaire. Her daughters Jeanine, Marie, and Priscilla remembered their mother and father always singing around the house. Priscilla Bellaire Tahtinen: "Mother spoke the French language, sang, and could read French. When they sang French songs to us in French they would always translate it in English for us so we knew what the song was about. Both mother and dad could sing nice English songs as well as in French" (Tahtinen 1991). Lomax filmed the two outside their home singing a duet in French. Priscilla and several of her siblings remembered that occasion. Several recording sessions also occurred in local homes, but the most performances were captured in Baraga's Holmes Hotel: "Alan came over to our house and he talked to my folks and dad and mother sang a few songs for him at our home, then he asked them if they would sing for him at the hotel and they agreed—so off we all went. . . . There were other people (French) who came to the hotel to sing too" (Tahtinen 1991).

This comic folksong featuring bilingual haggling is well known in Quebec by the titles "La fille d'un avocat" (The Lawyer's Daughter) and "I Went to the Market." Alfred Vandertie, a Walloon French singer recorded in Wisconsin by Helene Stratman-Thomas (Stratman-Thomas CD part 1, track 10), offers a rougher version involving broken arms, while echoing Quebec versions with a trip to market. Exilia Bellaire wryly substitutes "Marquette," a market city east of Baraga and named for the prominent seventeenth-century French priest and explorer, Jacques Marquette.

10 Pretty Polly; Those Western Shores

Sung by Fred Carrière, Champion, Michigan, October 10, 1938.
Recorded by Alan Lomax.

2426 A

It was in those western, in those western shores,
There lived a young damsel so handsome and fair.
She was courted by a young man who called her his dear
And was known as a traitor—a ship carpenter.

That soon-wanted seaman to go upon sea
What caused this young damsel to sob and to say,
"Oh William, oh William, don't you go on sea.
For don't you remember what you've told to me?"

Early in the morning before it was day,
He calls upon her those words he did say,
"Come Polly, come Polly, come go along with me,
Before we get married our friends for to see."

He led her through mountains and valleys so deep,
What caused this young damsel to sob and to weep.
She sobbed and she wept, those words she did say,
"I'm afraid to my heart you have led me astray."

"Tis true, tis true," young William did say,
"For many long nights I've been digging your grave."
When she saw her grave open and the spade lying by,
She wrung her poor hands and most bitterly cried.

"Oh pardon, oh pardon," pretty Polly did say,
"I lived no longer than to become your wife.
I'll sail this world round and set you quite free,
If you only will pardon my sweet babe-a-nee."

"No pardon, no pardon, there is no time to stand."
And for the time he drew a knife to hand.
He pierced her through the heart till her life blood it flowed
And into the grave her sweet body did throw.

He covered her over so snug and secure,
So no one would find her he thought he'd made sure.
He jumped upon board ship to sail this world round
Before this young murder would ever be found.

He had not sailed for over a day
When the captain came up and those words he did say,
"There's murderer on deck, boys, and the deed has been done
And the ship must be hunted or cannot be launched."

Up stepped a sailor who says, "It's not me."
Up stepped another and the same he did say.
Up stepped young William who stamps and he swore,
And he says, "It's not me, I will vow and declare."

As he was returning from the Captain with speed,
He met pretty Polly, which made his heart bleed.
She ripped him, she tore him, she ripped him in three,
Saying, "This is for the murder of sweet babe-a-nee."

Lomax: Where did you learn this one?

Carrière: I composed the biggest part of that.

Lomax's recorded conversations with Carrière reveal that he had a prodigious memory for traditional songs in both French and English, as he claimed to have once learned five songs in a single night. He had also composed several songs, as he explained to Lomax, by fixing "an air" in his mind and then working out lyrics in his head for several weeks until he was satisfied. This particular Carrière composition bespeaks his familiarity with a wide range of traditional ballads and stories. The murderous William lures "pretty Polly" with exactly the same "Come go along with me" found in the widely known ballad "Pretty Polly." The sea captain's misgivings about William echo the biblical Jonah, while the vengeful ghost exacting retribution resembles many in folk legends and ballads.

LUMBERJACKS

The heavily timbered northern half of Lower Michigan and the entirety of the Upper Peninsula spurred logging and sawmill operations that made Michigan the nation's leading lumber producer from 1869 to 1900. Cutting and moving felled logs demanded men, frozen ground, and teams of horses and oxen, so in late fall, hordes of workers entered the woods to toil until the spring thaw, when decked logs were rolled into rivers and "driven" downstream to mills. Cooped up in crudely built winter camps for months, with Sunday their only day off, Michigan's lumberjacks—some of them veteran loggers from back east—entertained one another and chronicled their existence through songs. Earl C. Beck (1891–1977), an English professor at Central Michigan University, began documenting lumber-camp folksongs and singers in the early 1930s (Beck 1942, 1960). In 1934 he organized a troupe of old-timers, billed as the Michigan Lumberjacks, to sing and dance in St. Louis at the first National Folk Festival.

11 No Sir
Sung by Bill McBride, Mount Pleasant, Michigan, August 1938.
Recorded by Alan Lomax.
2261 B3

As I walked out to Nottaway City,
Just at ten the other night,
There I spied this dark-eyed gypsy
Washing her snatch in the moon so bright.

CHORUS:
And she says, "No, no sir, no."
And all her answer, it was "No."

"Madam, if you'd loose your garter,
Tie it a little above your knee.
If I could, I would go higher—
Very angry you would be?"

CHORUS:
She says, "No, no sir no."
All her answers, they were "No."

"Blue it is a handsome color
When it gets your [?]
Like young men when they go courting,
They most gently [generally] get the slip."

"Madam when you're in your bedchamber
Where young maidens ofttimes be,
If I could I'd go and see you—
Very angry you would be?"

"Madam if I swell your belly,
Swell it big as big could be,
If I could I'd swell it bigger,
Would you father it on me?"

All that night we tossed and tumbled.
When it was the break of day,
"I'll have you protect me from all dangers,
Open your thighs and I'll fly away."

"My father, he was a London merchant,
He requested long ago.
And this request was all he asked of me—
Was to answer all men, 'No.'"

William "Bill" McBride (ca. 1864–1952) was born in Isabella City, Michigan. His mother was a native of the area, but his father, Samuel, hailed from New York State and perhaps had worked in the woods there. McBride wed sixteen-year-old Mary C. Beach in 1891, and by 1910 the couple had seven children, a challenging situation for a mother whose spouse was often gone from November through April.

As Earl Beck tells us, McBride had been "a chopper, swamper, teamster, top-loader, and riverhog for some of the biggest outfits of the Great Lakes pinewoods. On a log he was as agile as a cat, almost the equal of the famous Billy Girard of Gladstone [the era's champion birler]." McBride was also a fine woods singer with an astounding repertoire who was part of the Michigan Lumberjacks troupe and contributed more songs than anyone to Beck's collections: "Bill learned many songs in the shanties, on the decking grounds and along the rivers, and he seems to have remembered all of them. I rode with him once for twenty-four waking hours, during twenty of which he sang and recited with almost no repetitions. There were lumberjack songs, Civil War songs, Irish ballads, English ballads, slavery songs, barroom songs. Most of the material was printable. He must know as much more, or nearly as much more, that is not printable" (Beck 1942: 6–7).

Alan Lomax recorded three "printable" songs from McBride—"The Jam on Gerry's Rocks," "Turner's Camp on the Chippewa," and "Johnny Carroll's Camp"—that were issued on Beck's Library of Congress LP, *Songs of the Michigan Lumberjack* (1960). Yet unlike Beck, Lomax not only actively sought "unprintable" songs that were a small yet significant part of woods singers' repertoires, but also questioned singers about them. Regarding "No Sir," his notebooks set down this comment from McBride: "It don't speak it out so plain, but it p'ints it out so near that you'll know what it means. The chippies like these, just like the lumberjacks did. They'll give me a dollar + a drink to sing it in these places where they ain't no decent girls."

"No Sir," sometimes called "O No John," is an old English folksong. Cecil Sharp recorded four versions from English singers from 1903 to 1908 (Reeves 1958: 33–37, 162–163). The Stoneman Family of Carroll County, Virginia, recorded a coyly refined version, "The Spanish Merchant's Daughter" (Victor V-40206), in 1928 during the landmark Bristol Sessions in Tennessee, at which the Carter Family and Jimmie Rodgers also made their first records. The English traditional singer Sam Larner (1878–1965), who at eight left his Norfolk home to sail as a cabin boy, performed a bawdy version closely resembling McBride's (Larner 1961).

12 Joe Williams

Sung by Bert Graham, Newberry, Michigan, August 1938.
Recorded by Alan Lomax.

2344 A1

Oh my name it is Joe Williams and my age is twenty-one,
I'm a rambling wreck of poverty and a roving son-of-a-gun.
From driving ox teams in Comstock lumber woods,
To hear me curse and swear at them it'll do your asshole good.

Whoa Buck! Gee haw Diamond! You broad-horned son-of-a-bitch.
It's don't you dare to kish at me, or I'll slog you till you tip.
Come swamper, cut that knot off, you lobcocked son-of-a-whore,
Or I'll make you suck that off-ox tit till your upper lip gets sore.

Now I'm like any old bullpuncher, I like my lager beer.
Like any old bullpuncher, I like my whisky clear.
Like any old bullpuncher, I like my gin and tod,
For I'm a rambling wreck of poverty and a son-of-a-gun, b'god.

Oh it's now I go down to Cheboygan, I think I'm quite a man.
I promenade around the streets, my aleck in my hand.
In going up Broadway, I met a pretty lass.
I introduced her to my aleck and slap 'er up her ass.

Oh I tangled up her little guts till she was in a fit,
And when I pulled out old Reuben, he was covered in blood and shit.
Oh the spendings from her asshole would run a water mill,
And if you had a fatter sow, you'd a-got a barrel of swill.

For I'm like any old bullpuncher, I like my lager beer.
Like any old bullpuncher, I chase me whisky clear.
Like any old bullpuncher, I like my gin and tod,
For I'm a rambling wreck of poverty and a son-of-a-gun, b'god.

So now I go back to the woods, I found I've got the pox,
I wish to Christ I'd stayed at home and shagged that old off-ox.
Put on a little wagon grease and did it up in a rag,
For when I think of that old whore, I wish I were a stag.

So now my song is ended and I'll sing to you no more.
So health to all you shanty boys and hell to that old whore.
So now my song is ended and I'll sing to you, alas!
And if any of you don't like this song, you can kiss that off-ox ass.

Little is known about Albert Francis "Bert" Graham beyond his draft registration record from 1942, which lists his birthdate as May 12, 1883, and his residence as Newberry, Luce County, Michigan. Lomax recorded more than seventy performances in Newberry, in English, Finnish, German, Lithuanian, and Scandihoovian English. All of the performers were men, and most were either dwellers at Larsen's Luce Hotel or denizens of its barroom (see the notes below for track 15). Graham recorded a dozen songs and recitations for Lomax, including the dialect-inflected "Swede from North Dakota," John Henry Titus's maudlin 1872 poem "The Face on the Barroom Floor," and "The Jolly Tinker," a rasty seventeenth-century British ballad in which "old Reuben does his worst" (Randolph 1992a: 113–116).

Derived in part from "The Son of a Gambolier," a drinking song from 1870 or earlier that features "a rambling wreck of poverty" from Ireland's "Tipperary Town," this version portrays a lumber-camp teamster. Ox drivers in the woods were especially foul-mouthed by reputation and relied on oaths and a stick to goad their sometimes stubborn team, in this case "Buck" and "Diamond." In addition to common woods terms like "bullpuncher" and "swamper," the rarer "kish" is a "call to cows or calves" previously reported from Dutch and Flemish settlements in North Dakota and "on the Upper Delaware and in the Catskills"—perhaps indicating its route into the Michigan lumber camps (Cassidy and Hall 1996: 228). Presumably an ox that would "kish" at its driver is "talking back." "Old Reuben" and "aleck" are, of course, archaic male vernacular for penis. In 1941 Robert Draves, the student engineer who recorded "vulgar" lumberjack songs for Helene Stratman-Thomas, captured a similar version of "Joe Williams" from Lee Tester in Rhinelander, Wisconsin. Paul Gifford confirmed that this song persisted in Upper Midwestern oral tradition in the 1970s: "I taped a man named Orin Miller, of Scottville, MI (a fiddler). . . . His version had 'Ludington' instead of 'Cheboygan', but it was equally filthy ('swamper, cut that knot off, you lop-cock son of a whore, or suck my old snotty old fuck-stick until your upper lip gets sore,' etc.)" (Gifford 2007). About the same time, Guy Logsdon recorded a version from cowboy singer Riley Neal (b. 1891) of Gisela, Arizona (Logsdon 1989: 12).

13　Torch Lake

Sung by an unidentified man, St. James, Beaver Island, Michigan, late August 1938. Recorded by Alan Lomax.

2303 A3

There's a fine boarding house on the shores of Torch Lake
Where four fucking larrups would fit on your plate.
And more fucking larrups was sure to be there,
And in the rank butter you'd always find hair,
Derry-di-oh-day. Whack for the di-oh-diddle-oh-day.

Oh our cook, she's the daughter of Honest John Clark,
One taste of her biscuits would make an ox fart.
Her puddin's are tough and as green as the grass
And if you would taste 'em, you'd hock off your ass,
Derry-di-oh-day. Whack for the di-oh-diddle-oh-day.

Oh there's Peter, Joe, William, there's Frankfort and Knott,
And there's sweet little Mary with a wart on her twat.
There's Jumper, our push, he's a good one too,
But the long-legged bastard, he shit in our shoes,
Derry-di-oh-day. Whack for the di-oh-diddle-oh-day.

Oh here's to Tad Minton, the son-of-a-bitch.
May his ballocks rot off with the seven-year itch.
His pecker will turn on the point of screw,
And his arsehole'd whistle the red, white, and blue,
Derry-di-oh-day. Whack for the di-oh-diddle-oh-day.
[Spoken:] That's all.

Lomax: When was this composed?

Anonymous: In a lumber camp.

Lomax: Where?

Anonymous: Torch Lake, Michigan.

Lomax: And what was the name of the man they were singing about?

Anonymous: Tad Minton.

Lomax: He ran a boarding house?

Anonymous: No, a lumber camp.

Lomax: What did they do? Did they sing this song to him?

Anonymous: Yes, they sang it to him.

Lomax: And walked out.

This singer is the only anonymous performer recorded by Alan Lomax, presumably because all of his songs were raunchy: "Brown County Blues," "No Balls at All," "Oh Honey, Take Your Leg Off of Mine," a parody of "Red Wing," "Three Old Whores from Canada," and "The Wind Blew through Her Nightie."

Named for the torches used by Native peoples to spear and net fish at night, Torch Lake is Michigan's longest, deepest, and second-largest inland lake. Paralleling Grand Traverse Bay and situated in the pinery of northwestern Lower Michigan, its shores were the site of lumber camps as early as 1854. Beaver Islanders—many of them from Donegal and elsewhere in Ireland—often ranged from their homes to sail the Great Lakes or to work in lumber camps. This song, with its Irish "nonsense" refrain, includes several esoteric terms: "push" for foreman, "larrups" for syrup (Cassidy and Hall 1996: 293). Partly a versified "catalog" of characters that emerged in many a lumber camp during a season in the woods, it is also a satirical "needle," a song of witty complaint about overly hard work, poor pay, and bad food that flourished in lumber camps from the Canadian Maritimes and northern New England westward through the Great Lakes region (Ives 1964: 40, 143–146, 167–171). In the 1950s, after her marriage to Henry Cowell, Sidney Robertson Cowell recorded two such songs from Warde Ford of Crandon, "The Keith and Hiles Line" and "The River Drivers Song." One suggested that a cook's bakery was "harder than the hubs of hell," while another bid the boss a "to hell with" you farewell (Cowell 1956).

While the first three verses of "Torch Lake" appear to be original, they all resemble compositions from other camps, like this one from Ontario:

There's blackstrap molasses, squaw buns as hard as a rock,
Tea that's boiled in an old tin pail and smells just like your sock.
The beans they are sour, and the porridge thick as dough.
When we have stashed this in our craw, it's to the woods we go.
(Fowke 1970: 41)

The final verse, aimed at Tad Minton, relies on an old, still resilient toast, doubling as a curse, which dates back at least to the Spanish American War of the 1890s.

Here's to the Spaniard, the son-of-a-bitch,
May his balls rot off with the Cuban itch.

May his prick shrivel up like a bamboo cane,
And his asshole whistle "Remember the Maine."

Kaiser Wilhelm, Adolph Hitler, Emperor Tojo, Saddam Hussein, and Osama Bin Laden have been similarly pilloried in hopes that their assholes will all whistle "The Star Spangled Banner" (Randolph 1992b: 723).

There are other instances of disgruntled loggers, like those in the Torch Lake camp, taunting their boss with a "needle" once the season was through and they had been paid. In 1941, for example, Helene Stratman-Thomas recorded "Old Hazeltine" from Bert Taplin (b. 1854) in Wautoma, Wisconsin.

It's of the Eau Claire River, a stream I'm sure you know,
It's of a crew of shanty boys who worked through the snow,
And as to Old Hazeltine he's a lousy son-of-a-bitch,
For it is from the poor man that he has grown rich.

The cheating of his jobbers [subcontractors] and the starving of his crew,
I think he's an old whelp, boys, now my hearties, don't you?

Taplin elaborated: "God I hated him. I was in a saloon singing while I was drunk. And along came Hazeltine and I had to sing this song. They stood by the doorway, the boys, and wouldn't let him out. He had to listen."

14 Traverse City

Sung by Lester Wells, Traverse City, Michigan, early September 1938.
Recorded by Alan Lomax.

2307 B1

When I first come to Traverse town,
There was two houses scattered all around.
There was one place that I could stay
Overnight if I would pay.

CHORUS:
Oh dear, oh dear,
I never did see what a place
Traverse City is a-getting to be,
Oh dear.

Oh there was a blacksmith right in town,
Oh there you could get your horseshoeing done.
You'd prang on the tires when they're reading up the news
Or out in the street they's picking horseshoes.

Oh there's Mr. Gunton, I s'pose you all know,
You want good boarding, that's the place to go.
Little bit of cake and a little bit of gin
And a little back door for to step right in.

Oh there's Mr. Hannah, too, I like to forgot,
He's the best old man in the whole lot.
He'd go to a meeting, he'd preach and pray,
And when he come home the cards he'd play.

Lomax: Who made this one up?

Wells: Well, they was, oh, they was four, five of us. Get together, y'know. And we kept

a-getting one, get one thing, and [everybody?] made this up about Traverse City.

Lomax: How long ago was that?

Wells: Oh, Jesus, that was fifty years ago, anyway.

Lester Wells, according to murky census records, was born either in Canada or in southern Michigan in 1856 or 1858 to Canadian-born parents, Sarah and Elias Wells. In 1870 the family moved to a farm in the East Bay Township of Grand Traverse County, Michigan. Wells married Helen Lavanchie Hinkson (1859–1915) in 1878, and the couple had five children. A longtime farmer and logger, Wells is reported by Earl Beck to have done "his lumbering in the Saginaw Valley" (Beck 1960), but he also logged closer to home. On March 25, 1946, the *Record Eagle* of Traverse City published a photograph of lumberjacks atop a timber-laden sleigh: "Putting in the load of logs on the bunks in Clinch Park on Pioneer Days about 12 years ago. Veteran local lumbermen had charge of the loading and on the load may be seen Louie Lautner, Lester Wells, Bill Hoxie, Marty Newstead, Francis Ransom and others who are not identified." Wells was also active as a trucker and building mover after his wife's death. He lived in a boardinghouse from 1930 until his death in 1941.

Alan Lomax made this observation in his field notebooks: "found Lester Walls [Wells] in Lantner's [Lautner's?] Place (the hangout for sailors, lumberjacks, etc.)—another tough and intelligent oldster at 82—still active (moving, trucking, farming—number of songs + his friends know many more." Wells recorded nine songs for the

Library of Congress, two of which—"Michigan I-O" and "The Falling of the Pine"— were included on the Library of Congress LP *Songs of the Michigan Lumberjacks* (1960).

"Traverse City," with its incremental and collective composition and its focus on several local characters, draws upon methods and modes sharpened in many a lumber camp. Regarding particular verses, blacksmith shops in a prior era were hangouts for farmers and loggers awaiting the fashioning or repair of essential tools. Gunton's cake and gin shop figures as a favored boardinghouse, perhaps railed against by Mr. Hannah, the "best man" of the final stanza whose hypocritical behavior echoes widespread jokes and anecdotes regarding preachers drawn to the supposedly devilish practice of cardplaying.

15 Yulia and Olaf

Sung by Nils Larsen, Newberry, Michigan, September 14, 1938.
Recorded by Alan Lomax.

2340 A2

Now they call me a yolly good fellow
And I tink they been so many this.
If you ever have been a good fellow,
Then you know yust how costly it is.

Now I went out to the wood in November,
I come down with the drive in the spring.
And now I'll stay here in the city,
Yust a vatching my *pengar* [money/coins] takin' ving [wing].

I met a little blond, her name Yulia.
I tink that Yulia been Yew [Jew].
But she's spending up all of my pengar,
And a damn fine gold watch I had too.

Now Yulia, she called me good fellow.
She tink that going to help some,
But she's spending up all of my money
And putting me right on the bum.

Go back to the woods Mr. Olaf,
Driving your old team of mules.
Go put this in your pipe and please smoke it,
Good fellows been mostly damn fools.

Nils Larsen (1907–1973) was born in Värmland, a rural Swedish province, the second of Fridolf and Christina Larsen's five sons. He and his brother John (1903–1972) were brought to Newberry, Luce County, Michigan, where their parents ran a boardinghouse for single men. The 1930 census lists forty-seven boarders at Larsen's Luce Hotel, whose ages ranged from twenty-one to seventy-four; more than half were fifty or older. Besides those from Michigan and Sweden, there were men from seven states, as well as from Canada, Finland, Germany, and the Russian partition of Poland.

In the late 1940s, folklorist Richard Dorson described Newberry as "an inland community of under three thousand persons, which once manufactured thousands of tons of pig iron annually, but now depends for survival on a lone sawmill and a State Hospital for the insane." Ruled by "an economic boss, the owner of the sawmill," it was a place where, in Dorson's view, politics were "apt to degenerate from a high standard of lawlessness to petty boss rule" (Dorson [1952] 2008: 180). Alan Lomax arrived in Newberry a decade earlier, a little more than a year after a bitter strike against the sawmill owner led by Finnish workers seeking better pay and conditions. On June 4, 1937, a pro-company mob, enraged in part by the presence of avowed Communist Finns in the ranks of striking lumberjacks, attacked them with baseball bats and iron bars, killing one striker and destroying Newberry's Worker's Hall (Karamanski 1989: 237–241).

With Europe drifting rapidly toward war and the hirelings of bosses beating and killing militant workers almost with impunity throughout America, Lomax regarded Newberry and, by extension, the Larsens with a sense of righteous political indignation invested with his interpretations of Darwin, Freud, and Marx:

Newberry—the toughest little town I have seen in Michigan—Larsen's Luce Hotel—the young loafers, football players, fighters around the dreary bar, potential fascists, boasting about how the strikers had been beaten up and the Finn Workers Hall smashed.— We showed them reds—radio stations all over the country congratulated the little town of Newberry—whistles blowing at 6 a.m.—chased strikers for five miles out of town— beating them. "Hey boys, here's a Roosevelt man."—Dude Larsen [Sten (1917-1985)], the youngest, talks stupid, a boaster, soft, golden hair falling in forelock over high sloping Swede forehead—brother John the brightest complexion I've ever seen—reputed a terrible fighter—always drunk—dangerous—very handsome—a godlike selfish Nordic mouth—Old Man Larsen, hirsute, heavy, ape-like—short worn Neanderthal teeth—always drunk—his business gone to Hell and him indifferent—Mrs. Larsen is a perennial invalid—unseen—she hopes to die.

Lomax must certainly have heard the loud, vindictive bragging he describes, perhaps from one of the Larsen boys. Three of them performed for his recorder. Sten Larsen sang a pair of comic songs: "The Piece of Baloney" (2342 A1), a versified rendering of the international folktale "Dream Bread" (ATU tale type 1626) that combined stage Irish and Jewish dialect; and "My Wild Irish Nose" (2342 A2), a parody of "My Wild Irish Rose," delivered in an exaggerated Irish tenor. John Larsen delivered "To Save Myself from Hell, Boys" (2345 A2), a version of the whore-seeking song usually called "Canal Street" (Cray 1999: 212–214). But during this same recording session, Lomax encountered several participants in or supporters of the strike, conceivably from among the Larsens' boarders. Nils Larsen's song (2340 A2), for example, was performed immediately after Andrew Jackson, a Finnish American with an anglicized name, sang "Aina olen ilolla mä lähtenyt" (I Have Always Left with Joy) (2340 A1). Borrowing its tune and some phrases from "Lännen lokari" (The Logger of the West), recorded in 1930 by Hiski Salomaa—a Finnish immigrant songwriter whose witty compositions included anthems for the Industrial Workers of the World (IWW)—Jackson's song very likely invoked the previous year's strike in its third verse.

Kun kuuluu ne lakkohon kutsumus,	When the strike is calling,
Ulos metsistä me marsitaan,	We are marching out of the forests,
Ja kolkkien korpien hongistot vastaa	And the hallowed deep forests and pine trees answer
Jo laulumme kaiuntaan.	To the echo of our singing.
Kun nää [?] jumalauta antaudu ei,	When the [?] are, goddamit, not surrendering,
Ei vaikka perkele veis	Not, devil, even if they took us
Vaikka uhkaa jo vaarat ja vankilat,	When the dangers and prisons are threatening,
Vaikka kuulatkin lenteileis.	Even if they were shooting bullets.

(Transcription and translation by Susanna Linna Moliski)

The third generation of Larsens had quite different retrospective impressions of their grandparents and uncles in the 1930s. On October 2, 2009, Betty Theut of St. Ignace wrote to folklorist Hilary Virtanen: "I found the songs quite amusing, however the notes on the family were not what I remember. . . . My grandmother was a hard worker and cooked three meals a day for the hotel and lumberyard. My uncles were not as he describes them" (Theut 2009).

Both of Nils Larsen's songs were performed in Scandihoovian English of the sort flourishing in the Upper Midwest. Relying on *t* for *th*, and *y* for *j*, they also used a stereotypical male name, Olaf, as well as *pengar* (money), a Swedish loan word common in the Upper Peninsula's creolized dialect. His first song, included here, is set in a prior era of pine logging that required winter work and river drives. It shares several phrases and sentiments found in another Scandihoovian dialect sent to Robert Winslow Gordon— founder of the Archive of American Folk Song at the Library of Congress—by Bradford Shaw of South Carver, Massachusetts, in 1926: "Lumberyack faller ban yolly big fool," and

> Ven along come de spring ve drink and ve sing;
> Ve call de town faller gude friend.
> He help us to blow our whole vinter's dough,
> But he ain't got no panga to lend.
> *(Shaw 1926)*

Larsen's "Yulia and Olaf" also uses an all-too-familiar phrase, "on the bum," for the Depression's legion of homeless itinerant laborers, some of whom disdained working dangerous, backbreaking jobs for starvation wages. A few days before, Lomax set down this verse in his notebook.

> I met a man the other day
> I never met before.
> He asked me if I wanted a job
> A-shoveling iron ore.
> I asked what the wages were
> And he said, "Ten cents a ton."
> I said, "Ol' fella go chase yourself,
> I'd rather be on the bum."
> *(Jimmy Martin, St. Ignace)*

Intriguingly, Larsen's second song, "The Big State Fair" (2341 A1), better known as the "Swede from North Dakota," emerged around 1900 and was a particular favorite of hobos and harvest hands, including members of the IWW (Leary and March 1993: 261–262).

16 Long Barney

Sung by Lester Wells, Traverse City, Michigan, early September 1938.
Recorded by Alan Lomax.

2307 A2

Did you ever hear tell of Long Barney?
He lived near the town of Killarney.
With a blink of his eye the girls all would sigh,
And they all fell in love with Long Barney.
With a blink of his eye the girls all would sigh,
And they all fell in love with Long Barney.

He was going to the fair, it being Easter,
His pocket did hold many a taster.
He met with a Twig and with her danced a jig,
And they jigged it all 'round, did Long Barney.
He met with a Twig and with her danced a jig,
And they jigged it all 'round, did Long Barney.

Then into his tent he brought her.
He gave her a drop of the cratur.
Put his arms 'round her waist and her sweet lips did taste,
And she cried out, "Don't smother me, Barney."
Put his arms 'round her waist and her sweet lips did taste,
And she cried out, "Don't smother me, Barney."

Then in stepped Brian O'Darby,
Who had Biddy long desired.
Oh it's "Biddy," says he, "come over to me
And don't sit there listening to Barney."
Oh it's "Biddy," says he, "come over to me
And don't sit there listening to Barney."

"Oh," says Barney, "then you'd better toddle
Or I'll give you a belt o' the noddle."
Click-clack went the stick, on the floor Darby kicked,
And he kicked him around, did Long Barney.
Click-clack went the stick, on the floor Darby kicked,
And he kicked him around, did Long Barney.

Oh then into a tent he brought her,
He give her a drop of the cratur.

Put his arms 'round her waist and her sweet lips did taste,
And she cried out, "Don't smother me, Barney."
Put his arms 'round her waist and her sweet lips did taste,
And she cried out, "Don't smother me, Barney."

Oh says "Barney, there's no use resisting,
My father he's always a-listening.
My father and Twig said they'd give a pig
To a man that would marry me, Barney.
My father and Twig said they'd give a pig
To a man that would marry me, Barney."

Oh says Barney, "And mind, you've another.
We'll make them both sisters and brothers.
With Barneys and Twigs and children and pigs,
We'll soon stock the cabin," says Barney.

Lomax: Was that Barney a friend of yours?

Wells: Yeah, he was my first cousin.

Lomax: Where'd you learn that song?

Wells: Oh, in the camps, all in the camps. I went to the camps when I was fifteen years
old and I stayed there until I was pretty near ready to die. And then I quit.

Wells went into the lumber camps of northern Lower Michigan in the winter of 1873.
Many lumberjacks were Irish, and comic "stage Irish" songs flourished throughout
North America, especially in the late nineteenth century. No wonder Wells was able
to invest this song with a passable brogue. As in this song, the Irish were stereotypically
fond of whisky ("the cratur"), dancing jigs, fighting, and pigs, as evident in such proverbial expressions as "pig in a parlor" and "as Irish as Patty's pig." The many internal
rhymes in the third and fifth lines—Twig/jig, waist/taste, stick/kicked, etc.—are a hall-
mark of Irish ballad composition carrying over into English from prior Irish language
conventions.

No character in this song turns up easily in census records. "Long" typically applies
to a lanky fellow. "Twig" may be an English surname, but it has also been applied to
slender young men and women. "Biddy" is a common nickname for Bridget, a significant
name for Irish females, but also typically applied to slatternly stage-Irish maids.

17 Hayfoot, Strawfoot

Sung by Adolphus Delmas, Round Lake, Michigan, September 8, 1938.
Recorded by Alan Lomax.

2321 A2

Hayfoot, strawfoot, any foot at all,
Jenny lost her maidenhead a-going to the ball
She lost it in the weeds and she found it in the grass.
She wrapped it in a rag and she put it up her French ass.

Doot-de-doot-de-doot-de-dootle-do,
Doo-de-dootle-dootle-de-do-do
De-dootle-dootle-day,
Oh-de-dootle-dootle-do!

That's all.

Alan Lomax introduced Delmas on disc following a recording of "In New York Town" ("The Butcher Boy"): "This song was recorded near Round Lake, Michigan, in Emmet County on September 8, 1938, by Mr. Adolphus Delmas, seventy-seven-year-old former resident of Crossville [Cross Village], Michigan, who now lives in Mackinaw City." Born in Illinois in 1859, Delmas came to northwestern Lower Michigan sometime in the 1880s to work in the woods. He married an Odawa woman, Catherine Sequagua (or Schawajaw), who also appears in census records as Catherine (or Katherine) Williams (1867–1902). Delmas died in 1943 in Petoskey, just north of Round Lake, and is buried in Cross Village.

Lomax recorded Delmas during a session that included Ed Thrasher (track 18). The old men sang ten songs altogether, seven of them bawdy, and they evidently conversed about similar topics. As Lomax set down in his notebook: "This was in Crossville where Delmas married a squaw and raised his Indian family. . . . The people here have pioneer candor. Potter, Delmas and the rest loved their wives and loved them because they were good partners in the bed and say so. Delmas, the old man, was terribly sentimental about his dead Indian wife—proud of her ability to cook and her good body. He expressed disgust at the idea of sleeping with her when she was pregnant or menstruating. 'I'm no dog,' he said. And he swore he had not touched another woman since she died or at any time after they were married. 'Not that I've not had plenty of chances, but what comes so easy is bound to be dangerous.'"

"Hayfoot, Strawfoot" is a dance call sometimes associated with quadrilles or square dances, and bawdy calls were common in lumber camps or at house parties. Jennifer C. Post recorded a tamer version from New Hampshire in 1988 from a singer who associated it with Saturday-night house dances in the 1940s.

> Left foot, right foot
> Any foot at all
> Sally lost a bustle
> Coming home from the ball.
> *(Post 2004: 205)*

Delmas set his words to the tune of a schottische, a German couple dance form popular throughout the Upper Midwest. Paul Gifford (2011) identified the melody as "Rainbow Schottische," which often figured in schottische quadrilles requiring four couples who formed a "square." Composed about 1852 by Henry Kleber, a German immigrant to Pittsburgh, it was published in nineteenth-century omnibus tune collections and widely performed, turning up, for example, in a manuscript from the Idaho goldfields (V. Williams 2008: 61).

18 Shoot the Cat

Sung by Ed Thrasher, Round Lake, Michigan, September 8, 1938.
Recorded by Alan Lomax.

2321 B1

'Twas Nelly the milkmaid, so handsome and so gay,
So fond of a dance and going to a spree.
It's one joke to give and another for to take.
Says Nelly to the Mrs., "May I go to the wake?"
With my hol-fol-di-lain.

Says the mistress to Nelly, "I'd have you to beware,
For sure as you go, young Roger he'll be there.
He'll take you in his arm and he'll do to you some harm,
And you'll be sorry coming home in the morn,"
With your hol-fol-di-lain.

Nelly she got ready, was out upon the way,
Wishing all the time that Roger he'd be there.
"He'll take me in his arm and he'll shield me from all harm,

And I won't be sorry coming home in the morn,"
With my hol-fol-di-lay.

Early in the morning, before the break of day,
Roger threw Nelly down beside a stack of hay.
Says Roger to Nelly, "I'll lay you here so deep,
And I'll play to you the game that they call Shoot the Cat,"
With my hol-fol-di-lain.

Three months passed and the fourth month had come,
The rose and Nelly's cheek, they both grew into one.
Her apron wouldn't tie and her corset wouldn't lap,
And they laid it to the game that they call Shoot the Cat,
With my hol-fol-di-lay.

Eight months passed and the ninth month had come,
Born unto Nelly a fine young son.
Says mistress to Nelly, "We'll name him for your sake,
And we'll call him Shoot the Cat Coming Home from the Wake,"
With your hol-fol-di-lain.

This young devil grew up to be a man.
He run around town with his codger in his hand.
And every lady that he'd meet, at her he would shake it,
And he says his mama shot a cat coming home from the wake,
With her hol-fol-di-lay.

Adolphus Delmas: By God, Ed, that's good!

Edward E. Thrasher was born in 1877 in Millington, Michigan, a small town in the vicinity of Saginaw and Bay City where lumber camps and mills flourished. His father, Lyman Thrasher, hailed from Ohio, while his mother, Catherine Brown Thrasher, was born in Canada. He married Nora Evans in 1906 and the couple had two children.

Thrasher and Adolphus Delmas (track 17) were clearly friends who enjoyed bawdy songs and, besides those included here, Lomax recorded "Big White House in Larktown," "Bonny Black Hare," "I Met Miss Monroe in the Morning," "Keyhole in the Door," and "One-Eyed Riley" from Thrasher. "Nelly the Milkmaid" has a well-known Irish tune, and the wakes in Ireland were not only vigils for the dead but also social occasions that sometimes included drinking and boisterous behavior. Lusty milkmaids and plowboys likewise figure in rural folksongs from Ireland and England. This particular song is well known on both sides of the Atlantic, although the phrase "shoot the cat" seems to be unique to North American versions (Randolph 1992a: 170–171). In 1890 the English immigrant O. J. Abbott (1872–1962), who worked as a hired man on farms and in the woods of Canada's Ottawa Valley, learned a version very similar to Thrasher's from an Irishman, Patrick Whelan, of South March, Ontario (Randolph 1992a: 171; Fowke 1965: 11–13, 36–37, 168). Thrasher's penis-wagging episode, resembling verse 4 of "Joe Williams" (track 12), does not appear in other recorded performances and may be the singer's addition.

The phrase "shoot the cat" comes from sailors' jargon. Volume 16 of an 1869 London publication, *The Shipwrecked Mariner: A Quarterly Maritime Magazine*, included this explanation: "That which for many years past we have decided upon calling the ship's *cargo* [from the Portuguese] . . . was in earlier days sometimes designated by the Dutch name of *katt*, the tradition of which still remains in our naturalised *tea-caddy* and katty-packages employed to this day; and also in the English word *cat*, which is used for a coasting vessel, the name of the thing carried being given to the vessel carrying, just as *packet* is short for *packet-boat*. To shoot the cargo is a common expression for disburdening a ship of its load; and I need not insist further upon the aptness of the metaphor to the misery of the sea" (158). A euphemism for vomiting, the phrase "shoot the cat" was clearly also used for a male ejaculation.

LITHUANIAN

Lithuanians settled in the Upper Peninsula of Michigan in the early decades of the twentieth century, often as secondary migrants from communities in Illinois and Wisconsin. By the 1930s they could be found in every county of the U.P. except Baraga, and especially in the Copper Country, where they logged, mined, farmed, and occasionally owned shops (Grazulis 2009).

19 Russian Gigue

Played by Charles Ketvirtis on concertina, Newberry, Michigan, September 14, 1938. Recorded by Alan Lomax.

2337 A2

Charles Ketvirtis (1893–1968) was born in Lithuania, as was his wife, Mary A. Dubulski (1896–1959). The couple settled in Newberry, Michigan, where they raised eight sons and two daughters. Charles played the boxy German, or Chemnitzer, concertina throughout his long life and is remembered for performing and leading his sons in singing at family reunions. Ketvirtis played for social occasions from the 1930s into the 1950s. *The Evening News* of Sault Ste. Marie, Michigan, reported on the Newberry wedding of Mary Serafin to James Leazier Jr., for which Mary Ann Ketvirtis was a bridesmaid: "A reception was held at the home of the bride's parents from 5–8 p.m. with 150 guests present. . . . Music was furnished by the Charles Ketvirtis orchestra" (Thursday, August 21, 1952).

Lithuanians were few in the Newberry area, and a dance musician seeking an audience had to learn songs and tunes from several cultures. Lomax recorded nearly a score of performances from Ketvirtis. Six were Lithuanian, including his only vocals, while the others were instrumental versions of American, Finnish, German, Polish, and Russian tunes. It is not clear whether the French spelling *gigue*, from the original English "jig," comes from Ketvirtis or Lomax. The Russian word for jig simply uses Cyrillic characters for the same sound.

20 Buffalo Gals

Played by Charles Ketvirtis on concertina, Newberry, Michigan,
September 14, 1938. Recorded by Alan Lomax.
2337 B2

Ketvirtis interjects a nonlexical epithet—"Opa(h)elia!"—during the last phrase of this tune that resembles such exclamations as *lelija* that end numerous Lithuanian folksongs from what was likely Ketvirtis's home region, Aukštaitija [this annotation by Debra Raver]. The original tune is likely of eighteenth-century German origin, but by the nineteenth century it was widely known by Anglo-American fiddlers prior to its acquisition of lyrics for the minstrel show stage in 1844 (Bayard 1945: 1; Meade, Spottswood, and Meade 2002: 754–755).

21 Mother Song

Sung and played by Charles Ketvirtis on concertina, Newberry, Michigan, September 14, 1948. Recorded by Alan Lomax. Transcription by Vita Ivanauskaite-Šeibutiene of the Lietuvių literaturos ir tautosakos institutas (Institute of Lithuanian Literature and Folklore), with assistance from Guntis Smidchens; translation by Guntis Smidchens and Aurelija Tamosiunaite with assistance from Debra Raver; annotations by Ivanauskaite-Šeibutiene, Raver, and Tamosiunaite.

2337 A1

Motiniute meilioji,	Beloved mother,
Augin(ai) mani, nešiojai.	You raised me, you rocked me in your arms.
Augin(ai) mani, nešiojai.	You raised me, you rocked me in your arms.
Auginai mani meiliai,	You raised me lovingly,
Kodėl dabar negaili?	Why don't you pity me now?
Kodėl dabar negaili?	Why don't you pity me now?
Grait atskyrė nug tavi	I have been separated from you so soon,
Un didžių vargų mani.	And taken into great troubles (suffering).
Un didžių vargų mani.	And taken into great troubles (suffering).
Ant didžiojo vargelio,	Into great trouble (suffering),
Užu jauno bernelia.	Married to a young man.
Užu jauno bernelia.	Married to a young man.
Motiniute, kur guli?	Dear mother, where do you lie?
Aukštam svirni, lovelėj.	In the high granary, in a bed.
Aukštam svirni, lovelėj.	In the high granary, in a bed.
Kad turėčiau sparnelį,	If I had a wing,
Ti aš tinai nuskrisčia.	Then I would fly there.
Ti aš tinai nuskrisčia.	Then I would fly there.
Tai aš tinai nuskrisčia.	Then I would fly there.
Kaip gegutė kukuočia.	I would cuckoo like a cuckoo-bird.
Kaip gegutė kukuočia.	I would cuckoo like a cuckoo-bird.

Kaip gegutė kukuočia,	I would cuckoo like a cuckoo-bird.
Man(o) vargelis rokuočia.	And I'd tell you about my trouble.
Man(o) vargelis rokuočia.	And I'd tell you about my trouble.

Ketvirtis: [not clear what's being said but perhaps—] Well, I've sung a few words, but I've got to go now.

Lomax: What's the name of that song?

Ketvirtis: Well, what they call in English, "Mother." The mother was old with a young kid who left. The mother died, you cried.

The singer is singing in the Aukštaičiai dialect and maybe a little bit with an English accent, therefore it is hard to hear the exact endings of some of the words.

Widows and orphans are common figures in Lithuanian laments like this one, as are cuckoos who typically herald disaster or death with cries akin to human sobs (Rudalevičiūtė 2008: 4). In other Lithuanian versions of this song, which are associated with weddings—and hence the separation of a daughter from her mother—the fifth verse replaces the mother's resting place—"Aukštam svirni, lovelėj" (In [a] high granary, in [a] bed)—with "Aukštam kalne, smėlely" (In [a] high hill, in [the] sand), a clear reference to a cemetery, which, in Lithuania, is usually situated on a small sandy hill.

GERMAN

Germans are Michigan's largest ancestral group, having settled the rich farmlands bordering Ohio and Indiana prior to the Civil War, where Frankenmuth and Gaylord remain known for their Bavarian heritage. Yet in the Upper Peninsula—dominated by mining, logging, mill and dock work, and hardscrabble farming—Germans were not particularly numerous, especially in relation to Nordic, Slavic, French Canadian, and Italian settlers.

22 Was war an diesem Baum? / What's on This Tree?

Sung by Herman Meyers, Newberry, Michigan, September 16, 1938.
Recorded by Alan Lomax. Transcription, translation, and annotation by Antje Petty, 2011.
2349 A1

Was war an diesem Baum?	What was in this tree?
Ein wunderschönes Nest.[1]	A beautiful nest.
Nest am [im] Baum,	Nest in the tree,
Baum in d[e]r Erd.	Tree in the ground.

CHORUS:	*CHORUS:*
Drunten auf grünigsche[2] Weide	Down in the green meadow
Da steht ein schöne[r] Werre[3] Baum,	There is a beautiful tree,
schöner Werre Baum.	Beautiful tree.
Right, right[4]	Right, right.

Was war in diesen[m] Nest?	What was in the nest?
Ein wunderschönes Ei.	A beautiful egg.
Ei im Nest,	Egg in the nest,
Nest im Baum,	Nest in the tree,
Baum in d[e]r Erd.	Tree in the ground.

Was war in diesem Ei?	What was in this egg?
Ein wunderschöner Dotter.	A beautiful yolk.
Dotter im Ei,	Yolk in the egg,
Ei im Nest,	Egg in the nest,
Nest im Zweig,	Nest on the twig,
Zweig am Ast,	Twig on the branch,
Ast im Baum,	Branch on the tree,
Baum in d[e]r Erd.	Tree in the ground.

Was war in diesem Dotter?	What was in this yolk?
Ein wunderschöner Vogel.	A beautiful bird.
Vogel im Dotter,	Bird in the yolk,
Ei im Nest,	Egg in the nest,
Nest im Zweig,	Nest on the twig,
Zweig am Ast,	Twig on the branch,
Ast im Baum,	Branch on the tree,
Baum in d[e]r Erd.	Tree in the ground.

Was war an diesem Vogel?	What was on this bird?
Ein wunderschöner Bill[5]	A beautiful bill.
Feder im [am] Vogel,	Feather on the bird,
Vogel im Dotter,	Bird in the yolk,
Ei im Nest,	Egg in the nest,
Nest im Zweig,	Nest on the twig,
Zweig am Ast,	Twig on the branch,
Ast im Baum,	Branch on the tree,
Baum in d[e]r Erd.	Tree in the ground.

Was war an diesem Bill?	What was on the bill?
Ein wunderschöner Gwand[6]	A beautiful frock.
Gwand am Bill,	Frock on the bill,
Feder am Vogel,	Feather on the bird,
Vogel im Dotter,	Bird in the yolk,
Ei im Nest,	Egg in the nest,
Nest im Zweig,	Nest on the twig,
Zweig am Ast,	Twig on the branch,
Ast im Baum,	Branch on the tree,
Baum in d[e]r Erd.	Tree in the ground.

Lomax: Mr. Meyers, where did you learn this song?

Meyers: I learned this as a boy in Canada. When I was a boy eight years old, I learned this song from my mother.

Lomax: Was she from Germany, or was she born in this country?

Meyers: She was born in Germany.

Lomax: What part? Do you know?

Meyers: Don't know what part. She come over when she was a young woman, to this country.

———

1. The singer has a southern German (possibly Austrian) accent, saying, for example, *wunderscheyn* rather than *wunderschoen*, but the language is basically standard German with a few exceptions.
2. *Gruensche* is standard for "green."
3. Most versions of this song concern a *Birnenbaum* (pear tree), but Meyers seems to sing *Werrebaum*.
4. Here Meyers uses English words.
5. Meyers seems to use the English "bill" for a bird's beak, although he also interjects *Feder* (feather) inconsistently.
6. *Gwand* is an Austrian term.

Born in Canada in 1877 to German immigrants, Herman Meyers arrived in Michigan in 1891. The 1900 census lists him as an unmarried inmate of Newberry's Upper Peninsula Hospital for the Insane, and perhaps he remained in the area for the rest of his life. In 1940 he was listed as the divorced head of a small household that included three older boarders: an Irish immigrant, Michael O'Gorman, 73; and two fellows born in Michigan, James Peake, 65, and Archie McLaughlin, 76.

Meyers sang seven songs for Lomax, three in German and four in English, the latter including the sentimental western song "Home on the Range" and a popular minstrel show ditty, "I'll Never Leave Old Dixie Land Again." With its cumulative structure and incremental repetition, "Was war an diesem Baum?" is just the sort of song an eight-year-old might remember, however imperfectly, from his immigrant mother's singing. Well known in the Old World, it was included by Ludwig Erk and Franz Magnus Böhme in their three-volume collection *Deutscher Liederhort* (German Nursery Songs), published from 1893 to 1894 (2: 531–532). And it has flourished in German American communities, especially among the Pennsylvania Dutch (Brendle and Troxell 1949: 72–77; Boyer, Buffington, and Yoder 1964: 46–51).

POLISH

Polish immigrants arrived in Michigan mostly in the late nineteenth and early twentieth centuries. Second only to Germans among the state's ethnic groups, Poles were mainly industrial workers and farmers. The Dodge Brothers automotive plant drew many to the Detroit area, where the immigrants established Poletown and dominated Hamtramck. Others toiled in the iron and copper mines of the Upper Peninsula. In the early 1870s, Poles from Poznan and Kashubia were lured to Presque Isle County by lumber companies seeking to populate logged-off acres. Clearing rocks and stumps, the newcomers planted rye and potatoes, worked winters in the woods, and labored in limestone quarries on the nearby shores of Lake Huron. Some of their neighbors were Anglo-Americans and Anglo-Canadians, but more were Prussians and Pomeranians, with whom they had rubbed shoulders in Europe. Their relative isolation, rural occupations, and general conservatism—combined with a regular influx of fellow immigrants escaping the Pennsylvania coal mines and Chicago factories—contributed to the sustenance of Old Country traditions, especially in the communities of Metz and Posen.

23 Chodźcie gąski moje / Come My Little Geese

Sung by Edwina Lewandowski and Stephanie Lewandowski, Posen, Michigan, September 1938. Recorded by Alan Lomax. Transcribed and translated by Paulina Michalewicz.

2320 A2

Nad wodą wieczornej porze	At night by the water
Za gąskami chodziła	She walked tending the geese
Dziewczyna śliczna jak zorze	A girl as beautiful as the dawn,
I tak sobie nuciła	And this is what she sang to herself

Chodźcie, chodźcie gąski moje	Come, come my little geese,
Chodźcie ze mn do domu	Come home with me
A powiem wam troski moje	And I will tell you all my worries
Nie powiedzcie nikomu	You will not tell them to anyone
Chodźcie, chodźcie gąski moje	Come, come my little geese,
Chodźcie ze mną do domu	Come home with me
A powiem wam troski moje	And I will tell you all my worries
Nie powiedzcie nikomu	You will not tell them to anyone

Edwina Lewandowski (b. 1918) and her sister Stephanie (1920–2012) were born in the Posen area of Presque Isle County to Peter and Joanna Lewandowski, who had five daughters and four sons. Raised on a farm, the sisters loved to sing at home and in school, with Edwina on soprano parts and Stephanie on alto. One brother, Steve, played the violin, while another, Ted, was adept on banjo and piano. Both entertained for weekend dances around Posen and Metz in a band that included Felix Kania (tracks 24 and 29). And there were other musical Lewandowskis in the area, including Philip and Casimir "Cash," a pair of fiddlers who from roughly 1908 until the early 1930s "traveled to Rogers City, Metz, and Hawks and around the country, usually by the familiar horse and buggy, to play for the famous two day weddings" (Posen Centennial Committee 1970: 98). Stephanie married Philip Smolinsi in 1946, and they raised six children on a dairy farm in Leer, Michigan, with Stephanie working later as a cook at the Posen School. Edwina married Stanley Switek in 1956, and the couple had two children and ran a bean farm near Pinconning, Michigan.

Alan Lomax visited the Posen area by design. Konrad Bercovici, a Romanian Jewish immigrant journalist, traveled there in the early 1920s. The United States had recently restricted immigration, Prohibition was in place, the resurgent Ku Klux Klan had commenced attacks on Catholics, Jews, and Slavs in the Upper Midwest, and there was considerable debate within the nation's Anglo-Protestant ruling class over the value of "foreigners" in the American fold. Bercovici stressed the value of Old World customs, while championing the contributions of immigrants to American life, including those who had settled in Posen: "The Pole is a very good farmer and a very good cattleman, but he believes in doing things as his father and grandfather did them. He, too, believes in small farm villages instead of a baronial estate for each farmer, as was [Thomas] Jefferson's original dream" (Bercovici 1925: 124). Lomax read Bercovici in preparation

Joanna and Peter Lewandowski family: *(top row, left to right)* Anthony, Bernice, Martha, Bernadine, Edwina, Stephanie, and Steve; *(front row, left to right)* Ted, Joanna, Blanche, Peter, and Leo, Posen, Michigan, ca. 1938. (courtesy of April Miller and Janet Albosta)

for his Michigan fieldwork. Having successfully recorded Polish performers in Detroit, he sketched dour initial observations in his notebook regarding Presque Isle County.

I wd have liked to have seen more of the Poles around Gaylord but they were having a picnic under the aegis of the [sootrags?] of hell + were much too drunk and excited to even sing—Drove on to Posen (a bare + frozen little country town), no place to stay, no place to eat—In Metz a dance—happy girls and red faced boys and the worst jazz I ever heard—unbelievable—Rogers City the next morning, empty, gray and on the edge a big

> calcite plant + standing on the edge of Lake Michigan [actually, Lake Huron] like a big
> daddy long legs—Posen. Rev. Czyper [Casimir Szyper, pastor of St. Casimir's Catholic
> Church in Posen], stern, clean cut, owning all the Poles, cold and empty like a drum that
> beats itself. [Boleslaw] Centala, the organist, young yellow pale + toothless—knows
> no folk music and no folk musicians—hated superstitions when young—farmers still
> putting [?] in the fences to scare witches—to cure warts bury a cucumber under the
> drip from an eave—as c. rots w. rots.

Lomax succeeded nonetheless in finding many fine folk singers and instrumentalists.

The Lewandowski sisters' "Chodźcie gąski moje" (Come My Little Geese) is a venerable folksong from the Poznan region. From 1857 to 1890 the Polish folklorist Oskar Kolberg (1814–1890) published thirty-three volumes documenting Polish regional folklore, including twelve thousand folksongs. Originally entitled *Lud* (people or folk) but republished as *Dzieła Wszystkie* (Complete Works), Kolberg's massive compilation included a version of this song (Kolberg [1880] 1961: 51). Geese were important in the rural economies of Old and New World Poles, providing eggs, meat, down for pillows and comforters, and wing feathers that served as pastry brushes and dusters. The task of tending geese typically fell to young girls.

24 Wedding March
Played by Felix Kania on clarinet, Posen, Michigan, September 1938.
Recorded by Alan Lomax.
2311 A1

Felix Kania (1882–1966) was born in Poland and immigrated in 1900, working successively in Massachusetts, Rhode Island, Illinois, and Minnesota before settling in the Metz/Posen area, where his son Edward recalled that "he liked the seasons" (Kania 1989). According to Ed, Felix learned to play the clarinet in the United States from Lithuanians who taught him to play from notes; he later picked up other tunes for himself. He was a fixture in the Rogers City Band, whose repertoire included Sousa marches. More often, echoing the village bands of Posen, the elder Kania matched his clarinet with a pair of violinists, including Anthony Strzelecki, and a drummer to play for local weddings, which were typically held in the summer, when an empty barn or granary—or perhaps a temporary plank-covered frame with a tented ceiling—might serve as a dance floor. Many guests arrived by horse and buggy, and the festivities extended for several days: "We got the food, we got the beer. Might as well make it last until it was all gone" (Kania 1989).

Edward Kania (1926–2011), a clarinetist and accordionist who also worked at Michigan Limestone in Rogers City for thirty-five years, was twelve years old when Alan Lomax recorded his father: "We didn't have any power, and the guy that come and recorded was with a 78 rpm record. And he was cutting with a six-volt battery outfit, I think. I remember the battery stood out on the porch and he brought the wires in the house and everything, brought the recorder into the house. And my dad played and sang" (Kania 1989).

The march featured here figured prominently in weddings, as Ed Kania recalled: "They were called to the family's home. They played before they went to church. And then they had another march that they played upon return from church. . . . And the one that was recorded in 1938 was the one from before they went to church." At the wedding itself, Felix and fellow musicians mostly performed such couple dances as polkas, obereks, mazurkas, and waltzes, but their repertories also included square-dance tunes.

25 Irish Washerwoman

Played by Tony Strzelecki on lead fiddle and by a second fiddler,
possibly Tony Wasylk, Posen, Michigan, September 1938.
Recorded by Alan Lomax.

2312 A1

Anthony "Tony" Strzelecki (1882–1969) was born in Posen, Michigan, to Polish immigrant parents. He was a farmer who, like an Old World agrarian villager, lived on Posen's main street. A respected fiddler, Tony had learned to play by ear from his father, Jacob, and was in demand for local weddings through the 1950s, sometimes joined by Antony "Tony" Wasylk (1889–1954), by his brother Walter Strzelecki (1880–1967), who bowed chords on bass fiddle, and by a younger generation of musicians. Strzelecki's sons, Joseph (1910–1999) and Jacob (1920–2005), both learned their father's tunes on fiddle and button accordion, respectively. Joe especially favored old Polish marches: "At the wedding, before they were leaving for church, some of the older ladies that knew that song,

FOLLOWING PAGES: Felix Kania (with clarinet) and two fiddlers play for a wedding on a farm, Posen, Michigan, ca. 1920. (author's collection, courtesy of Ed Kania)

the orchestra played and the ladies were singing that" (Joseph Strzelecki 1989). Joe's wife, Louise, also fiddled, and sometimes the two played twin fiddles at weddings and parties. When his father was dead and his wife could no longer play, Joe taped a second fiddle part and played along with those recordings (Jacob Strzelecki 1989).

In his field notes Lomax referred tersely to "Tony W." (Tony Wasylk?) as "a comic— caperer." He also mentioned a fellow named "Sehelestika" who was "a cream buyer" who "let me record in his house." Perhaps this fellow was Tony Strzelecki? No name remotely resembling Sehelestika turns up in local church and community records, and both Joe and Jacob Strzelecki distinctly recalled their father being recorded at home.

"The Irish Washerwoman" was a favorite dance tune all across the Canadian– American border region from the East Coast through the Great Lakes region (see also Stratman-Thomas CD part1, track 30). Associated with Irish famine refugees of the 1840s, the tune dates to the eighteenth century and is probably English. The two Tonys likely encountered the tune locally, where their Polish style of lead fiddle and chording second fiddle had parallels among local Anglo- and Scots-Canadian fiddlers. Lomax noted cross-cultural connections in a report to the Librarian of Congress: "A visit to Posen, Michigan, brought the Library an interesting collection of Polish ballads and fiddle tunes. Many of the latter had been learned from local [Anglo-Celtic] fiddlers when the Polish settlers arrived and now among young people are passed under Polish names as Polish tunes" (A. Lomax 1939). This rendition of "Irish Washerwoman," with its skittery melody and rhythmic syncopation, evokes the musical dialect of village ensembles from Poland's Poznan region.

26 Polish Polka
Played by Tony Strzelecki on fiddle, Posen, Michigan, September 1938.
Recorded by Alan Lomax.
2312 B2

Polka means a Polish woman, just as *polak* is either a Polish man or a generic term for a Polish person. The polka dance, however, is in 2/4 time and originated in the Czech-Polish border area around 1830. Like the Austrian waltz and other couple dances emerging in that era, it captivated dancers throughout Europe and the Americas, where it was often performed to the accompaniment of fiddles or accordions or brass-and-reed ensembles. Perhaps this particular tune had a name, but if so, it remains to be discovered.

27 W żelaznej fabryce / In the Steel Mill

Sung by Adolph Romel and Sylvester Romel, Posen, Michigan, September 1938. Recorded by Alan Lomax. Transcribed and translated by Paulina Michalewicz.

2320 A3

A sam się zabieram	And I myself choose to go
Do tej Ameryki.	To that America.
Przyjochałem ci ja do tej Ameryki,	I came to that America,
Znalazłem robote	I found a job
W żelaznej fabryce.	In the steel mill.
Jak robie, tak robie, roboty pilnuje	I work, that's how I work, I watch my job
A anglik nade mną	And the English (American) boss
Jeszcze godamuje.	Still goddamns me.
Niech on godamuje, roboty nie rzuce.	Let him goddamn me, I will not quit my job.
Gdy Pan Bóg da zdrowie,	When the Lord God will give me health,
Do kraju powróce	I will return to my country
Bo w tej Ameryce, odbierają chłopcom lata	Because in that America, they take youth from boys
A młodem dziewczętą odbierają wianki.	And they take wreaths from young girls.
Bo w tej Ameryce	Because in that America
To są same niedowiarki.	There are only unbelievers.

Adolph Romel (1909–1986) and his younger brother Sylvester (1913–1994) were the sons of Valentine Romel (1880–1962) and Anna Losinski Romel (1884–1953), both of whom were born to Polish immigrant parents in Posen, Michigan. In 1989 Anna Romel's last surviving son, Syl, recalled his mother as constantly singing around the family home and farm: "She was a good singer. She did know, oh, about a hundred songs. And not from the papers, she had that in her head. Just like we did. We didn't sing from the paper, just from [the head]. That's the only way" (Romel 1989). The family included five boys and five girls, yet only "the boys were the singers," joining their mother and learning her repertoire while walking the dirt roads to school or to neighbors' homes, at weddings, around the house, and especially in the barn. With no radio and milking by hand, Anna Romel sang daily to relax the cows, with her sons chiming in.

Lomax set down brief field notes regarding the Romels and Michigan's Polish farmers: "Always something to do on a farm. Young boys stay at home, quit school to help with farm. The Romel boys have not married. Four Keller boys in Cross Village the same. But country knows result of work. Six or seven big sturdy outbuildings around every farm. The farm yard looks swept." Syl Romel married a few years later, farming and working at the Rockport Quarry on Lake Huron, where he was called a canary and was asked to sing and whistle by the foreman when work was slow. Fond of dancing with his wife, Josephine, he "never liked square dances, but waltzes, hop waltzes [polkas], two steps, obereks." Interviewed fifty-one years after the 1938 Lomax recording session, Romel's recollections were rough: "He came to the Strzeleckis, Strzeleckis asked us to come sing. That's all." The session included fourteen songs, four by Anna, two more that she sang with Adolph, four by Syl and Leo, including one with fiddle backing by Tony Strzelecki, two by Adolph and Syl, and a pair featuring four brothers: Adolph, Leo, Syl, and Ted.

"W żelaznej fabryce" is a folksong, probably from the early twentieth century, known in both Poland and the American Midwest. Sometimes the sojourning husband returns to his wife and children; sometimes there is only wishful thinking; sometimes the worker's exile is permanent. Syl Romel's rendition, with its mixed-language phrase "godamuje" (goddamns me), ends with a bitter vow to return since America makes young men old and takes the "wreath," a symbol of fertility and virginity, from young women. Three years after the Romels sang "W żelaznej fabryce" for Alan Lomax, it was published by Chicago's Wladyslaw Sajewski and attributed to Jan Piwowarczyk (John the Drinker), a regular performer with the Makowska Orchestra and on the Windy City's *Polish Barn Dance* program. In the 1960s the Starlights released a 45 rpm record, "Iron Foundry Polka" (Ampol 507), that matched an English title with Polish lyrics, the final of which (translated here) offer a bleak conclusion.

> Go ahead and love another, I don't forbid you,
> Because from America I am not returning to you.
> *(Leary and March 1993: 278)*

> Sylvester and Bill Romel, Posen, Michigan, 1989. (photo by author)

28 Turkey in the Straw

Played by Tony Strzelecki on lead fiddle and by a second fiddler,
possibly Tony Wasylk, Posen, Michigan, September 1938.
Recorded by Alan Lomax.

2313 B2

"Turkey in the Straw" emerged on the American minstrel stage in the late 1820s, where it was often associated with the bumpkin blackface character "Zip Coon." Arguably the best-known American fiddle tune from the early nineteenth century through the present, it was performed in inimitable Polish village style by Strzelecki and his second fiddler.

29 Czerwono posiadło, a zielono zniszło / Red When It Was Planted, Green When It Bloomed

Sung by Felix Kania, Posen, Michigan, September 1938. Recorded by
Alan Lomax. Transcribed and translated by Paulina Michalewicz.

2310 B2

Czerwono posiadło, a zielono zniszło.	Red when it was planted, green when it bloomed.
Nie wie łojciec, matka do kogoż mnie tęskno.	My father and mother don't know who I am longing after.
Oj tęskno, nie tęskno do Jasia mojego. Bym troszke; wiedziała, poszła bym do niego,	Oy, I remember, I long after my Jack. If only had some knowledge, I would go to him,
Ale dróżki nie wiem i pisać nie śmieje	But I don't know the way and I'm afraid to write
Bo mnie nie powiedzom jego przyjaciele.	Because his friends will never tell me.

Lomax: Would you say in Polish what that song is? [Lomax likely meant to say "in English."]

Kania: [surprised] *Czerwono posiadło, a zielono zniszło* [Red when it was planted, green when it bloomed].

Lomax: Who sang it in Polish?

Kania: I don't know.

Lomax: What's your name in Polish?

Kania: Huh?

Lomax: What's your name?

Kania: Felix Kania.

In his Posen field notes, perhaps prompted by this incident and unaware of his saying "Polish" when he meant "English," Lomax wrote: "They find it practically impossible to translate Polish even so much as song titles—They are extremely brusque—seem hostile—when you first approach them, they say little and that curtly—They all work like Hell + are very conscious of this fact."

"Czerwono posiadło, a zielono zniszło" relies on a familiar agrarian metaphor to convey the poignant fate of a young woman who has given birth to a child whose father is far away in some unknown place. The song is not included in folklorist Oskar Kolberg's massive collection of Polish folksongs. Might it have been composed during the great Polish American migration that largely occurred following Kolberg's death in 1890? Many sojourning Polish males, like the fellow in the Romel brothers' factory song (track 27), left wives and sweethearts behind.

30 Goldmine in the Sky

Sung by Edwina Lewandowski and Stephanie Lewandowski, Posen, Michigan, September 1938. Recorded by Alan Lomax.

2320 A1

There's a goldmine in the sky far away.
We will find it, you and I, some sweet day.
There'll be clover just for you down the line,
Where the skies are always blue, pal of mine.

Take your time old mule, I know you're going lame,
But you'll pasture in the stars, when we strike that claim,
And we'll sit up there and watch the world roll by
When we find that long lost goldmine in the sky.

Far away, far away,
We will find that long lost goldmine some sweet day,
And we'll say hello to friends who said goodbye
When we find that long lost goldmine in the sky.

This sentimental western song, endearingly performed in the Lewandowski sisters' Polish-influenced English, was written by the brothers Charles and Nick Kenny, subsequent composers of the 1950s pop song "Love Letters in the Sand." Although "Goldmine in the Sky" was recorded by many performers, including Pat Boone, Horace Heidt, and Nat "King" Cole, it was first recorded by and is fundamentally associated with Gene Autry, doubtless the Lewandowski sisters' source. Autry (1907–1998) was born in Tioga, Texas, but won national acclaim while performing for the *National Barn Dance* from 1929 to 1934. Broadcast on Chicago's WLS radio and featuring Southern hillbilly and Midwestern polka performers who sometimes fused each other's sounds, the *Barn Dance* could be heard throughout Michigan. Autry's bands included several accordionists, among them Frank Kuczynski, better known as Pee Wee King, recruited in 1934 after Autry heard him playing on the *Polish-American Hour* over WRJN in Racine, Wisconsin (Hall 1996: 30–31). Autry first recorded "Gold Mine in the Sky" in 1937 on Vocalion (03358), and then, backed by Frank Kuczynski on accordion, sang it in an eponymous film released by Republic Pictures in early July 1938, just two months before Lomax's visit to Posen.

FINNISH

Between 1880 and the onset of World War I, more than three hundred thousand Finns immigrated to the United States, variously fleeing evictions from peasant homelands, a population surplus, unemployment, class strictures, a domineering state church, and the political oppression of Swedes to the west and Russians to the east. Roughly half settled in the Lake Superior region. Toiling as miners, loggers, fishers, dock workers, small farmers, millhands, craftsmen, cooks, and maids, they established rural communities and "Finn towns" in industrial cities, especially throughout the western half of the Upper Peninsula of Michigan.

Like other newcomers and their descendants, Finnish Americans sustained Old World musical traditions. Hymns, ballads, and patriotic, class-conscious, and sentimental songs—rendered a cappella or accompanied by a pump organ or kantele—echoed from homes. Polkas, waltzes, and other dance tunes—performed on fiddle, harmonica, and accordion—dominated house parties and lumber-camp frolics. Institutions fostering music soon thrived. Suomi Synod Lutheran churches, aligned with Finland's state church, fostered sedate choirs with standard part-singing, while members of the charismatic, democratic Laestadian or Finnish Apostolic Lutheran church composed new hymns and adapted American gospel songs. Temperance and workers societies built halls, formed brass bands, staged musical plays, and sponsored dances (Leary 2001a).

31 Kulkurin valssi / Vagabond Waltz

Sung and played on harmonica by Yalmer Forster, Calumet, Michigan, September 27, 1938. Recorded by Alan Lomax.

2384 B22

Lomax: Where'd you learn that?

Forster: I learned that in this country. It's an old country song, Finnish country song, but I learned it in this country from the Finnish people. Down in Newberry I learned that from a Finlander come from the old country. He started learning to play the piano 'cordion. I helped him with the mouth organ then, see. That's how I got started on these.

Yalmer Eino Forster was born in 1892 to Finnish immigrant parents. He married Lillian Amala (b. 1902) in 1921. By 1938 they were living in Calumet with their five children and a boarder, Abraham "Aapo" or "Abo" Juhani (see track 33). Draft records from 1942 place the Forsters in nearby Laurium. Little else is known about Forster beyond the fact that he was bilingual and assisted Alan Lomax in communicating with Aapo Juhani. Forster's wife, Lillian, wrote affectionately to Lomax in December 1938: "I had Abo tell my fortune and see [he] said your thinking a lot of comeing down to see us, Oh! I wish you would. . . . Alex and Yalmer are so lonesome for you and, so am I. . . . Best regards from everyone, Abo too. He's sewing his cap so his ears won't freeze."

Lomax recorded more than a dozen harmonica performances from Forster, including a quadrille, a French jig, the popular waltz "Over the Waves," a Norwegian tune, and several Finnish polkas and waltzes. All of them were ably delivered in an "accordion style" achieved through rhythmically blocking and unblocking reeds with one's tongue, thus simulating the left- and right-hand sounds of a button accordion. This particular tune, identified as "The Traveling Boy" in the Library of Congress records, is "Kulkurin valssi," best known in English as "Vagabond Waltz." Along with "Orpopojan valssi," which Forster also performed, it is a well-known composition of J. Alfred Tanner (1884–1927), a Finnish entertainer who combined folk and popular melodies with humorous lyrics. The Finnish American singer Juho Koskela (1879–1942) recorded "Kulkurin valssi" in 1920 (Victor 72910) and again in 1921 (Columbia E7241); he also recorded "Orpopojan valssi" in 1923 (Victor 73870). Meanwhile, in 1922, Tanner toured the Upper Midwest's Finnish communities in Michigan, Wisconsin, and "everywhere in Minnesota where there was a hall available for him to perform in" (Wasastjerna 1957: 299). "Kulkurin valssi," which celebrates a homeless yet cheerful and idealistic wanderer, resonated powerfully with Finnish Americans, many of whom had been landless workers in both Finland and America. In the twenty-first century many Finnish Americans informally regard it as their cultural community's "national anthem."

32 Kaurapellon pientareella kasvoi kaunis kukka / On the Side of an Oat Field Grew a Beautiful Flower

Sung by Amanda Härkönen, Calumet, Michigan, September 29, 1938.
Recorded by Alan Lomax. Translated by Susanna Linna Moliski.

2394 B3

Kaurapellon pientareella kasvoi kaunis kukka.	Alongside an oat field grew a beautiful flower.
Kaurapellon pientareella kasvoi kaunis kukka.	Alongside an oat field grew a beautiful flower.
Sinisilmä, punaposki, kullan kiertotukka,	Blue-eyed, red-cheeked, golden-haired beloved,
Sinua lemmin, omanani armaanani lemmin.	You I love, as my own beloved I love.

Misidentified in the Library of Congress records as "Amanda Heikkinen," Amanda Härkönen (1888–1959) was born in Ristijärvi, a small village in the Kainuu region of northern Finland. She immigrated to America with a sister in 1905, settling in Cloquet, Minnesota, where she married Anselm Maki. Her daughter, Evelyn Palosaari, in a letter written to folklorist Hilary Virtanen, offered poignant details of a hard yet rich life: "There was a tragic fire in Cloquet, where her husband, after fighting the fire, died from smoke inhalation. She came to Pelkie, Michigan, where she lived with her sister Aina and family. She married Karl Suomi and had three children. They lived in Pelkie on a farm. Life was difficult trying to make a living and there were no conveniences. . . . She was a cook at a lumber camp at one time—making three meals a day on a wood fire stove with no water on tap—it was in a well away from the cook's camp. After Mr. Suomi passed, she cared for her children and farm with the kind help of loving neighbors. . . .

After a few years she married Henry Harkonen [no relation], and had one child, Evelyn, who joined a family of nine children" (Palosaari 2008).

Amanda was almost forty-seven years old when her last child was born. The Harkonens farmed, with Amanda milking cows, gardening, and cooking. She was noted for making a dozen loaves of bread at a time, and for her *juusto*, a Finnish baked cheese. Active in her church and the local temperance society, "she had a happy disposition, told jokes," and sang.

Härkönen described "Kaurapellon pientareella kasvoi kaunis kukka" as a ring-dance song, or *rinkkitanssi laulu*, that young people in her home village danced in a circle while holding each other's hands (another such song is on the Robertson CD, track 28). A well-known Finnish folksong, it has become regarded as emblematic of rural childhood through, for example, an exhibit, *Lapsuuden huoneet* / Childhood Rooms at the Helskinki Art Museum (2007), as well as its quotation and cover image evocation in Eila Peltonen's rustic novel, *Minun onneni minttumaa* (1984: 299).

33 Juliana

Sung by Aapo Juhani, Calumet, Michigan, September 27, 1938. Recorded by Alan Lomax. Transcription and translation by Susanna Linna Moliski.

2386 A

"Sun tullee isääs kuulla, kun olet ainoa lapseni. Et taida rikkautta, eikä arvoa alentaa."	"You should heed your father, since you are my only child. You won't inherit riches or anything of value."
"Lempeä ei saa multa, edestä tavaran Mitä hyödyttää minua kulta suuressa surussa."	"You can't get my love with material things. What does gold matter amidst deep sorrow?"
Puistolle viheriälle Juuliaan käveli. Viikunapuitten alle hän siellä istahti.	To a green park Juliana walked. Under the date tree she sat down.
Elonsa ilottoman hän siellä lopetti. Myrkyn nautittuaan elosta erkani.	Her joyless life she ended there. After taking poison, she left her life.
Kun isänsä sai kuulla Juliaanan kuolleena: "Juliaana, Juliaana, miksi saatoit minut suremaan."	When her father heard of Juliana's death: "Juliana, Juliana, why did you make me mourn?"

Kiireesti kirjoitettiin meripojalle.	Rapidly the sailor boy was written to.
Iloinen ettei ollut se kirje hänelle.	It wasn't a happy letter to him.
Sinetin kun hän rikkoi ja näki sanoman,	When he broke the seal and saw the message,
Niin tunnotoinna vaipui maassa makaamaan,	He fell senseless on the ground.
Taas suuren Luojan hän kohta virkoisi,	Again—great Lord—he soon recovered,
Haudalle Juliaanan Indianaan matkusti.	And to Juliana's grave in Indiana he traveled.
Kätensä kylmeneet hellästi pusersi.	Her cold hands he pressed tenderly.
Pois kuolon kalpeuden poskilta suuteli.	He kissed death's paleness from her cheeks.
Kyllä uskollinen oli sinun rakkautesi suuri.	Your grand love was faithful.
Kiitos kiitos suuri minun rakkaimpani.	Thank you, thank you grandly, my beloved.
Ei nuorta sydäntäni ei voinut satuttaa	My young heart couldn't be hurt by the power
Ylivalitiaan voima eikä maailman tavara.	Of the Almighty or the things of the world.
Tässä isä sekä äiti tulee näkemään	Her mother and father will see that
Että uskollinen lempi on valta väkevä.	Faithful love is a powerful force.

We know very little about Abraham "Aapo" Juhani, a lifelong bachelor, who was born in Finland in 1867. The 1920 census lists him as a boarder with the family of John and Katherine Tuoriniemi in Houghton County, Michigan. In 1938 he was seventy-one years old and living with Yalmer and Lillian Forster in Calumet, where Alan Lomax referred to him jocularly as the family's "singing neurotic nursemaid."

Juhani was a font of magico-religious lore, which Lomax documented on film and in his notebooks (see commentary on the film *Alan Lomax Goes North*). He was also a fine button accordionist, invariably scatting as he played. Lomax recorded a score of performances from Juhani, including the children's folksong "Kiikkuri kaakkuri," dance tunes—mazurkas, polkas, and schottisches—and several long ballads, including "Juliana" or "Kauppias Intiassa" (The Merchant in India). The Finnish ballad scholar Anneli Asplund includes this narrative folksong as number 24 in her concordance *Balladeja ja arkkiveisuja: Suomalaisia kertomalauluja / Ballads and Broadsides: Finnish Narrative Popular Songs*: "The central theme of 'The merchant from India' is faithful love between different social classes. The oldest known version appeared in 1895, published by O. W. Mattsson, who was a productive broadsheet creator. The text is based on a Swedish-language broadsheet and was probably translated by Mattsson. In all 14 impressions are known, the latest dating from 1915" (Asplund 1994: 835). In 2010 the Finnish musician J. Karjalainen recorded a new version of Aapo Juhani's 1938 performance for his chart-topping album *Polkabilly Rebels: Ameriansuomalaisia Lauluja / Finnish-American Folksongs* (Poko CD 380).

34 Kauhavan Polka

Played by Henry Mahoski on concertina, Amasa, Michigan, September 22, 1938. Recorded by Alan Lomax.

2361 A

Henry Mahoski was born in Milwaukee in 1917, the son of Polish immigrants. The family moved to Amasa, Michigan, where the elder Mahoskis ran the Brown Mill Bar following the end of Prohibition in 1933. There were Polish concertina players in the area, as Mahoski's son, Henry Jr., informed folklorist Hilary Virtanen: "He learned to play the concertina on his own when he was a teen attending Amasa High School and got to be good enough to be invited to play at dances out in 'Finn Country,' which was a few miles out of Amasa" (Mahoski 2008). After World War II the Mahoskis moved to Davenport, Iowa, where Henry Sr. ran a succession of taverns and played concertina for local events. Mahoski and his wife retired in Amasa in the early 1980s, and he died there in 1986.

Viola Turpeinen and John Rosendahl, promotional brochure, Kimball, Wisconsin, 1981. (photo by author)

Lomax recorded two Polish dance tunes, a polka and a "galop," from Mahoski, along with a Finnish schottische and "Kauhavan Polka," misidentified as "Karttula's Polka." In 1928 this fast, distinctively Finnish polka, which has become a standard in the region, was recorded for Victor (80587) and probably composed by John "Jukka" Rosendahl (1891–1932) and Viola Turpeinen (1909–1958). Rosendahl was a Finnish immigrant fiddler, while Turpeinen was a stellar piano accordionist who had grown up just a few miles southwest of Amasa in Stambaugh, a mining location. Turpeinen won a local reputation while playing for dances in her early teens. After being "discovered" by Rosendahl, she recorded more than forty tunes for Victor from 1928 to 1938, while touring incessantly throughout the Upper Midwest's Finnish settlements (Leary 1988). It is likely that Mahoski saw her perform and listened to her definitive recording.

35 Pikkulintu erämaassa lauleleepi suruissana / A Little Bird in the Desert Sings Sadly

Sung by Selma Elona Halinen, Allouez, Michigan, September 30, 1938. Recorded by Alan Lomax. Transcription and translation by Susanna Linna Moliski.

2398 A1

Pikkulintu erämaassa lauleleepi suruissana.	A little bird in the desert sings sadly.
Kylman talven vaiheella edestä kaipailee.	In the cold winter it longs for summer.
Minä olen yksin täällä, niin kuin hanhet vetten päällä.	I am alone here, like geese over the water.
Ei oo mulla perintöjä, eikä muuta tavraakaan.	I have no inheritance, nor other things.
Sinä leipäni ja rauhani?	Is that my bread and my solace?

Halinen: That's the end of that.

Lomax: What's your full name?

Halinen: Selma Elona Halinen.

Lomax: Where were you born?

Halinen: I guess you could say in Allouez, Michigan. It's a mile away from here.

Lomax: Can you tell me how old you are?

Halinen: Thirty-six.

Lomax: Did you go to high school?

Halinen: Sure, I've got the diploma here. I can show it to you if you don't believe it.

Lomax: Who taught you all of your songs?

Halinen: My mother taught me these songs.

Lomax: Did she know a lot of them?

Halinen: Ohhhh, I wish she was living and I could sing just like her. And she had a good voice too. My sister [Lempi] has a pretty good voice. Go down there, she'll sing you some nice songs.

Lomax: What part of Finland was your mother from?

Halinen: Sievi, Oulu Land [an Anglicization of *lääni* (province)].

Lomax: And when did she come to this country?

Halinen: She was eleven years old. She was fifty-five when she died.

Lomax: And she taught you all those songs when you were a little girl?

Halinen: Yeah.

Selma Elona Halinen (1902–1971), best known as "Elona" (anglicized from the Finnish "Ilona"), was the daughter of Finnish immigrants, Moses and Selma Halinen. As a young woman she traveled downstate to Detroit, where she permanently injured her arm while working in an industrial laundry. Returning to the family home in Allouez, Elona lived with her parents until their deaths and never married. Her great nephew, Dwayne Palos, informed folklorist Hilary Virtanen that "the whole family was musical." Besides her mother Selma (1878–1933), the source for most of the fourteen songs Elona recorded, Moses Halinen (1874–1938) was a copper miner who also crafted violins, violas, and banjos (Palos 2010).

Elona Halinen inspired this vivid sketch in Lomax's field notes: "Ilona Halenin [*sic*]—blond, crisp hair, broad, full prominent cheek bones splashed with pink—and a hearty male laugh cracking at the end—her rt. hand which she had paid $200 to send to commercial art school, continually trembling—it went into an electric wringer up to the elbow and when she sits now with her short pipe in hand, thinking, her mouth turns grey and weary and the lovely eyelids droop with hopelessness—When she begins to think about her arm too much she goes out and gets a bottle."

"Pikkulintu erämaassa lauleleepi suruissana," with its peasant's evocation of birds and bread, is a traditional Finnish lament. The eminent Finnish folksong scholar Ilmari Krohn (1867–1960) included versions in a massive compendium under the auspices of the Finnish Literature Society and now available online as the Suomen Kansan e Sävelmät (Digital Archive of Finnish Folk Tunes), which is maintained by the University of Jyväskylä (http://esavelmat.jyu.fi/index_en.html, accessed April 13, 2014). It was also included in such popular song collections as *Laulurastas Suomen Nuorisolle* (Song Thrush of Finnish Youth), which was published in Tampere in 1904.

36 Meripojan laulu / Sailor's Song

Sung by Frank Maki, Amasa, Michigan, September 23, 1938. Recorded by
Alan Lomax. Transcription and translation by Susanna Linna Moliski.

2363 B

Oli kaunis kuutamoilta	It was a beautiful moonlit night
Tuolla merellä.	On the sea.
Laivamme kulki hiljaa	Our ship was sailing slowly,
Keinuellen laineilla.	Swinging on the waves.
Minä vahtina seisoin siellä,	I was standing watch.
Kompassia tarkastelin	I looked at my compass,
Mielessäin ajattelin,	My thought was,
Että missä on kultani?	Where is my love?
Kuin sitten saavuimme me	And when we arrived
Liverpoolin satamaan	At Liverpool harbor
Minä kysyin konsulilta	I asked the consul
Onko kirjeitä Suomenmaan.	If there were letters from Finland.
Siel oli yksi kirje,	There was a letter,
Vaan se ei ollu kullaltani.	But it wasn't from my love.
Äitini vanha ja hellä	My mother, old and kind,
Ilmoitti ikävää.	Had sad news to tell.
Ves' virtana vierähteli	Water ran like a stream
Meripojan kasvoilla.	Down the sailor's face.
Hän muisti ajan entisen	He remembered old times,
Petturikultansa.	His traitor love.
Hyvästi synnyinmaa,	Goodbye my homeland,
Suomi on minun synnyinmaa.	Finland, my homeland.
Hyvästi petturi kulta	Goodbye traitor love
Ja rakkaat vanhemmat.	And my dear parents.

The surname "Mäki," meaning "hill," is so common in the Upper Peninsula of Michigan
that it has been used in a generic phrase for Finnish Americans, "sauna Maki" (Leary
2001b: 97). Since the late nineteenth century, several Frank Makis have lived in various
parts of Iron County, but sadly little is known about the only one who clearly resided
in Amasa. This Frank Maki (1892–1944) was born in Finland and was married at the
time of his death at age fifty-two. His songs all had a working-class sensibility, including
one wherein a young man is beaten up and called a "Red" by his sweetheart's father, and

another about a powerful underground miner who can "twirl tool handles." Perhaps this is the Frank Maki who placed a Christmas greeting to fellow workers in the *Työmies* (Working Man) annual in 1929?

Alan Lomax recorded seven songs from Maki on September 22–23, 1938, in Amasa, where he also recorded concertinist Henry Mahoski and two other Finnish singers, Frank Viita (1889–1906) and Vernon Rautanen (b. 1901). The experience prompted brief incisive field notes: "Amasa—Sept. 22—clean, bare little town, gray and deserted, surrounding the Finnish Co-op—the people grave, intelligent and well-informed like the other Finns I've met—the old songs are going but their intelligence persists—the houses have books and toilets—even in the country, the floors are of hard wood and the farmers talk like they've been to college."

There are many Finnish traditional and popular songs about a *meripoika*, or sailor, and this particular song's theme of a wandering lover spurned by his sweetheart back home is likewise common in the folksongs of many people. The opening lines of Maki's song, "Oli kaunis kuutamoilta tuolla merellä" (It was a beautiful moonlit night on the sea), closely match those of an old song still circulating among the Kven people, Finnish peasants and fisherman who settled in northern Norway: "Yks kaunis kuutamoilta Atlantin Merellä" (One beautiful moonlit night on the Atlantic sea) (*Kvensfinsk Tradisjon i Norge* 2013). Yet Maki's tune, intriguingly, is the same as that of the American cowboy song "When the Work's All Done This Fall," which was documented by Alan Lomax's father, John A. Lomax, in his pioneering anthology *Cowboy Songs and Other Frontier Ballads* (1910: 23).

37 Oli mulla ennen punaset posket / I Used to Have Red Cheeks

Sung by Amanda Härkönen, Calumet, Michigan, September 29, 1938. Recorded by Alan Lomax. Transcription and translation by Susanna Linna Moliski.

2394 A2

Oli mulla ennen punaset posket, vaan päivä on ruskottanut.	I used to have red cheeks, sunburnt.
Ja ruskan punasilla poskilla olen poikia uskottanut.	And with red cheeks I made boys believe.
Ja sain minä illalla jäniksen kiinni ja silitin sen selkää.	I caught a rabbit tonight and I petted its back.

| Ja tyttö on viiden kolmatta niin | And the girl is fifteen and the boys |
| pojat ne sitten jo pelkää. | are already afraid of her. |

Like "Kaurapellon pientareella kasvoi kaunis kukka" (track 32), this is a ring-, or circle-, dance song, with feisty lyrics that might appeal to a self-reliant country girl. Härkönen learned it in her home village in northern Finland prior to 1905, the year she immigrated at seventeen with her sister. Asked by Lomax about how the song was performed, she replied: "Ne pyörii, käsistä pitelee kiinni. Joo. Kaksin käsin pyöritään, niin ja käsistä pidetään kiinni." (They swing, and hold hands. Yes. You whirl it with both hands, yes and you hold hands.)

38 Kuule sinä Hiltu kun laulelen / Listen Hiltu When I Am Singing

Sung by Kalle Kallio, Newberry, Michigan, September 14, 1938. Recorded by Alan Lomax. Transcription and translation by Susanna Linna Moliski and Tom DuBois.

2335 A

"Kun kuule sinä Hiltu kun laulelen mä sullen	"Oh listen, Hiltu, when I sing to you
Että paina sinä rintaasi vasten	Press this close to your breast
Kun pleijatamme fonia ja rakastellaan	When we listen to records and make love
Eikä mennä me pappilaan.	And don't go to church.
Kun pleijatamme fonia ja rakastellaan	When we listen to records and make love
Eikä mennä me pappilaan."	And don't go to church."

Kun Hiltu se hiivas ja kulkurista tykkäs	Hiltu really liked the tramp
Kun kulkuripoika oikein lykkäs	When the tramp boy really bounced her,
Kun yhreksän kertaa yhtenä yönä	When nine times in one night
Hän tussun kylyvetti	He bathed her pussy;
Kun yhreksän kertaa yhtenä yönä	When nine times in one night
Hän tussun kylyvetti.	He bathed her pussy.

Ja jos meidän asiat vikahan mennee	And if things should go wrong
Niin mennään me tohtoriin	We will go to the doctor
Kun tohtori [?]	When the doctor [?]
Eikä maksa kun komekymppii.	And it doesn't cost more than a thirty.
Kun tohtori [?]	When the doctor [?]
Eikä maksa kun kolmekymppii.	And it doesn't cost more than a thirty.

| Kalle kalliin otti tiketin suoraan Helsinkiin | Kalle Kallio took a ticket straight to Helsinki |
| Tililili lillili lillili lii | Tililili lillili lillili lii |

Otti suoraan Helsinkiin	And took [a train] straight to Helsinki
Ja siellähän hämärässä rehvailtiin [?]	And there they dated in [?]
Ja suutelot antoi häll'.	And he gave her a kiss.
Tililili lillili lillili lii	Tililili lillili lillili lii
Ja suutelot antoi häll'.	And he gave her a kiss.
Kun vuoren ne yhressä koppasivat	They had been together for a year
Niin menivät ne naimisiin.	So they got married.
Tililili lillili lillili lii	Tililili lillili lillili lii
Ja menivät ne naimisiin.	They got married.
Kun pentukin heille ko	And a kid was born to them
Ja sen nimi oli Vilhelmi.	And he had the name Vilhelmi.
Sillala raitti ja sullala raa	Sillala raitti ja sullala raa
Ja sen nimi oli Vilhelmi.	And he had the name Vilhelmi.
Tilulu lullu lii . . .	Tilulu lullu lii . . .

Thus far we know little about Kalle Kallio beyond World War II draft records from 1942 listing him as born in 1887 and living in Newberry, Michigan—the town where Lomax recorded him on the first of three days spent recording in Larsen's Luce Hotel: "The bar is dreary—the hangout for the bums and the Finns—Kali [Kalle] Kallio—the Ape Man—lank straw colored hair—stubby hands—thick low body—hard pale blue eyes."

Lomax referred to Kallio's performance as a Finnish lumberjack song. This bawdy immigrant's song, with its preference for records rather than church services, sympathy for tramps and maids, and exuberant celebration of lovemaking was likely sung by Kallio in Michigan lumber camps, and perhaps he composed it. The tune, however, as well as the theme of a lusty wandering tramp were drawn from Hiski Salomaa's "Lannen Lokari," released as a 78 rpm record in 1930 (Columbia F 3158). Salomaa (1891–1957), aptly dubbed the Finnish Woody Guthrie because of his populist songwriting, lived in the Upper Peninsula of Michigan from 1910 to 1919, where he worked as a tailor and was involved with the Industrial Workers of the World (Pitkänen and Sutinen 2011). Kallio closes his performance by scatting in a fashion suggesting his familiarity with strident marches played by the many Finnish brass bands found throughout the Upper Midwest (Niemisto 2013).

39 Kylläpä kai / I Guess So

Sung and played on kantele (zither) by Wäinö Hirvelä, Ironwood, Michigan, October 15, 1938. Recorded by Alan Lomax. Transcribed and translated by Susanna Linna Moliski.

2467 A

Vekkulit, kyläpä kai.
Funny ones? I guess so.

Siitä se syntikin alkusa sai.
That is the origin of sin, too.

Elämä vieläkin paratiisi ois
Life would still be the paradise

Eeva se melkeinpä vietteli pois.
Eve almost seduced away.

Kesä oisi aina, ja sunnuntai.
Summer would be always,
    and Sunday too.

Naisitko, naisitko, kylläpä kai.
Would you marry, would you
    marry? I guess so.

Jos minä naisin niin akka se löis
If I should marry, my wife would heat

Kahvia möis.
And sell coffee.

Pirttini täyteen lapsia tois.
My cottage she would fill with children.

Rikkana, ristinä kaikessa ois.
Everything would be troublesome,
    a cross to bear.

Entä se rakkaus, hui minä hai.
What about love? Who would care?

Naisinko sittenkin, kylläpä kai.
Would I still marry? I guess so.

Aamusta iltaan liikkuis sen suu.
From morning to night her
    mouth would move.

Yölläkin löis tämä kylkeeni luun.
Even at night she would
    poke me in my side.

Naristen nälkää se voihkisi: "voi!
She would whine about hunger like: "Oh!

Miksi mun Luoja sun luoksesi toi?"
Why did God bring you to me?"

Hupsu se ukko ja poika ken nai.
Foolish is the man and boy who marries.

Oisinko hupsu? No, kylläpä kai.
Would I be a fool? I guess so.

Silkissä aina se kulkisi vaan.
She would walk around in silk.

Saattaisi velkaan talon ja maan,
She would bring the house
    and land into debt,

Fiininä kylillä kulkiessaan.
Walking in the village dressed so finely.

Kiskurin nimen mä kuulisin vain,
I would be known as a frugal man,

Vaikka näin sopuisan miehen hän nai.
Even though I am so mild.

Naisinko sittenkin? No, kylläpä kai.
Would I still marry? I guess so.

Kuolinvuoteella maatessaan
Lying in her deathbed she would whisper:

kuiskais "Se alkaa niin kaivoissa vaan
"It begins . . .

Unessakin hahmona vieress käyn."
Even in dreams I will be by your side."

Kuun valon varjossa puuhkaisen näin:
In the moonlight I will whisper like this:

"Kuhnuri, vieläkö makaat vain?"	"Lazy, are you still asleep?"
Naisinko sittenkin? No, kylläpä kai.	Would I still marry? I guess so.
Jos taas minä kuolisin pois,	And if I was the one to die,
pillit ja viulut haudalla sois.	The pipes and fiddles would
	play on my grave.
Peijaisissa se leikkiä löis,	She would joke at the funeral,
sormusta vaihtais ja sananasa söis.	Change her ring and break her word.
Hyvä mun on yksin aikoja kai.	It's better for me to be alone.
Minäkö se naisin? No, kylläpä kai.	Would I marry? I guess so.

Lomax: What the name of that song?

Hirvela: Bachelor's Song. It's a humorous song.

Lomax: And where did you learn it?

Hirvela: Finland. In Tyrnävä, it's the name of the town.

Lomax: Did you learn it from a book?

Hirvela: There was a humorist in Finland. He made his own songs, and this was one of them. He just sent me the words of his song.

Lomax: What was his name?

Hirvela: Pasi Jääskeläinen.

Lomax: Did he live in your town?

Hirvela: Well, he didn't live in our town, but he used to come and do concerts.

Lomax: Was he a theatrical person? Did he work in the theater?

Hirvela: No, he was just amateur, but he used to give concerts. He did some folk songs with the kantele. He was the best known kantele player in Finland at that time.

Wäinö Hirvelä (1880–1949) was born in Tyrnävä, a small town in the Oulu province of northern Finland. He immigrated as a young man, practicing a photographer's trade in Chisholm, Minnesota, prior to settling in Ironwood, Michigan, where he operated his own studio from 1908 until moving to California upon retirement in 1946. He married Nelma Heikka of Laurium, Michigan, in 1915, and together "they conducted mainly a portrait service but managed to do commercial work as the demands were numerous from logging camps . . . mining crew groups, family weddings, funerals, and panoramic pictures so popular in those days" (*Ironwood Daily Globe*, June 20, 1985). The Hirveläs were especially active in the Kalevainen movement and supported fund-raising events for Finns affected by the Winter War with Russia. Wäinö served on the organizing committee for a Kaleva concert on February 28, 1940, for which his daughter, Helen, was featured as a piano soloist (*Ironwood Daily Globe*, February 13, 1940). Six weeks later, the Ironwood paper announced that "Mrs. Waino Hirvela will present a kantele solo" for an event in support of Finnish Relief (April 10, 1940).

As he told Alan Lomax, Hirvelä learned "Kylläpä kai" from a performance by Pasi Jääskeläinen (1869–1920), a noted kantele builder, instructor, and performer from Haapavesi, not far south of Wäinö Hirvelä's birthplace (Hakala 1997: 224–226). Jääskeläinen toured America in the early twentieth century, performing folksongs, his own compositions, and other popular numbers (Wasastjerna 1957: 299). Perhaps Hirvelä saw him play on one such tour or acquired his songbook, *Lauluja* (1908). This particular song, however, was composed by Karl Gustaf Larson (1873–1948), the son of Swedish restaurateurs in Helsinki who, although inspired by the Swedish populist poet Carl Michael Bellman, nonetheless adopted Finnish language and culture to write plays, poems, and songs under the pen name Larin-Kyösti. As for Hirvelä's instrument, although he referred to it and probably thought of it as a Finnish kantele, it is actually a zither made in a curved design prominent in the Baltic region.

40　Yli kymmenen vuotta Korpiinissa oli jo asuttu / Ten Years We've Lived in Corbin

Sung by Kusti Similä, Fulton, Michigan, September 28, 1938.
Recorded by Alan Lomax. Transcription by Susanna Linna Moliski;
translation by Tom DuBois.
2392 B2, 2392 A1

Kymmenen vuotta Korpiniissa oli jo asuttu	Ten years we've lived in Corbin,
Eikä täällä kauppapuotia viel oo näkynyt,	But not a store we've seen,
Vain Kovaniemi se elelee siellä	Just Kovaniemi's living there, that
se kello-Peslevi.	time-card tracking thief.
Hän tuumaili että tuostahan se oli reformi?	He thinks he'll be able to
	reform us that way?

CHORUS:	*CHORUS:*
Vaik on long way to Ewlettiin,	But it's a long way to Eveleth,
Mistä jauhosäkin saa.	Where you can buy a sack of flour.
It's a long way to Ewlettiin	It's a long way to Eveleth
Kun ei ole kauppapuotia.	Since there isn't any store.
Goodbye jo kirkollitkii velverron rakentais.	Goodbye church league, we're going
	to build a chapel [store].

Kusti and Esther Similä, with their son Toivo, Calumet, Michigan, ca. 1909. (courtesy of Leo Holmberg)

Kotmannin kolikin roppia
  Kauppapuotis myydän kai.
	Gottman's Colic Syrup might
	  even be sold at that store.

[Note: The chorus follows each verse, but after the first rendition "where you can get a rag crate" replaces "where you can buy a sack of flour."]

Ja liikkeen hoitelijaksi ne laittoi Rookerin. Joka nimeltään oli Mäkinen ja aika täkyri. Ne tavaraa nyt ostelivat tuolta juutalaisilta	And as the manager they choose a crook. His name is Mäkinen and he's a schnook. They were buying all their stuff from that "Jew"

Ja se arveli että hintaa niille
  korottaa vain saa.
	And he felt he could hike the price
	  just as much as he pleased.

Elwettissä sulkatalkona.	In Eveleth we're at a feather bee [fund-raiser for the store].
Kyllä niistä Korpiinissa taalan aina saan.	Sure you can always get a buck for one of those in Corbin.

Uusia siellä lasilla ompi näytteillä,
Vaikka puolet hintoja kohottaa
  ei judat tyvitä.
	New eyeglasses are on display there,
	Even at half the price they
	  wouldn't be a deal.

Kun metsätyöt niin pirusti runnailee	While we're slaving over lumber work
Niin Mäkinen se kierosilmässä	That cockeyed Mäkinen is fixing prices.
hintoja määräilee.	
Puolentoista taalan paidasta se	A dollar-and-a-half shirt he wants
pyysi kahta ja varttia.	to sell for two and a quarter.
Vielä vakuutti, meillä oo tuota	And still he insists it's no cheapskate goods.
juutalaisten tavaraa.	

Kusti (Gust) Similä (1880–1958) was born in Muhos, a small town in the province of Oulu, northern Finland. As a young man he traveled south to Helsinki, where he loaded salt onto ships before immigrating in 1903 to Michigan's Keweenaw Peninsula. There he worked in a copper mine and lived in a boardinghouse where, fortuitously, his wife-to-be cooked, served, and cleaned. Similä married Esther Kero (1888–1961) around 1907. The couple would have thirteen children. Sometime between 1915 and 1917, perhaps motivated by the tumultuous Copper Country strikes of 1913, the family moved to northern Minnesota, where they owned a small farm and Kusti worked for a logging company. In 1922 or 1923 they resettled in Michigan for good, although Kusti sought seasonal employment during the Great Depression. Despite a life of hard work, he was beloved by his children and descendants for his cheerful, resilient personality and extensive repertoire of songs (Virtanen 2010; Holmberg 2013).

Alan Lomax was especially moved by Similä's sojourns, as evident in this passage from his field notebook: "The tale of Kusti Simola's [*sic*] job hunt—the burly handsome blond fellow shambling across 12 mtn ranges + up to climax 14,000 ft. 3000 above tree level, criss-crossing Montana, Dakota, Oregon + Washington looking for harvest job—down to Calif to pick grapes + the Negroes at 35 cents a day—to the site of the gov. dam and the 5000 people waiting in their tent city—the employment . . . agencies . . . —his college educated pal who had lost his job because he had been accused of blackmail. . . . Of him—shivering in shoes, blue overalls + shirt on the Canadian border: 'You can't buy a Job.'"

Lomax recorded five songs from Similä, the last three of which reveal a decided working-class sensibility (Frandy 2010): a paean to the beauty of Finland, the well-known lullaby "Pium, paum," a comic account of a wild rural dance party, a ditty about a defiant servant inclined to drink, and the fiercely satirical "Yli kymmenen vuotta Korpiinissa oli jo asuttu," which is included here. This last song memorializes the struggles of the Similäs and other settlers in Corbin, Minnesota. Created "as a small, speculative venture by the Corbin Improvement Company in 1907," Corbin disappeared around 1970

Esther and Kusti Similä, Fulton, Michigan, ca. 1950. (courtesy of Leo Holmberg)

"when open pit mining operations consumed the site" (Alanen 2005). In 1905 John Mäkinen and John Kovaniemi, the villains of Similä's song, established a post office and store in Corbin. Like many company stores exploiting the era's immigrants, this Iron Range enterprise charged its isolated customers excessive prices, resulting in the unfortunate yet common characterization of the decidedly Finnish miserly manager as a "Jew." The recurrent mention of colic syrup in the song's chorus suggests parental concern for an infant's health, while the long trek for equitable prices indicates that the Similäs and their neighbors were probably involved with the 1917 creation of a Finnish cooperative store in Eveleth (Virtanen 2010: 48–49). The song's tune, verse structure, and part of its language come from "It's a Long Way to Tipperary," the 1912 British music-hall composition of Jack Judge, whose grandparents hailed from Tipperary, Ireland. In 1914, as World War I commenced, the Connaught Rangers, an Irish regiment, were witnessed singing this song while marching in France. Recorded that year by the world-renowned Irish tenor John McCormack (Victor 64476), the song became extraordinarily popular in Great Britain and North America. Parodies of "It's a Long Way to Tipperary" were frequently composed, in both English and Finnish, by members of the Industrial Workers of the World, the "one big union" especially active among Finnish miners, timber workers, and partisans in the cooperative movement on the Minnesota Iron Range during the Similäs' tenure in Corbin (Virtanen 2010: 50–51).

41 Oi Herra, jos mä matkamies maan / Oh Lord, if I, a Wanderer of the Earth

Sung by Lillian Aho, Calumet, Michigan, September 26, 1938. Recorded by Alan Lomax. Transcription and translation by Susanna Linna Moliski, with assistance from Tom DuBois.

2379 B1

Oi Herra, jos mä matkamies maan,	Oh Lord, if I, a wanderer of the earth,
Lopulla matkaa nähdä sun saan,	In the end of my journey should see you,
Oi, jos mä kerran näkisin Herran	Ah, if I once saw the Lord
Ja kunniaa.	And the glory.
Sinua kaipaa sydämeni,	For you my heart longs,
Sun puolees huutaa mun henkeni—	For you my spirit calls—
On yksin tästä sen ikävästä	Alone in this misery
Jo kyynellaan.	And in tears.

Lillian Aho, Calumet, Michigan, 1935. (courtesy of family of Lillian Aho Aukee)

Muut kaikki hyljää, vaan sinä et.	All others will abandon me, but not you.
Autuuden särkyneen sydämen	You will comfort the broken heart.
Sinulta saavat, sä luet haavat	You will heal the wound
Ja kyynellaan.	And their tears.
Mua auta, Herra, mä toivon vaan,	Help me Lord. I will hope
Vaikk' ei ois toivoa ollenkaan.	Even if there is no hope.
En päästä sua, ennen kuin mua	I won't let you go before
Käyt siunaamaan.	You will bless me.

Lomax: What's your name?

Aho: Lillian Aho.

Lomax: How old are you?

Aho: Twenty-one.

Lomax: Where did you learn this?

Aho: I don't know. I just heard it from somebody else.

Lomax: What's it called?

Aho: Oh God, I am a traveling man with you.

Lillian Aho Aukee (1917–2011) was born in Gogebic County, Michigan, to Finnish immigrant parents. Her father, Pekka Aho, was a lay preacher and kantele player who ministered to rural Finnish Lutheran congregations (see track 42), and Lillian grew up immersed in church activities, including hymn singing. In 1944 she married Lauri Aukee (1917–1998), likewise the child of Finnish immigrants, in Ironwood. The couple moved to the Detroit area after World War II, where Lauri worked for the Ford Motor Company and they raised four children. Frequent visitors to the Upper Peninsula, the Aukees were active in their local Finnish Center of Farmington Hills, Michigan.

"Oi Herra, jos mä matkamies maan" is among the best-known Lutheran hymns in Finland, where it has been performed especially for funerals. It was composed by Wilhelmi Malmivaari (1854–1922), a leader in the pietistic "Awakened" movement within the Finnish state church. Lilian Aho's performance closely matches the first four verses found in printed hymnals, but she did not sing the last two verses, perhaps in keeping with customary practices in Michigan.

Oi Herra, suothan sä minulle	Oh Lord, grant me
Sun armos voimaksi matkalle.	Your grace to strengthen me on the way.
Anteeksi anna, mua nosta, kanna,	Forgive me, raise me, carry me,
Vie perille.	Bring me to my destination.
Oi saanhan joukkoon autuaitten	Oh I will attain the company of the blessed
Kanss' ystäväini ja omaisten.	With my friends and family.
Mä päästä kerran luo armon Herran,	Bring me to the grace of the Lord,
Oi saanhan sen.	Oh I will receive it.

42 Mun kanteleeni kauniimmin /
My Kantele Will Sound More Beautiful

Played by Pekka Aho on kantele, sung by Lillian Aho, Calumet, Michigan,
September 27, 1938. Recorded by Alan Lomax. Transcription and
translation by Susanna Linna Moliski.

2388 B

Mun kanteleeni kauniimmin
  taivaassa kerran soi.
Siel uusin äänin tuhansin mun
  suuni laulaa voi.

One day my kantele will sound
  more beautiful in heaven.
There my voice will sing
  thousands of new sounds.

Nyt halleluja rakkaalle mun Jeesukselleni.
Ah autuas on päivä se kun pääsen luoksesi.

Now, hallelujah to my beloved Jesus.
Blessed is the day when I come to you.

Pekka "Peter" Aho (1884–1959) was born in Kurkijoki, a Finnish Karelian village on
the shores of Lake Ladoga that was later seized by the Soviet Union during the Winter
War of 1939. He learned to play kantele by ear and, as an immigrant in 1912, brought
a thirty-string kantele to Ironwood, Michigan. There he met Helmi Jokela from Kemi,
a port village in Finnish Lapland, whose extended family included kantele players. The
couple married in 1915, with five of their six children surviving to adulthood.

As Joyce Hakala tells us in her landmark chronicle of Finnish American kantele
players, Pekka Aho "was a skilled upholsterer, carpenter, and mason. In the 1930s he also
operated a public sauna in Calumet, Michigan." But most of all, he was a lay preacher
and religious performer: "When lay preacher Pekka Aho conducted religious services,
he often sang hymns and played his kantele. His daughter said that 'he could reach
more people by playing and singing than he could by preaching.' [Lillian Aho Aukee,
Dearborn, Michigan, contacted by Hakala in 1994 and 1996.] Pekka traveled to small
communities throughout Michigan and in other states for the Suomi Synod, to preach
in communities without a full-time minister. His mission work was enriched by his kantele music, 'and that's why he played it in the first place,' said daughter Lillian Aukee.
'No one really gave concerts with kanteles years ago'" (Hakala 1997: 125). An excerpt
from the *Ironwood Daily Globe*, published a few weeks after Alan Lomax recorded Aho,
offers testimony: "Finnish Lutheran Churches . . . Services with Pekka Aho of Calumet
preaching, also local speakers, Monday through Friday next week at following places:
Covington, Trout Creek, Paynesville, North Bruces, and Ewen" (October 12, 1938).

Pekka Aho, Calumet, Michigan, 1920s. (courtesy of family of Lillian Aho Aukee)

Pekka Aho, traveling lay preacher, with his car, 1930s. (courtesy of family of Lillian Aho Aukee)

Lomax offers a terse description in his field notebook: "Mr. Aho, Pine Street, kantele, very religious—blond daughter, Lillian." Pekka Aho recorded three songs for Lomax: "Oi terve Pohjola Isäimme kotimaa," a romantic paean to Finland by the classical clarinetist Bernhard Henrik Crusell (1775–1838); "Ole kanssani," a Finnish rendering of "Abide with Me," a deathbed composition by the Scottish Anglican hymnodist Henry Francis Lyte (1793–1847) that soon entered funeral repertoires across a range of Christian denominations; and "Mun kanteleeni kauniimmin," with Lillian Aho Aukee on vocals. At once an expression of Christian sentiments and a tribute to the kantele— the mythical instrument of Finland's epic, the *Kalevala*—this song is the most famous composition of Kreeta Haapasalo (1815–1893), a peasant woman from the Perho River valley who was celebrated by Finnish nationalists in the mid-nineteenth century and performed throughout the country (Hakala 1997: 75).

43 Suun kloorin kloorin halleluuja! / Oh Glory, Glory Hallelujah!

Sung by Emil Maki, Newberry, Michigan, September 14, 1938.
Recorded by Alan Lomax. Partial transcription and translation by
Susanna Linna Moliski, with additions from Arttu Tolonen.

2334 B1

Siellä Iisakka ja Jaakoppi ja Taavetti,	There was Isaac and Jacob and David,
Mooses, Pilatus ja Koljatti,	Moses, Pilate and Goliath,
Piljaani, aasi ja profeetat muut	Baalam's ass and all the prophets
Siellä hohottelivat naurussa suut.	There laughing with a smile on their faces.
Pitkät parat siellä keikkuivat ja kaljutkin kiils	Long beards were swinging and bald heads shining
Pelivärkkein humina mun korviani viils.	And all that musical humming hurt my ears.
Pyhä Pietari janiteeri innostu kans	Saint Peter, the janitor, got really excited
Löi tahtia avainknipullans.	And tapped the rhythm with his keys.
Suun kloorin kloorin halleluuja!	Oh glory, glory hallelujah!
Suun kloorin kloorin halleluuja!	Oh glory, glory hallelujah!
Suun kloorin kloorin halleluuja!	Oh glory, glory hallelujah!
Siellä harput ja hanurutkin soi.	The harps and accordions were playing.

Emil Maki (1893–1957) was born in the vicinity of Turku in southwestern Finland, and settled in Newberry, Michigan, sometime after 1900. He married fellow immigrant Olga Koivisto in 1914, and the couple had seven children. But sadly that is as much as we know about him. Quite likely he was a friend of the equally elusive Kalle Kallio, since their 1938 performances sequentially leapfrog one another.

Alan Lomax recorded four songs from Maki during one of his marathon sessions in Newberry, presumably at Larsen's Luce Hotel. Three were of Old World origins—two wistful laments and a fragment from a courting song fraught with class conflict:

Voi teitä heilani vanhemmat,	Oh you, my sweetheart's parents,
Voi surrako teitin pitää	Should you be in mourning
Kuin se tämmönen renttu on	Because this kind of trash is
tyttärenne henttu ja	your daughter's lad
Eikä teidän auta mikään?	And you can't do anything about it?

Maki's fourth performance boisterously asserts similar working-class sentiments, yet is solidly grounded in Finnish America. Borrowing its melody and most of its chorus from the most important Union song of the American Civil War—Julia Ward Howe's 1861 composition "The Battle Hymn of the Republic"—"Suun kloorin kloorin halleluuja" imagines heaven quite differently than either Kreeta Haapasalo (see track 42) or neighboring pietistic Lutherans. As Tim Frandy astutely commented: "With paradise painted as a dancehall filled with worker-prophets and saints, Maki defies the Suomi Synod's social politics and paints the afterlife exquisitely in terms of vulgar sensual pleasures" (Frandy 2010: 35). Seven decades later, Maki's imagining of St. Peter as a swinging celestial janitor, and not a vigilant border guard, captivated Finland's foremost roots musician, J. Karjalainen, who covered this song as the closing track of his 2008 recording *Paratiisin Pojat* (Paradise Boys) (Poko Records 367).

Print by Isabella Leary

ALAN LOMAX GOES NORTH
"THE MOST FERTILE SOURCE"

"The Upper Peninsula of Michigan proved to be the most fertile source of material. After six weeks of recording a mass of lumberjack, Finnish, and French folksongs, I felt that there was enough material in the region for years of work."

So wrote Alan Lomax in a report to the Librarian of Congress chronicling the capture of "about a thousand songs" on disc from Michigan singers (1939: 221). Celebrated for creating extraordinary sound recordings commencing in the 1930s, Lomax has been scarcely remembered for making silent film footage—often in color, some of it remarkable—throughout that decade. He began in Haiti in 1936, filming singers and ceremonies together with his wife, Elizabeth Goodman Lomax (Averill 2011; Szwed 2010: chap. 5). The couple also filmed performers in Kentucky, Ohio, and Indiana in 1937 and 1938. Lomax's Upper Midwestern filmmaking, however, was undertaken alone in a remote area while simultaneously managing bulky recording equipment and a stock of blank records.

Neither synchronized with sound nor edited into a finished document, his 1938 cinematographic efforts also lacked accompanying notes, in sharp contrast to the 1936 footage, which was supplemented with a list of "records that can be played as musical accompaniment," as well as fifteen pages of "Descriptive notes pertaining to the Archives' Haitian film" (Averill 2011: CD5). Haphazardly indexed, eventually spliced willy-nilly onto a single reel with clips from his earlier fieldwork and that of other researchers in the American West, it languished in obscurity for decades.

In the late 1970s, thanks to Carolyn Lipson-Walker's *American Folklore Films and Videotapes: An Index*, I happened on an entry for "The Archive of Folk Song: Being a Collection of Amateur Films Made by Alan Lomax and Others from 1936–1940" (1976: 291). The twenty-three "segments listed in sequence" began with: "1. Mrs.

Otis Rindlisbacher of Rice Lake, Wisconsin, playing on a 'viking cello.'" Eight other Upper Midwestern segments (nos. 4–6 and 18–22) were scattered thereafter. Some compounded the erroneous designation of Otto Rindlisbacher as "Otis," "concertina" rather than button accordion, "Ladrium" for Laurium, "John Frederickson" instead of Aapo Juhani, and "Odanah, Wisconsin" for a sequence filmed during the National Folk Festival in Washington, D.C. Yet other descriptions provided accurate information on people, places, ethnic groups, and activities. In the 1980s I viewed all twenty-three segments at the Library of Congress's Motion Picture, Broadcasting and Recorded Sound Division, subsequently purchased a video copy, and began working incrementally with Lomax's Upper Midwestern sound recordings, field notes, and correspondence to discover just who had been filmed, where, and what they might have performed.

There are gaps in time and space in the film record. We see and hear Wisconsin lumberjacks, Serbs in Detroit, and Croatians, French Canadians, and Finns in the Upper Peninsula, but the many performers and cultures Lomax recorded in Michigan's Lower Peninsula are conspicuously absent. There is evidence that Lomax's Michigan filmmaking efforts were more extensive and ambitious. In an August 27 letter, he asked his Library of Congress boss, Harold Spivacke, to "Purchase a dozen reels of film and I'll let you know where to forward it. This country & the people are very photogenic" (Cohen 2011: 97). Presumably he filmed more of them than we know. Nearly a month later, a September 28 excerpt from his field notebooks tells us: "When my film was stolen—Aapo [Juhani] read the cards and after considerable mumbling told me that the film was stolen at nine o'clock + by two blond young men—then the finger of suspicion was laid more + more heavily on Jenkelin as the séance proceeded." Sadly the film was never recovered.

Hence we produced what we imagine as approaching Lomax's original intention. In no case are we absolutely certain that audio tracks align exactly with filmed performances, but in every case our correlations stem from reasonable surmise. Crucially, since filmed excerpts were invariably much shorter than recorded songs, Guha Shankar duplicated and extended key footage. The result is a narrative sequence organized by cultural groups. Each section matches silent-film footage with field recordings to convey something of the performers' personalities, power, and grace amid gritty surroundings. New recordings of excerpts from Lomax's field notes and correspondence, read by fellow Texan Bill C. Malone, complement his pithy on-disc introductions to filmed performers; and throughout we have added text identifying places and people, along with English subtitles when necessary.

THE WISCONSIN LUMBERJACKS: FROM RICE LAKE AND LADYSMITH

The film footage begins with two stills. Pairing image and text, "Mr. Lumberjack Goes to Washington" anticipates the title of Frank Capra's 1939 film, *Mr. Smith Goes to Washington*. Culled from an unidentified Wisconsin newspaper (mid-April 1938) in Charles Brown's National Folk Festival papers at the Wisconsin Historical Society, it offers selective background eliminating Iva Rindlisbacher: "A Bangalo, made from a washtub and a lumberjack's peavey, an Irish bull fiddle and a squeeze box will be among the 40 musical instruments dating from the logging camp days which will be taken to Washington, D.C., by four northern Wisconsin men when they leave for the national folk festival April 21. The men, billed as The Lumberjacks are (left to right) Otto Rindlisbacher, Rice Lake; Frank Uchytil, Haugen; and Earl Schwartztrauber and Ray Calkins, Ladysmith."

A more inclusive publicity photo made in Rice Lake follows. Front: (*from left to right*) Otto Rindlisbacher, Iva Rindlisbacher, Ray Calkins. Back: (*from left to right*) Earl Schwartztrauber, Frank Uchytil, Dr. J. H. Wallis. As Rice Lake's mayor but no musician, Wallis helped secure funding while contributing "stories of Paul Bunyan" to the group's performances (*Oshkosh Daily Northwestern*, April 30, 1938). The recording in the background, commencing with "In 1871 to Swamp for a Go-Devil We Begun," is "Fred Sargent's Shanty Song" (Wisconsin Lumberjacks CD, track 1).

Alan Lomax recruited the Lumberjacks and several other performers—notably Captain Pearl Nye, "Bard of the Ohio Canal," and W. C. Handy, "Father of the Blues"—to visit the Archive of American Folk Song in the Library of Congress during their stint at the National Folk Festival. Recording inside the library's Jefferson Building, Lomax squeezed performers onto an outside balcony to film silent footage. The Lumberjacks-on-film commences with Ray Calkins brandishing a homemade guitar colorfully nicknamed the "Paul Bunyan harp," then features Calkins plucking his "harp" while Otto Rindlisbacher push-pulls a button accordion and Frank Uchytil fingers a rustic string bass facetiously dubbed the "Irish Bull Fiddle" (the once popular term "Irish bull" means an exaggerated malapropism). Since Lomax never recorded the particular instrumentation featured on film, we accompanied this segment with a Calkins solo he called "Shantyboy Tune," a Swedish melody better known as "Kväsarvalsen" (Wisconsin Lumberjacks CD, track 3).

In the next sequence, pivoting on one stiffened leg, while cavorting with the other, the otherwise fully ambulatory Earl Schwartztrauber commemorates the jigging of a peg-legged woods worker propelled by the trio of Rindlisbacher, Calkins, and Uchytil. Again Lomax recorded no such instrumental combination, so this segment, with its prominent button accordion, relies on a Sidney Robertson recording at Chicago's 1937 National Folk Festival that includes John Giezendanner's yodeling (Wisconsin Lumberjacks CD, track 8).

The final Wisconsin Lumberjack footage is of Iva Kundert Rindlisbacher, resplendent in peasant dress and beaded cap, fingering and bowing the Viking cello, a variation on the single-string Norwegian psalmodikon fashioned from a pitchfork. Its cigar-box tone chamber is decorated with the Star of David, while the tune is heavily Irish, "The River in the Pines" (Wisconsin Lumberjacks CD, track 4).

In August and September 1938, Folklorist Alan Lomax Traveled Michigan, Recording "a Thousand Songs" for the Library of Congress

Lomax's silent film sweeps across fall foliage on Cliff Drive (old Highway 41) in the Upper Peninsula of Michigan's Keweenaw Peninsula and was evidently shot through his car windshield. Did Lomax manage simultaneous driving and filming, or did some local person (Yalmer Forster?) assist at the wheel? We don't know. The tune in the background is "Kulkurin valssi" (Vagabond Waltz), arguably the best-known Finnish American tune, expertly played by Yalmer Forster, who assisted Lomax's Finnish American fieldwork in the Calumet area (Lomax CD, track 31). In the sonic foreground, Bill C. Malone reads an excerpt from a letter written by Alan Lomax on July 2, 1938, to his sister, Bess, who was traveling in Europe at the time. Commencing with "I expect after this summer to be much more cosmopolitan than you, despite your European tour," he explained his impending cultural sophistication by parodying the series of official letters of introduction and inquiry he had sent that summer to folksong collectors and state-historical-society officials in Michigan, Wisconsin, and Minnesota.

> Dear Sir: The Archive of American Folk Song plans a rapid recording survey of Michigan, Wisconsin and Minnesota during the summer. If you know of the location of any Jugoslavian baroto blowers or any Swiss chantey singers, I would

greatly appreciate your calling me by long distance before morning. By the middle
of September, I hope to be speaking an interesting dialect composed of Norwegian,
Swedish, Icelandic, German, Canuck, Hungarian, Finnic, Polish, Russian and Oshkosh.
You may expect to receive an autographed photo of me holding up my first muskie by
at least the end of this month. The work is going to be very interesting. I'm going to
Detroit armed with letters of introduction to all the factions of the United Automobile
Workers and to the Massaba Iron Ore Range of Minnesota and the I.W.W. [Industrial
Workers of the World] of Duluth for union material, that assuming a galaxy of all sorts
of exotic songs and instruments plus all their Americanizations.

Facetiously imagining seagoing chantey singers from landlocked Switzerland, while
conflating the name of the Menominee's Chief Oshkosh with a language, Lomax did
in fact succeed in recording Serbian flute players, singing Finnish I.W.W. members, and
both "exotic" and intriguingly Americanized sounds. We do not know if he caught a
muskellunge or even went fishing, but his East Texas dialect remained intact.

SERBS: DETROIT AREA

In the twenty-first century, the Detroit area's American Serbian Hall is still just a few
blocks west of the Chrysler assembly plant. In the twentieth-century film, Lomax fixes
his camera on seven men arrayed before their Serbian (*Srpske*) hall, a modest tree-shaded
building with lettering across the front gable. His on-disc introduction sets the scene:
"This record is being made at Claire Pointe [a neighborhood in St. Claire Shores],
Michigan, on the outskirts of Detroit, August 5, 1938. The section here is almost solidly
Serbian. In the shadow of the Chrysler plant you find the Serbians still playing their
native shepherd's flutes and the *gusle*, singing the heroic ballads of the old days in Serbia
(2238 A1)."

The camera shifts to Stefan "Steve" Trivanovich dressed up for Sunday in a white
shirt and fedora playing flute outside a clapboard building, perhaps the Serbian hall,
with a painted bentwood chair nearby and a water tower looming in the distance. The
matching Lomax field recording is "Pastirska pesma" (Pastoral Song), played on the *svi-
rale* (shepherd's flute) by Trivanovich (2238 A2). Six days later Lomax wrote to Harold
Spivacke, his boss in the Library of Congress Music Division, about the recording

session: "Sunday a Serbian played his shepherd's flute for me—virtuoso performance by a steel chipper who reads and writes little and still plays his pipe for his amusement in the shadow of the automobile work. Goatlike, leaping. Really I could stay here in Detroit for a couple of months and never run out of material." Lomax jotted terse biographical notes on the record's sleeve: "Stephan Trivanovich, 47 years old, [born] on a farm in Y. [year], Glina, Jugoslavia, 1910 immigrant (567 Clairepointe)." A "Steve Trivanovich" born in 1892, immigrating in 1909, and living in Detroit is listed in the 1930 census as the husband of a widow, Mary Pontich, and father of two stepchildren.

Following Trivanovich, Pajo Tomic displays and then plays his beautifully carved horse-head gusle against the same backdrop. Again Lomax wrote on the record sleeve: "Paul Tomitch, a poem, gusla, about 1912 war with Turks. . . ." We hear Tomic, speaking in Serbian, introduce himself—"I am from Bosnia, Pajo Tomic"—before playing the gusle and singing a song from the Balkan Wars (1912–1913), when Bulgaria, Greece, Montenegro, and Serbia allied against the Ottoman Turks.

> In fall 1912
> The Serbian army assembled
> On the border of Novi Pazar
> To save our brothers from slavery,
> Led by "Djikan,"
> A born general.
> (August 5, 1938; 2239 A; translation by Richard March)

This performer is likely the same Paul Tomich (1896–1967) who census records show as immigrating to Detroit from Serbia in 1912. In 1920 he was the single head of a household that included a quartet of Slavic boarders from Austria, Montenegro, and Serbia.

The four singers seen in the next film excerpt, situated alongside the same building as Trivanovich and Tomic, remain unidentified, although three of them may be singers—Stjepan Basrak, Petar Bangac, Stjepan Vujuanovic—listed for the accompanying recording, "Marko Kraljević."

> Marko Kraljević is strolling.
> It isn't a flat field,
> Nor is he wearing armor,
> But rather a cotton shirt.
> He strapped on a military belt.
> (August 5, 1938; 2240 B; translation by Richard March)

A warrior prince of the fourteenth century, Marko Kraljević became a legendary Serbian hero who championed the oppressed in battles with the Turks. Accounts of his exploits figured heavily in epic song cycles performed on the gusle (Lord 1960).

One of the probable singers, Petar Bangac, remains elusive, but "Steve Vujanovich" (born ca. 1882) and "Steve" Basrak (born 1880) both appear in the 1940 census wherein Vujanovich is listed as single and living in a boardinghouse and Basrak is a widower.

Lomax's final silent-film footage featuring Serbians shows a second gusle player, Stevan Raicevich, in front of a brick wall. When the camera shifts to a side view, however, we see the clapboard Serbian hall of prior footage. Grape leaves and a trellis—common features of halls built by wine-loving South Slavs—offer a lush backdrop for a bloody song: "Smrt čekaj pašu" (Death Awaits the Pasha):

> Sing, oh mountain spirits,
> The Serbian gusle calls you.
> Don't flee down the road,
> Don't sparkle on peasant hearths,
> But fly to the battle field,
> Fly with the eagles,
> Fly to Kosovo,
> With Obilić the Sultan-killer.
> *(August 5, 1938; 2245 A; translation by Richard March)*

Like Marko Kraljević, Miloš Obilić was a legendary Serbian hero of the fourteenth century who figured ever after in epic songs. According to tradition, Obilić killed the Ottoman sultan Murad I. We know from Lomax's 1938 field notebooks that Raicevich was born on a farm in Montenegro in 1885 or 1886. One of ten brothers, he sojourned to the United States in 1904, working for six months in Pittsburgh, then toiling for a decade with fellow Serbs in the coal mines of Raton, New Mexico. Thanks to his pay, he sent home for a mail order bride. Stevan and Angeline Raicevich raised nine children. The family returned to Europe from 1915 to 1920, as Stevan served as a volunteer with the Serbian army, fighting the Turks in conflicts that claimed the lives of his nine brothers. In the 1920s the Raiceviches settled in the Detroit area. Stevan was a laborer for the Works Progress Administration when recorded by Lomax. He played the gusle until his death in 1957. In 2014 two grandsons, including namesake Stevan D. Raicevich, are the proud keepers of their anecstor's instrument.

CROATIANS: COPPER COUNTRY
(THE FLORIANI TAMBURITZA GROUP)

Far from Detroit, across the Straits of Mackinac, Lomax filmed forests, farms, and mines throughout the Upper Peninsula. Here his camera captures the head frame of the Eureka mine shaft no. 4, an iron-ore mine at Ramsay, Michigan, on the Gogebic Range. The song is "Thirty-First Level Blues," sung and played by two brothers, Veko and Vladimir Floriani Jr., of Ahmeek in the Keweenaw Peninsula's Copper Country.

> I've got the thirty-first level blues, from my head down to my shoes.
> In the morning I mope around, in the evening my sorrows I drown.
> When the boss comes down and says, "Get up, don't stall around."
> Shows I'm paid to try and keep his rep.
> Work makes my back ache, and someday his head I'll break,
> 'Cause I've got those blues, those thirty-first level blues.
> *(September 25, 1938; 2374 A1)*

For this musical complaint of a miner toiling far underground, the Florianis favored a swinging string sound with jazzy vocals. Vladimir Jr. was born in 1906 and Veko in 1911. Their Croatian-born parents, Margaret (b. 1885) and Vladimir Floriani Sr. (b. 1881), had immigrated to Michigan in 1905. Inspired by clear broadcasts from Chicago's WLS *National Barn Dance* more than four hundred miles to the south, the elder Floriani and three of his sons joined the Keweenaw Barn Dance Troupe in 1935. Their variety shows—featuring "vocal numbers, musical acts, comic skits, dances, clogs, and other features"—entertained capacity crowds in Ahmeek's Rex Theater. The Barn Dance Orchestra included "Vladimir [Sr.] and Lado [Vladimir Jr.] Floriani, mandolins; Fritz Geissler, violinist; Veko Floriani, bass violin; John Polancich, concertinist; and Joseph Floriani, guitar" (Wesley Williams Scrapbooks, Upper Peninsula Regional Digitization Center).

Composed by Vladimir Jr., "Thirty-First Level Blues" was a local hit, performed on the Barn Dance stage, over area radio stations, and at house parties. Decades later, his son, James V. "Jim" Floriani, contributed a new first verse "to explain why this copper miner has the 'blues'" and a third verse "to give the song a happier ending" (Floriani 2013).

> There's copper underground, as pure as can be found.
> Sometimes, it's a mile below, a mine can be hot or cold.
> Oh—the dangers there are several, death waits for you at any level,
> But I've got a wife and kids at home to feed.

Lake Linden Road, Houghton County, Michigan, 2013. (photo by Hilary Virtanen)

> I light up my gas lamp, to go down into this slave camp,
> I'm feeling low as this thirty-first level hole.
>
> The blues I always find, working down in this mine.
> Gonna quit this job today, wanna live like the other kind.
> When the boss came down today, told him another he'd have to find
> To work so hard for the good old C&H.
> Work makes my back ache, I'm going fishing in the lake,
> And no longer get the thirty-first level blues.

"The good old C&H" is the Calumet and Hecla, the region's largest copper mining company.

The elder Floriani was likewise a tamburitza musician who formed a family ensemble with his sons. On April 14, 1938, five months before Lomax's recording, the region's *Daily Mining Gazette* published a story, "Tamburitza Music Scores Hit Here," regarding a performance by the Slavonic Tamburitza Orchestra of Duquesne University in Pittsburgh. Featuring "15 skilled artists," each "attired in a colorful costume of the Jugoslavs," the orchestra included "two young Ahmeek men, Joseph and Veko Floriani . . . students at Duquesne University."

With his car in the background, Lomax filmed Vladimir Sr. and Jr. and Veko performing outside their home in Ahmeek as Margaret Floriani looked on. We hear the trio's rendition of "Majko moje" (My Mother). A saucy daughter deflects maternal pressure.

> "Oh, my child, to whom should I marry you?"
> "Oh, my mother, I would like to tease."
> *(September 25, 1938; 2375; translation by Richard March)*

As the song plays out, the film footage shifts to railroad tracks, the Lake Linden–Calumet Road, and its descent to Lake Linden.

FRENCH CANADIANS: BARAGA

The scene shifts from Slavs and mining to French Canadian farmers and loggers. Lomax pans Baraga's hills and houses alongside Lake Superior. As the camera settles on Mose and Exilia Bellaire, seated outside their home with a young girl beside them, Bill Malone reads Lomax's reflections: "In Champion and Baraga I found French ballad singers who still enjoy ballad fests that lasted all night." Beyond the singing Bellaires, we glimpse decked and peeled logs, a conical haystack, and countryside. And as the Bellaires' tempo increases, a grinning boy step dances on the family porch.

The Bellaires were easily the most prolific French singers in Baraga, performing more than fifty songs between them, including three duets that included the song featured here, "Dis-moi pourquoi, une?" (Tell Me Why, One?), recorded on October 13, 1938 (2441 A1). As evident from Anjili Babbar's transcription and translation (with assistance from Stephen Winick), the song offers a rapid-fire question-answer catechism with incremental, numerical repetition.

Descendants of French Canadian singers listen to ancestral voices: *(left to right)* John Cadeau, Anne Cadeau, Ed Cadeau, Ron Jestila, and grandchildren, Ron Jestila home, Baraga, Michigan, 1989. (photo by author)

Exilia: Dis-moi pourquoi une	Exilia: Tell me why one
Dis-moi pourquoi une	Tell me why one
Mose: Il n'y a qu'un seul Dieu	Mose: There is but one God
Il n'y a qu'un seul Dieu	There is but one God
E: Dis-moi pourquoi deux	E: Tell me why two
Dis-moi pourquoi deux	Tell me why two
M: Deux testaments	M: Two testaments
Il n'y qu'un seul Dieu	There is but one God
Il n'y qu'un seul Dieu	There is but one God
E: Dis-moi pourquoi trois	E: Tell me why three
Dis-moi pourquoi trois	Tell me why three
M: Les trois Hébreux	M: The three Hebrews

Deux testaments	Two testaments
Il n'y a qu'un seul Dieu	There is but one God
Il n'y a qu'un seul Dieu	There is but one God
E: Dis-moi pourquoi quatre	E: Tell me why four
Dis-moi pourquoi quatre	Tell me why four
M: Quatre évangélistes	M: Four evangelists
Les trois Hébreux	The three Hebrews
Deux testaments	Two testaments
Il n'y a qu'un seul Dieu	There is but one God
Il n'y a qu'un seul Dieu	There is but one God
E: Dis-moi pourquoi cinq	E: Tell me why five
Dis-moi pourquoi cinq	Tell me why five
M: Cinq livres de Moise	M: Five books of Moses
Les quatre évangélistes	Four evangelists
Les trois Hébreux	The three Hebrews
Deux testaments	Two testaments
Il n'y a qu'un seul Dieu	There is but one God
Il n'y a qu'un seul Dieu	There is but one God
E: Dis-moi pourquoi six	E: Tell me why six
Dis-moi pourquoi six	Tell me why six
M: Six urnes rendu, placé	M: Six urns arrived
Aux Noces de Cana	At the Marriage at Cana
Cinq livres de Moise	Five books of Moses
Les quatre évangélistes	Four evangelists
Les trois Hébreux	The three Hebrews
Deux testaments	Two testaments
Il n'y a qu'un seul Dieu	There is but one God
Il n'y a qu'un seul Dieu	There is but one God

[Note: The remaining verse sung by the Bellaires is not in the film.]

E: Dis-moi pourquoi sept	E: Tell me why seven
Dis-moi pourquoi sept	Tell me why seven
M: Sept sacrements	M: Seven sacraments
Six urnes rendu, placé	Six urns arrived
Aux Noces de Cana	At the Marriage at Cana
Cinq livres de Moise	Five books of Moses
Les quatre évangélistes	Four evangelists
Les trois Hébreux	The three Hebrews
Deux testaments	Two testaments
Il n'y a qu'un seul Dieu	There is but one God
Il n'y a qu'un seul Dieu	There is but one God

Sometimes known as "Il n'y a qu'un seul Dieu" (There Is One Great God), this song was well-known in Quebec. In *Negro Folk Singing-Games and Folk Games of the Habitants*,

Pete and Mose Bellaire with a heifer calf, Baraga, Michigan, 1930s. (author's collection, courtesy of Priscilla Bellaire Tahtinen)

Grace Cleveland Porter called it an "Old French-Canadian Folk-Singing Game" and described its performance on a roadside by a ring of children (1914: x–xi, 34–45). The song's origins are in Europe, where it developed as a Christian adaptation of a Jewish ritual song, "Echad mi yodea?" (Who Knows the One?). Widely known since at least the seventeenth century, it has been reported frequently in English versions throughout North America (Newall 1891; Eckstrom 1935; Randolph 1980, vol. 4: 34–35), including in Michigan's Upper Peninsula. Writing in the *Journal of American Folklore*, the children's game scholar William Wells Newall cited a "complete version" in *Bizarre Notes and Queries* (1889) contributed by Rev. J. H. Hopkins who, "during a residence on the southern shore of Lake Superior, had caught it by ear from Cornish miners employed in the copper mines of that region" (Newall 1891: 215).

Edward King, a recent arrival in Baraga from Quebec, sang and fiddled in lumber camps and for entertainments hosted by the Bellaires. We see King seated and singing on the porch of a frame house with split firewood nearby. Wearing mid-calf logger's boots, he keeps time with his feet. On October 12, 1938, King recorded several songs for Alan Lomax accompanied by rhythmic foot percussion. "Le Jour de l'an" (New Year's Day), matched here with silent film footage, appears on the Lomax CD (track 5).

> I rest, and I see your heart
> while looking at your portrait.
> And I hung up my pants.
> And every time that she shivers,
> for goodness sake—but in winter
> it's damn freezing.
> *(2446 B1)*

"Ida Goyette" (2446 A2; Lomax CD, track 6), a fiddle tune from King, accompanies the ensuing film sequence, which presumably was made in the Baraga area. We see in succession: a farmer in shirt-sleeves and suspenders pausing in a field to lean on a hoe handle; a woodsman with an ax felling an aspen amid trees and stumps; an apron-clad old woman sitting outside, possibly singing, as cattle graze; and a serious mother and coy daughter framed in a doorway. The mother is Matilda Auge Cadeau (1880–1958), who farmed and raised ten children with her husband, John (recorded leading his neighbors in a rousing drinking song, Lomax CD, track 7). The daughter is likely Madeline Cadeau (1918–2004), who would marry a neighbor, Lawrence J. Vizina Jr., in 1941 and live her life in Baraga.

FINNS: UPPER PENINSULA

Alan Lomax recorded more songs and tunes from Finns, and in more locations, than from any other group in the Upper Peninsula. As he reported to the Library of Congress: "Everywhere through the Copper Country and south of it, Finnish singers generously furnished me with more material than I had time to record." His camera focuses briefly on the blacksmith shop of J. Fredrickson & Son, a Calumet business with a unique rooftop sign fashioned from the smithy's products: a wagon wheel, a plow, and an anvil encircled by a horseshoe. Inside the Fredrickson home, John and his second wife, Kaisa Kipina, sing "Herran haltuun" (Dear Brethren) from a Finnish Apostolic Lutheran songbook with lyrics only, as the tunes were learned by ear.

Herran haltuun veljet raakkaat,
   jääkäät veljet, menemään.
Uskolliset siitä taitaa meitä.
Oi, kuin on se kallista, että siellä
   kohdata saamme kerran varmahan,
   luona Heran Jumalan.
(ca. September 26, 1938; 2377 A)

Let us endeavor, dear brethren,
   unto the Lord.
We faithful shall pass home into his arms.
Oh, how precious it is that we shall meet
   again in the home of God, our Father.

John Fredrickson (1856–1940) was born in Kauliranta, a village on the Finnish side of the Tornio River that forms the border with northern Sweden. Before his death Fredrickson wrote an autobiography in Meänkieli, the Finnish dialect of the Tornio Valley. Thanks to a translation by E. Olaf Rankinen of Suomi College (now Finlandia University), we know that Fredrickson's parents were landless crofters on a large estate, where his father was respected as a skilled workman and his mother was renowned for spinning and weaving. Fredrickson learned net making and sign painting before settling on the blacksmith's trade. An avid hymn singer schooled in the verses and melodies of Lutheran services, he was a *lukkari*, or cantor, throughout his adult life. In 1876 Fredrickson was swept up in a religious revival inspired by the pietistic Swedish Sami pastor Lars Levi Laestadius (1800–1861), whose followers formed Finnish Apostolic Lutheran congregations in the New World.

Fredrickson married Kaisamarja Mella (1848–1936) in 1877. An established blacksmith thereafter in Finland and, subsequently, across the river in both Kuivakangas and Haaparanta, Sweden, Fredrickson was affected by an economic depression from 1901 to 1902. Michigan beckoned and the Fredricksons departed for Calumet in 1903,

John Fredrickson, Calumet, Michigan, ca. 1938. (courtesy of Corey Fredrickson)

John Fredrickson and son at their home and shop in snowy Calumet, Michigan, 1930s. (courtesy of Corey Fredrickson)

where "many friends, and acquaintances, a large delegation of smiling and happy people awaited." After working for a year in the woods and on a streetcar line, Fredrickson and his son, Eemeli, opened their blacksmith shop on Pine Street. Soon after, Fredrickson took on responsibilities as cantor for the local Apostolic Lutheran congregation (Fredrickson 2013).

Lomax had recorded impassioned religious trance music from African Americans in the South and in Haiti and was likewise familiar with the "holy rollers" of Southern white Protestant tent revivals. A terse entry from his field notebook hints that he may have hoped to capture something similar in Michigan: "The Lutheran Apostolics started in N. Finland where people were living in a very wild state—drinking + fighting—the founder of the Apost. C. started to reform them + painted such a picture of Hell + Heaven that they joined the church—Lars Levi Laestadius. It is powerful in Oregon + Washington states—the older branch here in Calumet still goes in for hysterics almost every meeting." John and Kaisa Frederickson's singing, however, was dignified and sedate.

The songbook Fredrickson holds on-screen is likely *Amerikan Siionin laulut ja virret sekä kirkkokäsikirja* (American Songs and Hymns of Zion, as well as a Church Handbook), published in Calumet, Michigan, in 1930 by the Amerikan suomalainen apostolis-luterilainen kirkkokunta (Finnish American Apostolic Lutheran Church). The hymn matched with film footage is number 165, typically sung to close a service (Linna 2009). Although the woman on film with Fredrickson is his second wife, Kaisa Kipina (1877–1950), she was not listed by Lomax as a singer. Indeed, the woman recorded with Fredrickson may be Aina Pitkänen Pohjola, who also sang an Apostolic Lutheran hymn at the same session. Pohjola (1886–1953) was born in the Kuusamo area of northeastern Finland, along the Russian border. She immigrated to Calumet in 1909, where she married Aleksanteri Pohjola (1870–1940) in 1913 and was active in the local Finnish Apostolic Lutheran Church (Kurtti 2007).

The camera moves from Frederickson's place to a home where a woman rocks in a chair, sometimes with a lap dog, as a kettle heats on a nearby wood-fired kitchen stove. She is likely Selma Elona Halinen, matching the description read by Bill Malone from Lomax's notebook: "Ilona Halenin—blond, crisp hair, broad, full prominent cheek bones splashed with pink—and a hearty male laugh cracking at the end." Halinen, whose biography is sketched in the Lomax CD notes (track 35), performed several poignant laments, including "Pikkulintu erämaassa lauleleepi suruissana" (A Little Bird in the Desert Sings Sadly).

We do not know for certain who is seen after Selma Halinen, but the older woman wearing a traditional Finnish peasant head scarf, or *huivi*, may be Mathilda Herraniemi. Born in Finland in 1881, she settled in Calumet, where, sometime in the 1930s, she married the widower Mikko Herraniemi, who was fifteen years her senior. "Sun henkesi kasteen alle" (My Weary Soul) was the only song she recorded for Alan Lomax.

Sun henkesi katseen alle,	My weary soul will take
Mun sieluni uupunut vie.	Your spirit beneath the dew [i.e.,
	will accept baptism].
On kirkasta vakavalle	The narrow road of the blessed cross
Ristin siunatun taitotie.	Is clear for the solemn.
(September 26, 1938; 2378 B1)	

Invoking the "narrow road" to salvation that figures prominently in Apostolic Lutheran theology, the song was relatively new at the time: a 1929 composition of the Laestadian hymnodists Yrjö Karanko (1883–1957) and Vilho Rantanen (1889–1978), which was published in *Sävelsilta: Tekstikirja* (Oulu: 1934).

The scene shifts from homes in Calumet to log outbuildings in a rural area before settling on a powerful older man leaning on crutches in front of a frame house, with

Lomax's Plymouth sedan, a frame house, a milk can on a cart, an inverted washtub, and an unknown woman in the background. A passage from Lomax's notebook, part of which Bill Malone delivers as a voice-over, suggests who the man is: "John Hyvönen, 73, Pewabic—paralysis in right arm + left eye—square + powerful—a chuckler of huge swelling laughter—a miner for 49 years in the same mine—looks like a great redfaced bear, kindly + a lump of strength—knows a lot more songs than he sang but they are all dirty and he was solid, firm though friendly, in his refusal to sing them—He says he can stop blood with his formula of Mary, Jesus."

Born in the Finnish village of Piippola in Northern Ostrobothnia, Hyvönen (1865–1945) immigrated to Michigan's Copper Country in 1887. He married Matilda Aho (1870–1933) shortly after she immigrated in 1894, and the couple had nine children. Hyvönen's blood-stopping power, brought about with a magico-religious formula, was sufficiently common among Finns and other immigrant workers in the Upper Peninsula to figure in the title and an entire chapter of folklorist Richard Dorson's *Bloodstoppers and Bearwalkers: Folk Traditions of Michigan's Upper Peninsula* ([1952] 2008). On September 29, 1938, Hyvönen was living with his son, Emil, when he sang six songs for Lomax, including "Pääskynen se on taivaan lintu" (Swallow, the Sky Bird), a fragment of which is heard in the film.

Pääskynen se on taivaan lintu,	The swallow is a sky bird,
Pääskynen se on päivän lintu.	The swallow is a daytime bird.
(2395 B1)	

Hyvönen also performed several rollicking songs from his youth in Finland, including "Ja pojat ne lähtivät hotelliin" (And the Boys Left for the Hotel):

The guys went to a hotel,
They headed from Oulu to a hotel.
With all sorts of joking,
Like guys they were poking.
They got there at church-going time
While the minister was preaching
And the cantor beseeching.
But they just got down to business and headed for the tap.
And the price of a shot was a mark.
Pretty steep when a whole bottle costs three.
But the bottle was fine and the label new.
They just pull out the cork and out pours fine wine.
(2396 B2; translation by Susanna Linna and Tom DuBois)

Contrary to Lomax's assertion, he also sang one "dirty song," although as Tim Frandy observes, during the recording of "Ja kun minä kerran illalla lähin" (Once I Left in the Evening) "Hyvönen's modesty overtakes him, and he struggles to finish the song's last verse" (Frandy 2010). The song concerns a young man's welcome by a woman on a cold night. From the final verse:

Likka se heti lahvista veti mursi ja putelin	The girl pulled a bottle from the drawer.
Sitten me siinä ryypittiin ja	There we drank and enjoyed the flight,
lentävästä nautittiin,	
Niin alkoipa likan vetinen vika	And the girl's wet place flickered in lust.
halusta häpättää.	
(2395 B2)	

The film footage shifts from the Copper Country westward to Ironwood on the Michigan–Wisconsin border, where Wäinö Hirvelä was a professional photographer. We see him seated in his studio, nattily dressed with a vest and tie, playing a tabletop zither in kantele style and singing into Lomax's bulky microphone. Chiefly focused on Hirvelä's singing and playing of a song by Pasi Jääskeläinen, the camera fleetingly zooms out to offer glimpses of painted trees and bushes on a canvas backdrop used for studio portraits. For biographical information on Hirvelä and the song heard on-screen, see the Lomax CD notes (track 39).

Pasi Jääskeläinen songbook and "Kulkurin valssi" sheet music, Ironwood, Michigan, 1981. (photo by author)

Lomax spent several days northeast of Ironwood in Green, an Ontonagon County hamlet on the shore of Lake Superior where he filmed Finnish dancers and recorded an immigrant fiddler and singer, Charles Korvenpaa. Named in 1904 for the general manager of the area's McMillan Brothers Sawmill, Green was settled in 1903 by seven Finnish families who purchased cutover land from the McMillans and began to establish farms. Soon joined by other immigrant Finns, many of them former spool-mill workers from the Lappeenranta vicinity in southeastern Finland, the residents of Green built a farmers hall in 1915 where meetings, gymnastics, and dancing were regular pastimes (Hokkanen

1976; Karttunen 2002; http://www.facebook.com/Green1904, accessed November 4, 2013). In 1938 the Green Tercentenary Dancers were formed in commemoration of the strong Finnish presence in the 1638 Swedish settlement in the Delaware Valley.

Evidently charmed by his visit to Green, Lomax filmed Korvenpaa fiddling outdoors under a hardwood tree on the Ruuttila farm while the dancers, dressed in matching male and female folk-inspired clothing, performed on a well-mown grassy field. The carefully planned sequence offers an elevated distant view with farm buildings, a road, and a creek-spanning bridge, followed by ground-level footage and close-ups of couples and individual dancers. Lomax penciled the dancers' names on a disc sleeve, and we are fortunate that Korvenpaa's grandson, Doug Karttunen, corrected misspellings and added the maiden names of several women. By couple, they include Mrs. Wesley (Anna Store) Broemer and Eli Kangas, Leonard and Bertha (Ruuttila) Kekke, Eva Kangas and Theodore Ruuttila, Oiva Niska and Alma Davis, Lempi Hill and John Wiittala, Charley and Elma (Wettberg) Bolo, Eli and Lydia (Karttunen) Perttunen, Soley and Ruth (Bolo) Carlson, and George Savola (or possibly Leonard Kekke) and Mary Jane Immonen.

In its edition of Tuesday, October 11, 1938, the *Ironwood Daily Globe* reported: "The Finnish folk dance group of Green was pleasantly surprised when it was requested to dance two folk dances of which Alan Lomax of the congressional library of Washington, DC, made a techni-color movie. A phonographic record was also made of the music and songs used in the dances. Charles Korvenpaa played the violin for the dances as well as a number of old Finnish folk dance tunes which were recorded. The movie and records will be sent to the congressional library. The weaver's dance was one of the folk dances in the movie. It is an old dance dating back many generations." Sadly all of the recordings from this session, including "Kankurin tanssi" (Weaver's Dance), were damaged. There are several versions of a weaver's dance performed in the twenty-first century by Norwegian and Swedish dancers in North America and accessible via YouTube. Each is a contra dance variation performed to different tunes, and we have no way of determining a connection with the Finnish "Weaver's Dance." Lomax's film footage is paired, consequently, with "Finnish Medley," including "Kauhavan Polka," by solo fiddler Helmer Toyras of Aura, Michigan (1981).

The original fiddler, Kalle V. "Charles" Korvenpaa (1885–1973), was born in Finland where he learned to fiddle by ear. He immigrated to Ontonagon County, Michigan, in 1910 with his wife, Hilda M. Pietila Korvenpaa (1887–1936). The Korvenpaas lived in White Pine, where Charles worked as a miner and in lumber camps. He continued to

Charles Korvenpaa, fiddler, with the Tercentenary Dancers, Green, Michigan, 1938. (courtesy of Douglas D. Karttunen)

toil in the woods after the family settled in Green in 1916 to farm and raise four children (Karttunen 2013).

Finnish footage concludes with Lomax's finest Michigan filmmaking as he documents the magico-religious practices of erstwhile accordionist Aapo Juhani. This carefully planned sequence begins with Juhani and a neighbor boy, "Sonny" Kvarup, gathered at a stone-ringed spring to buy, bless, and fetch water on the outskirts of Calumet; proceeds to a nearby alder grove where Juhani cuts leafy twigs; follows him and Kvarup down a railroad track and across barren windswept dunes to a row of mining company houses where Juhani boarded with the Forster family; lingers in the Forster kitchen where Juhani makes alder twig/spring water tea, praises its virtues, and offers the concoction to young Kvarup; and concludes with Juhani playing button accordion on the steps of his home as small children look on.

We have paired two of Juhani's button accordion tunes, each featuring his incessant scatting, with the film footage: "Kiikkuri kaakkuri kirjava lintu" (Cuckoo Speckled Bird), a Finnish folksong well known into the present on both sides of the Atlantic (September 27, 1938; 2384 A1), and an unnamed Finnish schottische (September 27, 1938; 2384 B1).

A vivid description from Lomax's field notebook—heard on-screen through Bill Malone's reading as the sequence commences—notes Juhani's traditional merging of magical thought, animism, Christianity, and folk science via attention to cardinal directions, right and left hands, tripartite repetition, the spring's spirit, Christ's power, and alder's medicinal virtues as an astringent and tonic.

Sept. 28—Aapo—at the spring—Mrs. Kvarup + son, Forster, Aapo + me. Aapo can cure people who are cursed. He can also curse people who insult him. To cure a burn, he brings ice from the North to cool the burn.

1) Chipped silver coin into the spring, because money is evil if shined up

2) Knelt over and blessed the spring, putting something much stronger than money into the water.

3) The moss had to be in the middle of the water. Why?

4) The bucket—dipped up the water from behind the water. We all must drink because it was very powerful and would cure all ailments.

5) Then Sonny + old Aapo went into the bush to get twigs. He cut *leppä* [alder] twigs. The twigs had to be cut from the right hand side in front of him.

6) He cut the branches from 3 different trees and then prayed over them. He bathed Sonny then in the spring water—3 hands full—Sonny had to take the water with his right hand and bathed the right side of his face first—3 times.

Sonny told to face the East—towards Christ—had to kneel on the special stones at the West end of the spring.

He felt we should all bathe in the spring because the water was powerful. He wanted to take Sonny to the bath house [sauna] + bathe him all over to make him strong—Tea of leppä had to boil until it was coffee colored—then a wineglass full taken in three gulps would cure you of anything whatsoever.

The bath wouldn't do in the house—must be in the sauna—stand in the tub then twigs
+ Aapo bathed him + gave him tea—(the twigs were boiled after most of the leaves
had been stripped off).

Lomax interviewed Juhani concerning the entire process, with particular attention to
the use and meaning of his magico-religious *loitsu* (spell). Hence we hear Juhani speaking, accompanied by Susanne Linna's translated subtitles, as he chips silver into the
spring, and later in the kitchen as he proclaims the power of ceremonially acquired tea.
At the spring:

> You carve a piece of silver coin into the water.
> You say: "A gift I give, help I receive."
> You say the Lord's Prayer across the spring:
> "Our Father, who art in Heaven . . ."
> Prayers make the water precious.
> *(2381 A)*

In the kitchen:

> You pray at home.
> Prayer has a lot of power.
> Doesn't the word of God have power?
> Nothing's as powerful and healing.
> Just apply the spring water . . . it'll heal.
> *(2381 A)*

Such powers were not confined to a few remarkable folks like Aapo Juhani. Besides
mentioning in his notebooks that John Hyvönen invoked Jesus and Mary to stop
blood, Lomax made extensive observations about Finnish American magico-religious
practitioners.

Scratch a F [Finn] + you'll find a superstition—this applies to everyone I've met here,
from Dr. Nisonen [Martii Nisonen (1891–1946), music professor, Suomi College,
Hancock, Michigan] to Aapo—When I tell ed. of paper about Aapo's tricks, he
responds with tales about magical blood clotting . . . by telephone in Finland and he
claims this is a trick he himself has seen performed + can perform himself on occasion—no one in the office says him nay. When this tale is brot to Dr. Nisonen sympa-
thetically, he says because his gr.father cd disappear at will + he tells a circumstantial

Aapo Juhani's spring, Calumet, Michigan, 2013. (photo by Hilary Virtanen)

tale of the time his gfather vanished before his father's eyes—Mrs. [illegible] in her vague shiftless + absentminded way says well of course I don't follow any of these superstitions but they do say that spring water is good for you and medicinal baths.

When my film was stolen—Aapo read the cards and after considerable mumbling told me that the film was stolen at nine o'clock + by two blond young men—then the finger of suspicion was laid more + more heavily on Jenkelin as the séance proceeded—Forster then volunteered information that when anyone stole anything from him he could make them bring it back. How? Oh, I cut a stick out in the brush and do things with it.

He promised to do something for me and the next morning he went fooling around the car with what looked like a willow stake about 2 feet long + sharpened at both ends behind his back and under his elbows—he told me that the person wd either bring it back or the blood would rush out of his forehead—Wd he tell me how to do this trick— No, because if he did he would lose his powers. But he could tell me how to prevent my stuff from being taken. Make a watchman take a piece of string and measure a dead body and put the string in your car.—If a thief tries to take anything the watchman will hold him there until you come and given him a boot behind and send him away.

Forster also recalled how once Aapo used to jinx him and he went about turning Aapo's little tricks until they all turned back on him. Finally Aapo apologized for trying anything—Again Forster helped his brother's employer out—this farmer was being persecuted by an Italian neighbor + F's brother wasn't able to help him. So F went about through the brush tearing the stuff down—little wooden crosses with chains around them and bunches of keys and every time one would come down it would roar like the brush was falling.

"Enough Material for Years of Work"

Pressed for time and exhausted yet exhilarated by a long productive trip, Lomax left Michigan thoroughly convinced that it was a many-splendored, barely explored storehouse of traditional music. As the camera returns to autumn's trees along the Copper Country's Cliff Drive, Bill Malone reads from Lomax's ensuing report to the Librarian of Congress: "The Upper Peninsula of Michigan proved to be the most fertile source of material. After six weeks of recording a mass of lumberjack, Finnish, and French folksongs, I felt that there was enough material in the region for years of work." Henry Mahoski's spirited accordion rendition of "Kauhavan Polka" offers sonic background as the credits roll (Lomax CD, track 34).

Print by Isabella Leary

WHEN THE DANCE IS OVER
THE HELENE STRATMAN-THOMAS RECORDINGS, PART ONE

HO-CHUNK

The Ho-Chunk (People of the Big Voice)—formerly known by the outsider's term, "Winnebago"—have made what is now south-central Wisconsin their home for millennia, living in villages alongside lakes and rivers. In the mid-nineteenth century, the federal government forced them to resettle successively on reservations in Minnesota, South Dakota, and Nebraska. Yet many Ho-Chunks refused to leave, while others returned to Wisconsin. The warrior tradition has been especially strong among Ho-Chunks, carrying over into service in the United States military. Land claims by veterans under the Homestead Act of 1862 enabled Ho-Chunks to establish legal residence in Wisconsin, especially along the Black and Wisconsin Rivers, where they eventually won federal recognition, with Black River Falls as their site of tribal government.

1 Flute Song

Spoken and sung by Stella Stacy, with flute by Henry Thunder, Black River Falls, Wisconsin, August 15, 1946. Recorded by Aubrey Snyder. Partial transcription and translation by Stella Stacy (Mountain Wolf Woman), with the assistance of Frances Perry, 1948.

8411 B1

This is a flute song. This is a love song. A young fellow was sick and his sweetheart heard that he died. And she cried. Then he heard about it, and made a song about it: "I didn't die, but you cried. If I died, I wouldn't be knowing that you cried."

W d ttete deAeke dX K Kiti dtetke	I didn't die but you cried.
W d) bete diri t te kittiti kettete—te!	But if I had, I wouldn't have known that you cried for me—hey!

At Black River Falls we had made arrangements to record music of the Winnebago Indians. Mrs. Frances Perry, city librarian, and Nancy Oestreich, an anthropologist living at the Indian mission, had consented to contact the Indians for us. During the day I received word of my brother's illness and consequently returned to Madison. However, Aubrey Snyder, the recording technician, stayed to work with Mrs. Perry and Miss Oestreich. The recording equipment was set up in a room in the city library. Henry Thunder and Stella Stacy came from the Indian village to sing a variety of Winnebago Indian songs—war dances, moccasin game songs, peyote religious songs, love songs, lullabies, "Green Corn Song," "Calumet Song," and "Swan Song." (Stratman-Thomas 1940–1960: August 15, 1946)

The song featured here was composed by Stella Stacy's brother, Jasper Blowsnake, or Warudjáxega (Crashing Thunder), whose "Personal Reminiscence" figures in *The Winnebago Tribe* (1923: 399) by the anthropologist Paul Radin. Because Radin deemed the English translation of Blowsnake's Ho-Chunk name as especially colorful, he used it for the title of *Crashing Thunder: The Autobiography of an American Indian* (1926), even though the book concerned Jasper's younger brother, Hágaga (a birth-order name), also known as Sam Blowsnake and as Big Winnebago. The song is based on a rumor circulating about his supposed death and the reaction of a young woman who wept at hearing the news.

The singer, Stella Stacy, became well known as Mountain Wolf Woman, the English translation of her Ho-Chunk name, Xéhachiwinga. Born near Black River Falls in 1884 and a member of the Thunder Clan, she offered tape-recorded reminiscences to the anthropologist Nancy Oestreich Lurie, resulting in *Mountain Wolf Woman, Sister of Crashing Thunder* (1961), published a year after her death. Raised as a traditionalist, she later converted to the Peyote Religion, or Native American Church, as did many Ho-Chunks. Although her autobiography mentions only singing while fasting as a young girl (Lurie 1961: 21), Mountain Wolf Woman recorded twelve songs altogether

> Ho-Chunk singers with bone whistle and hand drum, Wisconsin Dells, 1946. (Wisconsin Historical Society, WHi-25204)

in 1946, including "49 Song"—performed with hand drum, vocables, and English lyrics (see track 4, below)—and a Native American Church, or "peyote religion," version of the Christian "Lord's Prayer" in addition to those mentioned by Stratman-Thomas. Several of her performances figure in the soundtrack of a video biography, *Mountain Wolf Woman, 1884–1960*, by Jocelyne Riley (1990).

The seven-hole end-blown flute in this performance is of a sort commonly made of cedar to accompany love songs, particularly courting songs, by Ho-Chunk and neighboring Woodland Indian peoples through the mid-twentieth century. Henry Thunder, born in the Black River Falls vicinity around 1866, was "one of several flute players in the area," including Adam Thundercloud and Mitchell Red Cloud Sr., the father of World War II veteran and Congressional Medal of Honor winner Mitchell Red Cloud Jr. (Stratman-Thomas 1940–1960: Winnebago file). Thunder was mentioned often in the "Indian News" column of the Ho-Chunk writer Charles Round Low Cloud, which was published in the Black River Falls and La Crosse newspapers (Clark and Wyman 1973). These brief passages show regard for a prominent elder, traditionalist, and healer.

Sunday, February 8, 1948
The Indians had another religion dance last Saturday night at Indian Mission by Joe
Thunder of Wyeville, Wis., Tom Thunder of Hunters Bridge, Charles R. Lowe Cloud,
Henry Thunder, Benjamin and Eli Young Thunder, Alex and Adam Thunder Cloud and
family. We have some more to come. There will be another week from next Saturday
night at Wyeville by the Decorah family and too many Decorah and we don't know who
will be there when time come but this is who believe the right way to worship by the
Indian way and this way the old Indian way they called prepared every things for our
future.

June 9, 1948
The Indian dances and feast last Saturday and Sunday night, and old man Henry
Thunder said he has been try to make a rain, and old people they used to make rain at
any time they wanted. We have only one old man can do that.

The Stacy-Thunder recordings relied on assistance from Frances Perry (1897–ca. 1990) and Nancy Oestreich Lurie (b. 1924). Perry—whose performance of the locally composed "Cranberry Song" was included on Stratman-Thomas's Library of Congress LP,

Folk Music from Wisconsin—was the city librarian for Black River Falls and a lifelong chronicler of Ho-Chunk life. Her reminiscences, recorded in 1986 by Robert Andresen for his *Northland Hoedown* radio program, are permanently archived on the Andresen Collection site of the Mills Music Library (http://music.library.wisc.edu/wma/Andresen/frances.htm, accessed December 28, 2013). Perry's preservation of the glass negatives for portraits of Ho-Chunks made by photographer Charles van Schaick in the Black River Falls area form the basis of *People of the Big Voice: Photographs of Ho-Chunk Families by Charles Van Schaick, 1879–1942* (T. Jones et al. 2011). Born in Milwaukee and formerly a professor of anthropology at the University of Wisconsin, as well as the retired head curator of anthropology at the Milwaukee Public Museum, Nancy O. Lurie has been a distinguished scholar of and a tireless advocate for the Ho-Chunk Nation since the 1940s.

2 War Dance

Spoken and sung with hand drum by Winslow White Eagle, Wisconsin Dells, Wisconsin, July 24, 1946. Recorded by Helene Stratman-Thomas, Aubrey Snyder, and Charles Hofmann.

8376 A2

This is Winslow White Eagle singing a war dance.

Haylushka, or warrior songs, are a venerable Ho-Chunk genre that became part of the powwow repertoire in the twentieth century, wherein they are performed typically on the big drum rather than on the small-frame, or hand drum, featured here.

Railroad transportation, proximity to Milwaukee and Chicago, and H. H. Bennett's evocative photographs of the Wisconsin River and Ho-Chunk people combined to make the Wisconsin Dells a popular tourist attraction (Hoelscher 2008: 28). By 1916 the brothers Sanborn and Winslow White Eagle were performing dances on a sandy beach for tips from tourists on river steamers. Three years later a group including Captain Glen Parsons (a pilot and general manager of the Dells Boat Company), local entrepreneur George Crandall, and Russell Decorah of the Ho-Chunk Nation launched the Stand Rock Indian Ceremonial, a nightly summer event from 1919 to 1997 featuring the songs and dances of Ho-Chunk and other American Indian peoples (http://sarweb.org/?tallmadge_exhibit_hochunk_tourism, accessed December 28, 2013).

Winslow White Eagle, river-view guide, wears a feather bonnet on the *North Star* excursion boat, Wisconsin Dells, Wisconsin, 1931. (postcard, author's collection)

Hence Stratman-Thomas and others seeking the traditional performances of American Indians frequented this site: "We took our equipment to Wisconsin Dells, where we were assisted by Charles Hofmann of New York, who had come to Wisconsin for a similar purpose, and Mrs. Phyllis Crandall Connor, director of the Indian Ceremonial at Wisconsin Dells. With Mrs. Connor's permission recordings were made in the Indian village which is the summer quarters of the Indians participating in the Ceremonial. . . . There were war dances sung by Winslow White Eagle" (Stratman-Thomas 1940–1960: July 24, 1946).

Phyllis Connor, the daughter of George Crandall, had been managing the Stand Rock Ceremonial since 1929, while Charles Hofmann, who would soon write about his Wisconsin recording experiences (Hofmann 1947), was inspired by the 1920s "Winnebago" recordings made in the area for the Smithsonian Institution by Frances Densmore (1867–1957), the most prolific recorder of American Indian music (1928, 1929, 1930, 1940).

Highly respected as a traditional singer by fellow Ho-Chunks, Winslow White Eagle (1896–?) had previously performed the Fish Dance, Green Corn Dance, Horse

Dance, War Dance, Women's Dance, Medicine Lodge, Moccasin Game, Night Spirit Bundle, and Peyote Lord's Prayer songs for cylinder recordings made by Densmore in 1928 and 1930, and by Huron Smith in 1928 (Gray and Lee 1985: 279, 285, 287–288, 324). Besides the songs recorded by Hofmann and Stratman-Thomas in 1946, he also sang eight songs on March 1, 1958—including "Air Raid on Iwo Jima" and "Korea War Song"—which were reissued on a CD one hundred years after his birth as "Winnebago Tribal Songs" (1996). Not content to sing for his own people, for visitors to Wisconsin Dells, and for the occasional folklorist, White Eagle sometimes ventured farther afield in Wisconsin as a Ho-Chunk cultural ambassador. In summer 1953, for example, he headed a delegation of ten families to camp and offer cultural presentations in Oshkosh for that city's centennial. In early July, as reported by the *Oshkosh Daily Northwestern*, representatives of the region's "various German, Danish, Finnish, Norwegian, and Swedish Lutheran churches" were welcomed by "Indian Chief Winslow White Eagle" and "with the Indian and immigrants kneeling, the combined choirs sang melody in a foreign tongue" (Monday, July 6, 1953).

Ken Funmaker Sr., a formidable singer who knew more than three hundred traditional songs, as well as being the first director of the Ho-Chunk Nation's Language Division, offered vivid memories of Winslow White Eagle when I interviewed him in 1995.

> My neighbors were Sam Carley, Ed Whitebear, Mark Henry, Sanborn White Eagle, Winslow White Eagle. . . . There was quite a few Ho Chunks who were living in Lyndon Station at that time. The other thing about it was that there was work at that powder plant [the Baraboo Munitions Plant]. So all these people were working there. They had buses that were going right to the plant. That made it nice. Since there were so many Ho Chunks living in Lyndon, it became a regular stopping place for our tribal members from other districts. . . . The songs that they sang, that's where I got my start singing. Haylushka songs, we call them powwow songs. . . . Then my neighbor, Winslow [White Eagle], he was an excellent singer. . . . He could really control his voice. He had that kind of flutter in his voice. He could really sing. He'd go right up to falsetto and right down to a real deep bass. Even in the same song, he could go with that range. He could start a song, probably about middle range. Then he could go down to bass like that. Then where the women come in, he could sing falsetto. Jump right into that, make it sound just like a woman. And he had that quiver in his voice. Man, that guy was good.

As a fledgling singer whose sons now sustain his legacy through their drum group, the Wisconsin Dells Singers, Ken often traveled to Wisconsin Dells in the summer when Stand Rock Ceremonials featured fine singers every evening. And so he was present on July 24, 1946, when Helene Stratman-Thomas and Charles Hofmann arrived: "I remember there was some singing going on. . . . They were recording. . . . They had it right in the middle of the village. They weren't hiding, so the singers, they just went down. Whoever wanted to watch, they could watch. There was no secret about it. And I liked that approach. . . . It was a really good way to do it" (Funmaker 1995).

ONEIDA

The Oneida, an Iroquoian people, were refugees to Wisconsin from western New York State in the early nineteenth century. Settling near Green Bay, many had converted to Christianity prior to their arrival. Mainly Episcopalians initially, some Oneidas had become Methodists by the early twentieth century.

3 Tsyatkatho

Sung by Wallace Smith and Albert Webster, Oneida, Wisconsin, September 1, 1946. Recorded by Helene Stratman-Thomas and Aubrey Snyder. Transcription and translation by Floyd Lounsbury, 1947.

8468 A

Tsyat-kat-ho tsi ni-shoñ-kwa-wi	Behold what He hath given us,
Ne yoñ-kwe-ti-yo-se	To our Christian people:
Ne ya-ka-we-lyah-si-yo-se	Pure hearts
Ska-ni-koñ-lat i-keñ.	And one mind.
Te-yoñ-ta-te-no-loñ-khwah-se	Loving one another
Ke-li-stos sha-ko-wi	Christ has given them
Tsi tyoh-na-wa-tet ne yo-skatst	As a flowing stream, glorious,
Wa-toñn-he-tse-li-yo.	A very good life.
Ka-ya-ne-leñ ka-loñn-ya-ke	Heavenly portals in heaven,
Ne sa-ne-leñ-hoñ-tsa,	Thy glory on high,
Eñh-sa-thi-teñ-steñ eh noñ-kwa	That Thou will understand
Ne tsi tkoñ-ti-tyeh-se.	Where they are flying [Where the angels are].

Ne ne yo-na-toñn-ha-he-le	It is a happy life
O-neñ eh ye-ya-kov ,	When one gets there,
O-neñ ye-ko-noñ-ta-la-oñ	When one has reached that city
Tsi noñ-we ne Ni-yo.	Where God is.

Stratman-Thomas's Oneida field notes are unusually rich and include particular mention of the singers heard here, Wallace Smith and Albert Webster. Their harmonies, as well as Webster's assertive bass vocal, were influenced by Southern part-singing. Indeed, Oneida Methodist male quartet and jubilee groups flourished in the 1930s after some Oneidas attended Virginia's Hampton Institute, a hotbed of African American religious singing (O'Grady 1991: 69–70, 80).

Several months before starting out our summer field trip we had sent an article to newspapers in the various county seats, asking for information about folk singers. One reply to this article came from Mrs. I. O. Sessman of West De Pere, who told of her pleasure in hearing the Oneida Indians sing in their native tongue at the Oneida Methodist Church. At Mrs. Sessman's suggestion, we wrote to the pastor, Reverend J. H. Wenberg. Rev. Wenberg replied, "We have often wished we could get phonograph recording of Oneida songs. In another generation few of the Oneida will be left who sing in their native tongue." A joint meeting was planned by Rev. Wenberg and Father William Christian of the Oneida Episcopal Church for Sunday evening, September 1st, when the Oneida would be back from cherry-picking in Door County.

Early Sunday morning we drove from Green Bay to Oneida to attend worship at Reverend Wenberg's church. Since Rev. Wenberg had written, "We hear the Oneida songs every Sunday morning," we were at first disappointed inasmuch as the choir sang an anthem in English and the congregational hymns were sung in English. However, as the offering was being taken, a single male voice, that of Wallace Smith, started an Indian hymn in which the others soon joined. "O Sayanel" (O Savior, hear my prayer; O Lord, hear while I pray. Own my soul forever.) This thrilling music was sung in parts with no accompaniment. The parts had been learned by rote and handed down traditionally in the families of the Oneida Indians for many generations.

From Reverend Wenberg we learned that the Oneida Indians in Wisconsin do not sing any native tribal music. The hymns in the Oneida language constitute practically the only music in their native tongue. He showed us a handwritten book of translations of hymns into Mohawk, a dialect kindred to the Oneida.

In the evening the Oneidas from the Methodist and Episcopal churches gathered at the Methodist Church. They were very serious and cooperative. There were
some beautiful voices among them, particularly the bass voice of Albert Webster. The
Oneida seemed to sense that the older traditional songs were those in which we were
most interested, for they sang them with an unforgettable fervor.

We recorded "O Sayanel" which we heard during the morning worship.
"Tsyatkatho" (Behold What He has Given to Us) was sung to four different
tunes. . . . The Oneida were enthusiastic participants; after the evening meeting had
been dismissed, several of the men gathered around the microphone for more recording . . . (September 1, 1946)

"Tsyatktho"/"Jatgato" (Oh Lord) was published as number 15 in a songbook compiled
through the Works Progress Administration by two linguistic anthropologists, Morris
Swadish and Floyd Lounsbury, in collaboration with a respected Oneida singer, Oscar
Archiquette (1941). Originally "Psalm 133," composed by the English hymnodist Isaac
Watts (1647–1748), it had been translated into Oneida and published in a Methodist
hymnal by Abraham Sickles, a Canadian Oneida (1855).

Wallace Smith (1882–1962) and Albert Webster (1882–1969) were among nine
Oneida hymn singers recorded by Stratman-Thomas. Webster attended Hampton
Institute as a young man, where he "became versed in Gospel music" (Campisi and
Hauptman 1981: 446).

PAN-INDIAN

Inter-tribal powwows began to flourish in the early twentieth century, drawing upon
older tribally specific practices but also fostering new dances, dance regalia, songs, and
the development of a pan-Indian repertoire.

4   49 Song

Sung by Margaret "Laughing Eyes" Edaakie (Eagle) and Phyllis Lewis,
with hand drum, Wisconsin Dells, Wisconsin, July 24, 1946. Recorded by
Helene Stratman-Thomas, Aubrey Snyder, and Charles Hofmann.
8376 B2

When the dance is over,
You must wait for me
I will take you home on my burro.

When the dance is over
You must wait for me.
I will take you home in my flivver.

"49 songs" emerged in the 1920s among the Kiowa in Oklahoma. Originally related to the songs of women as they linked arms to send men on war journeys, they supposedly acquired the "49" reference soon after a burlesque show with a Gold Rush "Girls of '49" theme played the Caddo County Fair. By the 1930s such songs—invariably characterized by nonlexical "vocables" and English lyrics sung to a hand drum or big drum—were "after hours" mainstays at powwows and other late-night social gatherings of young men and women. Much like the era's blues and honky-tonk country songs, they concerned courting, cars, drinking, and sex.

Although the Stand Rock Indian Ceremonial in Wisconsin Dells primarily involved Ho-Chunk performers, it also attracted Native peoples from the Great Plains and the Southwestern Pueblos. Margaret Lewis Edaakie (1921–2011), also known as Margaret Eagle and as Laughing Eyes, was a Zuni from New Mexico whose family performed for the Chicago World's Fair in 1933 and thereafter for the Stand Rock Ceremonial, where Margaret was a regular from 1933 to 1972 (http://www.k-jon.com/member/blogentry. aspx?mjid=5574&mid=345737, accessed October 27, 2014). She was joined on this song by Phyllis Lewis, "her ten year old niece" (Hofmann 1947: 293).

FRENCH CANADIAN

French Canadian families emigrated from Quebec to northern Wisconsin in the late nineteenth century, settling in communities where fur traders and French-Indian peoples had been a presence for generations: in Florence, Marinette, Oconto, and Brown Counties, which extend north from Green Bay along the Michigan border; and in the Chippewa, St. Croix, and upper Wisconsin River valleys, where logging and sawmill operations flourished.

5   Good for the Tongue

Played by Leizime Brusoe, fiddle; Robert McClain, clarinet; Walter Wyss, string bass; and Emery Olsen, accordion; Rhinelander, Wisconsin, August 14, 1941. Recorded by Helene Stratman-Thomas and Robert F. Draves.
5015 B2

Leizime Brusoe (1870–1949) learned to fiddle in his native Canada from an elder brother at roughly age six. He operated Brusoe's Dray Line in Rhinelander for forty years and later was the custodian at the city's logging museum. When meeting Brusoe on August 31, 1940, Stratman-Thomas seemed unaware that he had been recorded earlier by Sidney Robertson, perhaps because Alan Lomax had referred to him as "Rousseau" (Robertson CD, tracks 1–3).

> From Antigo we went to Rhinelander and stopped at the Logging Museum. When we asked the attendant there if he knew anyone who could sing old ballads or play old dance music, his reply was, "You're looking at the man right now!" We learned that we were addressing Leizime Brusoe, who was indeed the champion old-time fiddler of the Midwest. He had earned this title in the *Chicago Herald and Examiner* old-time fiddle contest in 1926. A loving cup in the parlor of his home was proof of the fact. However, when we heard Mr. Brusoe play, we didn't need the loving cup to prove to us that he was unusually gifted.
>
> Mr. Brusoe began fiddling at the age of six. He came to Wisconsin from Canada as a young man and has played for dances in the northern part of the state for fifty years. He carried an astounding number of dance tunes in his head, for he played entirely by ear and did not know one note from another. Mr. Brusoe took great pride in his playing and he was confident that if there had been a national contest of old-time fiddlers, he would have been champion of that too. He had much to tell us about how the quadrille, the Sicilian Circle, and the French Four should be danced. He objected greatly to speeding up the tempo so that the dances lost all grace and beauty.

When Stratman-Thomas sent recordings of Brusoe's solo fiddling to Alan Lomax at the Library of Congress, he deemed them among the best performances of old-time dance tunes yet recorded for the Archive of American Folk Song. Alan Jabbour, as director of the American Folklife Center and a stellar fiddler, concurred thirty years later and included four tunes by Brusoe among the twenty-eight in a definitive anthology, *American Fiddle Tunes* (1971). At Lomax's request, Stratman-Thomas arranged for a second recording session on August 14, 1941. This time "Mr. Brusoe organized a little dance orchestra. . . . The men played for us from eight-thirty in the evening to well past midnight. All of the orchestral arrangements were made by ear. Mr. Brusoe could not read music; the clarinet and string bass players were blind; the accordion player much preferred not to read music."

"Good for the Tongue" earned Brusoe's victory in the *Chicago Herald Examiner*'s old-time fiddler's contest of 1926. A version appeared in Elias Howe's *Musicians Omnibus Complete* (1863). The tune was especially popular among French Canadian and métis fiddlers in the Upper Midwest, where it was also called "Whitefish on the Rapids." A performance by Coleman Trudeau figures in Michael Loukinen's film on Indian fiddling, *Medicine Fiddle* (1991), with additional examples and fiddlers' biographies offered on *Paul Gifford's Collection of Old-Time Fiddling, Dulcimer Playing, and Songs from Michigan and the Great Lakes Region* (http://www.giffordmusic.net, accessed July 3, 2012).

6 Je ne veux pas d'un avocat / I Do Not Want a Lawyer

Sung by Ernest Joseph Belisle, Somerset, Wisconsin, August 8, 1946. Recorded by Helene Stratman-Thomas and Aubrey Snyder. Transcription, translation, and annotation by Anjili Babbar, with assistance from Sylvain Gaillard and Florence Théroud, 2012.

8393 A1

Je ne veux pas d'un avocat,	I do not want a lawyer,
Je ne veux pas d'un avocat,	I do not want a lawyer,
Car trop souvent faire des contrats,	For too often you make contracts,
Car trop souvent faire des contrats.	For too often you make contracts.
Souvent (ils ne) sont pas bien faits,	Often they are not well made,
Marions malurette.	Let's marry.
Souvent (ils ne) sont pas bien faits,	Often they are not well made,
Marions maluré.	Let's marry.
Je ne veux pas d'un ouvrier,	I do not want a laborer,
Je ne veux pas d'un ouvrier,	I do not want a laborer,
Car trop souvent des clous à planter,[1]	For too often [you have] nails to hammer in,
Car trop souvent des clous à planter.	For too often [you have] nails to hammer in.
Souvent j'y plante pas drette,[2]	Often I don't hammer them in straight,

Marions malurette.	Let's marry.
Souvent j'y plante pas drette,	Often I don't hammer them in straight,
Marions maluré.	Let's marry.
Je ne veux pas d'un cordonnier,	I do not want a shoemaker,
Je ne veux pas d'un cordonnier,	I do not want a shoemaker,
Car trop souvent les clous à planter,	For too often [you have] nails to hammer in,
Car trop souvent les clous à planter.	For too often [you have] nails to hammer in.
Souvent j'y plante pas drette,	Often I don't hammer them in straight,
Marions malurette.	Let's marry.
Souvent j'y plante pas drette,	Often I don't hammer them in straight,
Marions maluré.	Let's marry.
Je ne veux pas d'un habitant,[3]	I do not want a farmer,
Je ne veux pas d'un habitant,	I do not want a farmer,
Car trop souvent aller aux champs,	For too often you go to the fields,
Car trop souvent aller aux champs,	For too often you go to the fields,
Souvent en grande charrette,	Often in a big cart,
Marions malurette.	Let's marry.
Souvent en grande charrette,	Often in a big cart,
Marions maluré.	Let's marry.
Je ne veux bien d'un officier,	I don't much want an officer,
Je ne veux bien d'un officier.	I don't much want an officer.
Toujours de quoi sur l'bas d'son pied,	Always something on the bottom of his foot,
Toujours de quoi sur l'bas d'son pied.	Always something on the bottom of his foot.
Tout drette à la couchette,	Directly to bed,
Marions malurette.	Let's marry.
Tout drette à la couchette,	Directly to bed,
Marions maluré.	Let's marry.

---

1. The singer might have made an understandable slip here, since he attributes hammering nails to both the laborer and the shoemaker. This characteristic probably belongs to the shoemaker.
2. More properly rendered as "Souvent je les plante pas droit."
3. *Un habitant* is quite literally an "inhabitant," but in Quebec it is used to refer to someone from the country—in this case, a farmer.

Nestled alongside the Apple River, a tributary of the St. Croix, Somerset, Wisconsin, was substantially settled by farmers and loggers from Quebec in the late nineteenth century and continues to honor its French Canadian heritage with an annual Pea Soup Days festival. The Franco-American singer and folklorist Mary Agnes Starr put Stratman-Thomas in touch with Marie Donalda Lagrandeur, who organized a gathering of performers (see

> Ernest Belisle, garage mechanic, at his workplace, Somerset, Wisconsin, 1946. (Wisconsin Historical Society, WHi-25296)

track 9): "In the evening the French singers gathered at the La Grandeur home. They were Adelord Joseph Vanasse, the village druggist, and Dr. Phaneuf, who included with other songs the old French *Malbroque* as a duet in the manner to which the Somerset folks were accustomed. Mrs. C. Diotte was persuaded to contribute a voyageur song. These singers took turns with younger members of the group [including] Ernest Joseph Belisle, who had learned his songs from his grandfather" (Stratman-Thomas 1940–1960: August 8, 1946). Ernest Joseph Belisle (1900–1964), an auto mechanic, was born in Somerset to Paul Belisle and Sophie Tremblay, both of whom had grown up along the St. Lawrence River in Berthierville, Quebec, before immigrating to Wisconsin.

Belisle recorded nine songs for the Library of Congress, ranging from tragic ballads to comic love songs like "Je ne veux pas d'un avocat." Because of its refrain, this song is best known as "Marions marulette" in many versions found in western France, as well as in Quebec, with the rejected suitors also including a peddler and a doctor. Conrad Gauthier (1885–1964), a native of Quebec who performed folksongs on radio, recorded a version in 1928, which may be heard online (http://www.youtube.com/watch?v=VxXFsT5pU4Y, accessed July 4, 2012).

7   How They Sang the Marseillaise in Chippytown Falls

Spoken and sung by Charles Cardinal, Chippewa Falls, Wisconsin, August 13, 1946. Recorded by Helene Stratman-Thomas and Aubrey Snyder.
8409 A2

Now folks, I would like to tell you something about in the early nineteen hundreds, oh I should judge about nineteen hundred and six or seven, I run across French Canadian old lumberjack. And he met me one day, in the old saloon days, and he says: "Howdy do, your name is Cardinal, hain't it?"

I says, "Yes sir, it is."

"Well," he says, "you know, Mr. Cardinal, I hused to know your fader pretty well. And I know our honcle too, used to keep the hotel. And say, you know Mr. Cardinal, I'm like to tol' you somet'ing. You know how dey used to sing da 'Marseillaise' in Chippytown Falls?"

I say, "No, I do not."

"Well," he says, "dis is da way dey used to sing da 'Marseillaise' in Chippytown Falls."

Ol' Mose Sarazan
And Felix Cardinal
Johnnie Theriault
And Johnny Martineau,
Likewise h'ol Pete Lego

Charles Cardinal (1889–1983) was born in "Frenchtown" on the south side of Chippewa Falls to French Canadian immigrant parents. A house painter by trade, who in his sixties was president of Local 259 of the Brotherhood of Painters, Decorators, and Paperhangers of America, he fathered seven children with his wife, Frances Bergeron. A sociable fellow, Cardinal spent three months in jail for serving "intoxicating liquors" during Prohibition, a "light sentence" in view of his otherwise upright nature and many dependents (*Manitowoc Herald Times*, Thursday, August 8, 1929).

Cardinal's performances for the Library of Congress, all of them in a theatrical French-English dialect, included comic stories, recitations like "Little Bateese" by the Canadian dialect poet William Henry Drummond (1854–1907), and songs, including his localized version of the "Marseillaise." The original song, which became the French national anthem in 1795, was composed in 1792 by Claude Joseph Rouget de Lisle (1760–1836). The Chippewa Falls rendition omitted valiant French soldiers to intone the names of local French Canadians: Mose Sarazan owned the Ottawa House, a prominent hotel; Felix Cardinal was Charles's uncle and owned a saloon; Johnny Theriault owned a brickyard; and Pete Lego (Legault) was a noted French Ojibwe logger who figured in a cycle of comic anecdotes.

Pete Legault, now spelled Lego, of Chippewa Falls. Like Sevier Forcier, he could not read nor write, but starting in as a common woodsman by sheer ability he became a successful logger and in later years was interested in one of the large companies of Chippewa Falls. He was an interesting character, but unfortunately it is somewhat difficult to separate fact from fiction in the numerous stories that are told about him. Another old Frenchman, an intimate acquaintance of Legault, expressed the situation to me thus: Said he, "Pete's back was broad and when anyone heard a good story they would lay it on him."

One story that I heard many years ago, attributed to Legault, I am inclined to accept as true. It was told that once when in charge of a driving crew up river, and the water went so low that they had to quit work, his message to his superiors down river was a sketch of a peavey sticking upright in a log. (Bartlett 1929: 202)

The saloon where Cardinal heard the song featuring Lego was run by Eli Hodge (b. 1840) from the 1880s through the early 1900s and was a favorite gathering place for old lumberjacks of all nationalities (Cardinal 1981).

8 Michaud

Spoken and sung by Mary Agnes Starr, Waukesha, Wisconsin, August 28, 1946. Recorded by Helene Stratman-Thomas and Aubrey Snyder. Transcription, translation, and annotation by Anjili Babbar, with assistance from Sylvain Gaillard and Florence Théroud, 2012
8447 A2

Another play song is "Michaud est monté dans un pommier," or Michaud climbed up in the apple tree. The version which I sing came to me from my aunt, Eugenie Leroux Bachand. This song was described by Mrs. Kinzie in *Waubun* as sung by the voyageurs. In singing it every type of tree could be described.

Michaud est monté dans un pommier	Michaud climbed up in an apple tree
Pour trier[1] des pommes.	To pick some apples
La branche est cassée. Michaud est tombé!	The branch broke. Michaud fell!
Ou est-il Michaud? Michaud est sur le dos!	Where is Michaud? Michaud is flat on his back!
Ah réveille, réveille, Michaud.	Ah wake up, wake up, Michaud.
Ah réveille, réveille, Michaud.	Ah wake up, wake up, Michaud.
Michaud est monté dans un prunier	Michaud climbed up in a plum tree
Pour trier des pruniers.[2]	To pick some plums.
La branche est cassée. Michaud est tombé!	The branch broke. Michaud fell!
Ou est-il Michaud? Michaud est sur le dos!	Where is Michaud? Michaud is flat on his back!
Ah réveille, réveille, Michaud.	Ah wake up, wake up, Michaud.
Ah réveille, réveille, Michaud.	Ah wake up, wake up, Michaud.
Michaud est montée dans un Poirier	Michaud climbed up in a pear tree
Pour trier les poires.	To pick some pears.
La branche est cassée. Michaud est tombé!	The branch broke. Michaud fell!
Ou est-il Michaud? Michaud il est en haut!	Where is Michaud? Michaud is up high[3]
Bon!	Good!

Ah réveille, réveille, Michaud.   Ah wake up, wake up, Michaud.
Ah réveille, réveille, Michaud.   Ah wake up, wake up, Michaud.

------

1. *Trier* literally means "to pick out or screen" in France and Quebec. Perhaps it also means literally "to pick" (*cueillir*) in Starr's dialect, or perhaps she confused her verbs. On the other hand, if Michaud is choosing the best apples among many, *trier* makes sense.
2. Here the singer clearly means that Michaud wishes to pick *des prunes* (plums) and not *des pruniers* (plum trees).
3. Since Michaud has fallen for the *third* time, after having lost consciousness the first two times and having to be called to "wake up," it may be that Michaud is *en haut*, not in the tree, but in heaven.

Our itinerary took us to Waukesha, where we planned to record Mrs. Mary Agnes Starr's Canadian French songs. In 1871 Mrs. Starr's Grandmother and Grandfather Leroux came from the province of Ontario to settle in Oconto. Of Helen Nicholas Leroux's thirty-four grandchildren, Mrs. Starr believes she is the only one who has carried on an interest in the French songs. Her love for the songs she heard in the homes of the French people led her not only to preserve those which she had learned by rote, but also to make a study of the survival of French songs along the trails of the French explorers in America.

Out of her store of French songs she has developed fascinating lecture-song recitals, which she has presented to numerous organizations, schools, and colleges in the Midwest. For recording, Mrs. Starr selected carefully those songs which were her own family heritage. Among them . . . "Michaud," a favorite of her aunt, Eugenie Leroux Bachand. (Stratman-Thomas 1940-1960: August 28, 1946)

Mary Agnes Starr (1902–1999) was raised in the French Canadian logging community of Oconto, Wisconsin, the daughter of Edward and Elizabeth Leroux Barber. According to family tradition, her grandmother Julien Langlois Nicholas was singing her traditional lullabies minutes after her birth. Prior to marrying Morton Hull Starr in 1937, she worked as a rural schoolteacher and as a housemother for sororities at the University of Wisconsin–Whitewater and University of Wisconsin–Madison. Starr's autobiographical account of Franco-American folklore, *Pea Soup and Johnny Cake* (1981), details her lifelong passion for French songs as both a performer and an amateur folklorist. Her papers regarding this topic are in the archives of the University of Wisconsin–Milwaukee (http://digital.library.wisc.edu/1711.dl/wiarchives.uw-mil-uwmmss0028, accessed April 17, 2014).

Mary Agnes Starr

Diseuse and Interpreter

of

French-Canadian Folk Songs

in

Programs That Are Delightfully Different

Mary Agnes Starr, "Interpreter of French-Canadian Folk Songs"
brochure, 1930s. (Helene Stratman-Thomas Collection, Mills Music
Library, University of Wisconsin–Madison)

Well known in French Canada as a folksong for children (Mills 1960), "Michaud"
was, as Starr's spoken introduction attests, sung during the fur-trade era. Juliet Kinzie
(1806–1870), the wife of Indian agent John Kinzie, set down this account from a trip
between Portage and Green Bay in 1830.

The Canadian boatmen always sing while rowing, or paddling, and nothing encour-
ages them so much as to hear the *bourgeois* [boss] take the lead in the music. . . . The
Canadian melodies are sometimes very beautiful, and a more exhilarating mode of

travel can hardly be imagined than a voyage over these waters, amid all the wild mag-nificence of nature, with the measured strokes of the oar keeping time to the strains of "Le Rosier Blanc," "En roulant ma boule," or "Leve ton pied, ma jolie Bergere." The climax of fun seemed to be in a comic piece, which, however oft-repeated, appeared never to grow stale. It was somewhat after this fashion: "Michaud est monté dans un prunier." It was always a point of etiquette to look astonished at the luck of Michaud in remaining in the tree, spite of breaking the branch, and the joke had to be repeated through all the varieties of fruit-trees that Michaud might be supposed to climb. (Kinzie [1866] 1930: 47–49)

9   Bonsoir, mes amis / Good Night, My Friends

Spoken and sung by Marie Donalda Lagrandeur, Somerset, Wisconsin, August 8, 1946. Recorded by Helene Stratman-Thomas and Aubrey Snyder. Transcription, translation, and annotation by Anjili Babbar, with assistance from Sylvain Gaillard and Florence Théroud, 2012.

8390 B3

Here's a little French song that we sing when we've been gathered in the evening, and we're ready to say goodbye. Someone invariably bursts into song and starts singing, or else someone sits at the piano and plays this. And everybody sings.

Quand on est si bien ensemble,	When we get along so well together,
Quand on est si bien ensemble,	When we get along so well together,
Pourquoi donc, pourquoi donc se séparer?	Why then, why then part?
Bonsoir mes amis, bonsoir.[1]	Good night my friends, good night.
Bonsoir mes amis, bonsoir.	Good night my friends, good night.
Bonsoir mes amis, bonsoir mes amis.	Good night my friends, good night my friends.
Bonsoir mes amis, bonsoir.	Good night my friends, good night.
Au revoir, au revoir.	Goodbye, goodbye.

1. *Bonsoir* literally means "good evening," but it is used in this context to mark a parting at the end of an evening and hence is closer to "good night" in contemporary English.

Through Mrs. Mary Agnes Starr of Waukesha I had learned the names of singers of French-Canadian songs in Somerset on the St. Croix River. . . . Miss Lagrandeur not only

Marie Donalda Lagrandeur entertains Aubrey Snyder on her porch, Somerset, Wisconsin, 1946.
(Wisconsin Historical Society, WHi-25297)

persuaded others in Somerset to sing but also invited us to stay at her home and use
her living room for recording headquarters. . . . [She] concluded the evening with the
charming little "Au Revoir" which she had often heard the French guests sing as they
departed from her father's home. (Stratman-Thomas 1940–1960: August 8, 1946)

Stratman-Thomas recorded twenty-six French songs from eight singers that night. Marie
Donalda Lagrandeur (1894–1967) was editor of the *Somerset Courier* in the 1940s, as
well as a noted cook whose food traditions Mary Agnes Starr eventually documented
(1981: 25–28). Like her father, Henry Alfred Lagrandeur (1860–1923), Marie was born

in Somerset, but her songs came mostly from neighbors and the repertoire of her mother, Donata, who was born in Quebec in 1861 and immigrated to Wisconsin in 1886.

The French Canadian house party, or *veillée* (vigil), was a highly developed winter social institution with songs formalizing departures. The anthropologist Horace Miner mentions such a use of the song "Bonsoir" by Quebec's *habitants* (country folk) in the 1930s (1939: 164). Mary Agnes Starr described similar winter evenings in Wisconsin and Michigan's Upper Peninsula, especially at the New Year: "They called it *Courier le Vigne Allee*. One man would begin by calling on his neighbor and they would have a drink of wine together. Then they would proceed to the next house and have a drink with that neighbor. They would go on this way until there were about twenty or more in the group. The last house visited was that of the very richest man in the area as he alone would have enough glasses and wine to serve them all" (Starr 1981: 27). Elizabeth Baird (1810–1890), who settled in the old French fur-trading post of Green Bay in 1824, offers a vivid earlier account of a "bonjour" song that was the entrance counterpart to "Bonsoir's" leave-taking.

> On the eve of New Year's Day, great preparations were made by a certain class of elderly men, usually fishermen, who went from house to house in grotesque dress, singing and dancing. Following this they would receive gifts. Their song was often quite terrifying to little girls, as the gift asked for in the song was *la fille aine*, the eldest daughter. The song ran thus:

> | | |
> |---|---|
> | Bonjour le Maitre et la Maitresse, | Good day Master and Mistress, |
> | Et tout le monde du loger. | And everyone in the place. |
> | Si vous voulez nous rien | If you wish to give us nothing tell us, |
> | donner dittes le nous, | |
> | Nous vous demandons | We demand only your eldest daughter! |
> | seuiement la fille aine! | |

> As they were expected always, all would be prepared to receive them. (Frederick 1998: 4)

BELGIAN (WALLOON)

In the 1850s roughly fifteen thousand Walloon Belgians settled in northeastern Wisconsin, extending across parts of Brown, Door, and Kewaunee Counties and constituting the largest such enclave in the United States. Attracted by the availability of farmland, they also chose this area because their language closely resembled that of Green Bay's large French-speaking population. Here Walloon French flourished as the first language of rural Belgians well into the 1930s.

10 I Went to Market

Sung by Alfred Vandertie, Brussels, Wisconsin, August 24, 1940.
Recorded by Helene Stratman-Thomas and Robert F. Draves.
Transcription and translation by Francoise Lempereur, 1981.

4166 A1

I went to market with a *pania volant* [loose shirt].
The first one I met was *one fèye (d') on avocat* [a lawyer's daughter].

CHORUS:
And I love you *èt d'totes lès manires* [and in all ways].
And I love you *mais vos vos m'aimez pas* [but you don't love me].

I went to market with a *pania volant* [loose shirt].
I asked for fifty cents and she said *"Je n'avos pas"* ["I haven't them"].

She went upstairs *"po li trover sè papa"* [to find her father for me].
She came downstairs: *"le bounome i n'èst pus là"* ["The man isn't there"].

I squeezed her so hard that I *cassè les deux bras* [broke her two arms].
And it cost me five hundred for to get *er les deux bras* [her two arms back].

We had been directed to Al Vandertie, a young man with a very fine voice. His songs included love songs in the Walloon dialect. A little song, "I Went to Market," was typical of the mixture of the language from the old world with that of the new. The lines were composed of a smattering of both English and French dialect. Mr. Vandertie had learned the song from Gust Mathy, an old resident of Brussels. (Stratman-Thomas 1940–1960: August 42, 1940)

Alfred Vandertie's ancestors, whose surname was originally Vangindertaelen, came to Wisconsin from Belgium's Charleroi region in the 1850s. A relatively young man when recorded in 1940, Vandertie (1910–1998) was born in the Door County hamlet of Brussels and, for most of his working life, was a tavern keeper in nearby Algoma. He sang Belgian songs throughout his long life. In the early 1970s he was recorded by the Belgian folklorist Francoise Lempereur, who took him to Belgium in 1974, where he was given a hero's welcome. Lempereur subsequently took him to the National Mall in Washington, D.C., for the Smithsonian Institution's bicentennial Festival of American Folklife (Lempereur and Istasse 2011: 124). Vandertie was still singing for Belgian Days in Brussels when I first met him in 1993.

The 1880 census lists Gustave Mathy, Vandertie's source for this song, as a laborer who had been born in Belgium in 1851 and who was living with his fellow immigrant in-laws in De Pere. Mathy's mixed-language song of comic exaggeration about a country bumpkin's marketplace misadventures with a tricky lawyer's daughter has not been recorded in Belgium, however. According to Francoise Lempereur, who recorded identical lyrics from Vandertie in the 1970s, it is a "trilingual version of a bilingual song well known in French Canada" that was popularized by the *chanson* revivalist and Quebecois activist Gilles Vigneault (b. 1928). "It probably slid from Quebec to Wisconsin where Walloons transformed the text into French, a language not known to the performer, Alfred Vandertie" (Lempereur 1981; Lempereur and Istasse 2011: 120–124). Exilia Bellaire of Baraga, Michigan, recorded a French Canadian version of this song for Alan Lomax in 1938 (see notes to Lomax CD, track 9).

11 C'est l'café / It's the Coffee [the Kermiss Song]

Sung by Alfred Vandertie, Brussels, Wisconsin, August 24, 1940.
Recorded by Helene Stratman-Thomas and Robert F. Draves.

4166 A2

C'èst l'café, l'café, l'café	It's the coffee, the coffee, the coffee
Qui fait coqueter lè coméres.	Which causes women to chatter.
Abiye li coq'mwâr au fê	Now then—a kettle on the stove
Po fê one boune tasse dè café!	To make a nice cup of coffee!
Tchantez, l' djon—nèsse;	Young people—sing!
Tchantez lès bias! Tchantez lès bèles!	Sing, smart boys! Sing, pretty girls!
Vinoz danser à l' grande fièsse di Brussèle.	Come and dance at the great Brussels festival.

Po l' grande fièsse, dj'a l'èspèrance	For the great festival I expect
Qui l'timps f rè bia sins misères.	The weather to be perfect.
Dji vos-ègadje po l' preumêre danse.	I engage you for the first dance.
C'èst l' mia qui tot qwè qui dj' pou dîre.	It's the best thing I can say.

Alfred Vandertie and a Belgian friend, Belgian Days, Brussels, Wisconsin, 1993. (photo by author)

In late July 1993, seated in a car's front seat at the head of the Belgian Days parade and aided by a microphone with a speaker lashed to the car's windshield, Alfred Vandertie once again sang "C'est l'café," just as he had been singing it for at least sixty years. The November 21, 1933, edition of *The Manitowoc Herald-Times* reports on "the 75th anniversary of the 'First Kermiss' given by the Ernest Haucke Post of the American Legion Sunday afternoon and evening" with "old-time dancing," Belgian pies, a brief speech from Green Bay's Belgian consul on the "the migration of Belgians to America" and the "hardships endured by them in early days," and "Belgian folk songs" sung by "Alfred Vandertie, Brussels."

"C'est l'café" was used for generations in Wisconsin to invite people to the annual *kermiss* celebration, an Old World fall festival—featuring good food, dancing, and song—held by local Belgian and Dutch Catholic communities to raise funds for the church and have a good time. Vandertie's particular lyrics derive from words composed in 1854 by the Walloon poet Charles Werotte (1795–1870). The tune "C'est l'amour, l'amour" has been used for many folksongs in the Belgian region of Namur (Lempereur 1981).

Emile Boulanger, Dyckesville, Wisconsin, 1946. (Wisconsin Historical Society, WHi-25394)

12 Dance Tune

Played on fiddle by Emile Boulanger, Dyckesville, Wisconsin, August 31, 1946. Recorded by Helene Stratman-Thomas and Aubrey Snyder.
8461 A3

Emile Boulanger (1874–1965), a farmer and the son of Belgian immigrants, played many a quadrille for kermiss and other old-time dances. According to Louis Ropson—a farmer, church organist, and violin maker in the Dyckesville area who wrote to Stratman-Thomas on June 1, 1946—Boulanger possessed perfect rhythm "for old square dances" (i.e., quadrilles) favored by the immigrant generation of the 1850s. "Mr. Boulanger learn it from an old man who came from Belgium. He settle up in the village of Lincoln,

Kewaunee County. His name was Mr. Thiry"—very likely Constantine Thiry (b. 1824), who arrived in Wisconsin in 1857. Stratman-Thomas's field notes for August 31, 1946, tell us: "In order to have electricity, we asked permission to record in the village dance hall at Dyckesville. Snyder drove around to gather Mr. Ropson's friends, Anton de Beck and Emile Boulanger. . . . Without Louis Ropson's help as interpreter, we would have had difficulty, for although Mr. de Beck and Mr. Boulanger had been born in Dyckesville . . . and both were nearing eighty, they did not converse in English. . . . We recorded several dance tunes which Mr. Boulanger had played at dances ever since he was a boy. He too had made his own violin."

CORNISH

Between 1830 and 1850, roughly six thousand immigrants from Cornwall in the southwest of England, including many experienced miners, were drawn to southwestern Wisconsin's lead-mining district. Settling in such Grant, Iowa, and Lafayette County communities as Platteville, Hazel Green, Shullsburg, Linden, Mineral Point, and Dodgeville, they mined, farmed, built stone houses, practiced seasonal customs, made pasties and saffron buns, sang songs, and sustained legendary and jocular stories that extended Old World traditions. Stratman-Thomas, who hailed from Dodgeville and was of Cornish descent, was especially intrigued by Cornish tradition. In the late 1940s, after her work for the Library of Congress, she documented thirty-two Cornish cooks, carol singers, and storytellers from southwestern Wisconsin. Her unpublished Cornish field recordings and manuscripts are part of the Stratman-Thomas Collection of the Mills Music Library at the University of Wisconsin–Madison.

13 Cornish Story

Spoken by John Persons, Madison, Wisconsin, August 2, 1946.
Recorded by Helene Stratman-Thomas and Aubrey Snyder.
8378 B1

One of the characteristics of a Cornishman is the fact that he doesn't admit he doesn't know everything that you're talking about and has no knowledge of it, or that he can't understand or figure out anything that you're talking about.

REACHES 93 TODAY

John Persons

John Persons, 2318 E. Dayton St., celebrated his 93rd birthday today.

A former mail carrier at Dodgeville, Mr. Persons has lived in Madison for 20 years. He was awarded a plaque during Wisconsin's centennial year as a member of a family which operated a farm during the state's first 100 years.

Mr. Persons has two daughters, Mrs. Thomas Novick, with whom he and his wife, Nellie, make their home, and Mrs. James Soyde.

John Persons, Madison, Wisconsin, June 21, 1952. (newspaper clipping, *Capital Times*; Helene Stratman-Thomas Collection, Mills Music Library, University of Wisconsin–Madison)

And there was a couple young fellows that were working in the mine that decided they wanted to be captains in the mine. In order to be a captain, you must have a little education, to be able to keep time and figure some small sums.

So they decided to go to night school. And after having attended for some time, they met on the street, and one said to the other, he said, "Jack, how are you coming along with the schooling?"

"Oh, tolerably well, thank you. How are you?"

"Well, pretty well. Only one thing: I can't understand the problems."

"Huh! They're easy as pie for me."

"Well, then, I'll give 'e one."

"What is it?"

"Well, here are eleven pounds of mackerel, eleven cents a pound. What'll it come to?"

"Wait a minute, I'll have it for 'e." And he takes a little pencil and paper to figure, but he couldn't do it. And he says, "Jack, give me the problem once more, will 'e?"

"Eleven pound mackerel, eleven cents a pound."

"I'll have 'em in a minute. [Pause.] Now give me that problem exactly right. I want to git 'em for 'e."

"Well," he said, "eleven pound mackerel, eleven cents a pound."

"Mackerel, eh, mackerel?!? Well, no wonder I couldn't get it right. 'Ere all the time I been figuring eleven pound 'erring."

In keeping with English practice, New World mines throughout the nineteenth century were typically organized in quasi-military fashion with a mining captain presiding over a particular operation and wielding power over who was hired or fired. In the Upper Peninsula of Michigan's Copper Country, on the iron ranges of Michigan, Wisconsin, and Minnesota, and in southwestern Wisconsin's lead district, Cornish were most often the captains. This particular joke, sometimes involving codfish and shad, has also been told about fishermen (Johnson et al.: 1936: no. 934).

John Persons (1859–1954?) grew up in Survey Hollow, near Dodgeville, the son of Cornish immigrants. In the 1860s he and other Cornish boys went caroling at Christmas time, blackening their faces and turning their coats inside out "so the pixies wouldn't recognize them" (Stratman-Thomas 1940–1960: August 2, 1946). A farmer and rural mail carrier, he moved to Madison in 1932 to live with his daughter and son-in-law, sing occasional carols with Stratman-Thomas, and play golf.

WELSH

Welsh settled throughout southern Wisconsin mainly between 1840 and 1860, establishing farms, working alongside the Cornish in lead mines, and cutting stone in quarries. Steeped in traditions of choral singing and poetic recitation, they sustained annual *Eisteddfod*, or bardic competitions, in such Wisconsin cities as Milwaukee, Oshkosh, and Racine. In 1896, for example, the December 31 edition of the *Racine Journal* proclaimed that "Glees, choruses, and soloists are hard at work practicing for the great Eisteddfod to be given in this city on New Year's day," which was to be larger "than at any Eisteddfod ever held" in the region. Primarily Calvinistic Methodists, but including Presbyterians, Congregationalists, and Baptists, Wisconsin's Welsh also carried on the *Gymanfa Ganu*, a choral, nondenominational religious songfest that persists in the twenty-first century (Davies 2006: 23, 29–31, 42–43).

14 Cawn esgyn o'r / Paradise
Spoken by William Reese; sung by Reese and Selina Phillips, Dodgeville, Wisconsin, August 19, 1940. Recorded by Helene Stratman-Thomas and Robert F. Draves. Transcription, translation, and annotation by Maria Teresa Agozzino, Gwenan Puw, and Stephen Williams, January 2010
4159 A2

This verse [unintelligible]. It's hard for me to get all the syllables, hit all the notes, you know. There are too many notes or too many syllables. Now we'll see.

> William Reese and Helene Stratman-Thomas, Dodgeville, Wisconsin, 1940. (Wisconsin Historical Society, WHi-25174)

O fryniau Caersalem ceir gweled	From the hills of Jerusalem[1] can be seen
Holl daith yr anialwch i gyd;	The whole journey in the wilderness;[2]
Pryd hyn y daw troion yr yrfa[3]	At this period come events from the journey
Yn felys i lanw ein bryd;	Sweetly to fill our minds;[4]
Cawn edrych ar stormydd ac ofnau,	We can look at storms and fears,
Ac angau dychrynllyd a'r bedd,	The horror of death and the grave,
A ninau'n diangol o'u cyrhaedd,	While we are safe from their clutches
Yn nofio mewn cariad a hedd.	Swimming in love and peace.[5]

------

1. Regarding the translation of *Caersalem* as Jerusalem, a *caer* is a fortified city and a common prefix in many Welsh place names.
2. Journey in the wilderness is a common Christian metaphor from both the Old and New Testaments, from Moses and the Israelites' forty years in the wilderness to Christ's temptation by the Devil during his period of fasting in the wilderness.
3. Literally the "twist and turbulent events of one's metaphoric journey through life," *troion yr yrfa* is densely layered religious imagery common to many hymns.
4. Here "sweetly" connotes a sense of pleasure or triumph at having withstood successfully the challenges faced on life's journey.
5. This is an affirmation of Christian faith, echoing the standard human fears of death and suffering, with the reassurance that "we" are safe in God's love, "swimming in peace and love."

When we started out on our collecting tour, I suggested going first into the southwestern part of the state, which I knew best. Our first stop was in Dodgeville, where we called on Dr. William Reese, a Welsh tenor. Dr. Reese, who was then in his eighties, asked one of the sopranos of the old Welsh Presbyterian choir, Miss Selina Phillips, to sing some Welsh hymns with him. (Stratman-Thomas 1940–1960: August 19, 1940)

Set to the old Welsh folk tune "Crugybar," which takes its name from a village in Carmarthenshire, the song sung by Reese and Phillips was composed by the Calvinistic Methodist minister and hymnodist David Charles (1762–1834) of Carmarthenshire. It was published in 1918 in *Cân a Mawl: Llyfr Hymnau A Thonau Methodistiaid Calfinaidd Unol Dalaethau Yr America / Song and Praise: The Hymnal of the Calvinistic Methodist Church of the United States of America* (Protheroe 1918: no. 243). Phillips and Reese, who sang from memory, performed only the second of the song's two verses.

Selina Phillips (1871–1943) bequeathed her copy of the hymnal to Stratman-Thomas, and it is now in the Mills Music Library. William Reese (1858–1949), referred to in a Madison newspaper profile as "one of Wisconsin's pioneer horse doctors" (*Capital Times*, July 10, 1941), was not a veterinarian but a doctor who made house calls in the

Primitive Methodist Church, Jenkynsville, Wisconsin, 2011. (photo by author)

horse-and-buggy days. Highly respected in the Dodgeville area, he was buried nearby in the Welsh cemetery at Rockwell Mills.

15 My Welsh Relation

Sung by Dr. Daniel W. Wickham, Dodgeville, Wisconsin, August 19, 1940. Recorded by Helene Stratman-Thomas and Robert F. Draves. Annotations by Maria Teresa Agozzino, 2010.

4159 A2

I was born not far from Carmel
In a place called the Welsh Mountains,
When one day I and Mary
Went to ride upon the donkey.

CHORUS:
Yes, you never did see,
Yes, you never did see,
Yes you never did see
Such a big time before.

Then we went to railway station
For to meet a Welsh relation,
A William Jones a cwm y Henry,[1]
Come to see the open railway.

CHORUS:
Was you never did see,
Was you never did see,
Was you never did see
Such a big time before.

There was John and Sean and Mary
Drinking pie and eating sherry,
Dance away to tune o' fiddle,
Up the side and down the middle.

Then we went to see the engine.
It was puffin' and a-blowin'.
It were made o' wondrous power.
It could go three mile an hour.

It was puff and blow and whistle,
And making noise just like old Difil,[2]
And poor Mary was scairt all over,
Thought the Old Chap had come for her.

She is heavy, sister Bella.
She is heavy umbrella.
She is, thinks so much about it
She is never going without it.

------

1. "Cwm y Henry" or "Henry Valley," with its mixture of Welsh and English suggests a bilingual singer.
2. Wickham's *difil* sounds much like *diafol*, Welsh for "devil."

We then carried the recording equipment up three long flights of stairs to the dental office of Dr. Dan Wickham. Dr. Wickham had consented to sing a little song in Welsh brogue, "My Welsh Relation," which had circulated through Iowa County for many years. Dr. Wickham had a patient in the chair, but when she heard our conversation with Dr. Wickham, she called out, "Go ahead, Dan, sing. I'm in no hurry!" So when we had the equipment all set up, Dr. Wickham sang for us, with his patient as the audience. (Stratman-Thomas 1940–1960: August 19, 1940)

Daniel W. Wickham was born in the Dodgeville area in 1875. His parents, William Wickham (b. 1839) and Mary Griffiths (b. 1844), hailed, respectively, from Cardiganshire and Carmarthenshire, both in South Wales. Wickham learned this song from Tom Jones, an erstwhile Baptist, from the Garrison Grove neighborhood near Dodgeville, adding that it was well known throughout Iowa County. It uses the widely familiar Welsh tune for "Y mochyn du" (number 16 below), and with its comic account of an encounter by Welsh country folk with an early railroad train, it may well have been composed in Wales. In 1953, for example, Alan Lomax recorded another comic railroad song situated in the Aberdare Valley in 1846, "Cosher Bailey," set to the tune of "Y mochyn du" and sung by John H. Davies of Treorchy, South Wales (MacColl 1963). Its chorus and one of its verses closely resemble the chorus and fourth verse of "My Welsh Relation."

Cosher Bailey had an engine
It was always wanting mending,
And according to the power,
She could do four miles an hour.

CHORUS:
Did you ever saw,
Did you ever saw
Such a funny sight before?

16 Y mochyn du / The Black Pig
Sung by Hugh P. Jones, Redgranite, Wisconsin, July 20, 1941. Recorded by Helene Stratman-Thomas and Robert F. Draves. Transcription, translation, and annotations by Maria Teresa Agozzino, Gwenan Puw, Stephen Williams, January 2010. Agozzino added that "Welsh is far from standardized, and this version suggests North Wales origins." She and her colleagues also note, "Welsh can be rather nuanced. For example, in verse 5, the word $w\hat{r}$ is a lenited form of $gw\hat{r}$ [man] but can suggest gentleman or holy man. *Parchedig* means 'reverend' (as in 'respected one')—the context suggests Twm Gruffydd is a minister [or] man of the church."

4967 B1

Holl drigolion bro a bryniau	All inhabitants of the area and surrounding hills[1]
Dewch i wrando hyn o eiriau.	Come and listen to these words.

Fe gewch hanes rhyw hen fochyn
A fu farw yn dra sydyn.

CHORUS:
O mor drwm yr ydym ni,
O mor drwm yr ydym ni,
Y mae yma alar chalon
Ar ôl chladdu'r mochyn du.

Beth oedd achos ei afiechyd?
Beth roes derfyn ar ei fywyd?
Er mae blas oedd achos angau,
I'r hen fochyn i fynd adre.

Fe rônt fwy o faith i'r mochyn,[3]
Na allasai fola bach ei dderbyn,
Er main chydig o funudau
Dyma'r mochyn yn mynd adref.

Mofyn hers o Aberteifi
A cheffyla i chario'i fyny;
Y cyfylai'n llawn morwyni
Ro'l i ddangos parch i'r mochyn.

Y parchedig wˆr Twm Gruffydd
Ydoedd yno yn pregethu;
Pawb yn sobor anghyffredin
Ro'l i ddangos parch i'r mochyn.

Mar, ci Joseff Pigi Wyli,
Ydoedd yno yn blaenori;
Pawb o'r teulu yno'n canlyn

Ro'l i ddangos parch i'r mochyn.

Melys iawn i'w gael ei sleisen
O gig mochyn gyda tharten,
Ond yn awr rhaid fyw ag hynny
Mochyn du sydd wedi marw.

Bellach rydwyf yn terfynnu.
Nawr yn rhodio hebio ganu.
Gan dymuno peidiwch ddilyn

Siampl ddrwg wrth fwydo'r mochyn.

I'll tell you the tale of an old pig
That died very suddenly.

CHORUS:
Oh how heavy we are with sadness,
Oh how heavy we are with sadness,
Here is heart-piercing grief
After burying the black pig.

What was the cause of his illness?
What put an end to his life?
Indeed it was greed that caused his demise,
Causing the old pig to go home.[2]

They gave the pig too much nourishment,
More than his little belly could hold,
And in only a few minutes
The pig went home.[4]

They fetched a hearse from Aberteifi
With horses to draw it;
The verges were lined with maidens[5]
Come to show respect for the pig.

The reverend man Thom Griffith
Came there to deliver the sermon;[6]
Everyone was incredibly solemn
To show respect for the pig.

Mar, the dog of Joseph "Pigi Wili,"[7]
Was there as chief mourner;
The whole family was there to
    follow [the hearse]
To show respect for the pig.

It's very tasty to have a slice
Of bacon with a pie,
But now we'll have to live without it
Since the black pig has died.

Now it's time to conclude.
Now it's time to give up singing.
Here's hoping that you will
    avoid this bad example
Of how to feed a pig.

---

1. *Bro a bryniau*: an idiomatic phrase meaning "hills and vicinity," that is, the neighborhood.
2. "To go home": an idiomatic phrase referring to death and the prospect of heaven.
3. "Faith" may be a mutated form of *maeth* (nourishment) but could possibly also be *haidd* (barley).
4. A euphemism for death.
5. Probably serving maids, grieving women rather than literally virgins.
6. "The sermon," that is, the funeral address.
7. In Wales people are often known colloquially by the name of their farmstead, as here.

Stratman-Thomas recorded "Y mochyn du" from Hugh P. Jones in the village of Redgranite on July 20, 1941. Although her notes reveal only that Jones was born in 1888, he was also one of several workers in that area's stone quarries who were interviewed for the Wisconsin Historical Society in 1965. Jones learned to cut blocks at age thirteen from his father in a Welsh quarry. Following the advice of a childhood friend who had settled in Redgranite, a destination for immigrant stonecutters, Jones arrived there in 1909. Over the next thirty years he wielded an eight-pound hammer as a stone-cutter, mostly in Redgranite but also in the greater Milwaukee area and Cincinnati, Ohio. As asphalt and concrete all but eliminated demand for paving stones by 1940, Jones found work in various factories around Wisconsin, retiring in 1955. Through it all, he kept a family home in Redgranite, where his wife, Florence, an immigrant from Northern Ireland whom he married in 1917, was a cook and maid at the Western Hotel (H. Jones 1965).

When asked by Stratman-Thomas for the Welsh text of his song, together with a translation of it into English, Jones responded with a typescript, "committed to writing by Hugh P. Jones," consisting of twelve stanzas and a chorus, despite his having sung no more than eight stanzas in 1941. His transcription of the chorus matched his singing verbatim, and his rendering of the first stanza differed only in the third line from what he had sung then ("Cewch chi hanes rhyw hen fochyn" [You'll get the story of an old pig] instead of "Fe gewch hanes rhyw hen fochyn" [I'll tell you the tale of an old pig]). As for the other seven stanzas sung by Jones, however, they neither correlated easily with the any of the stanzas he provided nor were they accompanied by close translations. Stratman-Thomas's papers also include what appears to be a typeset broadside that corresponds exactly with the verse and chorus Jones "committed to writing," with the exception of one letter, a probable typographical error.

From an undated letter in her files, it is evident that Stratman-Thomas sought help from Moses Morgan, a renowned singer and choir director from Pickett, Wisconsin, from whom she also recorded Welsh songs. Morgan in turn consulted D. Jenkins

Williams of Wausau, who enlisted one T. J. Davies of Wales, Wisconsin, for additional help. The following letter from D. Jenkins Williams to Moses Morgan is worth quoting:

> My Dear Moses:
>
> "Y Mochyn Du" is really an interesting old Welsh folk song. It has a pathos to it as well as a humorous side, and the pathos is what I would not be able to preserve in trans- lation. And without the pathos, to my mind, it would be ridiculous, and we must not make it ridiculous.
>
> Even the title "Y Mochyn Du" has a deep pathos, for back there in the rural areas of Wales to lose a black pig was to lose a winter's living. It was a real loss, and, if you can express pathos by a translation such as "After Burying the Old Black Pig," you are a more expert translator than I am.
>
> D. Jenkins Williams

Williams appended to this letter T. J. Davies's "bravely offered" translation of the first five stanzas of the song, plus its chorus, in verses that stray from the literal sense of the Welsh text because of Davies's attempt to echo its meter and rhyme. Here is his transla- tion of the opening stanza and the chorus:

> All ye folks from vale and mountain,
> I'm about to raise a curtain
> On the tale of black piggy
> That died sudden. 'Twas a pity.
>
> Oh how gloomy we all were;
> Oh how gloomy we all were.
> We had real heartaches, watching,
> While they buried him out there.

In the end, Stratman-Thomas gave up the effort to obtain an accurate transcription and translation of this song.

Unbeknown to Stratman-Thomas, who wrote in her field notes that the song was "several hundred years old," "Y mochyn du" was composed about 1854 by John Owen (1836–1915) of Eglwyswrw, Wales. A shepherd and estate servant in his youth who was nonetheless proficient in music and literate in both Welsh and English, Owen based the song on the loss of a valued pig belonging to "one David Thomas, of Parc-y-maes, Brynberian." Soon after, Owen's employer, Mrs. Thomas James of Felin Wrdan (Jordan's

Mill), published "Y mochyn du" as a broadside: "The ballad was sung at local fairs by the well-known ballad-monger Levi Gibbon, who also added some of the verses. Soon it became one of the most popular of Welsh ballads, sung not only throughout Wales, but in all quarters of the globe where Welshmen gathered" (Welsh Biography Online, http://wbo.llgc.org.uk/en/index.html, accessed January 25, 2012). A twelve-verse version of the ballad, published about 1885 in Aberdare, Wales, by W. Lloyd and son, is identical, with the exception of a few words, to the one supplied by Hugh P. Jones. Made accessible thanks to the Library of Cardiff University, it is accompanied online by an undated twelve-verse English translation that is quite distinct from T. J. Davies's "bravely offered" rendition, albeit published by the Davies Brothers of Aberdare. Composer John Owen's autobiography, written after his career as a Calvinistic Methodist minister, offered this confession: "I wrote 'Y Mochyn Du,' now so well known throughout the land; a song that will continue to corrupt the tastes of our young people when the tongue that first sang it will have long been silent in the grave. Forgive, O Lord, the sins of my youth!"

17 Siani bach / Dearest Sian

Sung by John Williams and chorus at the Welsh Gymanfa Ganu, Pickett, Wisconsin, August 25, 1940. Recorded by Helene Stratman-Thomas and Robert F. Draves. Transcription, translation, and annotations by Maria Teresa Agozzino, Gwenan Puw, Stephen Williams, January 2010.

4183

Mi ddymunais fil o weithiau,	I have wished a thousand times,
Hob y deri dan do,	Hob y deri dan do,[1]
Fod fy mron o wydyr golau.	That my breast was of clear glass.
Dyma ganu eto	Let's sing again
Fel y gallo'r ddyn gael weled,	So that one can see,
Siân, w f'annwyl Siân,	Sian, oh my dearest Sian,
Fod fy nghalon mewn caethiwed.	That my heart is captive.
CHORUS:	*CHORUS:*
O dro mwyn, ddoi di'r llwyn	O[2] pleasant time, will you come to the woods[3]
Seinio'r fangre Siâni bach fwyn?	To make noise in this place, my sweet little Siani?[4]
O dro mwyn, ddoi di'r llwyn	O pleasant time, will you come to the woods

FOLLOWING PAGES: John Williams leads Welsh singers at a *Gymanfa Ganu* in the Peniel Church near Pickett, Winnebago County, Wisconsin, 1946. (Wisconsin Historical Society, WHi-7180)

Seinio'r fangre Siâni bach fwyn?	To make noise in this place, my sweet little Siani?
Trwm yw'r plwm a thrwm yw'r cerrig,	Heavy is lead and heavy is stone,
Hob y deri dan do,	Hob y deri dan do,
Trwm yw calon bob dyn unig.	Heavy is the heart of each lonely man.
Dyma ganu eto.	Let's sing again.
Trymaf peth rhwng haul a ddaear,	But the heaviest thing between heaven and earth,[5]
Siân, w f'annwyl Siân,	Sian, my dearest Sian,
Canu 'n iach lle byddo cariad.	Is saying goodbye to love.[6]
Hebddu yw dy lais yn canu,	Without her your voice when singing,
Hob y deri dan do,	Hob y deri dan do,
I hen fuwch pan fo hi'n brefu.	Is like an ancient cow mooing.
Dyma ganu eto.	Let's sing again.
Neu gi dall yn clepian cyfarth,	Or like a blind dog's incessant bark,[7]
Siân, w f'annwyl Siân,	Sian, my dearest Sian,
Wedi colli ffordd i'r buarth.	When it's lost its way (back) to the farmyard.

------

1. Traditional folksong refrain, commonly used as a filler line in folksongs.
2. Note risqué innuendo in chorus.
3. *Llwyn*, a small woodland, bushy area.
4. Diminutive, affectionate form of Sian.
5. Literally "between sun and earth."
6. The literal translation of this idiomatic phrase is "singing healthily," but in this context it is an expression of deep grief and loss.
7. *Clepian cyfarth* is an idiomatic phrase that has suggestions of loud resonant barking, almost like something banging. Note the onomatopoeic effects caused by the explosive consonant sounds.

We drove on to the Peniel Church, where the Morgans and all the other Welsh of that area were singing wholeheartedly the fine old Welsh hymns. We could scarcely get into the church as it was so crowded, but we soon made ourselves part of this hymn-singing festival. (Stratman-Thomas 1940–1960: August 25, 1940)

The rural church where Stratman-Thomas recorded John Williams and other singers in 1940 is in Winnebago County, not far from Oshkosh, in a part of Wisconsin where organized Welsh singing has flourished from the mid-nineteenth century to the present. Six years later, someone named John Williams was photographed leading Welsh singers from the pulpit of the Peniel Church amid another Gymanfa Ganu. We do not know for certain if it is the same person since John Williams is a very common name. We do know, however, that the racy love song "Siani bach" would not have been sung in church.

For this performance, rendered in call-and-response pattern, Williams is joined by two men and a woman as he takes the lead for the first, third, fifth, and seventh line of each verse, then forms a quartet with them on alternating lines and the chorus. "Siani bach" is an old Welsh folksong with considerable variation probably owing to a tradition, formalized by the Eisteddfod, that fostered poetic competition and improvisation. The Welsh composer Henry Brinley Richards (1817–1885), for example, published quite different texts of "Siani bach" from North and South Wales in his popular folksong collection *The Songs of Wales* (1873). Although thematically related, and sharing parts of the chorus and repetitive alternating lines in each verse, the performance by Williams and company is yet another distinct rendition. Intriguingly, the recurring "hob y deri dan do" refrain, which literally refers to a pig under the oaks, occurred, along with occasional invocations of "Siani bach," in the sea-shanty choruses of Welsh sailors in the era of sail (Hugill 1961).

AFRICAN AMERICAN

Wisconsin's small nineteenth-century population of African Americans swelled with the Great Migration from the rural South to the urban North that commenced during World War I and continued into the post–World War II era. Largely attracted by industrial and service jobs in Racine, Kenosha, Milwaukee, Beloit, Janesville, and Madison, African Americans brought with them a wealth of traditional song. The African American folksongs recorded by Stratman-Thomas, however, came from one of Wisconsin's two significant pre–Civil War rural black settlements, the Pleasant Ridge community between Beetown and Lancaster in Grant County (Cooper 1977: 19–26).

18 Hide Thou Me

Sung and spoken by Lillie Greene Richmond, Lancaster, Wisconsin, August 1946. Recorded by Helene Stratman-Thomas and Aubrey Snyder.

8432 A3

In Thy cleft, oh rock of ages, hide Thou me.
Be now my soul's eternal treasure, hide Thou me.
In the sight of Jordan's billows

Let Thy bosom be my piller.[1]
Hide me, oh Thou rock of ages, safe in Thee.

From the snares of sinful pleasure, hide Thou me.
And when in glory dawns the morrow, hide Thou me.

[Spoken:] How's that?

———

1. "Piller" is a common dialect rendering of "pillow" and, since bosoms typically figure poetically
   as pillows, that is likely what Richmond intended. Yet the identically pronounced "pillar" is also
   commonly used in such songs to suggest reliance on a powerful deity.

Lillie Greene Richmond (1862–1952) was born a slave on the Fourth of July in St. Charles County, Missouri. When she was a year old, her grandparents, John and Lillie Smith Greene, led their extended family to St. Louis, with help from the Underground Railroad, thence by train to Dubuque, Iowa, and overland to the Pleasant Ridge community, where free blacks had established farms in 1848 (Cooper 1977: 1–2). Dancing and both secular and religious singing flourished in the community, and Lillie Greene "was quite a singer in her day and also went to lots of dances" (Crichton 1946). She married a local man, Romulus Rufus Richmond, in 1880, and the couple moved to Chariton in south-central Iowa in 1887. The Richmonds raised ten children, while Romulus presided over a church and Lillie was a cook at the Burlington Depot Hotel. Throughout the years, they maintained connections with Pleasant Ridge, and as a widow with grown children, Lillie returned to Wisconsin in the 1940s.

Sharing the phrase "rock of ages" with the better-known song of the same name, "Hide Thou Me" was composed by Fanny Crosby (1820–1915), a staunch Methodist and prolific hymnodist whose works were especially popular in revivals and widely published in such anthologies as *Redemption Songs* (Sweeney et al. 1889). Richmond truncates the three-verse original and departs from it in word choice and phrasing, suggesting that she knew it chiefly through oral tradition.

19 Little Old Log Cabin in the Lane

Sung by Lillie Greene Richmond, Lancaster, Wisconsin, August 1946.

Recorded by Helene Stratman-Thomas and Aubrey Snyder.

8432 A2

I am getting old and feeble now and cannot work no more.
Lay aside the rust, the bladed hoe to rest.[1]
Old Mistress and Old Massa are lying side-by-side,
And their spirits are roving with the blessed.

The things, they have changed, the darkies dead and gone.
I cannot hear them singing in the cane.
All the friend that they have left me is that little dog of mine,
In the little old log cabin in the lane.

———

1. Richmond sings this confusing phrase confidently, suggesting she sang it this way regularly. In other
versions, the words are "That rusted bladed hoe I've laid to rest."

"Little Old Log Cabin in the Lane" was composed in 1871 by William S. Hays (1837–
1907) of Louisville, Kentucky, whose sentimental minstrel-show songs resembled the
popular creations of Stephen Foster. Widely appreciated by blacks and whites alike, the
song entered oral tradition. It was also frequently recorded by early hillbilly musicians,
most notably by Fiddlin' John Carson of Atlanta, whose version was issued on the Okeh
label in 1923 (Meade 2002: 345–346).

20 One More River

Sung by Lillie Greene Richmond, Lancaster, Wisconsin, August 1946.

Recorded by Helene Stratman-Thomas and Aubrey Snyder.

8434 A4

One more river,
And that's the river of Jordan.
One more river,
And that's the river to cross.

The animals came in two-by-two,
There's one more river to cross.
The elephant and the kangaroo,
That's one more river to cross.

Said the ant to the elephant, "Quit your pushing."
There's one more river to cross.

First published in 1881, with words by James Hosey and music by Thomas P. Westendorf, the much lengthier original song invokes both Moses leading the children of Israel toward the Jordan River and Noah loading his ark with two creatures of every kind. Intended for the minstrel stage and originally written in exaggerated eye-dialect ("Dar's One More Ribber to Cross"), this song—which is definitely not performed in "coon song" fashion by Lillie Richmond—had entered oral tradition by the late nineteenth century and was subsequently collected in numerous versions by folklorists in North Carolina, Ohio, and Arkansas. The prominent black bandleader Lt. Jim Europe also recorded a version in 1919, as did the Southern white banjo player Uncle Dave Macon in 1935 (Meade 2002: 575).

ANGLO-AMERICAN

Anglo-Americans from New England, New York, and Pennsylvania established towns and farms throughout southern Wisconsin in the first half of the nineteenth century, along with immigrants directly from England, especially in the agricultural and lead-mining district of southwestern Wisconsin. After the Civil War, northern New Englanders and Anglo-Canadians were prominent in northern Wisconsin's logging and sawmill industry, which also recruited Southern Appalachians around the turn of the twentieth century. Their rich repertoires included singing games, comic recitations, Old World riddling and murder ballads, and the lyric folksongs of farmers and laborers.

21 Chase the Buffalo
Sung by Preston Willis, Linden, Wisconsin, August 1946.
Recorded by Helene Stratman-Thomas and Aubrey Snyder.
8423 B1

Arise, my true love, and present to me your hand,
And we'll take a pleasant ramble through some far distant land

< Lillie Richmond (*right*) and an unidentified woman, Lancaster, Wisconsin, 1946. (Wisconsin Historical Society, WHi-25304)

Where Jim Hawkins shot Jim Buzzard, and Jim Buzzard shot Jim Crow.
And we'll rally 'round the wild woods and chase the buffalo.

And chase the buffalo, and chase the buffalo,
We'll rally 'round the wild woods and chase the buffalo.

Evidence of this song's English origin is offered by William Alexander Barrett (1836–1891), who included a version, "The Buffalo," in *English Folk-Songs* (1890: 18–19). As his preface declares, the songs Barrett published were "noted down from the lips of singers in London streets, roadside inns, harvest homes, festivals on the occasion of sheep shearing, at Christmas time, at ploughing matches, rural entertainments of several kinds, and at the 'unbending' after choir suppers in country districts." This particular song, however, "probably belongs to the early part of the eighteenth century" and "was very popular with Londoners."

Folklorists have reported many versions extending from the East through the Midwest to the Great Plains, where prior to the Civil War it had become a singing game, or "play party," for courting-age adolescents whose Methodist or Baptist or Presbyterian faith deemed dancing to the fiddle as sinful (Wolford [1917] 1959: 114, 225, 302). Stratman-Thomas tells us nothing about the song, its use, or its singer. From census and newspaper sources, however, we know that Preston Willis was born in 1883 in the hamlet of Mifflin in western Iowa County, Wisconsin. An educator and a farmer into the 1950s in the nearby Linden area, where he served as high school principal in the 1930s, he also sang the comic minstrel song "Old Dan Tucker" for the Library of Congress. Preston's "Chase the Buffalo" includes a line concerning Jim Hawkins, Jim Buzzard, and Jim Crow not found elsewhere. "Jim Crow" is the capering buffoon of blackface minstrelsy created by Thomas D. Rice in the 1830s; "buzzard lopes" were standard minstrel-show dances; whereas Jim Hawkins is the cabin-boy hero of Robert Louis Stevenson's *Treasure Island* (1883). Preston's particular rendering probably derived at some point from lines in versions of this song regarding a land "where the hawk caught the buzzard and the buzzard stubbed his toe" (e.g., Wolford [1917] 1959: 225).

22 Barker's Call

Spoken by Hamilton Lobdell, Mukwonago, Wisconsin, June 24, 1941.
Recorded by Helene Stratman-Thomas and Robert F. Draves.
4961 A2

And the next curiosity is Madame Sherwood, the great Irish giantess, weighing an enormous sight of 675 pounds. Exhibited here for the mere trifle of 25 cents, one quarter of a dollar.

We have here on exhibition large sticks of matrimonial candy. Sweet at one end and sour at the other. Striped way around once and half way back. Contains a quart of molasses and a half a pound of sugar. And here we are, squandering it away at half-price for the mere trifle of 10 cents a stick.

We also have here on exhibition large glasses of strawberry lemonade. Made five hundred feet below the surface of the earth and drawed up by a telegraph wire. Have a drink? [Laughter]

In response to a newspaper article concerning the recording project of the University of Wisconsin, we received a letter from a young woman, Mrs. Lee Lobdell, of Mukwonago, Wisconsin. Mrs. Lobdell wrote that she was sure some of the songs that her husband's grandfather sang should be preserved on records. We had gone to visit the grandfather, Mr. Hamilton Lobdell, in June of 1941. Although he was at the time eighty-seven years of age, blind and frail, he sang for us all afternoon. When we suggested that he rest now and then, he would lie back on the couch, but he kept on singing. His songs were those he had sung as a boy for entertainment at church and school "socials" and included a great miscellany of ballads and popular songs of earlier decades: "The Girl with the Waterfall," "Daisy Dean," "Little Nell of Narragansett Bay," and "Lost on the Lady Elgin." His prize offering was "Reuben Wright and Phoebe Brown." I have played Mr. Lobdell's recording of this yarn for many groups throughout Wisconsin since 1941. The delight of those who have heard it is proof of Mr. Lobdell's inborn ability as an entertainer. (Stratman-Thomas 1940–1960: June 24, 1941)

Hamilton Lobdell was born in 1854 in Waukesha County, Wisconsin, to parents who had come from New York State. His spoken and sung performance of "Reuben Wright and Phoebe Brown" that so appealed to Stratman-Thomas was issued on her

Helene Stratman-Thomas records Hamilton Lobdell, Mukwonago, Wisconsin, July 13, 1941. (newspaper clipping, *Wisconsin State Journal*; Helene Stratman-Thomas Collection, Mills Music Library, University of Wisconsin–Madison)

"Kentuck" ballad singer Ollie Jacobs in her rural Langlade County home, 1941. (Wisconsin Historical Society, WHi-25178)

Folk Music from Wisconsin (1960). It was likely acquired thanks to Hamlin's Wizard Oil, a cure-all created in 1861 by the Chicago-based Hamlin Brothers, who hired traveling medicine-show troupes to hawk their product throughout the Midwest with songs and comedy supplemented by such songbooks as *Humorous and Sentimental Songs: As Sung throughout the United States by Hamlin's Wizard Oil Free Concert Troupes* (1870). Lobdell's barker's call, included here, emulates the facetious hyperbole of traveling medicine-show and circus sideshow pitchmen that captivated him as a boy. Although billed as "The Giant Lady" rather than "The Irish Giantess," Madame Sherwood was a sideshow attraction in the 1850s and 1860s. Only five feet eight inches in height, she measured an astounding seven feet around the waist and did indeed weigh 675 pounds.

23 My Old Hen's a Good Old Hen

Sung by Pearl Jacobs Borusky, Antigo, Wisconsin, August 30, 1940.
Recorded by Helene Stratman-Thomas and Robert F. Draves.
4174 A3

My old hen's a good old hen,
She lays eggs for the section men.
Sometimes one, sometimes two,
Sometimes enough for the whole darn crew.

Cluck, old hen, cluck I tell you.
Cluck, old hen, or I'm a-gonna sell you.
Cluck, old hen, cluck I say.
Cluck, old hen, I'll give you away.

Pearl Jacobs Borusky (1899–1973) was born near Grayson in Carter County, Kentucky. In 1906 she traveled with her parents, Madison Green Jacobs and Ollie Jacobs, to settle on a farm near Bryant in Langlade County, Wisconsin. The Jacobs were part of a larger migration of Eastern Kentuckians who, beginning in 1903, sought farmland and woods work in northern Wisconsin. Their neighbors included Poles, one of whom, Rodney Borusky, Pearl married. The Jacobs were a singing family and, like other Kentucks (as they were called in the region), sustained an old-time repertoire.

In the 1930s fifty-six of the family's traditional songs were chronicled by Asher Treat (1907–2004) for an essay published in the *Journal of American Folklore* (Treat 1939; see also Stuttgen 1991). A 1925 graduate of Antigo High School along with one of the Jacobs children (Paul), Treat eventually became a professor of biology at City College in New York. An accomplished French horn player, who performed briefly with the New York Philharmonic, he had read Cecil Sharp's *English Folk Songs from the Southern Appalachians* (1932) and soon after, struck by parallel songs figuring in the lives of the Jacobs family, not only wrote down their words and tunes but also described the singers themselves, including Pearl Jacobs Borusky: "She is tall, thin, and dark, with a high forehead, high cheek-bones, large expressive eyes, and a thin, sensitive mouth. She possesses the same gentle and cheerful dignity which appears in the other members of the family and is reflected in her two children. During the past few years she has learned the importance of collecting and preserving the songs which form so intimate a part of

Asher Treat, Antigo, Wisconsin, 1940. (Wisconsin Historical Society, WHi-25411)

her and her people's experience. She became accustomed to singing the songs phrase by phrase, so as to make the notation of them easy; and she has gone to much trouble to refresh her own extensive memory by conferring with her relatives and writing down the words to many of the songs in advance of my infrequent collecting trips."

Borusky's concern with the precise words of songs likely accounts for the exact match between her recorded performance of "Cluck Old Hen" in 1940 and the words written down some years before by Asher Treat. More remarkably, she sang "Last Saturday Night I Entered a House" (the next song included here) exactly as her mother had performed it in the 1930s. She had learned "Cluck Old Hen" from her father, Madison Green Jacobs (1862–1935). The song, which exists in many versions, has been widely known throughout the Southern Appalachians. The "section men" in this version are part of a "section gang" charged with maintaining a particular stretch of railroad tracks.

24 Last Saturday Night I Entered a House

Sung by Pearl Jacobs Borusky, Antigo, Wisconsin, August 30, 1940.
Recorded by Helene Stratman-Thomas and Robert F. Draves.

4174 B1

Last Saturday night I entered a house
And through the dark way I crept like a mouse.
I opened the door and went straightway
Into a room where the girls all stay.
And it's hard times!

Such laughing and chatting as we did keep!
We waked the old widder all out of her sleep,
And in a few words she did address me,
"Such an impudent fellow before me I see!"
And it's hard times!

"O widder, O widder, you'd better keep calm
Until you find out who I am.
I'm Johnny the Carpenter, I go by that name.
A-courting your daughter, for the purpose I came."
And it's hard times!

"O daughter, O daughter, O daughter," said she,
"To think that my daughter would go before me
When I am so old and you are so young.
You can get sweethearts and I can get none."
And it's hard times!

"O widder, O widder, O widder at large,
If you are an old widder you are a great charge.
O widder, O widder, O widder by name."
She up with a broomstick and at me she came.
And it's hard times!

Such fighting and scratching! At last I got clear,
I mounted my horse and for home I did steer,
The blood running down, my head being sore,
There stood the old widder with a broom in the door.
And it's hard times!

FOLLOWING PAGE Pearl Jacobs Borusky with her mother, Ollie Jacobs, Langlade County, Wisconsin, 1941. (Wisconsin Historical Society, WHi-25176)

Come all young men, take warning by me,
And never a widder's daughter go see.
For if you do, twill be your doom.
They'll fight you like Satan and beat you with a broom.
And it's hard times!

This darkly comic account of a suitor's misadventures is called "Courting the Widow's Daughter" and classified as H42 in G. Malcolm Laws's concordance of traditional ballads originating in the United States (Laws 1964: 242). Dating to sometime in the nineteenth century, it has been documented by folklorists in the Appalachian South, the Ozarks, and Texas. Pearl Jacobs Borusky's mother, Mrs. Ollie Jacobs (b. 1862), sang this song for Asher Treat in 1933. She had learned it in Kentucky from a man named Walter Justice.

25 Did You Ever See the Devil?

Sung by Charles Dietz, Monroe, Wisconsin, September 1946.
Recorded by Helene Stratman-Thomas and Aubrey Snyder.
8458 A3

Did you ever see the devil
With his iron wooden shovel,
Scratching up the gravel
With his big toe nail?

Oh the dirt was so hard
That he couldn't get it up.
So away went the devil
With his tail curled up.

Through the late Charles E. Brown, curator of the State Historical Society museum, I had become acquainted with Mrs. Ralph Kundert of Monroe, a collector of stories of early Green County. As a result of her interest in reconstructing her family history, she had discovered that her father, Charles Dietz, not only had a wealth of information and tales of pioneer days, but also remembered folk ballads of the period. Mr. Dietz had been president of the Green County Normal School for many years. It was interesting to meet a prominent educator who still had room in his mind for all of the little ditties of his boyhood days. He had learned many English ballads from his pioneer mother who came to Wisconsin from New York State. Mr. Dietz reminisced, "She too was a school teacher. I was practically brought up in the schoolhouse, as my mother took off just enough time from her teaching for me to be born." In the style of a true ballad singer, Mr. Dietz recorded "Froggy Would A-Wooing Go," "Young Mary," "Three Dishes and Six Questions," "The Old Man Came Home Again," "Six King's Daughters," and "Old Willis Is Dead." He also recalled the play parties which substituted for dancing, which was frowned upon. He sang bits of songs that were used for play party games: "The Needle's Eye," "King William Was King James's Son," and "Come Philander." (Stratman-Thomas 1940–1960: September 2, 1946)

Born in 1870 to a Pennsylvania German father, Charles Dietz acquired his folksong repertoire from his mother, who was of English ancestry. His two-verse song regarding the devil and hard ground goes back to at least the early nineteenth century and has been reported, in many versions, from Cornwall to Labrador, from Alabama to California, and

Charles Dietz and Helene Stratman-Thomas, Monroe, Wisconsin, 1946. (Wisconsin Historical Society, WHi-25398)

among blacks and whites alike. Various renditions of the first verse also have been sung as "floating verses" associated with hornpipes, especially "Fisher's Hornpipe" and also "Stack of Barley" (e.g., Deane and Shaw 1975: 67–68; Scarborough 1925: 284; Smith 2007: 141–142; B. Taylor 1852: 175).

26 Three Dishes and Six Questions

Sung by Charles Dietz, Monroe, Wisconsin, September 2, 1946.
Recorded by Helene Stratman-Thomas and Aubrey Snyder.
8458 A2

"I'd take that fair maid in my arms
And roll her next to the wall."

"Oh go away, you silly man,
And do not bother me.
Before that you can lie with me
You must cook me dishes three.
Three dishes you must cook for me
And I will eat them all.
Then you and I in the bed will lie,
And you'll lie next to the wall.

"For my breakfast you must cook
A bird without any bones.
And for my dinner you must cook
A cherry without any stones.
And for my supper you must cook
A bird without a gall.
Then you and I in a bed will lie,
And you'll lie next to the wall.

"Oh go away, you silly man,
And do not me perplex.
Before that you can lie with me,
You must answer questions six.
Six questions you must answer me,
As I repeat them all.
Then you and I in the bed will lie,
And you'll lie next to the wall.

"What is rounder than a ring?
What's higher than a tree?

What is worse than a woman's tongue?
What's deeper than the sea?
What bird sings first and what one best?
And where does the dew first fall?
Then you and I in the bed will lie,
And you'll lie next to the wall."

"This world is rounder than a ring,
Heaven's higher than a tree.
The devil's worse than a woman's tongue.
Hell's deeper than the sea.
The lark sings first, the sparrow best,
And out does the dew first fall.
Then you and I in the bed will lie,
And you'll lie next to the wall."

This contest in riddles, consisting entirely of dialogue between a crafty woman and her quick-witted suitor, is a version of a Scottish ballad dating to at least the eighteenth century. Dubbed "Captain Wedderburn's Courtship," it is number 46 in Francis James Child's canonical *English and Scottish Popular Ballads* (1882–1898). Stratman-Thomas tells us: "This old riddle song . . . was handed down in Mr. Dietz's family through his mother. . . . Mr. Dietz's version does not tell of the courtship leading up to the asking of the riddles; however, most of the riddles found in the early printings of the song are included. Numerous variants have been collected in the United States." Although Dietz neglected to sing a crucial verse in which the suitor took up his sweetheart's culinary challenge, he knew it and subsequently provided it to Stratman-Thomas.

"Oh, while the bird is in the shell,
It surely has no bones;
And while the cherry is blossoming
It surely has no stones;
The dove is a gentle bird
And flies without a gall.
Now you and I in one bed will lie,
And you'll lie next to the wall."

LUMBERJACK AND IRISH AMERICAN

Wisconsin's vast north woods, the pinery, was harvested mostly between the 1860s and the first decade of the twentieth century. The shanty boys, or lumberjacks, worked in the woods from late fall through early spring, occupying camps and moving felled timber when the ground was frozen. When spring "breakup" or "mud time" came, some returned to farms and family, while others whiled away the time in the saloons and sporting houses of rough towns, awaiting a log drive when buoyant white pine logs were floated downstream to sawmills. Men of diverse indigenous and immigrant backgrounds toiled in the woods, including many Irish, some of whom had settled first in Canada's Maritime Provinces and Ontario or in Maine and especially New York State. Among them were musicians and singers aplenty. Folklorist Franz Rickaby, who sought out the Upper Midwest's woods singers in 1919, found "that in the logging camp the hegemony in song belonged to the Irish. Although the Scotch and the French-Canadian occur occasionally, the Irish were dominant, and the Irish street-song was the pattern upon which a liberal portion of the shanty-songs were made" (1926: xxv). An Irish-influenced singing style likewise prevailed in the camps, featuring solo unaccompanied vocals that were louder and pitched slightly higher than one's normal voice and sometimes included a spoken final line signaling a song's conclusion. In addition to songs about lumber-camp life that were affected by Irish poetic and performance traditions, comic "stage Irish" songs concerning the exaggerated characteristics and foibles of Irish immigrants were popular both in the woods and roundabout the Upper Midwest.

27 Snow Deer
Played on harmonica by Emery DeNoyer, Rhinelander, Wisconsin, July 26, 1941. Recorded by Helene Stratman-Thomas and Robert F. Draves.
4989 B2

At Rhinelander Bob [Draves] met Emery DeNoyer, aged sixty-three, who had been an entertainer in lumber camps since he was a young boy. As he had lost his sight and an arm in an accident, he was taken by his father to the various camps on Sundays. In the camps he both learned the lumberjack ballads and sang them to the lumberjacks. Mr. DeNoyer knew fine versions of "The Little Brown Bulls," "Jam on Gerry's Rock," "The Shantyman's Life" and a song of his own composition, "The Tomahawk Hem" [hymn]. We first learned of Mr. DeNoyer through Mrs. Isabel Ebert of Rhinelander, who had collected many of his songs. (Stratman-Thomas 1940–1960: July 26, 1941)

Emery DeNoyer (1878–1960) was born in Swamp Creek, Michigan, near Saginaw, to which his French Canadian father, Alexander DeNoyer, had come in 1867 to work in the woods. Steady employment and better wages drew the family to Merrill, southeast of Rhinelander, in 1892; a year later, fourteen-year-old Emery was permanently disabled in a hunting accident. In 1894 the family moved to Rhinelander, where "all of the children found work, even Emery." According to Isabel Ebert: "Many camps depended upon Rhinelander for their supplies and so many companies were logging at the same time that they were very close together. The men in the camps needed to be entertained and were being visited by salesmen and representatives of charitable organizations. They were liberally rewarding all who bore the rigors of the cold and the hardships of early travel to call upon them. So, just as an experiment at first, Emery and his brother began offering them diversion. They were so successful Emery made camp entertaining his profession" (Ebert [1940s] 1998: 206).

Besides singing, Emery played the harmonica, and around 1900 he purchased a Victrola and a stack of records, which he and his brother hauled on a sled from camp to camp. When logging dwindled in northern Wisconsin, he ranged into the Upper Peninsula of Michigan and northern Minnesota. In the 1940s, DeNoyer not only sang old woods songs for programs at Rhinelander's logging museum but also did some contemporary crooning. On July 23, 1948, an ad, "TEEN-AGE DANCE," in *The Rhinelander Daily News* touted "Music by 'Hodag Hepcats' / Featuring Singer Emery DeNoyer / Dancing Starts at 8:30 P.M. / Admission: 35c / Sponsored by C.Y.O. [Catholic Youth Organization] Councillors Club."

"Snow Deer," the only recorded example of DeNoyer's harmonica playing, was captured at his insistence, as it was very popular in the camps. The lyrics, composed by Percy Wenrich and Jack Mahoney in 1913 and which, mercifully, DeNoyer did not sing, concern a cowboy who steals his "pretty Snow Deer" from her irate Native would-be lover.

> Sweet Snow Deer mine, moon's a-shine through the pines
> While Mohawks sleep, let us creep through the vale.
> Your cowboy lover, your heart will cover.
> Don't hesitate, it is late, ponies wait
> For you and me by the trees in the dale.
> Hear tom-toms beating, let's hit the trail.

The song is one of several pseudo-Indian "deer" songs—"Golden Deer," "My Wild Deer," "Pawnee Deer"—composed in the early twentieth century (Schafer and Riedel 1973: 382–387).

28 Shantyman's Life

Sung by Emery DeNoyer, Rhinelander, Wisconsin, July 26, 1941.
Recorded by Helene Stratman-Thomas and Robert F. Draves.
4988 A, 4989 B1

Come all you jolly fellows, come listen to my song;
It's all about the pinery boys, and how they get along.
They're the jolliest lot of fellows, so merrily and fine,
They will spend their pleasant winter months in cutting down the pine.

Some will leave their friends and homes, and others they do love dear.
And into the lonesome pine woods their pathway they do steer,
Into the lonesome pine woods all winter to remain,
Awaiting for the spring-time to return again.

Spring-time comes, oh glad will be its day;
Some return to home and friends, while others go astray.
The sawyers and the choppers, they lay their timber low,
The swampers and the teamsters, they haul it to and fro.

Next comes the loaders, before the break of day;
"Load up your sleighs five thousand feet, to the river haste away!"
Noon-time rolls around, our foreman loudly screams,
"Lay down your tools, me boys, and we'll haste to pork and beans."

We arrive at the shanty; the splashing then begins,
The banging of the water pails, the rattling of the tins.
In the middling of the splashing, our cook for dinner does cry;
We all arise and go, for we hate to lose our pie.

Dinner being over, we into our shanty go;
We all fill up our pipes and smoke till everything looks blue.
"It's time for the woods, me boys," our foreman he does say;
We all gather up our hats and caps, to the woods we haste away.

We all go out with a welcome heart and well-contented mind,
For the winter winds blow cold among the waving pine.
The ringing of saws and axes, until the sun goes down.
"Lay down your tools, me boys, for the shanties we are bound."

We arrive at the shanty with cold and wet feet;
Take off our over boots and packs, at supper we must eat.
Supper being ready, we all arise and go,
For it ain't the style of a lumberjack to lose his hash, you know.

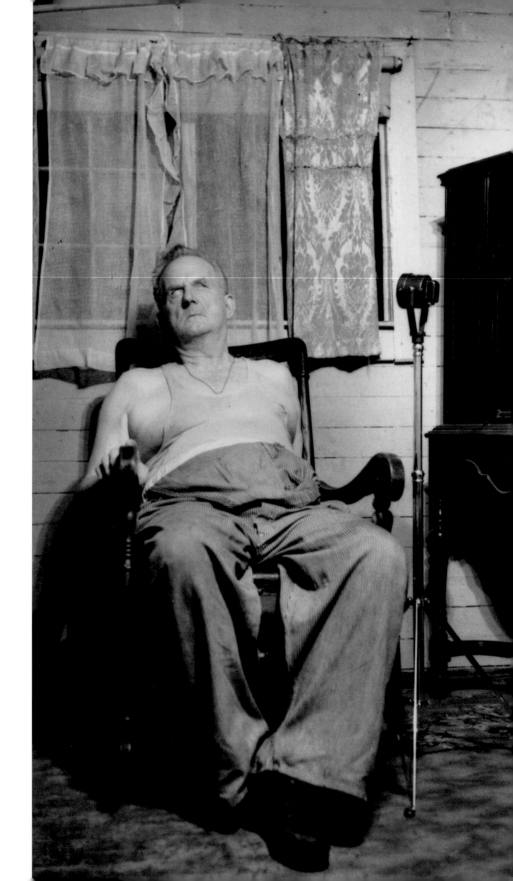

At three o'clock in the morning our bull cook loudly shouts,
"Roll out, roll out, you teamsters, it's time that you were out."
The teamsters, they get up in a fright and manful wail,
"Oh where's my boots, oh where's my packs, my rubbers have gone astray."
The other men, they then get up, their packs they cannot find;
And they lay it to the teamsters, and they curse them till they're blind.

Spring-time comes, oh glad will be its day.
"Lay down your tools, me boys, and we'll haste to break away."
The floating ice is over, and business now destroyed.
Three-hundred able-bodied men are wanted on the Pelican drive.

With jam pikes and peavies those able men do go,
All up that wild, dreary stream to risk their lives, you know.
Cold and frosty mornings they shiver with the cold;
So much ice upon their jam pikes they scarcely can them hold.

Now wherever you hear those verses, believe them to be true,
For if you doubt one word of them, just ask Bob Unson's crew.
It was in Bob Unson's shanties where they were sung with glee,
And the ending of my song is signed C, D, F, and G.

[Spoken] Melvin Seiden.

Folklorist Edith Fowke contended that this song, with its vivid description of daily and seasonal lumber-camp and river-drive experiences, originated in Maine or New Brunswick. It is widely known across the timbered borderlands of the United States and Canada as "The Shanty Boys and the Pine," "Cutting Down the Pine," and "The Lumbercamp Song"; it has also been localized frequently to describe "Jim Murphy's Camp," "Jim Porter's Camp," and "Turner's Camp on the Chippewa" (Fowke 1970: 34–36). Rickaby reported a version from Ladysmith, Wisconsin (1926: 69–76, 207–208), and Stratman-Thomas recorded the song from Charles Ring in Hayward. According to Ebert, the song was known in Wisconsin as early as the 1870s, but DeNoyer acquired it "in 1904 at a camp in Minnesota on the Cloquet River" (Ebert [1940s] 1998: 208). Perhaps Melvin Seiden, whose name is spoken at the song's close, was Rickaby's source? I failed to find Seiden in census records. Although Rhinelander's *New North* newspaper for February 1, 1918, tells us that DeNoyer returned that winter from "an extended trip in Minnesota," his version of "Shantyman's Life" sets the action in the Rhinelander area,

< Lumber-camp singer Emery DeNoyer, Rhinelander, Wisconsin, 1941. (Wisconsin Historical Society, WHi-25175)

where the Pelican is a tributary of the Wisconsin River. "Bob Unson's Camp" likewise refers to a logger active just down river in the Merrill area, as the 1895 census lists a Robert Unson living in Merrill. During the recording process only ten verses of this lengthy song fit on a single disc, hence the performance here retrieves the final two verses that Stratman-Thomas evidently neglected to remember when including only part of the song on *Folk Music from Wisconsin*.

29 Irish Jubilee

Sung by Emery DeNoyer, Rhinelander, Wisconsin, July 26, 1941.
Recorded by Helene Stratman-Thomas and Robert F. Draves.

4991 A

Just short time ago, boys, an Irishman named Doherty
Was elected for the Senate by a very large majority.
He felt so elected so he went to Denis Cassidy,
Who owned a barroom of a very large capacity.

He says to Cassidy, "Go over to the brewery
For a thousand kegs of lager beer, and give it to the poor.
Go over to the butcher shop and order up a ton of meat.
Be sure to see the boys and girls get all they want to drink and eat.

"Send out invitations in twenty different languages.
And don't forget to tell them all to bring along their sandwiches.
Tell them the music will be furnished by O'Rafferty,
Assisted on the bagpipe by Felix McCafferty.

"Whatever the expenses are, remember I'll put up the tin.
And everyone that doesn't come be sure and do not let them in."
Oh Cassidy at once sent out the invitations
And everyone that come was a credit to their nations.

Some come with bicycles for they had no fare to pay,
And those that didn't come at all made up their minds to stay away.
Two-by, three-by they marched into the dining hall:
Young men, old men, and girls that wasn't men at all.

Blind men, deaf men, and men that had their teeth in pawn.
Single men, and double men, and men that had their glasses on.
Before many minutes went every chair was taken,
Oh the front rooms, the mushrooms were packed to suffocations.

When everyone was seated they started to lay out the feast.
Oh Cassidy says, "Rise up, and give us each a cake of yeast."
He then says, "As manager, we will try and fill the chair,"
And then sat down. And we looked at our bill of fare.

There were pigs heads, goldfish, mockingbirds, and ostriches,
Ice cream, cold cream, Vaseline and sandwiches.
Blue fish, green fish, and fish hooks, and partridges,
Fish balls, snowballs, cannonballs, and cartridges.

We ate oatmeal 'til we couldn't hardly stir about,
Ketchup, hurry up, sweet kraut, and sauerkraut,
Dressed beef, naked beef, and beef with its dresses on,
Sody crackers, fire crackers, Limburger cheese with tresses on.

Beefsteak, mistake was down upon the bill of fare.
Roast ribs, spare ribs, and ribs that we couldn't spare.
Reindeer, snow deer, and dear me, and antelope.
The women e't mushmelon 'til the men said, "They cantaloupe."

Smoked herrings, red herrings, herring from old Ireland.
Boloney, fruit cake, sausages a half-a-mile.
Hot corn, corn salve, and honeycomb.
Red birds, read books, sea bass, and sea foam.

Baked liver, fried liver, Carter's Little Liver Pills.
And everyone was wondering who was going to pay the bills.
For dessert we had toothpicks, ice picks, and skipping ropes.
And washed them all down with a big piece of barber soap.

We ate everything that was down upon the bill of fare,
Then looked on the other side to see if any more was there.
Then the band played hornpipes, gas pipes, and Irish reels.
And we danced to the music of the wind that shakes the barley fields.

Old piper, he played old tunes, spittoons so very fine.
And piper Hudson, he came in, and he handed us a glass of wine.
We welted the floor 'til we could be heard for miles around.
And Gallagher was in the air, his feet was never on the ground.

The finest lot of dancers you'd ever set your eyes upon.
And them that couldn't dance was a-dancing with their slippers on.
And they danced jig steps, door steps, and highland flings
When Murphy took his knife out and he tried to cut a pigeon wing.

When the dancing was over, oh Cassidy then told them
To all join hands and sing in this good old chorus:
"Wherever old acquaintance may be forgotten, wherever you may be,
Just think of that good old time we had at the Irish Jubilee."

Composed by the Irish American singer and vaudeville performer James Thornton (1861–1938), "The Irish Jubilee" was published in 1890 by a New York City sheet-music firm, Witmark, with music by Thornton's show-business partner, Charles Lawler. William Williams links it with both a larger body of songs and the customs of New York City's Irish American Tammany Hall political machine: "A common feature of many of the common songs was a propensity towards exuberance, exaggeration, and excess, not merely in terms of drink and violence, but as exhibited by incessant lists of names, dances, and food. . . . 'The Irish Jubilee' (1890) describes a mammoth wingding to celebrate the rise of a local Tammany politico. When Doherty is elected to the Senate, he decides to celebrate" (W. Williams 1996: 144–145; see also Spaeth 1927: 225).

Folklorist Vance Randolph recorded the song in 1942 from Booth Campbell of Cane Hill, Arkansas, who reckoned he learned the piece about 1892 from the "between the acts" singing of a "stage Irishman" with a red wig and green whiskers (Randolph 1980: 232–235). Just about that time, while still living near Saginaw, DeNoyer pestered a "horse jockey" to sing the song over and over until he knew it. "It always took well with the lumberjacks" (Ebert [1940s] 1998: 215). Stratman-Thomas recorded another version in 1941 from a sixty-nine-year-old former lumberjack, F. S. Puty of Almond, who "picked this up from having heard others sing it. He didn't know whether this is folk or not, but has never known it to be published." Seven years later, amid fieldwork for the Library of Congress in the Upper Peninsula of Michigan, Henry Welliver recorded the song from another old lumberjack, Jim Kirkpatrick, of Brimley.

30 Irish Washerwoman

Called by John Muench with Ralph Weide on accordion, Lancaster, Wisconsin, August 23, 1946. Recorded by Helene Stratman-Thomas and Aubrey Snyder. Paul Gifford and Paul Tyler contributed critical information regarding singing calls, July 2012.

8433 A1

Lift your partner, right and left.
Join your hands and round [to] the left.

First couple out, then down the middle.
And with your right foot keep time with the fiddle.
It's when you come back, remember the call,
And swing in the corner, then promenade all.

Your little foot up and your big foot down
Say doodle-ee, doodle-ee, doodle-ee-um.

Same couple out, then down the middle.
And with your right foot keep time with the fiddle.
It's when you come back, remember the call,
And swing in the corner, then promenade all.

[Repeats previous verse.]

Your little foot up and your big foot down
Say doodle-ee, doodle-ee, doodle-ee-um.

Same couple out, then down the middle.
And with your right foot keep time with the fiddle.
It's when you come round, remember the call,
And swing in the corner, then promenade all.

Allemande, allemande, allemande left,
Then hand-over-hand and go right and left.

Meet your partner with a railroad swing,
And [pause] ee-oo-ee and a double-joint ee.
And a high-low, jack-in-the-gate.

Places all, and as you are.
Seat your ladies, I don't care.
Seat her in the higher chair.

[Spoken after the tune ends:] That's enough.

Mr. John Muench . . . of Lancaster, recalled numerous square dance calls, which were used to the tunes "The Irish Washerwoman," "Turkey in the Straw," "Grape Vine Twist," "Captain Jinks," "Over the Ocean Wave," "Pop Goes the Weasel," and "Little Brown Jug." Ralph Weide played the tunes on the accordion as Mr. Muench called, "Promenade all, 'round Beetown Hall," or "Calloway Hall." (Stratman-Thomas 1940–1960: August 23, 1946)

Muench (1886–1966) was a lifelong farmer in South Lancaster Township, where he raised hogs. A director of the Grant County Agricultural Society that oversaw the county fair, he was also active in the Grant County Coon and Fox Hunters Association. Less is known about accordionist Ralph Weide, a younger man who served in World War II. Stratman-Thomas learned of them through a letter (July 15, 1946) from Ida (Mrs. David) Crichton, the Lancaster correspondent for Madison's *Wisconsin State Journal*. Although mainly focused on the African American singer Lillie Richmond, Crichton also mentioned "a good many old-timers around here—lifelong residents— and some good fiddlers who played for dances 50–60 years ago." In a subsequent letter, she referred specifically to "John Muench, who did a fine job of dance calling one evening at his farm home." Muench's calls, intriguingly, invited dancers to promenade "'round Beetown Hall" in the community where Richmond had danced as a young woman.

Although square dances are popularly associated with the fiddle, the accordion was commonly used in the Upper Midwest for dance melodies over which "callers" offered instructions. Since on this occasion Muench was calling for imaginary dancers, his instructions are incomplete and he loses track in the penultimate verse. Meanwhile his use of "patter calls" in the first couplet, and "singing calls" thereafter may well have been influenced by radio broadcasts and recordings of regional musicians, particularly for this tune. Most famously, the fiddler Tommy Dandurand of Kankakee, Illinois, who performed on Chicago's WLS *National Barn Dance*, recorded the "Irish Washerwoman" in 1927 to support his "singing calls" (Berry 2008: 243). The tune itself dates to the late sixteenth century and may be of English origin despite its longstanding status as the quintessential Irish jig (Bayard 1982: 415–419). Widely known in America by the late eighteenth century, it became associated with working-class famine Irish in the mid-nineteenth century. Most frequently performed as an instrumental tune, it has lyrics lampooning stereotypical "shanty Irish" immigrants living with animals in drunken squalor. For example, Carol Ryrie Brink's *Caddie Woodlawn*, based on the experiences of her grandmother who lived along northwestern Wisconsin's Red Cedar River in the 1860s, includes a ten-line version of the "Irish Washerwoman" sung by the family's hired man, Robert Ireton (Brink 1936: 71–72). In 1989 I recorded a shorter rendition from a family band, the Gemmil Gang, in the vicinity of Posen, Michigan.

> Did you ever go down to an Irishman's shanty
> Where money is scarce but the whiskey is plenty?
> There's a three-legged stool and a table to match,
> A hen in the corner all ready to hatch.

31 Oh, It's Nine Years Ago I Was Diggin' in the Land

Sung by Noble Brown, Millville, Wisconsin, November 17, 1946.
Recorded by Helene Stratman-Thomas and Aubrey Snyder.
Brian Ó Broin, Kevin Conroy, and Dineen Grow collectively
provided note 2, and Ó Broin offered note 3.

8472 A2

Oh it's nine years ago I was diggin' in the land,
Me brogues[1] on me feet and me spade in me hand.
Said I what a pity it is for to see
Such a genius as I diggin' turf by the lea.
Mishen darn![2]

A darn tooranaddy, mishen darn toornan.
A right tooranaddy, mishen darn toornan.

So I pulled off me brogues, shook hands with me spade,
And off to the war like a dashing Irish blade.
The sergeant and the captain, they asked me to enlist.
By the great Graf de Grief,[3] give me hold of your fist.
Mishen darn!

A darn tooranaddy, mishen darn toornan.
A right tooranaddy, mishen darn toornan.

Oh the first thing they gave me it was an old gun.
Under the trigger I placed me thumb.
The gun being rusty went off with a shock.
Gave my poor shoulder most a darn devilish knock.
Mishen darn!

A darn tooranaddy, mishen darn toornan.
A right tooranaddy, mishen darn toornan.

The next thing they gave me it was an old horse,
All saddled and bridled and two legs across.
He kicked up his heels and I held him a-level
And the stiff-necked gally-gimme[4] ran to the devil.
Mishen darn!

A darn tooranaddy, mishen darn toornan.
A right tooranaddy, mishen darn toornan.

Oh it's nine years ago, thank God it ain't ten,
I'm back in Ireland diggin' murphies[5] again.
Success to the land, may God save the queen,
And when the war is ended I'll enlist again.
Mishen darn!

Darn tooranaddy, mishen darn toornan.
A right tooranaddy, mishen darn toornan.

———

1. Irish for a coarse, heavy laborer's shoe.
2. Likely a nonsense expression to Brown, who was not an Irish speaker, this phrase combines *Muise* and *darn*. The former is a mild expression of surprise (a corruption of *Muire* [the blessed virgin]) that one often finds in Connacht Irish; the latter is a polite version of "damn."
3. *Graf* is a German and Swedish term of nobility, the equivalent of "count" or "earl"; hence the Earl of Grief is an appropriate title for a commander whose common soldiers are cannon fodder.
4. *Gally* is a whale-fisher's term meaning "frightened" or "confused" that was likely interjected by the seagoing Brown. *Gally-gimme*, consequently, is something that gives someone a fright.
5. Potatoes.

Noble Bennie Brown (1885–1953) was born in Millville, a Grant County hamlet in the lower Wisconsin River valley. His father was English, his mother Scottish and Dutch. Brown found work at the age of fourteen in a Chippewa Valley lumber camp near Stanley, peeling hemlock bark essential for tanning hides. Over the next six years, he moved ever west, toiling in a succession of lumber camps in Wisconsin, Minnesota, California, Washington, and Oregon. Roaming to "the Barbary Coast of San Francisco before the earthquake and fire of 1907," as he wrote to Stratman-Thomas (January 9, 1947), Brown shipped out on sailing vessels for many years. "The wanderlust was always in my bones until I dropt [*sic*] anchor here at Millville Grant Co. Wis."

Most the twenty-two songs Brown recorded came from his saltwater sailing days, and three of them—"Blow Boys, Blow," "Reuben Ranzo," "Blow the Man Down"—were included on *American Sea Songs and Shanties*, a double-LP issued by the Library of Congress (L26/27). He also sang two "Dutch" dialect songs (see Stratman-Thomas CD part 2, track 1), and several comic Irish songs. The song included here was learned from his mother. Often called "The True Paddy's Song" or "The Kerry Recruit," this blarney-filled account of a potato-digging bumpkin's misadventures in the British army during the Crimean War is well known in Ireland. Classified as J8 in the War Ballads section of G. Malcolm Laws's *American Balladry from British Broadsides*, it circulated through broadsides, songsters, and oral tradition (1957: 132).

32 McNamar' from County Clare

Sung by Robert Walker, Crandon, Wisconsin, August 14, 1941.
Recorded by Helene Stratman-Thomas and Robert F. Draves.
5008 B2

My name is McNamar' and I came from County Clare,
From that darling little isle across the sea,
Where the mountains and the hills and the lakes and rippling rills
Are a-singing sweetest music all the day.

Our little farm was small, it would not support us all,
So one of us was forced away from home.
I bade them all goodbye with a teardrop in my eye,
And I sailed for Castle Garden[1] all alone.

For I'm an honest Irish lad, and of work I'm not afraid.
If it's pleasures, to you I will sing or dance.
I'll do anything you say, if you'll only name the day
When they'll give an honest Irish lad a chance.

I landed in New York, and I tried hard to get work,
And I wandered through the streets from day to day.
I went from place to place with starvation on my face,
And every place they want no help they say.

But still I wandered on, still hoping to find one
That would give a lad a chance to earn his bread.
But although it's just the same and I know I'm not to blame,
But it's often times I wished that I were dead.

For I'm an honest Irish lad, and of work I'm not afraid.
If it's pleasures, to you I will sing or dance.

I'll do anything you say, if you'll only name the day
When they'll give an honest Irish lad a chance.

But still I've one kind friend who a helping hand would lend
To a poor boy, and help him on at home.
I will bring my mother here and my little sister dear,
And nevermore again from them I'll roam.

Yes I'll do whate'er is right, yes I'll work both day and night,
Yes I'll do the very best I can.
And may God do help the heart that will take a poor boy's part
And make an honest Irish lad a man.

———

1. Castle Garden, situated on the southern tip of Manhattan, was New York's port of entry prior to Ellis Island.

We arrived at the home of Robert Walker in Crandon about ten in the morning. Mr. Walker was willing to sing for us but he asked us to return later in the day as he had a house full of company. When we returned in the middle of the afternoon, the guests were still there, so we suggested that perhaps they too would enjoy Mr. Walker's songs. They all agreed, and we made the recordings with some ten or fifteen listeners sitting around the room. The group included some small boys who were spellbound with the whole procedure of singing and recording. Mr. Walker's songs were all learned in the north woods. He sang his version of "The Little Brown Bulls" and many songs in Irish brogue which were typical of the songs which the lumberjacks sang for the entertainment of their fellows. (Stratman-Thomas 1940–1960: August 14, 1941)

Robert Walker's other "Irish brogue" songs on this occasion were well-known Irish American comic ballads: "Pat Malone," "The Pickled Jew," "Riley and I Were Chums," and "The Twenty Pound Dog." Born in 1883 in the Forest County community of Crandon, Walker learned these songs in the woods where he worked from his teens until retiring in 1955 at the age of seventy-two. Sidney Robertson recorded him in 1937 and again from 1952 to 1954 (Robertson CD, track 4).

County Clare is in the west of Ireland, and this immigrant's song is best known as "Give an Honest Irish Lad a Chance." Printed as a broadside in Belfast and Dublin and appearing in such American publications as *Delaney's Irish Songster* (New York: ca. 1887, p. 23), it has been recorded from Irish American singers in Canada and the United

States, including the Adirondack singer Sara Cleveland (1905–1992), who learned it from her father, Jerry Creedon, who was born in Cork and immigrated to New York in 1873 right around the time Robert Walker's parents left that state for Wisconsin (Paton [1977] 1995: 29–31; W. Williams 1996: 110, 263).

33 Fond du Lac Jail
Sung by Charles Robinson, Wautoma, Wisconsin, June 1941.
Recorded by Robert F. Draves.
4966 A2

In the morning you receive a dry loaf of bread
That's hard as a stone and heavy as lead.
It's thrown from the ceiling down into your cell,
Like coming from heaven popped down into hell.

Oh there's hard times in Fond du Lac jail,
There's hard times, I say.

Your bed it is made of old rotten rugs,
Get up in the morning all covered with bugs.
And the bugs they will swear that unless you get bail,
You're bound to go lousy in Fond du Lac jail.

Oh there's hard times in Fond du Lac jail,
There's hard times, I say.

Since I was scheduled to teach in summer school, Bob set out alone, going first into the lumberjack country of Waushara County. The lumberjacks whose songs he recorded were Charles Robinson, Charles Mills, Bert Taplin, Lewis Winfield Moody, Michael Leary, Henry Humphries, and F. S. Puty, whose average age was about eighty years: some of the last of the Paul Bunyans. (Stratman-Thomas 1940–1960: June 1941)

The youngster among these retired loggers, Charles Robinson was born in Massachusetts in 1865. He probably arrived in Wisconsin between the mid-1880s and the early 1890s, since his wife, Lacie, whom he married in 1894, was born in Wisconsin. Besides this song, the only one he recorded, Robinson performed a comic recitation in "Dutch" dialect, "Sockery's Cat" (Stratman-Thomas CD part 2, track 5). Robinson's singing reference to Fond du Lac, originally a lumbering and sawmill town at the southern end of Lake Winnebago, suggests that he might have worked in camps along the Wolf River, which flows into that lake from the north.

The song itself, however, originated in England in the late eighteenth or early nineteenth century. Recorded several times by folklorists from woods singers in New Hampshire, the home state of Robinson's father, it has a far wider circulation among itinerant workers from New Jersey to Texas (Lomax 1934: 138–143; Pike 1935: 337–351; Post 2004: 178–179).

34 Alphabet Song

Sung and spoken by Lewis Winfield Moody, Plainfield, Wisconsin, August 27, 1940. Recorded, with spoken interjections, by Robert F. Draves.

4972 A

Oh A is for asshole all covered with hair,
And B is for ballocks that long to be there.
C is for cunt of [?] and piss,
And D is a ding-darling as thick as your wrist.

CHORUS:
"Oh ding-darling, ding-darling, ding-darling," says she,
"I'll be your dear darling if you walk with me."
I wink and I blinked at her old magazine
And I shoved a dead bone in her scrogging machine.

E is the end of a long shittin' stick,
And F is for fucker who fucked off his prick.
G is for gobs all greasy and fat,
And H is the hairy old ass of a cat.

Oh it's I is an island one mile an' a half round,
And J is the jolliest old whore in the town.
L is a lousy old whore with the itch,
And K is a kiss-me-ass son-of-a-bitch.

[Moody sings the IJKL verse a second time.]

Moody: Guess I sang that before, didn't I? If you'd keep me track of the alphabet. That's what bothers me. Just keep me track of the alphabet.
Draves: M.

[Spoken] M is for maiden.

Oh M is for maiden with long curly locks,
And N is for nigs with flat-headed cocks.
O is for owl that fucks in the grass,
And P is for prick that goes down to your ass.
Draves: Q, R
Q is for queen that wanted to suck,
And R is for Rooshin [Russian] that wanted to fuck.
And S is for shithouse I ne'er did approach,
And T stands for turd that upset the mail coach.
Draves: U, V
U is an ulcer on an old whore's toe,
And V is a virgin, you very well know.
W, then X, and Y is a yard, one half of a stud,
And Z stands for zipper [zibber?] who fucked all he could.

One type of folk singer for whom we were constantly looking was the true lumber-jack. H. J. Kent of Wautoma, who had a great interest in local history, knew many of the older lumberjacks in Waushara and neighboring counties. He took us to visit John Christian of Coloma, Henry Humphries of Hancock, and Lewis Winfield Moody of Plainfield. Since not all lumberjack songs are intended for ladies' ears, it was some-times suggested that I "just wait in the car!" (Stratman-Thomas 1940–1960: August 27, 1940)

This field trip to Coloma, assisted by a local musician, Hubert J. Kent, was prompted by a letter from Alan Lomax to Leland Coon, Stratman-Thomas's Music Department chair, specifically requesting "Lumberjack songs" and "Vulgar ballads and songs" (July 18, 1940). The latter were a challenge Stratman-Thomas solved with quick thinking and the cooperation of Bob Draves, her student engineer: "The old lumberjacks looked embar-rassed and stared at Miss Thomas until she, suddenly understanding, tactfully wandered out of earshot. And then came the hardy old songs; the lusty old songs never recorded before and filled with life and living" ("Fading Folk Songs of Wisconsin Trapped on Discs," *Milwaukee Journal*, October 20, 1940).

Lewis Winfield Moody recorded a dozen such songs, more than any other Wisconsin singer: "Alec Brown" ("Highland Tinker"), "Alphabet Song," "As I Went Out Walking One Morning in Spring," "Big Brick House in a Georgia Town" ("One-Eyed Riley"), "Bob Goes Gunning," "Boring for Oil," "Everybody Has a Finger in the Pie," "Fisherman Have You Any Sea Crabs," "I Went Down to New Orleans," "Keyhole in the Door,"

"There Was an Old Woman," and "The Whore with the Curly Hair." He also sang, and perhaps knew more, workers' and Irish American songs common in lumber camps—"A Lumbering We Will Go," "The Dreary Black Hills," "Finnegan's Wake," "Miss Fogarty's Christmas Cake," "The Kerry Recruit"—suggesting that his "vulgar" emphasis may have been related to the context and what was expected. Moody (1861–1942) was born in Mukwonago, in Waukesha County, seven years after Hamilton Lobdell (see track 22), whose parents had also come there from New York. Moody married Lisetta Treutel in 1887, and the couple had five sons and a daughter. A blacksmith who had also worked in the woods, Moody operated shops mostly in the Plainfield area of Waushara County, but also to the northwest in the Wood County village of Nekoosa.

Songs featuring letters of the alphabet flourish in occupational traditions, including well-known sailors' and lumberjacks' alphabets. Moody's "Alphabet Song" is one of several bawdy A-to-Z ditties (Randolph 1992b: 616–621). Earl C. Beck, the Michigan-based collector of lumber-camp folksongs, clearly knew, but never published, such a song: "A folklorist might ask what manner of life does not have an alphabet song. The hobo has one; so does the queen of the red lights. In fact, the filthiest jingle I ever heard was the tenderloin madam's alphabet" (1948: 37). Alan Lomax neither recorded nor set down the lyrics for this song, although certainly he knew of it. Referring to the "Lumberjack's Alphabet" ("A is for axes . . .") in his 1938 Michigan field notebooks, he added: "The Alphabet Song was very popular + there was a companion piece that was often sung immediately after—'A is for asshole all covered with hair, etc.'"

35 Red Light Saloon
Sung by Bill Neupert, Schofield, Wisconsin, August 1941.
Recorded by Robert F. Draves.
5005 B1

I arrived in Muskegon the tenth of July,
For connections to make with a train I did try.

Got left in Muskegon and that was my doom,
When I paid a short visit to the Red Light Saloon.

< Unknown lumberjack singer, Waushara County, Wisconsin, 1940. (Wisconsin Historical Society, WHi-25420)

Oh the Red Light Saloon in Muskegon, I walked to the bar.
A red-headed maiden sold me a cigar.

I took my cigar and sat down in a chair,
And this red-headed maiden come trippin' and skippin' round there.

Oh she sat in my lap. She played with my mustache and mussed up my hair.
Old joy boy, old Reuben went up in the air.

Oh we tripped up the stairway a bedroom to find.
I done shucked my clothes and she pulled down the blind.

Oh I lay there a-puffing and a-panting awhile.
She said, "Get off me, you damn hobo, you've got me with child."

Oh she washed off my dodger and scrubbed out her cunt,
And she went right down stairs for some more jazzing to hunt.

If you should meet this fair maiden when the roses do bloom,
She'll jazz for two dollars in Muskegon at the Red Light Saloon.

In response to Alan Lomax's request for "the full version of 'Red Light Saloon' which I'd heard only in part" (May 1, 1941), Stratman-Thomas's student engineer Bob Draves accordingly captured three versions, making the "Red Light Saloon" second only to the "Little Brown Bulls," a Wisconsin lumber-camp ballad, as the song most recorded during Stratman-Thomas's three-year project. The "Red Light" refers of course to a lamp signaling the presence of prostitutes. This song is typically associated with Muskegon, Michigan, where "runners" lurked at railroad stations to coax shanty boys to the scores of saloons in notorious Sawdust Flats where "sporting women" would offer drinks, cigars, and a "little party" upstairs (Doerflinger 1972: 249–250; Kilar 2002: 71–75).

Bill Neupert's version is distinguished by two common lumberjack terms for penis, "old Reuben" and "dodger," as well as by his use of "jazz" in its original meaning as sexual intercourse. William B. Neupert (1888–1974) sang only this song for the Library of Congress, and we know little more than the fact that he lived and worked in Schofield, a logging and mill town just south of Wausau.

36 Red Light Saloon

Sung by John Christian, Coloma, Wisconsin, August 27, 1940.
Recorded by Robert F. Draves.

4167 B

Come all you young fellows, I'll sing you a song.
You pay good attention, it won't take me long.
I'll sing you a song while fortune on me fell
When taking a stroll to the White Hotel.

'Twas in the last days of the month of July,
For to make good connections with a train I did try.
While at Muskegon I was left there to doom
And pay a last visit to the Red Light Saloon.

I boldly walked in and stepped to the bar
When a pretty young damsel said, "Have a cigar."
I took a cigar and sat down in a chair.
Finally this maiden came tripping round there.

She boldly walked up and sat down on my knee,
Said, "You are a fine lad, and that I can see.
You are a shanty boy, for that I well know,
For your muscle is hard from your head to your toe."

Then she played with my mustache and curled up my hair.
My old boy got ugly, I vow and declare.
And I jumped and rised up, laying my cigar down,
Said, "My pretty fair maid, let us go have a round."

And she took me upstairs, to her bedroom we went.
Shutters was pulled down and at it we went.
I pulled out my dodger and I give it a shove.
Such glorious feelings from heaven above!

I bowed up my back while my dodger did play,
And then on her belly a-panting I lay.
Then she twirled with my mustache and on me did smile.
Said, "You upriver bummer, you've got me with child."

And I boldly rolled off and the sweat it rolled down.
To wash off my dodger she quickly flew round.
Some soap and some water to wash out her cunt,
While tripping downstairs another victim to hunt.

Now come all you young fellows, my song it is sung.
And if you've ever a chance to Muskegon to run,
Go seek this fair damsel, she's a rose in full bloom.
She fucks for five dollars in the Red Light Saloon.

John H. Christian was born in Ireland in 1872 and arrived in Wisconsin a decade later, presumably brought by his parents. His wife, Bessie, was born in Wisconsin, and the couple lived in Hancock, just north of Coloma where the recording occurred. Besides the "Red Light Saloon," he sang "Shantyboy on the Big Eau Claire," which was composed by the Irish American woods poet William N. Allen of Wausau, and "Paddy Miles the Fishermen," concerning sexual encounters with a mermaid.

Christian was recorded at the same session as Lewis Winfield Moody and another old lumberjack, Henry Humphries (also known as Henry A. Humphrey, b. 1866). Humphries, whose repertoire included such classic lumberjack ballads as "Harry Bale" and "Shantyman's Life," also performed a version of the "Red Light Saloon" (AFS 4977 A1) that departed intriguingly from Christian's mention of "the White Hotel."

Come ladies and gents, and I'll sing you a song.
Just give me your attention and it won't take me long.
It was of a misfortune, which to me did befall
By taking a trip to the noted Whitehall.

The intended destination, before being diverted to the infamous saloon, Whitehall was founded in the 1850s as a logging town, with a less unsavory reputation, in northern Muskego County.

37 Gambler's Blues

Sung by Bessie Gordon, Schofield, Wisconsin, August 13, 1941.
Recorded by Helene Stratman-Thomas and Robert F. Draves.

5008 A2

I was down in old Joe's barroom at the corner of the square,
And the drinks were served as usual, and a goodly crowd was there.

At my right stood Joe McCatty, his eyes bloodshot and red,
And he looked at the crowd all around him, and these were the words he said:

> Bessie Gordon plays the sawed-off organ in her bar, Schofield, Wisconsin, 1941. (Wisconsin Historical Society, WHi-6513)

"As I passed by the old infirmary, I saw my baby there,
All stretched out on a table, so cold and still and fair."

Yodel-ay-ee-oo, delady-ee-oo, de-leedle-lay-eeee.

"Sixteen coal-black horses all hitched to a rubber-tired hack
Took seven pretty girls to the graveyard, only six of them coming back."

Yodel-ay-ee-oo, de-leedle lady-ee-oo, de-lady-eeee.

"Now when I die just bury me, in a box with a coat and hat,
Put a twenty-dollar gold piece on my watch chain to let the Lord know I'm standing pat."

"Six crapshooters as pall-bearers, let a chorus girl sing me a song,
Put a jazz band on the hearse, to raise heck as we go along."

Yodel-ay-ee-oo, de-leedle-lady-ee-oo, delay-eeee.

"Now that you've heard my story, I'll take another shot of booze.
And if anybody happens to ask you, well, I've got those gambler's blues."

Yodel-ay-ee-oo, de-leedle-lay-ee-oo, delay-eeee.
Yodel-ay-ee-oo, de-leedle-lay-ee,
Yodel-ay-ee-oo, de-lay-ee,
Yodel-ay-ee-oo, de-lay-dee-oo, de-lay-dee.

We were directed to Schofield to see Mrs. Bessie Gordon. Mrs. Gordon knew many
of the sentimental American ballads, such as "The Baggage Coach Ahead," "Prayer
Meeting Time in the Hollow," and "The Wheel of the Wagon is Broken" [as well as "Just
Plain Folks"], which she had learned from her mother. Mrs. Gordon would sing these
songs for the entertainment of her customers at the tavern to the accompaniment of
a little reed organ which she had cut down to fit under the counter. (Stratman-Thomas
1940–1960: August 13, 1941)

The end of Prohibition in 1933 sparked a profusion of mom-and-pop taverns throughout
the rural and working-class districts of Wisconsin. In keeping with the Upper Midwest's
European peasant heritage, these were typically family places that served food along
with beer and featured live music. The tavern run by Bessie "Ma" Gordon (b. 1901) in
rural Marathon County near the mill town of Schofield was a tiny frame building where
she presided for more than forty years, "raised a large family and cared for a disabled

husband on the proceeds of the tavern," supplemented by a large garden and her earnings as a county clerk (Moen and Davis 2008: 77–78).

Gordon's sawed-off pump organ made creative use of an old-time instrument usually confined to churches and parlors. "Gambler's Blues" was a racy departure from her other performances, with warbling in the "blue yodel" style popularized in the 1920s by Jimmie Rodgers. Her lyrics and tempo are quite different from "Those Gambler's Blues" that Rodgers recorded in 1930, however, and closely resemble George Washington White's March 1932 recording, made in Grafton, Wisconsin, for the Paramount label. The song derives from a nineteenth-century British soldier's lament, "The Unfortunate Rake," which inspired the cowboy ballad "Streets of Laredo," as well as "St. James Infirmary," an urban underworld rendition to which Gordon's performance is closely related.

Print by Isabella Leary

MY FATHER WAS A DUTCHMAN
THE HELENE STRATMAN-THOMAS RECORDINGS, PART TWO

GERMAN AND AUSTRIAN

Immigrants from the many principalities that became the German nation, as well as from the old Austro-Hungarian Empire, began settling the Wisconsin territory in the 1830s, first arriving in the Milwaukee area via the Erie Canal and the Great Lakes or traveling down the Ohio River and up the Mississippi to make homes in southwestern Wisconsin. Outnumbering English-speaking settlers, they established farms, businesses, churches, schools, and towns, sustained and modified Old World cultural traditions, and spoke and sang in their dialects well into the twentieth century. Since descendants of German-speaking immigrants typically were bilingual, shards of their "lingo" often tripped off neighbors' tongues, sometimes with comic effect. Stratman-Thomas found mock German and German-Austrian performers among retired lumberjacks, immigrant tradesmen, and dwellers in such enduring Germanic strongholds as Wausau, Dodge County, and the greater Milwaukee area.

1   My Father Was a Dutchman

Sung by Noble Brown, Millville, Wisconsin, November 17, 1946.
Recorded by Helene Stratman-Thomas and Aubrey Snyder.
Transcribed and translated by Antje Petty, 2011.

8431 B2

Deutsch spreche[n]—verstehst du?	Speaking German—you understand?
Mein Vater was a Dutchman	My father was a Dutchman.
Verstehst du? Ja! Ja!	You understand? Yes! Yes!

Raised in the hamlet of Millville in heavily German Grant County, Brown could have heard this mixed-language song while growing up (see Stratman-Thomas CD part 1, track 31). He sang a similar comic dialect song, "Did You Call Me Vader?," featuring a stereotypical German immigrant, Fritz. Yet he may well have acquired it, like his repertoire of shanties, during his years at sea. Former sailor and sea-shanty scholar Stan Hugill categorized it as a "Pidgin-Dutch forebitter," or "sailor's song of leisure," and included variously titled versions—"Mein fader [alternatively "vader"] vos ein Dutchman"—in two publications (1961: 503; 1977: 23, 188). As Hugill explained: "The old-time sailing ship Johnny was very partial to 'furrin lingoes' but somewhat inadequate when he tried to use them. This song is a rather humorous attempt at Dutch, or perhaps German. A 'Dutchman' in the lingo of the old-time sailorman was any member of the Nordic race *except* a Hollander, who was called 'Holland Dutch.' The general term 'Squarehead' was used for all Germans, Scandinavians, and seamen from the Low Countries."

We will never know whether or not Brown—self-conscious about his rough ways and deferential to Stratman-Thomas as a woman and a university professor—knew any of the raunchy, bawdy verses Hugill reports. Among them:

> Mit mein niggerum, buggerum, stinkum,
> Vell, ve'll climb upon der steeples,
> Und ve'll spit down on de peoples.
>
> Und der polis-man, fireman, steepleman,
> Dey all climbs upon de steeple,
> Und dey laugh do all de peoples.
>
> Oh, ven I vos ein sailor,
> Vell ve trink up all der whiskey,
> Und it makes us feel damn frisky.
>
> Ve did all de bawdy houses,
> Und ve hitchum up de trousers,
> Und ve catchum all der louses.
>
> Ve chase all der bretty frauleins,
> Und ve chase 'em und ve tease 'em,
> Und ve catch 'em un ve kees 'em.

A variant of Brown's lone verse is well known in Australia, while the tune, called both "My Father Was a Dutchman" and the "Spanish Waltz," continues to be played as a stand-alone piece or to accompany the Spanish waltz figure for the Alberts quadrille set of dances popular in Victoria (Musgrove 2011).

2   Die Deutschmeister / The German Master [Regiment]

Played on zither and sung by Richard Taschek, with Laura Zenz and Louis Taschek, Darlington, Wisconsin, August 22, 1946. Recorded by Helene Stratman-Thomas and Aubrey Snyder. Transcription, translation, and annotation by Rudolph Pietsch, with assistance from Antje Petty, 2012.

8429 B2

A Friseur sagt zu sein G'hilfen,
    "Gottfried, nehmen's Ihnen z'samm!
In Fiesko schneid'n und stutzen, werd'ns
    kein Glück jetzt nimmer ham.
Richten's Ihna ein jetzt . . . nehmen's
    Rindschmalz und Pomad,
Ja wenn's sonst ja noch nix könnan,
    muaß i Ihnen wegtuan, tuat ma lad.
Mit die G'wiss'n, tan ma's fiara,
    hab'n 's uns eina, habt es ja."
	A barber says to his helper,
	    "Gottfried, bestir yourself!
	To make a short Fiesko[1] haircut, now
	    you won't succeed without
	Striving right now to get
	    lard and pomade.
	If you are not able to do this,
	    I have to fire you.
	Slick back some of the hair in front."

CHORUS:
Aber die Deutschmeister,
    die Deutschmeister, die
    Deutschmeister sein da, holl-ja,
Die Deutschmeister, die Deutschmeister,
    die Deutschmeister sein da, hull-ja,
	CHORUS:
	Hey, the Deutschmeisters,
	    the Deutschmeisters, the
	    Deutschmeisters are here, hull-ja!
	The Deutschmeisters, the
	    Deutschmeisters, the
	    Deutschmeisters are here, hull-ja![2]

Daß die Edelknaben[3] heute
    rücken in die Garnison,
Daß die Edelknaben heute
    rücken in die Garnison,
Jede Greisslerin mit da Butt'n, jeder
    Greißler bei [beugt] sein Stand,
Jeder Schuasta bei [beugt] sein
    Bankel, jeder Schneider bei
    [beugt] sein G'wand,
Jede Köchin in der Kuchl schreit
    beim Knödlsiad'n, hull-jå!
	Those noble pages conscripted
	    into the garrison,
	Those noble pages conscripted
	    into the garrison,
	Every [female] grocer with her basket,
	    every [male] grocer at his market stall,
	Every cobbler at his bench, every
	    tailor finishing a frock,
	
	Every [female] cook is whooping
	    while cooking dumplings, hull-ja!

Da laß ma uns're Dudler raus, Da gibt's a Hetzt, a G'stanz,	[Hey,] we will sing our yodeling There are funny verses.

Da hör ma harbe Tanz,	There we will listen to fancy dance melodies,
Da laß ma uns're Dudler raus,	[Hey,] we will sing our yodeling,
Und fahr (geh) ma mit an	And go home in a fancy
Edelschwamma z'haus, hull-ja.	Schwamma,[4] hull-ja.

----

1. Fiesko was a Genoese revolutionary with a distinctive short haircut. He figured prominently in Friedrich Schiller's *Fiesko: The Conspiracy of Genoa* (1783).
2. The Deutschmeister infantry regiment, whose recruits were drawn chiefly from Vienna, was the most celebrated unit in the Austrian army.
3. The regiment was referred to as the Wiener Edelknaben, which translates to "Vienna Pages." The sons of the Viennese ruling class sought positions in the unit and members included archdukes and imperial princes.
4. Schwamma was the surname of a famous Viennese coachman.

Born in 1891, Richard Taschek immigrated to Chicago in 1909, where Burgenlanders from Austria's easternmost province, bordering Hungary, made the Windy City home to the largest Austrian population outside of the home country. Newspaper obituaries and census records list Taschek's birthplace as being in both Austria and Hungary. Zither clubs and Austrian songs flourished in Chicago, perhaps inspiring Taschek to bring this instrument and a love of song to Darlington—the county seat of Lafayette County, Wisconsin—in 1917. There he set up a tailor's shop for thirty-two years and was known as T. Richards to his customers (*Wisconsin State Journal*, April 3, 1949).

There were like-minded Austrians in the community, and Stratman-Thomas learned of them serendipitously. As her field notes for August 22, 1946, tell us: "A University of Wisconsin music student, Elsie Taschek of Darlington, told me of the family parties at which Austrian dialect songs were still sung. Elsie's father, Richard Taschek, consented to sing and to play the zither. He arranged for a gathering of singers, among them Mrs. Laura Zenz, Louis Taschek, and [his wife, Irma Taschek]. Again the evening of recording was an occasion for merriment. The list of songs recorded that night is long. It includes: 'Wenn ich mein Heuserl verkauf' (When I Sold My House), 'Wenn ich dir in Auglein schaut' (When I Look in Your Eyes), and 'Mitzel, willst mit mir auf die Alme gehen?' (Mitzel, Will You Go with Me up the Alps?)." Stratman-Thomas went on to characterize "Die Deutschmeister" as a march, adding that the space on the recording disc ran out "before last singing of refrain was thru."

> Richard Taschek ("T. Richard") at his tailor shop, Darlington, Wisconsin, 1946. (Wisconsin Historical Society, WHi-25407)

The song's esoteric references to special haircuts, a Viennese coachman, the characteristics of the Deutschmeister, and the singers' regional dialect made the transcription and translation of this song a challenge. In 1984, when Judy Woodward of Wisconsin Public Radio sought help from the Deutsches Volksliedarchiv, she received this response from archivist Wiegand Stief: "Unverständlich. Ich kann auch über die Melodie keine Varianten finden." [Unintelligible. I also can't find a variant of the melody anywhere.]

Thanks to the Viennese ethnomusicologist Rudi Pietsch, we now know that Taschek's performance creatively combines and modifies two earlier songs. The first two verses and chorus are variations from "Die Deutschmeister san do!," composed by Johann Sioly and Wilhelm Wiesenberg. The third verse is a variation from a song by Carl Lorens, "Mir gengan heut nach Nußdorf h'naus." Both songs were performed in Viennese musical halls by traveling performers and entered into oral tradition aided by their publication in a *Liedflugblatt* (song pamphlet). Sioly (1843–1911), Wiesenberg (1850–1896), and Lorens (1851–1909) were all singers and prolific song composers—acknowledged as "poets of the people" because of their reliance on traditional song forms and themes—and especially active in Vienna from the 1870s until their deaths.

3   Wiener Fiakerlied / Viennese Coachman's Song

Played on zither by Hans Huber of Delafield, Wisconsin, at the
University of Wisconsin–Madison, September 1946. Recorded by
Helene Stratman-Thomas and Aubrey Snyder.
8467 A2

In 1946 John V. "Hans" Huber was a resident of Delafield in Wisconsin's Waukesha County, where he ran a tavern on Lake Nagawicki. Stratman-Thomas's notes and census evidence suggest he was born in 1900 or 1901, the son of Bavarian immigrants Hans and Elizabeth Huber. Prior to 1920 he lived for a time in Milwaukee, where his parents ran a boardinghouse that included immigrant men born variously in Austria, Bohemia, and Bavaria. It may be that the elder Huber was also a musician, as Hans Huber's Singspiel Ensemble put on comic musical performances in venues like Turner Hall in Monroe, Wisconsin, in the early twentieth century (*Monroe Weekly Times*, December 10 and 13, 1906). Another zither player who recorded for Stratman-Thomas, Albert Mueller (1913–1996), knew the younger Hans Huber as a fine musician and a "nice guy" of Bavarian/Austrian heritage (Mueller 1987).

Huber traveled to Madison, unplugging his amplified concert zither, to record ten Austrian and Bavarian tunes, along with the ragtime coon song "Dark Town Strutter's Ball" and a 1924 jazz composition, "Sleepy Time Gal," waxed by Harry James, Glenn Miller, and others. Huber's "Wiener Fiakerlied" is an instrumental version of a nostalgic composition by the Austrian industrialist Gustave Pick. Not unlike the minstrel-show songs of Stephen Foster, which portrayed African Americans with affectionate sentimentality and implicit condescension, Pick's song—celebrating an elderly "working class everyman" faithfully serving the Hapsburg Empire's "rich and famous"—was performed and translated widely following its 1885 publication, becoming "one of the most celebrated, imitated, and covered popular songs from the waning decades of the nineteenth century" (Bohlman 2002: 15–19). Featured prominently by Austrian performers of Viennese *schrammelmusik* at Chicago's Colombian Exposition of 1893, "Wiener Fiakerlied" was also recorded commercially by Austrian and German musicians in the United States (Bohlman 2002: 18; Spottswood 1990: 119, 141, 167, 237, 270).

4   Wir sitzen so fröhlich beisamen / We Sit So Merrily Together

Spoken and sung by Ella Mittelstadt Fischer, with an introduction by Helene Stratman-Thomas, Mayville, Wisconsin, August 27, 1946. Recorded by Helene Stratman-Thomas and Aubrey Snyder. Transcription, translation, and annotation by Antje Petty, 2011.

8444 A1

Stratman-Thomas: This is a conversation with Mrs. Ella Fischer of Mayville, and she's going to tell us about the days when she went to the Schlitz Palm Garten in Milwaukee.

Fischer: Well, my father used to be cooper there. And every Sunday he would take me down there. And the gang would be down there, all Germans, and then they would sing. The first one we generally sang was [begins to sing]:

Wir sitzen so fröhlich beisammen	We are sitting together so cheerfully
Und wir haben uns einander so lieb.	And we love each other so much.
Wir [er]heitern einander das Leben.	We enliven each other's lives.
Ach, wenn es doch immer so blieb!	Oh, if it were always to be like that!
Ach, es kann ja nicht immer so bleiben.	But things cannot remain as they are.
Hier, unter dem Wechsel des Monds,	Here, with the change of the moon,

Der Krieg muss den Frieden vertreiben.	War is dispelling peace.
Im Kriege wird keiner verschont.	Nobody is spared during a war.
Und da kommen die stolzen Franzosen Daher.	And there come the proud Frenchmen.
Und wir Deutschen, wir fürchten uns nicht.	And we Germans, we are not afraid.
Wir stehen so fest als wie die Mauern,	We stand firm like the walls,
Und weichen und wanken keinen Schritt.	And neither sway nor move a single step.
Oh Napoleon! Du Schustergeselle!	Oh Napoleon! You cobbler's apprentice![1]
Ei, du saßest so stolz auf deinem Thron.	Well, you so proudly sat on your throne.
In Deutschland da warst du so strenge.	In Germany you were so oppressive.
In Russland bekamst du deinen Lohn.	In Russia you got your reward.
Ach, hättest du nicht an Deutschland gedacht,	Oh, if you hadn't had Germany on your mind,
Und hättest du Frieden mit Russland gemacht,	And if you had made peace with Russia,
So wärest du Kaiser geblieben,	You would have remained Emperor,
Und hättest den allerschönsten Thron!	And you would have the most beautiful throne of them all!

---

1. This is the literal translation. The phrase is an invective.

Ella Mittelstadt Fischer (1871–1963) was born to German immigrant parents near Mayville in Dodge County, Wisconsin. In 1892 she married Otto Fischer, who had been brought to the area from Germany as a one-year-old in 1869. In 1946 the couple's daughter Leone Fischer Griesemer (b. 1898) wrote to Stratman-Thomas that she recalled her parents singing "in duet form when at feather stripping and neighborhood birthday parties" in their heavily German rural community. As a girl, Ella Mittelstadt had learned many German songs, not only in her parents' company, but also while tagging after her grandfather who tended the Schlitz Brewery's Milwaukee Gast Haus. She was likewise a noted herbalist, curing humans and animals with remedies that, according to family tradition, her mother had acquired from Menominee Indians in the 1860s and 1870s (Leary 1998: 323–324). The Schlitz Palm Garden, or *Palmengarten*, opened in 1896 as an opulent beer hall and hotel built by the Schlitz Brewing Company in downtown Milwaukee and was enthusiastically patronized by the city's substantial German-speaking populace.

Ella Mittelstadt Fischer flanked by her daughters Edna and Leone on Mother's Day, Mayville, Wisconsin, 1950. (author's collection, courtesy of Leone Fischer Griesemer)

Stratman-Thomas recorded Fischer at the home of her daughter Leone, who had learned about the Wisconsin Folksong Project by listening to public radio.

> We had arranged to call on Mrs. Ella Mittelstadt Fischer of Mayville that evening. In response to a broadcast over WHA Mrs. Fischer's daughter, Mrs. A. G. Griesemer of Lake Mills, wrote: "The announcement that the University School of Music is looking for more old tunes awoke in me a desire to preserve some of the many songs my mother sings of the Palm Garten era."
>
> When we arrived at Mrs. Fischer's home, she was convalescing from a serious illness, but she laughed at the thought that she was too ill to sing. Propped in a comfortable chair, she recorded her favorite German songs, which she had learned as a little girl when she went with her parents to the Schlitz Palm Garten in Milwaukee. We enjoyed Mrs. Fischer's stories of the *Gemutlichkeit* of the gatherings of the German families as expressed in her song, "Wir sitzen so fröhlich beisamen" (We Sit So Merrily Together). Mrs. Fischer not only knew the song of the "Milwaukee Fire" or "The Burning of the Newhall House," but she had also witnessed the tragedy. As a girl of twelve she had come to town the day of the fire to buy her confirmation dress. She remembered the occasion so vividly that she wept as she sang the song. (Stratman-Thomas 1940–1960: August 27, 1946)

Well-known in oral tradition as a soldier's song, with 103 variants held by the Deutsches Volksliedarchiv, "Wir sitzen so frohlich beisamen" harkens to the Napoleonic Wars of the early nineteenth century. The patriotic German lyrics, with their sympathy for Russia and scorn for Napoleon, were written in 1802 by August von Kotzebue (1761–1819), a prolific dramatist and essayist who had represented the German Federation as consul to Russia. The tune is attributed to Friedrich Heinrich Himmel (1765–1814), a Prussian composer (Stief 1984).

5 Sockery's Cat

Spoken by Charles Robinson, Marion, Waushara County, Wisconsin, April 20, 1941. Recorded by Helene Stratman-Thomas and Robert F. Draves.
4966 A3

Mine goot friends, I tell you little story 'bout what happened one day last veek. You see Katarina, dat was my *frau*, she go away, she make little picnic. And she say 'fore she go, "Sockery, you go up to barn about, see dat old blue hen don't lay some eggs pretty much already."

So I take the saw and the ax and the hammer, and I goes to work to make the house what was a hen house into a barn what was corn crib. And while I was sawing on a board, dat old blue hen she come out from round the barn. She say, "Cut-cut, cut-a-cut. Cut-cut, cut-a-cut." I thinks to myself, maybe she lay some eggs pretty much already.

So I creeps down under the barn and way back in the corner. I didn't see any eggs pretty much, but I saw little black and white *kat*. So I creeps up on my hands and knees, and I grabs him by the back of the neck. And oh, my goodness gracious me, what a schmell. I thought I had stepped on something which was dead. It was worser than a whole barrel of limburger. And I take it in mine arm, and I goes out in the front yard.

And along up the road come old Jake Moser. When he see me with dat kat he says, "You old fool, what you doing with dat schkunk?"

"Schkunk!" I say. And I drop him so quick as was half so quick as never was. "Mine goot friend Jake," I say, "what I do make dat schmell go 'way?"

Vell, he say he bury me up to the neck in the ground. Dat make the schmell go away. And he get a schpade, and he bury me up to the neck in the ground. And he say, "Vell, I got little business down by the willage. I go there."

So he vent, and pretty soon there was fly light on my nose. And I schpit and think and viggled. Fly he no go way. Pretty soon there was more flies. More than thousand flies. More than a hundred flies light on my nose. And I schpit and viggled, but the fly he no go 'way.

Pretty soon I look down the road, and there was men and women and schildrens. You see dat old fool, Jake, he go by the willage. He tell them there was man buried alive up to Sockery's. Vell, I see I couldn't keep dat schtory schtill any longer. So I tells them the whole business, and those fools, you can hear them laugh more than half mile.

Charles Robinson (*left*) and an unknown singer, Waushara County, Wisconsin, 1941. (Wisconsin Historical Society, WHi-25419)

> I think I not much longer vill schtay in this country. You see, everybody I meet on the road say to me, "Sockery, how you like to buy little kat?"

The performer of this comic story of an immigrant's misadventures with a skunk, Charles Robinson, worked in the woods as a young man before becoming a schoolteacher whose pupils included the children of German immigrants. Born in Massachusetts in 1865, Robinson also sang "Fond du Lac Jail" (Stratman-Thomas CD part 1, track 33).

Stratman-Thomas recognized "Sockery's Cat" as "a recitative of the type which was sometimes used in lumber camp entertainment. . . . There is a series of Sockery's stuff (all German dialects) in print." Stage German, or "Dutch," dialect songs and recitations became common in American music halls, tent shows, and comic anthologies in the mid-nineteenth century. Perhaps thanks to *Burdett's Dutch Dialect Recitations and Humorous Readings* (1884), Sockery's particular misadventures were very popular not only in informal storytelling sessions but also in schoolhouse recitations, newspapers and magazines, stage plays, and radio broadcasts from the late 1870s through the mid-1950s.

The search engine NewspaperArchive.com reveals roughly forty references to Sockery in mostly Midwestern newspapers between 1879 and 1954, including in such heavily German communities in Wisconsin as Appleton and Sheboygan. Most accounts of Sockery performances concern some variation of "How Sockery Set a Hen," which figures in the novel *Anne of Green Gables* (L. Montgomery et al.: 1997: 179). But there are also episodes regarding "Sockery's Day Off," "Sockery Joins the Lodge," and at least three versions of "Sockery and the Little Cat." In 1922, for example, Mrs. R. S. Beatty contributed two readings to upstate New York's *Westinghouse Radio Program*: "The Dutchman's Serenade" and "Sockery and the Little Cat" (*The Binghamton Press*, March 30). Presumably a mangling of "Zachary," Sockery is occasionally given the onomato-poeic surname Kadacut, in reference to his chicken call, but he bears a mock-German surname more often: Schneidelbecker, Schneldubecker, or Schtieidelbecker (see also Landon 1883; Newlin 1911; Leary 2008).

6 An einem Fluss daraus an Schuss / By a Rapidly Flowing River

Sung by Martha Steinbach, Wausau, Wisconsin, August 12, 1941.
Recorded by Helene Stratman-Thomas and Robert F. Draves.
Transcription and translation Antje Petty, 2011.
5005 B2, 5006 A1

An einem Fluss, der rauschend schoss,	By a rapidly flowing river
Ein armes Mädchen saß.	Sat a poor girl.
Aus ihren blauen Äuglein floss	From her blue eyes streamed
Manch Tränchen in das Gras.	Many tears onto the grass.
Sie wand von Blumen einen Strauß	She gathered flowers into a bouquet
Und warf ihn in den Strom.	And threw it into the current.
"Ach, guter Vater," rief sie aus.	"Oh, dear father," she cried.
"Ach lieber Bruder, komm!"	"Oh, dear brother, come!"
Ein reicher Herr gegangen kam	A rich gentleman walked by
Und sah das [des] Mädchens Schmerz,	And saw the girl's pain;

Sah ihre Tränen, ihren Gram	Saw her tears, her grief
Und dies brach ihm sein Herz	And this broke his heart.
"Was fehlet, liebes Mädchen, dir?	"What's wrong, dear girl?
Was weinest du so früh?	Why are you crying so early [in the day]?
Sag deine[r]Tränen Ursach mir	Tell me the reason for your tears.
Kann ich, so heb ich sie."	If I can, I will stop them."
"Oh seh[t?] dort jene Rasenbank.	"Oh see that grassy knoll over there.
Ist meiner Mutter Grab.	It is my mother's grave.
Und auch, vor wenig Tagen sank.	And a few days ago,
Mein Vater hier hinab."	My father died here, too."
"Der wilde Strom riss ihn dahin.	"The current pulled him in.
Mein Bruder sah [es] und sprang ihm nach.	My brother saw it and jumped after him.
Da fasst der Strom auch ihn,	There the current grabbed him, too,
Und ach, auch er ertrank."	And, oh, he also drowned."
"Nun ich im Waisenhause bin.	"Now I live in an orphanage.
Und wenn ich Rasttag hab,	And when I have a day of rest,
Geh ich nach diesem Flusse hin	I come to this river
Und weine mich [recht ab]."	And cry [my heart out]."
"Sollst nicht mehr weinen, liebes Kind.	"You shall not cry anymore, dear child.
Ich will dein Vater sein.	I will be your father.
Du hast ein Herz, das es verdient.	You have a heart that deserves this.
Du bist so fromm und rein."	You are so pious and pure."
Er tat's und nahm sie in sein Haus,	He did it and took her to his home,
Der gute reiche Mann.	The good rich man.
Zog ihr die Trauerkleider aus	Took off her mourning clothes
Und zog sie [sic] schönre an.	And dressed her in more beautiful ones.
Sie saß an seinem Tisch und trank	She sat at his table and drank
Von seinem Becher satt.	Her fill from his cup.
"Du guter Edler, habe Dank	"Oh dear nobleman, be thanked
Für deine edle Tat."	For your noble deed."

In 1891, the year of Martha Steinbach's birth, Wausau and surrounding Marathon County were 75 percent German, with settlers from Hesse-Darmstad having arrived in the 1850s, followed after the Civil War by immigrants from Pomerania, West Prussia, and Brandenburg. Although Mrs. Steinbach was born in Wisconsin, both of her parents, as well as her husband, Robert, were born in Germany. While Robert Steinbach recorded four songs for the Library of Congress, his wife sang only this one.

In a letter written April 28, 1947, to Stratman-Thomas, Martha Steinbach's son, Don, emphasized the pride his mother felt in singing this particular song. Stratman-Thomas's undated field notes go further: "Mrs. Martha Steinbach, age 51. She learned the song when nine years old from her mother, who was born in Germany. She says the song is about five hundred years old. She has never heard anyone else sing it. Great-grandmother has been an 'Amme,' a nursemaid, who learned the song from her grand-mother. Mrs. Steinbach's mother asked that she never let it die because it had been passed on from generation to generation. It is the story of an orphan child and a rich man who befriended her."

Thanks to the Deutsches Volksliedarchiv, we can trace the song—of which more than fifty variants are known—to 1781, when it was published with words attributed to Kaspar Friedrich Lossius (Stief 1984). Born in the Thuringian capital, Erfurt, Lossius (1753–1817) was a prominent clergyman, a prolific writer, and the editor of a Lutheran hymnal. The song, with its sympathy for an orphan and distress over the tragic loss of loved ones, resonates with Lossius's life, because he was orphaned and raised in difficult straits and later lost two young daughters to scarlet fever.

SWISS

In 1845 German-speaking immigrants from the Canton of Glarus settled in what would become Green County, Wisconsin, establishing the largest rural settlement of Swiss in the United States, centered initially on the village of New Glarus but expanding to include settlers from the Canton of Bern in and around the nearby city of Monroe. The late nineteenth-century expansion of the dairy industry in Wisconsin attracted another wave of Swiss immigrants, especially cheesemakers, who were often employed through-out the state by small cooperative cheese factories established by local farmers to process their milk. Wisconsin's Swiss included yodelers, button accordionists, and zither players from the outset, and Green County remains a stronghold of Swiss American music per-formed in local taverns and for such seasonal festivals as the performance of Schiller's play, *Wilhelm Tell*, produced annually since 1938 by the people of New Glarus.

7   Landjäger / Gamekeeper

Played on zither by Albert Mueller, New Glarus, Wisconsin,
August 20, 1940. Recorded by Helene Stratman-Thomas and Robert F. Draves.
4160 B2

Albert M. Mueller (1913–1996) was born in New Glarus where his father, Markus, a native of Glarus, Switzerland, had settled in 1910. His mother, Bertha, emigrated from the Swiss Canton of Appenzell in 1912, carrying with her a Glarner zither made by a craftsman named Oertli. Unable to play it herself, she encouraged her son: "She thought I should learn how to play that because I could play independently. You got your bass, you got your accompaniment, you got your melody all on one instrument" (Mueller 1987). For six months in 1924 eleven-year-old Albert traveled nine miles north each Saturday, taking two-hour lessons from a Mrs. Elmer in Belleville: "All by ear. She'd play and I'd watch her and listen and then I'd try to imitate." A few years later Albert bought a concert zither through an ad in a Swiss American periodical, *Die Hausfrau*, then sought help to play it from a Berner, John Aschliman, in Monroe: "Took the bus there on Saturdays to the Ludlow Hotel." After six months, Aschliman told him, "Well, Al, you can play as good as I can. So you're on your own from here."

From the late 1930s through the early 1940s, Mueller played zither between the acts for his home community's Wilhelm Tell play. Offered in German and English since its inception, the Tell play and related musical entertainments were well known to faculty at the University of Wisconsin, including Stratman-Thomas. As her field notes for August 20, 1940, tell us: "We arrived at New Glarus in the midst of preparations for the Wilhelm Tell play. Rehearsals for this annual Labor Day event precluded us from assembling groups of yodelers for recording, as we had planned. We were directed to a very talented Tyrolean zither player, Albert Mueller, who recorded many folk melodies, Tyrolean marches, and ländlers. We marveled at his dexterity. His mother too expressed her admiration and pride: 'Oh ja, his teacher says he hat a gut Schwung.'"

Mueller moved to Milwaukee in 1941, where he worked as a tool-and-die maker for a number of manufacturers, including Spincraft, occasionally returning home for music events like this World War II benefit: "Mrs. Ernest Zingg of Briar Hill will direct a Swiss dialect play, part of a Swiss-American entertainment and dance to be held at 8 p.m. Friday in Turner hall. The program is being sponsored by the American Committee for Swiss Relief to raise funds to help Switzerland care for refugee children from

Albert Mueller, his mother, and Robert Draves, New Glarus, Wisconsin, 1940. (Wisconsin Historical Society, WHi-25418)

German-occupied countries in Europe. Besides the Swiss play the program will feature Rudy Burkhalter and band, the Disch sisters, Albert Mueller and his zither, Madison Swiss chorus, the New Glarus yodelers, and Zimmerman's Swiss dance orchestra" (*Wisconsin State Journal*, Sunday, October 18, 1942). But after joining the Milwaukee Zither Club in 1942, Mueller's musical life was mostly in that city and, although he played for more than twenty years for Milwaukee Swiss Club functions, his repertoire shifted to German and Austrian tunes in keeping with his new home's dominant population. In the mid-1940s, while playing a solo job at the Golden Zither restaurant, he drew on his industrial trade to create an amplified zither with a gilded sound box. From the 1950s through the early 1960s, he was part of the Jolly Alpine Boys, combining zither, clarinet, button accordion, tuba, and occasional yodels. From 1966 to 1979, he was a full-time musician for the Golden Zither, and in the 1980s he performed with the Vienna Strings, an Austrian *schrammel* ensemble featuring zither, piano accordion, and twin violins.

"Landjäger," the tune he recorded for Stratman-Thomas, invokes an Old World gamekeeper, but a landjäger is also a dried sausage made in New Glarus and savored for more than a century by tavern patrons in Swissconsin.

8   Echo Yodel

Played on Swiss button accordion and yodeled by John Giezendanner,
with Albert Giezendanner, Barron, Wisconsin, August 9, 1946.
Recorded by Helene Stratman-Thomas and Aubrey Snyder.

8394 A1

John Giezendanner (1893–1975) and his brother Albert (1902–1994) emigrated from Switzerland in 1914 to Blanchardville, a community straddling Iowa and Lafayette Counties, just west of New Glarus and squarely within Wisconsin's Swiss heartland. A decade later the brothers had moved 250 miles north to join a burgeoning population of Swiss immigrants in Barron County. There Albert found work as a hired man for local farmers, while John rented his own land and began to make a name for himself as an innovative dairyman and Guernsey breeder ("Farm News" section, *Manitowoc Herald Times*, Wednesday, June 18, 1924). The brothers were active in local Swiss activities throughout their lives.

In summer 1975 some 175 Swiss Americans from northwestern Wisconsin gathered for an annual picnic at the Barron County fairgrounds in Rice Lake. At day's end John Giezendanner exclaimed, "I've got to play one more song." As the sound of his accordion and yodeling faded, Giezendanner collapsed. The *Rice Lake Chronotype* reported that, although rushed to nearby Lakeside Hospital, he "was pronounced dead on arrival. While the episode shocked and saddened the assembly, the summary of one member was generally recognized by all: 'He died doing what he liked most, and among friends.' Group singing continued on a subdued note" (August 6, 1975).

John Giezendanner's yodeling had been recorded by Sidney Robertson in 1938 when he performed as "Gits" with the Rindlisbacher-led Wisconsin Lumberjacks at the National Folk Festival in Chicago, yet Stratman-Thomas learned of him through correspondence with Lillian Hemstock Bowen, whose husband, John E. Bowen, the former mayor of Barron, was a former cheesemaker and cooperative creamery manager, as well as a cattle buyer (letter from Mrs. John Giezendanner to Stratman-Thomas, July 21, 1946; Curtiss-Wedge 1922: 553). Stratman-Thomas's field notes for August 9, 1946, reveal that: "John Giezendanner of Barron had been recommended as a very fine Swiss yodeler. When we arrived at his farm in the middle of the afternoon, Mr. Giezendanner was away from home helping one of the neighbors thresh. However, his wife sent one of the other men on the farm to take Mr. Giezendanner's place so that he could come home and yodel for us. Mr. Giezendanner was truly a virtuoso yodeler. His brother Albert joined him in an echo yodel."

Echo yodels, characterized by lead and answering voices, are a widespread subgenre of yodeling that simulate sonic reverberations in mountain valleys (Plantenga 2004).

9   Ländler

Played on Swiss button accordion by Otto Rindlisbacher, Rice Lake, Wisconsin, August 15, 1941. Recorded by Helene Stratman-Thomas and Robert F. Draves.

5018 A1

According to Otto Rindlisbacher (1895–1975), members of his mother's family "were musical. That's what they did" (Rindlisbacher 1973). His father, John Rindlisbacher, who once spelled his name "Rhiendeliousbeauchier," was an immigrant cheesemaker in Monroe and then Wiota in southwest Wisconsin before moving to Athens, in the central part of the state, where Otto was born. That same year the family moved to Rice Lake. Otto learned to play a wide range of instruments "just fooling around with them" and eventually made violins that were played in the La Crosse and Minneapolis symphony orchestras. He also worked in the woods and in all five of Rice Lake's sawmills before opening the Buckhorn Tavern, initially a billiard parlor, in 1920 with his brothers John and Louis. The Buckhorn was a classic northwoods "museum bar" filled with stuffed animals, curios, and musical instruments.

Rindlisbacher and his Swiss American wife, Iva, had a lifelong commitment to Swiss music. They hosted traveling Swiss performers like the Moser Brothers and the Jolly Rigi Boys (Leary 1991: 29–30), were regular participants in Monroe's Cheese Days celebration of Swiss artisanship and music, and, as Stratman-Thomas reported in her

field notes for August 15, 1941, "played their native Swiss instruments, the *Hand Orgeli* (button accordion) and the Swiss bells."

Named for Ländl, the mountainous region of Austria's Steiermark, the ländler is a gliding couple dance in 3/4 time. Originally Austrian, it has Bavarian, Czech, and Swiss variants.

LUXEMBURGER

Settlers from Luxemburg arrived in Wisconsin in the 1840s, establishing farms and inhabiting the villages of Port Washington, Lake Church, Belgium, Fredonia, Dacada, and Holy Cross in what would become Ozaukee and southern Sheboygan Counties, along the shores of Lake Michigan. Wisconsin's population of Luxemburger ancestry is second only to Illinois, and their distinctive Lëtzebuergesch language has persisted in Ozaukee County into the twenty-first century. Stratman-Thomas was fortunate to record from Jacob C. Becker songs that were composed by his father, Nicholas E. Becker, a prominent folk poet who chronicled the mid-nineteenth immigrant experience and was himself memorialized through a postage stamp issued by the Grand Duchy of Luxemburg in 1992, the 150th anniversary of his birth.

10 Onse gescht fu Chicago / Our Guests from Chicago

Sung by Jacob C. Becker, Belgium, Wisconsin, August 30, 1946.
Recorded by Helene Stratman-Thomas and Aubrey Snyder.
Transcription and translation by Jacob C. Becker, 1947.

8455 A2

Do, wo dem bloe Michigan	Here where the blue Lake Michigan
Seng Wale gent ons schlo'n	Sends high its waves ashore,
Chicago, kleng Port Washington,	Chicago and little Port Washington,
Milwaukee, sech ferdro'n.	And Milwaukee agree.
'T as enerle, a welcher Stat	No difference in what city,
A klenger Hett, am Schlass—	In a little hut or mansion—
All iwerall fent en eng Platz;	Everywhere you find a place;
Wo et gemittelech as.	Where it is comfortable.

< Otto and Iva Rindlisbacher in Swiss regalia, with instruments, 1930s. (author's collection, courtesy of Lois Rindlisbacher Albrecht)

Mir welle bridderlech hei sin,	We want to be like brothers here,
Ons rechen d' Brudderhand,	Like brothers we shake hands,
Well mir jo dach all Kanner sin	Because we are all children
Fum Letzeburger Land.	From little Luxemburg.
De Fremen, den heihinne kent,	The stranger who comes hither
Geseit mat heller Fred,	Sees always with delight.
Dat mir ons weisen him als Frend	We always greet him as a friend,
Wat d'Herz him schloen det.	That makes his heart beat.
An den do uowen, den ons let,	And He above who leads us all,
Wo mir och gin a stin,	Wherever we walk or stand,
Behitt ons ger fun allem Led,	Protects us from all sorrow and grief,
Well mir we Bridder sin.	Because we are all like brothers.
Si mir och hei am grosze Land	We are living in this land,
Guor weit a bret ferspret,	Scattered in the country,
So reche mir ons geren d'Hand	We greet Him and press his hand,
Foll Left, an Enegket.	Full of love and unity.

Jacob C. Becker (1872–1948) was a retired farmer in the town of Fredonia, living on the place his immigrant grandparents had settled and where his father, Nicholas E. Becker, had grown up. The journalist Fred Holmes had written about N. E. Becker in *Old World Wisconsin: Around Europe in the Badger State* (1944: 84–85), and perhaps for this reason, Stratman-Thomas assumed he was still living and wrote a letter accordingly. On July 13, 1946, she received this response from Jacob C. Becker: "Received your letter of June 24 addressed to my father, N. E. Becker, seeking information about Luxemburger songs and poetry. . . . [T]hey are often sung in neighborhood gatherings or even at weddings if you should come to Dacada, Random Lake, or Belgium . . . Please let me know a few days in advance and I will be home."

Six weeks later, Jacob Becker recorded seven songs for the Library of Congress. One of them, "Wanterlift" (Winter Song), was set to a traditional tune with lyrics he composed, but five were the work of his father. A short biography of the elder Becker, the first Luxemburger elected to the Wisconsin legislature (in 1898), appeared in the 1899 edition of the *Blue Book of the State of Wisconsin*.

Nicholas Edward Becker (Dem.) of Fredonia (P.C. address, Random Lake), was born
August 23, 1842, at Wormeldingen, in the grand-duchy of Luxemburg, and was educated at the boys' school—German and French—of his native place.

He came to Wisconsin with his parents in 1854, and settled on a farm in Fredonia, Ozaukee County, where he still resides. By occupation he is a farmer, but taught school from 1866 to 1882, and is widely known among the Luxemburgers in the United States by his poetical productions in their home dialect. He was town clerk from 1868 to 1877, and again from 1883 to 1887, and has been chairman of the town board since 1895. He was chairman of the Democratic county committee in 1887, 1888, 1889 and 1890, has been a notary public since 1879, and justice of the peace from 1867 to the present time. He was elected to the assembly in 1898, receiving 1,414 votes against 951 for W. H. Rintelman, Republican.

A Luxemburg–American blog, posted on November 22, 2012, included and extended the 1899 *Blue Book* account:

Nikolaus Becker (1842–1920), known as *Beckesch Klos*, was the son of Nicolas Becker (1799–1879) and Anna Maria Demuth (1804–1900). He later styled himself as Nicholas Edward Becker. In 1864 he married at Dacada, Wisconsin Germany-born Ottilia Schauer (1841–1909); seven children were born to the couple. *Beckesch Klos* was a poet, writing poems in the Lëtzebuergesch language. His most lasting contribution is to have recorded many of the nicknames of settlers from Luxemburg in Ozaukee County, Wisconsin, in his seminal *Lexicon der eigenthümlichen Benennungen vieler Bewohner des Nördlichen Theils von Ozaukee County, Wisconsin und Umgebung. Nebst einen Anhang Luxemburgischer Gedichte von demselbem.* (Keystone Printing Co., Chicago, Illinois, 1908) [Dictionary of the proper names of many inhabitants of the northern part of Ozaukee County, Wisconsin, and surrounding area. Next to an appendix of Luxemburgish poems by the same] (*Luxembourgensia: Today in Luxembourg-USA History*, luxembourgensia.blogspot.com/2012/11/22-november-1898-n-e-becker-beckesch.html, accessed December 20, 2012)

Stratman-Thomas focused in particular on Nicholas Becker's songs in her field notes of August 30, 1946.

Many of the immigrants to Wisconsin from Luxemburg settled in Ozaukee County. Near Belgium, on the farm cleared by his grandfather in 1854, Jacob C. Becker, seventy-four, related stories of this immigration which he had heard from his father, Nicholas E. Becker. The father had ability at writing poetry. In his native Luxemburg dialect he penned verses which told of incidents of the life of the Luxemburgers in Wisconsin. These verses were often sung to some familiar folk melody. "Zur Erreneronk" (For Remembrance) told how hard the immigrants worked when they first came here and how proud they were when they had cut their first path through the trees. "De Pier mat de gescheiten Ochsen" (Peter and His Smart Ox) related an incident which took place on Nicholas Becker's farm. A farmhand who came from Luxemburg about 1860 could drive horses but not oxen. When he got into the corner of the field, he couldn't turn the oxen round. He called to them in German and in French but to no avail. Mr. Becker, observing the difficulty, called to the oxen, "Gee! Haw! Back!" and the oxen responded. The bewildered farmer said that he wished he understood English as well as the oxen did.

"Onse Gescht fu Chicago" (Our Guests from Chicago) was written for a Luxemburg assembly at Port Washington [July 15, 1900]. Many of the guests came from Milwaukee and Chicago. Mr. Becker's verses were sung to the tune of "Ons Hemecht" [Our Homeland], the Luxemburg national hymn. Nicholas Becker was also alert to the American songs and made a translation of "Paddle Your Own Canoe" into the Luxemburg dialect.

DUTCH

Immigrants from the Netherlands, Catholics and Protestants alike, began settling in Wisconsin in the mid-1840s. The latter included members of the Calvinist Dutch Reformed faith in particular, who established farms and villages like Oostburg along the shores of Lake Michigan in southern Sheboygan County, as well as in and around the Fond du Lac and Dodge County communities of Alto, Brandon, Randolph, and Waupun. Late-summer "mission fests"—featuring all-day singing and preaching, and concluding with offerings in support of missionaries—were common in Dutch Reformed areas, sometimes drawing far-flung participants. Stratman-Thomas recorded singers at one such fest. As she wrote in her field notes for August 27, 1946:

The next morning we drove to Brandon to attend a Dutch Mission Fest. We had learned about this gathering from Mrs. Harman Hull of Waupun. Although she could not be present that day, she asked her sister-in-law, Miss Marion Hull, to introduce us to the Dutch people and tell them our purpose.

The Mission Fest was held outdoors on the church grounds. During the course of the meetings it is still customary to sing the traditional Dutch psalms. Miss Hull had arranged with the leader of the singing that we might place our microphones to best advantage to pick up the voices. The leader, Dick Kok, seemed to sense that this was an opportunity for recording a custom which had been an inherent part of Dutch religious life in Wisconsin. The Dutch people sang fervently the slow, steady, long tunes of the familiar psalms, one verse of which filled a full side of a record.

During the noon intermission, through the courtesy of one of the neighbors, we set up the recording equipment in a house across the street and passed around word that anyone who knew a Dutch song should come over and sing it. Neither we nor the neighbor lady were prepared for the enthusiasm with which this suggestion was received. Since the noonday intermission was short, we decided to take people in turn and let them come to the microphone without even questioning them as to what the song might be. We recorded everything from an epitaph on a tombstone to "Daisy, Daisy," which sung in Dutch so convulsed Snyder that he could scarcely keep his mind on the recording machine. . . .

Following the afternoon session of the Mission Fest we played from the speaker's platform all the recordings we had made that day. As so often happened, hearing some of the old songs freshened the memory of those in the gathering; we regretted that our schedule did not permit us to stay and record more Dutch music.

Regarding Stratman-Thomas's local contacts, Harmon and Marion Hull were the grandchildren of Dutch immigrants who farmed in the Alto and Brandon area. Dr. Harmon Hull had met his wife, Cornelia, a native of New York State, when the two were studying medicine. Cornelia Hull was active in the League of Women Voters and was a particular advocate for the Mexican American seasonal migrants who harvested sugar beets in the Waupun area (http://sflivingtreasures.org/index.php/treasures/2-treasures/70-mary-lou-cook.html?showall=1, accessed December 21, 2012).

11 Schaarensliep! / Knife Grinder!

Spoken and sung by Rika Tuinstra Enhoff of Kenosha, Wisconsin, at a
Dutch mission fest, Brandon, Wisconsin, August 28, 1946. Recorded
by Helene Stratman-Thomas and Aubrey Snyder. Transcription and
translation by Jolanda Vanderwal Taylor, 2010.

8449 B3

This is a little street cry what a man sings in Holland when he goes on the street with
the little *scharensliep* wagon to sharpen his knives and scissors and so on.

Scharensliep!	Knife grinder!
Mensen, zoek nu bij mekeaar	Folks, now collect
Al wat stomp is, mes en schaar.	All that's dull, knife and shears (scissors).
Maak wat spoed, want ik moet	Do make haste, for I must
Gauw weer verder en ik kom	Continue on soon, and I won't
(Te) morgen niet weerom.	Return again tomorrow.
Scharensliep!	Knife grinder!

Hendrika "Rika" Tuinstra (1896–1988) was born in Holland in 1896 and immigrated to
Wisconsin in 1914, a year earlier than her Austrian-born husband to be, Adam Enhoff.
The couple lived in Kenosha, a considerable distance from Brandon.

Street criers selling wares and services were common in Old and New World cities,
as revealed in this passage from a memoir of life in the Dutch city of Gouda in the early
twentieth century: "There were others that came occasionally, like the coal deliveryman,
and the *scharensliep* (knife and scissors sharpener) with his fascinating foot-powered
grinding wheel that threw sparks all around and made an ear-splitting, penetrating
noise. . . . Some of the regulars, like the ragman and the food scrap collector, had a special
cry that you could hear from half a street away, so that you knew they were coming and
could get things ready" (Maas 2007: 20).

12 Bokkie / Billy Goat

Sung by Marvin Fennema at a Dutch mission fest, Brandon, Wisconsin, August 28, 1946. Recorded by Helene Stratman-Thomas and Aubrey Snyder. Transcription, translation, and annotation by Jolanda Vanderwal Taylor, 2010.

8451 A2

Mijn vader kocht een bokkie,	My father bought a billy goat,
En een bokkie zonder staart.	A billy goat without a tail.
Hij ging er mee uit wandelen	He went out walking with it
Al in de Kalverstraat.	In the Kalverstraat.[1]
Daar kwamen twee agenten	There came two police officers
En die namen het bokkie mee.	And they took the goat with them.
En Vader begon te huilen,	And Father began to cry,
en het bokkie huilde mee.	And the billy goat cried with him.
Bokkie! Bokkie! Bokkie!	Billy goat! Billy goat! Billy goat!
Bèh. Bèh. Bèh.	Baah. Baah. Baah.
Bokkie! Bokkie! Bokkie!	Billy goat! Billy goat! Billy goat!
Bèh. Bèh. Bèh.	Baah. Baah. Baah.

----

1. The Kalverstraat is a high-end shopping street in Amsterdam.

Born in 1919 in the town of Salem in Kenosha County, Marvin Fennema was a fine tenor singer who earned BA and MA degrees in 1941 and 1942 from the School of Music at the University of Wisconsin. A sought-after soloist for weddings and concerts in the Madison area in the 1940s, he also directed several choirs (*Wisconsin State Journal*, May 5, 1942; August 2, 1942; July 18, 1947). Perhaps he learned this playful song from his parents, Andrew and Sarah, immigrants from the Netherlands.

Anna Gysbers Scholten, Oostburg, Wisconsin, 1946. (Wisconsin Historical Society, WHi-25410)

13 Moeder, moeder de beer ist los / Mother, Mother, the Bear Is Loose

Sung by Anna C. Gysbers Scholten of Oostburg, Wisconsin, at a Dutch mission fest, Brandon, Wisconsin, August 28, 1946. Recorded by Helene Stratman-Thomas and Aubrey Snyder. Transcription and translation by Jolanda Vanderwal Taylor, 2010.

8440 B2

Hop, zei Jantje, "De beer was los."	Hey [?] said Johnny, "The bear got out."
Hij niet heur hem brommen.	He did not hear him growling.
Mine de Turk z'n ketel het was,	I think the Turk's kettle it was,
En 't was de Turk zijn trommen.	And it was the Turk's drum.[1]

1. Small paired kettledrums called *naqqa-ra* reached Europe by the thirteenth century via the Crusades and became known as nakers. In the mid-fifteenth century, the large paired kettledrums of the Ottoman Turks were taken to Europe, principally by way of Hungary and Germany.

Anna Gysbers Scholten (1880–1965) was born in Winterswijk, Holland, and died in Grand Rapids, Michigan, a strong Dutch Reformed community where two of her daughters, Johanna Heenstra and Greta Scholten, made their homes. She married Gerhard Scholten in 1909, and the couple immigrated to Canada sometime before the birth of their second child in 1914. The Scholtens moved subsequently to Sheboygan County in 1922, farming in the Oostburg area, with Anna residing in that village after her husband's death in 1927.

Stratman-Thomas's notes reveal that this was one of the "Dutch songs she learned when a child," and likely she sang it for her own children. "Moeder, moeder de beer ist los" is a well-known children's song in the Netherlands that exists in several variations and had been published in such anthologies as *Klein, klein, kleutertje en anderen: Hollandsche kindereuntjes, No.1* (de Haan 1881) and *Moeder de Gans. Baker- en kinderrijmpjes* (Hildebrant 1915).

14 Epitaph

Spoken and sung by Mary Tillema Smedema of Randolph, Wisconsin, at a Dutch mission fest, Brandon, Wisconsin, August 27, 1946. Recorded by Helene Stratman-Thomas and Aubrey Snyder. Transcription, translation, and annotation by Jolanda Vanderwal Taylor, 2010.

8440 A1

This is Mrs. J. J. Smedema, Randolph, Wisconsin. I'd like to sing a little epitaph that was put on my mother's great-grandfather's tombstone in Holland. And she often sang the little song for us. I will now try and sing it.

Verlopen was mijn levensweg	Completed was my life's way
Als ik naar huis ging uit de kerk.	When I went home from church.
Wel spoedig had mijn leven naam [?],	Quite soon my life had ended,
Zelfs eer ik in mijn woning kwam.	Even ere I came into my house.
Nu ligt alhier mijn vlees en been	Now lies here my flesh and bone
Begraven onder dezen steen.	Buried under this stone.
En hoop om eens weer op te staan	And I hope some day to rise again
En met mijn Jesus in te gaan.	And to enter in with my Jesus.

Although Stratman-Thomas attributes this song to "Mrs. J. J. Schmedema," it was sung by Mary Tillema Smedema (1876–1958), born in Randolph to Dutch immigrant parents, Tjisse Douwes Tillema and Saapke Vander Velde. Her husband, John J. Smedema, with whom she had eight children, was a trustee in the 1940s for the village of Randolph.

Mary Smedema told Stratman-Thomas that her maternal ancestor "died suddenly while leaning upon a fence." This epitaph is clearly a variant of another, accessible through many Internet sites, commemorating the death of Klaas Jans de Waard (1757–1819), a church warden and mayor, who perished when he fell from his horse and whose inscribed tombstone is in the Dutch Reformed Church cemetery in Grijpskerk, Holland.

15 Wiene Wederslweh bloed volksrang / Blood of Netherland Flows; Vlaggelied / Flag Song

Sung by Dick Kok at a Dutch mission fest, Brandon, Wisconsin, August 27, 1946. Recorded by Helene Stratman-Thomas and Aubrey Snyder. Transcription and translation by Jolanda Vanderwal Taylor, 2010.

8440 B5, 8441 A1

Wien Neerlands bloed door d' ad'ren vloeit?	Who has Dutch blood flowing in his veins?
Wiens 't hart klopt fier en vrij.	[He] whose heart beats proud and free.
Wie(n) voor zijn volk van liefde gloeit?	Who glows with love for his people?
Verheff' den zang als wij:	May he raise the song, as [do] we:
Hij roem' met allen, welgezind	May he be well-disposed to praise
Den onverbreekb're(n) band	The unbreakable bond
Die hier Oranje en Neerland bindt	Which here binds Orange and the Netherlands
Voor land en Koningin.	For country and Queen.
Voor land en Koningin.	For country and Queen.
Bescherm, o God, bewaak den grond	Protect, oh God, defend the ground
Waarop onz' adem gaat [?],	On which our breath goes [we live and breathe],
De plek waar eens onz' wieg op stond	The spot where once our cradle stood
Wellicht ons sterfuur slaat [slaan?].	And perhaps our hour of death will come.
Wij smeken van Uw vaderhand	We beg of your father-hand
Met blijden kinderzin:	With joyful childlike spirit:
Bewaar, o lieve Heer ons land,	Protect, o dear Lord, our country,
Ons land en koningin.	Our country and our Queen.
Ons land en koningin.	Our country and our Queen.

Gij schitterende kleuren van Nederlands vlag,	Thou bright colors of the Netherlands' flag,
Wat wappert gij fier langs den vloed,	How you wave proudly along the water,
Hoe klopt ons het harte van vreugd en ontzag	How our heart beats with joy and respect
Wannneer het uw baren begroet.	When it greets your waves.
Ontplooi u, waai uit nu bij nacht en bij dag.	Unfurl, fly forth now by night and by day.
Gij blijft ons het teken o heilige vlag,	Thou remains to us the sign, oh sacred flag,
Van Trouw en van Vroomheid,	Of faithfulness and piety,
Van Vroomheid en Moed,	Of piety and bravery,
Van Trouw en van Vroomheid en Moed.	Of faithfulness and piety and bravery.

Dick Kok (1888–1985) was born in Holland and came to Wisconsin in 1910, settling in Alto, where he and his wife, Eike, also from Holland, lived their long lives. In 1965 their fifty-fifth wedding anniversary was a community-wide celebration, held in the Alto school (*Fond du Lac Reporter*, July 31, 1965). The Koks were members of the Bethel Reformed Church of Brandon, with Dick and several of the couple's seven children participating in church choirs and sponsored choruses (*Fond du Lac Reporter*, Saturday, June 30, 1973).

Performing at a time when the Netherlands was occupied by the Nazis, Kok combines a pair of Dutch nationalist songs frequently associated with one another. The first two verses are from "Wiene Wederslweh bloed volksrang," Holland's official national anthem from 1815 to 1932, which was composed by the Dutch poet Hendrik Tollens (1780–1856). Tollens's original includes "Van Vreemde smitten vrij" (From foreign stains free) in the second line of the first verse, a reference to pure Dutch blood. Socialists, anti-fascists, and racially mixed Dutch loyalists objected to assertions of racial purity, however, and the song exists in many versions. Kok's rendering closely resembles the (Dutch West) "Indies" version. His appended final verse is the patriotic "Vlaggelied," composed around 1865 by the Dutch physician and poet Jan Pieter Heije (1809–1876).

16 Daisy, Daisy

Sung by Henry Kempers at a Dutch mission fest, Brandon, Wisconsin, August 27, 1946. Recorded by Helene Stratman-Thomas and Aubrey Snyder. Transcription and translation by Jolanda Vanderwal Taylor.

8440 A5

Daisy, Daisy	Daisy, Daisy
Geef mij uw jawoord, doe!	Give me your "yes," oh do!
Aan jou denk ik bij alles bij wat-dat ik doe	I think of you whatever I'm doing
Maar kend ik niet rijk te trouwen,	But I wouldn't be able to marry richly,
Want een rijtuig kan ik niet houden.	For a carriage I cannot keep.
Maar wel een fiets	But I do have a bike
En dat is toch wel iets.	And that is something.
En je zult wel eens kijken hoe!	And you surely will see how!

Henry Kempers (1878–1953) was born in Holland and arrived in Wisconsin sometime prior to 1900, when census records note he was a "single boarder" with the Hinkamp family, Dutch immigrants farming in the Alto area of Fond du Lac County. By 1905 he had a wife named Johanna, also a Dutch immigrant, and was living on his own farm. Kempers served as town constable and, in the 1930s, was celebrated in syndicated newspaper stories for thwarting burglars who had broken into Melvin van Buren's store (*La Crosse Tribune and Leader-Press* and *Wisconsin State Journal*, November 11, 1934).

"Daisy, Daisy," the Dutch performance of which so convulsed sound engineer Aubrey Snyder, was composed with the title "Daisy Bell" in 1892 by the English songwriter Harry Dacre (1860–1922). It was immediately successful on the London music-hall stage and soon after was a hit in the United States. The song was also translated into Dutch and sold as a broadside in several versions, two of which are held by the Meertens Institute in Amsterdam and may be viewed through the *Doozoek het Geheugen van Nederland* / Memory of the Netherlands site. Since Dutch versions were circulating prior to Kempers's emigration, he likely learned this song in Holland.

ITALIAN

Italians arrived in Wisconsin and the surrounding Upper Midwest in the late nine-teenth century. Mostly landless peasants, they found work in the iron and copper mines in the Lake Superior region, as well as in the industrial cities of southern Wisconsin, where Milwaukee, Kenosha, Racine, and Madison each had a Little Italy fostering singers, accordion players, dancers, and Italian halls. Cumberland, in northwestern Wisconsin's Barron County, was also home to some three hundred Italian families, the largest Italian rural settlement in the United States. Immigrants from the Abruzzo and Molise regions of east-central Italy came there in the late 1870s and early 1880s, some working in lumber camps, others recruited in St. Paul by the Omaha railroad company in the wake of a strike. Many "settled south of town where they bought some shanties the railroad company had built and converted them into homes." Having established their own Catholic church, St. Anthony's, in 1885, they built Columbia Hall in 1907 for parties, dances, and community gatherings in the midst of the farming district (Cotone and Cotone 1974).

17 L'America è tanto bella / America Is Most Beautiful

Sung by Thomas St. Angelo, Mr. and Mrs. Ambrose DeGidio, and Michael Ranallo, Cumberland, Wisconsin, August 9, 1946.
Recorded by Helene Stratman-Thomas and Aubrey Snyder.
Transcription and translation by Thomas St. Angelo, 1947, with corrections by Luisa Del Giudice, 2010.

8395 A2

L'America è tanto bella,	America is most beautiful,
L'Italia è piccolina.	Italy is very small.
Son scritto alla mia biondina,	I have written to my little blonde,
All'Italia non ci ritorno più.	To Italy I will return no more.
Son scritto alla mia biondina,	I have written to my little blonde,
All'Italia non ci ritorno più.	To Italy I will return no more.
O-i mamma e fammi la dota,	Oh mother make ready my dowry.
O-i mamma e fammi la dota,	Oh mother make ready my dowry.
O-i mamma e fammi la dota,	Oh mother make ready my dowry.
All'America voglio andar,	To America, I want to go,

O-i mamma e fammi la dota,	Oh mother make ready my dowry.
All'America voglio andar.	To America, I want to go.

[Note: St. Angelo and company ceased singing after two verses, yet when asked to provide lyrics for the performance, he sent two additional verses to Stratman-Thomas.]

Io vad' alla stazione	I go to the station
E ordin al machinista,	And ask the engineer,
E ordin al machinista	And ask the engineer
Che prepa il vapore.	To make ready the boat.

L'America è tanto bella,	America is most beautiful,
L'Italia è piccolina.	Italy is very small.
Siamo scritto nostri carini,	We have written to our dear ones,
All'Italia non ritorniamo più.	To Italy we will return no more.

The children of immigrants, Thomas St. Angelo (1899–1967), Ambrose DeGidio (1901–1984), and Michael Ranallo (1905–1990) were raised on farms near Cumberland, whereas DeGidio's wife, Mary Lou Velotta (1906–1994), whose parents were from Italy, grew up in Owensboro, Kentucky. Ambrose DeGidio and Thomas St. Angelo were especially prominent Cumberland citizens. DeGidio studied voice in Minneapolis in the early 1920s, where he sang on KSTP radio prior to moving to Chicago in 1926 and performing with the Chicago Civic Opera. He and his wife moved to Cumberland in 1946, where they established the Ambrose Motel. Thomas St. Angelo, the local Italian community's second high-school attendee, worked in succession as a timekeeper for the railroad, a manager for the Gedney Pickle Company, as well as for a DuPont munitions plant, and a teller for the Island City Bank until it failed in 1930 amid the Great Depression. Thereafter he worked for the Federal Land Bank. St. Angelo also took correspondence courses in law and engineering, served on numerous local boards, was active in Republican Party politics, and represented Barron County in the state assembly from 1960 to 1964 (Cotone and Cotone 1974).

Stratman-Thomas had written in advance to St. Angelo, and he responded on July 22, 1946: "We have a few Italian folk songs that we will be able to give for recording, and I feel sure at this time that we will be able to be prepared with five or six voices. I would give you the names at this time but have not had time to contact them yet.... We have melodies of the songs I now have in mind but we have no written compositions and I doubt very much that they are obtainable in our country. I have learned them from my mother by memory who had a good voice and was musical." Stratman-Thomas's subsequent field notes for August 9, 1946, emphasized folksongs and food: "After supper with the Giezendanners, we drove on to Cumberland where Thomas St. Angelo had arranged for the recording of Italian songs. . . . Among the songs was "L'America è tanto bella" (America is so beautiful), which Mr. St. Angelo had learned from his mother and which he had never heard anyone else sing. . . . Good food often followed a session of recording folk songs, and this evening ended around the St. Angelo's dining table. It was early morning when we drove back to the hotel at Cumberland."

St. Angelo's parents, Gennaro Sant Angelo (1852–1943) and Angelina Carlascio (1856–1932), hailed from the village of Cantalupo in Italy's Molise region. Gennaro immigrated in 1883, working in the woods and on the railroad to earn money for land and his wife's passage. Angelina arrived in 1886 and Thomas, the couple's first child, was born three years later. She was remembered as cheerful, a fine cook, and a frequent singer. Although St. Angelo never heard anyone but his mother sing this song, it shares features with other songs from the Italian diaspora: a young man writing from America that he will not return to Italy; an emigrating child requesting an inheritance from a mother; and a ship ready to depart (Bianco 1974: 37–40, 146–149). Meanwhile Italian folksong specialist Luisa del Giudice, who transcribed and translated this performance, notes that the song "sounds like a typical Po [River] valley/Alpine style northern Italian song" in its choral performance, perhaps the result of the DeGidios' contribution, along with the development of group singing in the local church and hall.

18 Sona la mezzanotte / It Is Midnight

Sung by Irene Ruffolo, Kenosha, Wisconsin, August 28, 1946.
Recorded by Helene Stratman-Thomas and Aubrey Snyder.
Transcription by Vito Intravaia, 1947, with corrections by Luisa Del Giudice, 2010; translation by Del Giudice, 2010.

8449 B1

Sono la mezzanotte [*sic*] e l'aria scura
Vedo calar fra l'ambrose piante.
Del campo sento, barchero le mure,

Piangendo sulla tomba dell'amante:
Povera Giulia,

It is midnight and the dark night
I see fall all around the shady plants.
From the [church] yard I hear,
  jumping over the wall,
Weeping over the tomb of my love:
Poor Julia,

Da che moristi tu?	How did you die?
Ora, senza tu amore,	Now, without your love,
Non posso viver più.	No longer can I live.

Although Stratman-Thomas attributes this song to "Irene Ruffalo," this performance is almost certainly by Irene Ruffolo (1924–2009), who was born in Kenosha to parents who had emigrated in 1921 from Italy and who later married Peter Imbrogno. Her brother Edward E. Ruffolo (1923–2012) was a music student at the University of Wisconsin in the mid-1940s. Indeed, the *Wisconsin State Journal* reported on December 9, 1945, that Edward Ruffolo and Stratman-Thomas were two of the four vocal soloists featured in a performance of Handel's *Messiah*. She wrote to him in early August of the following year: "I have not forgotten our conversations about the old Italian folksongs which you and your mother sing. . . . We (my helper, Aubrey Snyder, and I) plan to spend Wednesday afternoon and evening in Kenosha, and I am hoping that you and your mother will be able to make some records on the folk songs. I personally am always happy when I find songs from the families of our own Music School students. I will call your home when we reach Kenosha."

We do not know why neither Edward nor his mother, Mary (b. 1902), sang for Stratman-Thomas. Perhaps Edward was away at the time, perhaps he knew fewer traditional songs than his sister, and perhaps twenty-two-year-old Irene was in better voice than her mother? Whatever the explanation, there was a vibrant Italian musical scene in Kenosha in the 1940s that involved the Ruffolos. In May 1948 the *Wisconsin State Journal* reported that the University of Wisconsin's Italian Club would offer an Italian comedy, *The Boors* by Goldini, with Edward Ruffolo of Kenosha in a prominent role and also featured as a tenor vocalist "between acts." In addition, "The play will be repeated Sunday afternoons in the Italian American lodge at Kenosha."

Identified by its first line, the verse Irene Ruffolo performed in August 1946 most frequently concludes a longer ballad known as "Povera Giulia" (Poor Julia). According to Italian folksong scholar Luisa del Giudice: "Normally it is a soldier who has returned from war and finds that the woman he was to have married has died. He wanders the cemetery, finds her tomb, and weeps." Variants of "Povera Giula," which is classified as a *canto narrative*, are in the Archivi di etnomusicologa dell' Academia Nazinale di Santa Cecilia.

19 Tiki-ti, Tiki-ta!

Sung by Joseph Accardi, Beloit, Wisconsin, August 21, 1946.

Recorded by Helene Stratman-Thomas and Aubrey Snyder.

Transcription and translation by Luisa Del Giudice, 2010.

8425 B2

Bella, me neghi un bacio tu?	My beauty, you deny me a kiss?
Ma perchè? Ma perchè,	But why? Oh why,
Un bacetto neghi a me?	Do you deny me a kiss?
Furba, tu dici sempre no!	Sly one, you always say no!
Ma lo sai che ti va	But you know that you want to,
Già pensi eme lo dai!	You think of it and you give it!
Pure i colombi fan così,	Even doves do it,
Va di qua, va di là,	They go here, they go there,
Quelli baciano e che fa?	They kiss, and what of it?
Dolce è baciar con volontà,	Sweet it is to kiss willingly,
Mia Ninì, mia Ninì,	My Ninì, my Ninì,
Bocca e bocca star così!	Lips to lips like this!
Chorus [sung twice each time]:	Chorus [sung twice each time]:
Gira e rigira, biondina.	Turn and turn again, my blonde one.
L'amore, la vita godere ci fa,	Love makes us enjoy life.
Quando ti veggo, piccina!	When I see you, little one!
Il mio cor sempre fa:	My heart goes like this:
Tiki-ti, tiki-ta!	Tiki-ti, tiki-ta!
Quando è stasera aspetterò	When tonight comes I'll wait
Che papà, che papà	Until father, until father
A dormire se ne va.	Goes to sleep.
Su, come un gatto lì per lì	Upstairs, like a cat, right there
Salterò, salterò	I'll jump up, I'll jump up
E del topo in cerca andrò.	And in search of the mouse I'll go.
Zitto le scale salirò.	Quietly, up the stairs I'll climb.
Verrò su, verrò su,	I'll come up, I'll come up,
Ma la porta m'apri tu?	But will you open the door?
Ah! se si sveglia il tuo papà?	Oh! If your father awakes?
Già lo so, già lo so.	I already know, I know,
Che d'un colpo abbasso andrò.	With one swat I'll be knocked down.
Dice il proverbio, o mia Ninì	Oh my Ninì, the proverb says
Gioventù, gioventù	Youth, youth
Se ne va e non torna più!	Flees away and returns no more!
Passa la vita tua così	Your life in this way flees
Tra l'età di mammà	Between your mother's years

Giuseppe "Joseph" Accardi, Beloit, Wisconsin, 1940s. (Helene Stratman-Thomas Collection, Mills Music Library, University of Wisconsin–Madison)

E la pipa di papà!	And your father's pipe!
Rose e garofani e che so	Roses and carnations and what else
Che bouquet, che bouquet	What bouquets, what bouquets
Ci vorrebbero per te.	You should have.
Ma se un marito sogni tu,	But if you dream of a husband,
Già si sa, già si sa.	One knows, one already knows.
Il marito eccolo qua!	The husband is right here, before you!

Giuseppe "Joseph" Accardi (1889–1956) was born near Marsala, Sicily's westernmost city, which is famed for its wine. He was a wine inspector as a young man, but the musty cellars affected his lungs and opportunities beckoned in the United States. He immigrated in 1921, along with his wife, Rosa (1889–1986), his father-in-law, Nicolò Passalaqua (1863–1941), and two children, daughter Rosaria (Sadie) and son Giacomo (Jack). The family settled in Beloit, where Giuseppe worked as a core finisher for Fairbanks and Morse, a company specializing in industrial-engine production. He was also very active in the local Italian community as a singer, with his performances charming Vito Intravaia, who would become a student in the School of Music at the University of Wisconsin.

Stratman-Thomas sketched details of her visit to Beloit on August 21, 1946: "We had been referred to the Italian singers, Joseph Accardi and Mrs. John De Noto, by Mrs. Vito Intravaia, wife of one of our former music school students. The Intravaias arranged to be present and encouraged the singers to record the songs which the Intravaias had heard so often.... Mr. Accardi's songs were full of drama and comedy.... *Tic ti, Tic ta* ... describes how the young lover's heart beat when he met his sweetheart."

This well-known song, originally entitled "Tic-ti, Tic-ta," was composed in standard Italian by the Neapolitan poet and songwriter Francesco Feola (1871–1945), founder in 1901 of the publishing house Canzonetta in Naples, with music by Gaetano Lama. The Italian immigrant Raoul Romito, whose operatic tenor resembled that of Enrico Caruso, recorded the song in 1918 (Columbia E-76221), and Giuseppe Accardi, who owned a copy of the recording, delivered a performance closely resembling Romito's. In the late 1940s the Slovenian American "polka king" Frankie Yankovic recorded "Tic Tock Polka" (Columbia 42731), preserving Lama's original melody but with completely different lyrics in English.

Giuseppe Accardi's grandson and namesake, Joseph Accardi (b. 1951) created a fine website in tribute to his grandfather, http://accardiweb.com/grandpa/ (accessed April 17, 2014), along with a thorough and illuminating listing of the elder Accardi's extensive collection of Italian American 78 rpm recordings, which included comic and dramatic songs and skits aplenty (http://accardiweb.com/grandpa/78rpm.htm, accessed April 17, 2014).

CROATIAN

Croatians were late nineteenth- and early twentieth-century immigrants to Wisconsin and the surrounding Upper Midwest. Like Italians, as well as fellow South Slavs—Montenegrins, Serbs, Slovenians—from the old Austro-Hungarian Empire, they found work in the region's iron and copper mines, and in industrial cities along the Wisconsin, Illinois, and Indiana shores of Lake Michigan: Sheboygan, Milwaukee, Kenosha, Racine, Chicago, and Gary. Tamburitza groups flourished among Croatian and Serbian workers in mining communities and urban ethnic neighborhoods, while others, like the Elias Tamburitzans, played professionally for a regional circuit of venues that included both South Slavic immigrant and more various "American" audiences.

... The ...

Croatian Tamburitza Ensemble

Presenting Exotic Music of Jugo-Slavia

● In Jugoslavia, it is the custom for families to assemble and furnish their own music and entertainment. For many years Chas. Elias Sr., and his family played together the music they so dearly loved. Later this family migrated to America. Here, their music was found to be so beautiful and novel and their long years of playing together had produced such perfection of ensemble playing, that they were persuaded to enter the professional filed. The company now consists of four members namely; Chas. Elias Jr., director; Martha Elias; Anne Elias and Mary Filipovich. All are accomplished musicians on the tamburitza as well as other well known instruments, being graduates of musical colleges of America.

The Croatian Tamburitza Ensemble, "Presenting Exotic Music of Jugo-Slavia" brochure, ca. 1940. (Helene Stratman-Thomas Collection, Mills Music Library, University of Wisconsin–Madison)

20 Introduction to Tamburitza Instruments

Spoken by Charles Elias Jr., Madison, Wisconsin, November 15, 1940.
Recorded by Helene Stratman-Thomas and Robert Draves.
4950 A1

Here we have a model of a tamburitza, which we claim was invented long before the guitar, ukulele, or banjo. The shepherds claim in the olden days, when they couldn't read nor write, people came to the country, took models of an instrument like this away, and made guitars and other string instruments. So please remember when I tell you that a tamburitza of this type is really one of the oldest string instruments. We also have six strings on this tamburitza and it's tuned in the G chord, the only tamburitza that is tuned different [strums the strings]. We use this to play chords and accompaniment. And they call it a very simple name in the Yugoslav language. I'm sure you'll all be able to understand it. It's called *druga bugaria*.

21 Medley: Da nije ljubavi ne bi svjeta bilo / If Not for Lovers There Would Be No World; Vinca ca / Wine, Wine

Sung and played on *biscernica, brac, druga bugaria*, and *berdo* by the Elias Tamburitzans (Charles Elias Jr., Ann Elias, Martha Elias, and Mary Filipovich), Madison, November 15, 1940. Recorded by Helene Stratman-Thomas and Robert Draves. Transcription and translation by Richard March.
4950 A2

Da nije ljubavi ne bi svjeta bilo,	If it weren't for love, there wouldn't be any world,
Ni mene ni tebe, moja bijela vilo.	Neither me nor you, my white fairy.
Noćas mi s snilo, moje bijela vilo,	Last night I dreamed, my white fairy,
Da je tvoje srce potkraj moga bilo.	That your heart was beside mine.
Kad ja čujem tambure, skočim na bure	When I hear tamburitzas, I jump up on a barrel
I natočim litru dve, pijem do zore.	And I pour a liter or two, I drink until dawn.
Moram da idem da se napijem.	I have to go to get drunk.
Moram da idem da se napijem.	I have to go to get drunk.
Hej ha vinca ca, vinca rumena!	Hey ha wine, wine, wine red wine!
Hej ha vinca ca, vinca rumena!	Hey ha wine, wine, wine red wine!

The Elias Tamburitzans were founded by Dragutin Ilijaš (1886–1937), who was born in Suhopolje, a village in the Slavonia province of Croatia, immigrated to Milwaukee in 1902, and Americanized his name to Charles Elias. A barber by day, he took night classes from the Meyer Music School and eventually organized tamburitza ensembles both in Milwaukee and on the Minnesota Iron Range, where he lived from 1915 to 1922. In 1924 the Elias Serenaders included his two oldest children, Martha (b. 1906) and Charles Jr. (b. 1908). The group toured the Midwest on the Chautauqua circuit, presenting programs on South Slavic music and culture to communities, schools, and colleges. After the death of his father, Charles Jr. took charge of the group, which included another sister, Anna (b. 1913), as well as "Mary Filipovich" (probably Marija Filipovic, born in Milwaukee in 1922). Inducted into the Tamburitza Hall of Fame in 1982, he was an active performer who also taught a pair of youthful ensembles—Milwaukee's Silver Strings Tamburitzans and the Waukegan Junior Tamburitzans—until his death in 1984 (March 2013: chap. 5; http://www.tamburitza.org/TAA/bios/elias.html, accessed December 28, 2013).

The Elias Tamburitzans were recorded in Madison, thanks to the efforts of another undergraduate music student, as Stratman-Thomas tells us in her notes for November 15, 1940: "During the ensuing school year we made a number of recordings of folk music at Music Hall on the University campus. A student, Anthony Bacich of Eagle River, had told me about native Croatian music which he had heard in his home. He was eager to have recordings made of the Elias family of Racine. Arrangements were made and in November this group of young Croatians came to Music Hall in Madison. They were Martha, Anna, and Charles Elias, Jr., and Mary Filipovich. The father, Charles Elias, Sr., had taught his children to play the Croatian folk instruments, the *tamburica*. The *tamburicas* were of varying sizes and had fascinating names—'*Biscernica*,' '*Contrsica*,' '*Brac*,' '*Druga bugaria*,' and '*Berdo*.' The scintillating quality of the *tamburica* made a brilliant background for the voices as they sang dance songs, love songs, and Christmas carols."

Charles Jr.'s polished introduction to the ensemble's instruments testifies to his experience as an education-oriented ambassador for South Slavic folk music in the United States. Likewise, as folklorist Richard March observed upon transcribing and translating the group's medley: "Accustomed as they were to performing for school programs and mixed audiences, the Elias Tamburitzans censored part of the first song in this melody by substituting 'da je tvoje srce potkraj moga bilo' (that your heart was beside mine) for the usual version: 'ni mene ni tebe moja bijela vilo' (that my body was beside yours). Likewise they left out two potentially salacious verses of the second song" (March 2012).

Ja leg'o do zida, žena do kraja,	I laid down by the wall, my wife by the side,
Dođe komšija pa me otjera.	My neighbor came along and chased me away.
Nije prošla godina, žena rodila.	Less than a year passed by, my wife had a baby.
Žena rodila isti komšija.	My wife had a baby who looks just like the neighbor.

Both of these songs are in polka tempo and remain popular in America's Serbian and Croatian communities. The legendary musician, vocalist, and bandleader Dušan Jovanović recorded the first, which is associated with Dalmatia, in 1925 (Columbia 23014-F), while the second, a Slavonian tribute to wine, was recorded by Chicago's Skertich Brothers in 1941 (Columbia 1236-F).

CZECH

Czechs from the German-ruled region of Bohemia began immigrating to Wisconsin in the late 1840s, forming neighborhoods in Milwaukee but also moving north along Lake Michigan's shores in the 1850s to establish farms in Manitowoc and Kewaunee Counties. Aided by rail travel, Czechs likewise moved west along the Wisconsin River valley to agrarian communities in Richland, Vernon, and Crawford Counties. The subsequent availability of logged-off, or "cutover," land in the late nineteenth and early twentieth century prompted Czechs, many of whom had been industrial workers elsewhere in the Midwest, to settle in such northern Wisconsin communities as Ashland, Cornell, Haugen, Moquah, and Phillips. In keeping with the proverb "Co Čech, to muzikant" (Every Czech is a musician), they sang traditional songs, formed brass and reed ensembles, played button accordions, and built taverns and community halls that fostered music and dance (Leary 2014).

22 Švestková alej / Prune Song

Sung by Charles Pelnar, John Pelnar, Bill Slatky, and Louis Kasal,
Kewaunee, Wisconsin. August 23, 1940. Recorded by Helene
Stratman-Thomas and Robert Draves. Transcription and translation
by Joe Grim Feinberg and Tereza Smejkalová, 2010.

4163 B2

V tej naší aleji švestky se válejí.	Plums lie along our tree-lined street.
Já dneska nehlídám, já dneska nehlídám,	I'm not guarding them, no I'm not guarding them,
Oči mě pálejí.	For my eyes are burning.

This quartet of Czech singers comprised half the members of a Bohemian band, the Straight Eight, named in part for powerful eight-cylinder automobile engines heavily promoted by American companies in the early 1930s. Louis P. Kasal (1894–1972) was a cornet player and violinist; John T. Pelnar (1895–1953) played bass horn, with his brother, Charles V. Pelnar (1902–1982), on flügel horn; while Bill Slatky was a baritone horn player. The parents of Kasal and the Pelnars were Bohemian immigrants. Kasal had been a corporal in World War I and an active member of the 121st Field Artillery Band, part of Wisconsin's combat-tested 32nd "Red Arrow" Division. His fellow bandmates were all military veterans, and perhaps some were active in the Field Artillery Band. The *Manitowoc Herald-Times* of June 17, 1932, chronicles a dance involving the Kewaunee post of the American Legion: "Houdek's straight eight band, made up of members of the Legion, furnished the music."

Stratman-Thomas's notes reveal her discovery of the band, its Old World connections, and its individual members.

I first learned of Bohemian music at Kewaunee through one of my former students, Dorothy Taddy (Mrs. G. D. Thoreson). At our request Mr. and Mrs. Thoreson gathered together the "Straight Eight" Bohemian band. It was nine-thirty in the evening before they all assembled at the high school, where they played Bohemian polkas and waltzes until long after midnight. The instrumentation of this little band was typical: clarinets, cornet, flügel horn, alto, bass, and baritone. The music they played, from well-worn handwritten manuscripts, was brought to Wisconsin by the parents or grandparents of the players.

Not only the music but also the names of the players were evidence of the genuineness of this Bohemian music—Albrecht, Slatky, Kacerovsky, Pelnar, Houdek, Ramesh, Kasal. It can be said of the Bohemians of Wisconsin that they truly are a dancing people. Polkas and waltzes such as the ones in this collection are played by small bands at the community dances and are danced by young and old alike.

Excerpts from the *Manitowoc Herald Times* show that Kasal and the Pelnars were particularly active in vocal ensembles, one of which included Gordon (G. D.) Thoreson, the husband of Stratman-Thomas's former student:

—January 17, 1933, the funeral of a farmer and former cheese factory and saloon operator includes vocal numbers "by Henry and Louis Kasal of Kewaunee."
—February 23, 1933, the Parent-Teacher's Association's regular monthly meeting features "a men's double quartet composed of Rev. E. T. Phillips, John Pelnar, W. E. Nyhus, Prin. R. A. Licking, Louis Kasal, M. F. Masse, Walter Kacerovsky, and J. P. Wood."
—July 26, 1933, "a quartet made up of John Pelnar, Henry Konop, Louis Judae, and Charles Pelnar rendered a group of selections" for the Kewaunee County Council of the Knights of Columbus.
—July 31, 1933, the Kewaunee Legion Post's Stag Party will feature "the male quartet composed of John Pelnar, Henry Konop, Louis Judae, and Charles Pelnar."
—May 29, 1935, Kewaunee's Memorial Day observance includes "selections by the male quartet: Gordon Thoreson, John Pelnar, Louis Kasal, and Charles Pelnar."
—November 3, 1945, Kewaunee's Armistice Day Program offers the public a "Medley quartet—Mrs. Mashek, Mrs. Cherney, Louis Kasal, and John Pelnar. . . . Following the program a booya will be served and later in the evening there will be dancing. The public is invited."

A year later Louis Kasal and Gordon Thoreson were featured performers in a three-act play, *Memories of Bohemia*, produced as "a tribute to early day Czech settlers in Kewaunee County" (*Manitowoc Herald Times*, November 2, 1946).

"Švestková alej," the song Stratman-Thomas recorded, has circulated widely through oral tradition, sheet music, and sound recordings on both sides of the Atlantic. Consisting of three verses in full versions, it draws metaphorically on blossoms, ripe plums, and withered prunes to sketch the trajectory of a young man's love affair. Intriguingly the single verse sung by the Straight Eight's quartet is the same lone verse sung on the 78 rpm recording made in 1933 by the Manitowoc County–based but nationally known "polka king" Romy Gosz and his Bohemian orchestra (Columbia 225-F).

23 Popelka polka / Cinderella Polka

Played by the Yuba Bohemian Band (Otto Stanek and Wencil Stanek, clarinet; George McGilvery and William Tydrich, cornet; Anton Stanek, horn; Nick Rott, trombone; Martin Rott, baritone; and Alfred Stanek, tuba), Yuba, Wisconsin, August 25, 1946. Recorded by Helene Stratman-Thomas and Aubrey Snyder.

8436 B2

The first Yuba band was formed in 1868. In 1888 the members included Michael Dedrick, clarinet; Frank Novy Sr., violin; Matthew Picha, cornet; Wencil Pliner, cornet; Martin Rott Sr., bass horn; and Wencil Rott, clarinet. In 1916 eleven of the band's thirteen members were Rotts. The Stanek family formed its own band sometime later, but the two groups had merged into a single Yuba Bohemian Band by the time Stratman-Thomas recorded them in Robert Novy's tavern and dance hall. The band was active until 1950, performing for weddings, an occasional funeral, and the annual pre-Lenten *Maso Pust* (Without Meat) festival, the Czech Mardi Gras (Braithwaite 1998: 69–77). Martin Rott Sr. (1850–1932) and his son Martin Jr. (1886–1977) were constant members. The former emigrated from Bohemia as a young man to farm in the Yuba area, an occupation pursued by Martin Jr., who also served as the president of Yuba's village board in the early 1950s. Yuba and its neighboring community, Hillsboro, sustain Czech American culture, including music and song, through *Český Den* (Czech Day), a festival held each June.

Stratman-Thomas had plenty to say in her retrospective 1946 field notes:

> Many years ago I had heard about the Bohemian bands at Yuba from my cousin at Richland Center, Mrs. Lee Dobbs. Mr. and Mrs. Dobbs were well-acquainted with many of the Yuba musicians. Snyder and I left Madison early one Sunday morning. The Dobbs joined us at Richland Center and we drove on through the hills to Yuba. Shortly after noon the Bohemian musicians began to assemble at Robert Novak's [Novy's]

The Yuba Bohemian Band, Yuba, Wisconsin, 1946. (Wisconsin Historical Society, WHi-25376)

Opera House and Dance Hall. There was Joe Yansky, who was a one-man band with an accordion [actually a concertina] and drums, played the polkas "Baruska" (Barbara) and "Zvojni domu" (Home from the War). Mr. and Mrs. Joe Viagelt sang "Ochi cerny" (Black Eyes) and "Virny Pravik" (True citizens of Praha/Prague). The song asks, "What does a true citizen of Praha love?" The answer is, "Mary, Praha, and the world."

Since the Bohemians first came to Yuba, they played at dances, weddings, and funerals. Most of the members of the Yuba band which we recorded had played together for forty years. The members were Otto and Wencil Stanek, clarinet; George McGilvery and William Tydrich, cornet; Anton Stanek, horn; Nick Rott, trombone; Martin Rott, baritone; and Alfred Stanek, tuba. The dances they played for us were "Litomericka," "Popelka polka," and "Samec galop."

I was particularly curious about the use of Bohemian band music at funerals. In reply to my inquiries I was told that the band would precede the hearse and march from the church to the cemetery, a distance of mile and a half. When I asked the band if they would record one of the funeral marches, they selected "Bohemul," which was the march played for the funeral of the uncle of one of the band members, Martin Rott, in 1932. Although this custom is passing, one elderly lady who was standing near me remarked: "When my husband died, the children didn't think we should have the band, but I insisted. I knew their father wouldn't think it right to be buried without the band marching and playing in the funeral procession.

Popelka, literally "little ashes," is the Czech name for Cinderella of fairy-tale fame. There are several "Cinderella Polkas," including one published in sheet music form by Boston's E. H. Wade Company in 1850. Wisconsin's Lawrence Duchow recorded a 78 rpm version of "Cinderella Polka" for RCA Victor (447-0128), while fellow Wisconsin Czech polka-band leader Romy Gosz recorded a different tune with a similar name, "Poor Cinderella Polka."

24　Pod našima okny / Underneath Our Windows

Sung by Emily Bauer McClure and Mayme Bauer Doser, Prairie du Chien, Wisconsin, August 19, 1941. Recorded by Helene Stratman-Thomas and Robert Draves. Transcription and translation by Joe Grim Feinberg and Tereza Smejkalová, 2010.

5021 A1

Pod našima okny teče vodička.	Underneath our windows water runs.
"Napoj že, má milá, mého koníčka."	"Will you water my horse, my dear loved one?"
"Já ho nenapojím, ja se koně bojím,	"I won't water him, I am afraid of horses,
Ja se koně bojím, že jsem malická."	I am afraid of horses, I am so small."
Pod našima okny opad růže květ.	Underneath our windows, petals fall off the rose.
"Pověz ty, má milá, proč tě mrzí svě?"	"Tell me my dear, why does the world weigh down on you?"
"Mně svět nic nemrzí, mně jen srdce bolí,	"It is not the world that weighs on me, it is my heart that aches,
Mně jen srdce bolí, plakala bych hned."	It is my heart that aches, so much that I could cry."
Pod našima okny roste oliva.	Underneath our windows grows an olive tree.

"Pověz ty, ma milá, kdo k vam chodívá."
"K nám žádnej nechodí, k nám se každej bojí,

K nám se každej bojí, že jsem chorobná."

"Tell me my dear, who comes to see you?"
"No one comes to see us,
     everyone is afraid of us,
Everyone is afraid of us, for I am so sick."

Mayme Doser (1894–1975) and Emily McClure (1896–1979) were sisters whose parents, Mary Zlabek and John Bauer (also spelled "Bower"), were immigrants from Bohemia in the old Hapsburg Empire. The couple lived in Cook County, Illinois, for a time in the 1880s, where John Bauer was a saloonkeeper, before settling among Czechs in the Prairie du Chien area where Mayme and Emily were born. Mayme owned and operated a beauty shop.

Stratman-Thomas was quite busy on August 19, 1941, as she recorded fourteen songs in Prairie du Chien, not only with Czechs but also with the French Canadian singer Virginia LaBonne Valley and the Irishman Patrick Sheehy. Her notes, sadly, say nothing about the Bauer sisters, except to mention their married names: Mrs. George McClure and Mrs. Mayme Doser. She also mentions Mrs. Frank Stevens—Rose Novak Stevens (1891–1978), whose mother, Elizabeth Novak, was born in Bohemia.

Rose Novak Stevens also performed a version of "Pod našima okny," one of the best-known Czech folksongs, with its peasant village setting and melancholy allusions to poverty, sickness, and heartache. Stratman-Thomas's notes for this song include a citation for *Kytice Společenských Písní* (Bouquet of Social Songs), published by the Bohemian Benedictine Press of Chicago, although it is not clear whether this songbook was owned by the Bauer sisters or was tracked down by Stratman-Thomas.

25 Když jsem šel cestičkou úzkou / As I Walked That Narrow Path

Sung by Emily Bauer McClure and Mayme Bauer Doser, Prairie du Chien, Wisconsin, August 19, 1941. Recorded by Helene Stratman-Thomas and Robert Draves. Transcription and translation by Joe Grim Feinberg and Tereza Smejkalová, 2010.

5021 A2

Když jsem šel cestičkou úzkou, trajdá,
Potkal jsem holčičku hezkou, trajdá.
Malou, nevelikou, ale hezkou, bobelatou,
Kukú kukukú,
Malou, nevelikou, ale hezkou, bobelatou.

As I walked that narrow path, try-da,
I met a pretty girl, try-da.
Small, not big, pretty, plump,
Coocoo, coocoocoo,
Small, not big, pretty, plump.

Když jsem se jí počal ptáti, trajdá,	When I went to ask her, try-da,
Jestli by se chtěla vdáti, trajdá,	If she would like to get married, try-da,
Ona povidala, za rok a za dvě léta,	She said in a year and after two years,
Kukú kukukú,	Coocoo, coocoocoo,
Ona povidala, za rok a za dvě léta.	She said in a year and after two years.
"Spěchej ty vojáčku, spěchej, trajdá,	"Hurry, soldier, hurry, try-da,
Kapičky do země tlačej, trajdá,	Drops are pushing against
	the ground, try-da,
Nedaleko dveří a paní máma leží,"	Not far from the door, and
	mother lies there,"
Kukú kukukú,	Coocoo, coocoocoo,
"Nedaleko dveří a paní máma leží."	"Not far from the door, and
	mother lies there."
"Paní máma nejmilejší, trajdá,	"Mother dearest, try-da,
Náš kocourek chytil myši, trajdá,	Our tomcat was catching mice, try-da.
Skočil na poličku a zlámal si nožičku,"	It jumped on a shelf and broke its foot,"
Kukú kukuku,	Coocoo, coocoocoo,
"Skočil na poličku a zlámal si nožičku."	"It jumped on a shelf and broke its foot."
Když mu to bolelo tuze, trajdá,	When it hurt him bad, try-da,
Křiklo to ubohé zvíře, trajdá.	The poor creature cried out, try-da,
Aj já mu křikla, "č— ts—,	And I called to him, "Ch— tss—,
kocourku jdi do pekla!"	tomcat, go to hell!"
Aj já mu křikla, "č— ts—,	And I called to him, "Ch— tss—,
kocourku jdi do pekla!"	tomcat, go to hell!"

Lusty wandering soldiers, fair peasant maids, and watchful mothers are staples in Czech and other European traditional repertoires, as is the feckless cuckoo—onomatopoeically invoked through the Bauer sisters' playful harmonies—which lays its eggs in other birds' nests. This song exists in many Old World versions but does not appear among songbooks, commercial recordings, or field recordings from Czech America.

26 Voják od Prairie du Chien / Soldier from Prairie du Chien

Sung and played on button accordion by Albert Wachuta, Prairie du Chien, Wisconsin, August 19, 1941. Recorded by Helene Stratman-Thomas and Robert Draves. Transcription and translation by Joe Grim Feinberg and Tereza Smejkalová, 2010.

5025 B

Ještě já se podívám, podívám	One more time I will look, I will look
K prérdučinským zahradám.	Over the orchards of Prairie du Chien.
Ješte já se podívám, podívám	One more time I will look, I will look
K prérdučinským zahradám.	Over the orchards of Prairie du Chien.
Spatřím-li tam ještě modrooké děvče,	If I see that blue-eyed girl,
Já si na něj zavolám.	I will call out to her.
A když ho tu nevidím, nevidím,	But if I don't see her, don't see her,
Ani o ňom neslyším,	And I don't hear of her,
S kým pak já se tady, s kým pak já se tady,	With whom then,
S kým pak já se potěším?	With whom will I enjoy myself?
Ty se budeš těšívat, těšívat	You will enjoy yourself, enjoy yourself
S mládencema v hospodě.	With the boys in the barroom.
Já se budu těšit, já se budu těšit	I will enjoy myself, I will enjoy myself
S vraným koněm na vojně.	With a black horse in the war.
Teče, teče potůček, potůček,	The creek is running, running,
Je celý zkrvácený.	Red with blood.
Teče, teče potůček, potůček,	The creek is running, running,
Je celý zkrvácený.	Red with blood.
To je z mého chlapce, to je z mého chlapce,	It's from my boy, from my boy,
Z jeho upřimný hlavy.	From his fair head.
To není z jeho hlavy,	It's not from his head,
To je z jeho koníčka.	It's from his horse.
To není z jeho hlavy,	It's not from his head,
To je z jeho koníčka.	It's from his horse.
Posekala mu ho, posekala mu ho,	Cut down, cut down
Ocelivá šavlička.	By a steel sword.
Ocelivá šavlička, šavlička,	A steel sword, a sword,
Na dvě strany broušená	Sharpened on both edges.
Ta mně bude chránit, mé srdéčko hájit,	It will protect me, defend my heart,
Až bude velká vojna.	When the great war comes.
Ta mně bude chránit, mé srdéčko hájit,	It will protect me, defend my heart
Až bude velká vojna.	When the great war comes.

Albert Wachuta (1875–1953) was born in Prairie du Chien, the son of Albert (1826–1908) and Barbara (1834–1906) Wachuta, who immigrated with the two eldest of their eventual five children. The younger Albert Wachuta sketched his biography and musical influences in a June 1948 letter to Stratman-Thomas:

> I was born in Prairie du Chien Oct 19, 1875 and never went to Bohemian school and hardly any to a English school. Them days boys had to work, that I mean, boys born on the farm of poor family, work was more important than school. Well my parents came to Prairie du Chien in 1864. Czechoslovakia city Bechene [Bechyně], County Tabor and in the city that my mother used to sing about in place of Prairie. I had learned the songs mostly from my mother, but some from other people too because them days there was a lot of Bohemian singing. But now there is none. It breaks my heart because I love to sing and I believe the Czech melodies is the tops. Don't you think so. I am gone to write out the words of the one I sang latter now in summer I am kind of busy mostly fishing. We are out at the camp our son had taken it over, so it's just the same as it was before.

A farmer for many years, Wachuta had an extensive rabbit farm in the early twentieth century, supplying fur buyers with pelts and selling the meat locally. In a syndicated rural news story, he championed rabbit-raising as "more profitable than hens" (*Postville [Iowa] Herald*, January 10, 1929). He also operated a resort on the Mississippi River, the camp mentioned in his letter.

Wachuta began playing the button accordion as a twelve-year-old for local Czech house parties. Stratman-Thomas's 1946 field notes focus on his localized version of a soldier's song: "In the midst of Mr. Wachuta's Bohemian song, I heard something that sounded like 'Prairie du Chenska.' In reply to my questioning, he said, 'Yes, that's right. I'm singing about a soldier. My mother sang about a soldier of the town in Bohemia where she was born. Since I live in Prairie du Chien, I sing about the soldier from Prairie du Chien.'" Unreported elsewhere in the United States, "Ještě já se podívám" is a well-known Czech folksong, existing in many variations and often performed as an instrumental polka tune in the twentieth century.

< Albert Wachuta, Prairie du Chien, Wisconsin, 1941. (Wisconsin Historical Society, WHi-25194)

POLISH

America's largest rural Polish settlement spans north-central Wisconsin's Portage and Marathon Counties, and Polish Americans are second only to Germans in population among Wisconsin's ethnic groups. Although Poles arrived in Wisconsin as early as the 1850s, they immigrated substantially from the 1890s until the onset of World War I. Hailing mostly from the German partition of northernmost Poland along the Baltic Sea, but also including southern mountaineers from the Austrian partition, Wisconsin's Poles dominated Milwaukee's south side. Whether farmers or factory hands, the predominately Catholic Poles celebrated weddings with songs in church halls as well as with polkas, waltzes, obereks, and krakowiaks that were likewise features of tavern dances. Portage County remains a stronghold of Polish music, song, and dance in the twenty-first century, while such summer galas as Milwaukee's Polish Fest and Pulaski Polka Days, held in a village northwest of Green Bay, testify to the continued regional vitality of Polish American folk music.

27 Zbojniki / Bandits' Dance

Spoken and played on fiddle by John Ciezczak, Stevens Point, Wisconsin, July 23, 1941. Recorded by Robert Draves.

4978 A

Bandit song! You know, those bandits, outlaws, they used to be just like Jesse James, you know, long time ago, [like] they have in this country. They have Janosik, in our country, Janosik, that something like Jesse James. Janosik in his day didn't have no guns. They have tomahawks or something. They'd go like this [brandishes an imaginary hatchet] and set to robbing and everything. Yah!

John Ciezczak (1888–1976) was born in the Tatra Mountains of southern Poland. Sometime around 1900 he traveled with his parents to Chicago, where the thriving Polish community included fellow "highlanders," most of whom "worked in the stock yards, slaughterhouses, meat packing companies, and iron foundries" (Gromada 2012: 66). Some immigrant Polish peasants cum industrial workers in Milwaukee and Chicago subsequently sought land in rural Wisconsin, including the Ciezczaks, who settled in the town of Hull, near Stevens Point. John learned a watchmaker's trade, which he practiced until retiring in 1952.

We do not know how Stratman-Thomas learned of Ciezczak, although her files mention "Mr. Bachleda, a farmer" living near Mosinee, between Stevens Point and Wausau, who "can play highlander fiddle music and sing." Stratman-Thomas's student engineer, Robert Draves, recorded Ciezczak by himself and described the circumstances in a June 23, 1941, letter to her: "People say they are surprised that I should ever have gotten the old fellow to open up, but didn't have much trouble. I visited him in the morning and found him unwilling, saying that he couldn't sing anymore, that he was too busy anyhow. But after awhile he was telling me I had better record him 'cause I wouldn't find anything like it anywhere else. . . . After he got going, he was so enthusiastic there was no stopping him. I thought it would be best to let him keep up the flow, so I recorded the whole seance."

Jerzy Janosik (1688–1713), the bandit invoked by Ciezczak, is a legendary Robin Hood figure who was executed for robbing the rich but was beloved by Slovak and Polish peasants of the Tatras. Continuously featured in poems, paintings, and films, Janosik and other highlanders have been celebrated in cycles of "bandit" songs. Ciezczak's Stevens Point neighbor, Adam Bartosz, sang one such song, "W murowanej piwnicy" (In a Cellar Made of Brick), for Draves that he had also performed for folklorist Harriet Pawlowska in 1940 (Pawlowska 1983: 188, 225). Meanwhile fiddler Karol Stoch and singer Stanisław Bachleda, both immigrants to Chicago from the Tatra Mountains, recorded "Piesni zbojnikow" (Song of the Bandits) in 1928 for Victor (V-16050).

The dance recalled and played by Ciezczak remains traditional in Poland's mountainous Podhale district as a men's dance, nowadays performed for exhibitions as a "flashy crowd pleaser" that involves walking, squatting, and leaping, with each man brandishing a characteristic hatchet, or *ciupaga* (Dziewanowska 1997: 268–269, 278–297).

28 In the Style of Sabała

Spoken, sung, and played on fiddle by John Ciezczak, Stevens Point, Wisconsin, July 23, 1941. Recorded by Robert Draves. Transcription, translation, and annotation by Marcin Gąsienica-Byrcyn, with assistance from Timothy J. Cooley, 2012.

4978 B

That Sabała, a famous musician, used to have that corn fiddle.[1] And one time those professors used to come from Kraków to Zakopane. Zakopane is the biggest summer resort in Poland. It's something like in Switzerland. So Sabała, he was the first one to get acquainted with those big professors. And he played that corn fiddle. You know, it's got only three strings on it. Then he used to play for them. Let's see, how did that go?

Kie jo sie podeprem,	When I lean on
Rajowom[2] ciupagom	The mountain hatchet,
To jo se zajadem	Then I will travel
Jaz ku piynci stawom.	All the way to the Five Lakes.[3]

1. The corn fiddle (*złobcoki* or *gęśle*) is pear-shaped bowed stringed instrument, longer and narrower than a conventional fiddle, that was made and played in the Tatra Mountains through the nineteenth century.
2. The word *raj* means "paradise." *Rajowom ciupagom* could possibly mean a hatchet from paradise. It could also mean either belonging to or made by someone named Raj.
3. The Valley of the Five Lakes is a place in the Tatra Mountains.

The fiddler Ciezczak memorializes, Jan Krzeptowski Sabała (1809–1894), was a farmer, hunter, and musician in the Tatra Mountains. Imprisoned briefly for participating in the 1846 Chochołów Uprising of highlanders against imperial Austria, Sabała in his later years became a hunting guide for wealthy visitors to the Zakopane area. The novelist and 1905 Nobel Prize–winner Henryk Sienkiewicz (1846–1916) was one of the "big professors" who befriended and wrote about Sabała; another was the Polish painter and writer Stanislaw Witkiewicz (1851–1915), who celebrated the old mountaineer as the "Homer of the Tatra Mountains." The illiterate Sabała was a superb traditional storyteller whose tales have been widely anthologized (e.g., Dorson 1975: 100–108). Likewise, his tunes are synonymous with the distinctive music of Polish mountaineers.

< John Ciezczak, Stevens Point, Wisconsin, 1941. (Wisconsin Historical Society, WHi-25186)

Regarding Ciezczak's particular performance, the ethnomusicologist Tim Cooley observed (2012): "The *nuta* (tune-family) type is a Sabałowa, named after Sabała . . . characterized by the descent in the second phrase to a G, requiring the use of the D string. Most require only the A and E. We don't really know if Jan Krzeptowski Sabała actually played any of these *nuty*, but they are considered an older style of tune-family. Note also that the poetry consists of six-syllable lines typical of the greater Poland, Slovakia, Hungary area. The tune, however, has 10 beats per phrase, usually conceived of as 5-bar phrases. This is typical of the Tatra region and very unusual elsewhere."

29 Matuś moja, matuś / Mommy, My Mommy

Sung by Bernice Bartosz, Stevens Point, Wisconsin, August 11, 1941.
Recorded by Helene Stratman-Thomas and Robert Draves.
Transcription, translation, and annotation of first two verses by Adam Bartosz, 1947, with editorial corrections by Paulina Michalewicz; additional transcription and translation by Michalewicz, 2010.
4976 B2

Matuś moja, matuś,
Wydaj[1] mnie za Jasia!
Spodobały mi się,
Kołeczka u pasa, oj dana!

CHORUS:
Oj dana, oj dana!
Oj dana, oj dana![2]

Kółeczka u pasa,
I włosy kręcone,
Matuś moja, matuś,
Wydaj mię za zonę, oj dana!

"Matuś moja, matuśm
Wydaj mnie za Jasia
Spodobały mi sie
Kółecka u pasa.

Oj dana [reapeated nine times]

Mommy, my mommy,
Give me out to Johnny!
I like the rings,
At his belt, oj dana!

CHORUS:
Oj dana, oj dana!
Oj dana, oj dana!

The rings at his belt,
And his curly hair.
Mommy, my mommy,
Give me away as a wife, oj dana!

"Mommy, my mommy,
Give me to Johnny [in marriage].
I have liked
The rings on his belt.

Oj dana [reapeated nine times]

Kółecka u pasa I włosy kręcone, Matuś moja, matuś, Wydaj mnie za żone."[1]	Rings on his belt And curly hair, Mommy, my mommy, Give me away as a wife."
Oj dana [reapeated nine times][2]	Oj dana [reapeated nine times]
"Córuś moja córuś, Już nie gadam wiele. Weż sobie chłopaka, Za tydzień wesele, oj dana!"	"Daughter, my daughter, I won't talk anymore. Take the boy, Wedding will be in a week, oj dana!"
Oj dana [reapeated nine times]	Oj dana [reapeated nine times]

---

1. To give out in marriage.
2. A common repetitive phrase in many Polish folksongs, but with no specific meaning.

Bernice Dombrowski Bartosz (1904–2004) and her husband Adam (see track 31 below) were prominent citizens of Stevens Point, where they were tireless advocates for Polish culture. During the American bicentennial of 1976, for example, "Mrs. Bartosz . . . was in charge of the painting of murals with Polish themes on [City] Square buildings last year" (*Stevens Point Daily Journal*, February 22, 1977).

Bernice Bartosz was born in the ancient northern Polish city of Toruń, which is on the

Bernice and Adam Bartosz, July 28, 1973. (courtesy of Jerome Bartosz)

Vistula River in part of what was then partitioned "German Poland" and in a region where the Kashubian dialect prevailed. The daughter of an architect who had previously sojourned to the United States, she graduated from a business college in Toruń prior to immigrating in 1926 to Baltimore, where she met her husband, a fellow immigrant. The couple moved to Stevens Point in 1937, when Adam was recruited by a pair of Polish American newspapers, *Gwiazda Polarna* (Northern Star) and *Rolnik* (Farmer). Adam edited these papers, with Bernice proofreading and covering women's topics, until 1973 (*Stevens Point Daily Journal*, July 28, 1973).

The couple's reputation likely attracted Stratman-Thomas's attention. Yet on June 23, 1941, while on a solo recording trip, Robert Draves reported to his boss: "I would have moved on to Wausau last night but for two problem-Poles. Mrs. Bartosz has songs, I know, but they're difficult people. Her husband is a little, self-satisfied, crew-cut, wiseacher [*sic*]. I'm going back there this morning. I'll get 'em or bust." Draves added an exultant postscript following his second visit: "We've won the Bartoszes. Even invited me for dinner. We will come back, you and I." Although we can only speculate on the turnabout, perhaps the Bartoszes were wary since prominent faculty from the University of Wisconsin had publicly scorned Portage County's Polish Catholics. Notably Edward A. Ross (1866–1951), a professor of sociology at the UW from 1906 to 1937, targeted Wisconsin Poles for a chapter, "The Alarming Prospect of Slavic Immigration," in his influential *The Old World in the New: The Significance of Past and Present Immigration to the American People* (1914). Fortunately Draves's persistence and purpose won out.

Both of the Bartoszes were fine singers in a village style who were visited subsequently by Harriet Pawlowska, a folklorist from Detroit who recorded folksongs in Wisconsin in 1946 and 1947 (Pawlowska 1983: 247). Despite her well-to-do urban background, Bernice grew up in an era when Polish schools were forced to use German rather than their own language. Hence her formative Polish-language experience was bound up with oral tradition. Indeed she had "never read a Polish book before emigrating" (*Stevens Point Daily Journal*, July 28, 1973). "Matuś moja, matuś" is a well-known folksong in Poland and Polish America, while the exclamatory "Oj dana" of the chorus figures in many traditional songs. A five-verse variant, featuring "Stash" and his red cap rather than "Johnny" and his rings, had been printed decades earlier by the Stevens Point publisher employing the Bartoszes, *Lutnia polska: Czyli, śpiewnik, największy ze wszystkich wydanych dotychczas* (The Polish Lute: Greatest of All Previously Issued Songbooks [Bracia Worzałłowie (Worzalla Brothers) 1917: 249]). The first two verses of Bartosz's performance closely resemble those gathered for a songbook in the 1940s by Poles in Minnesota (Contoski 1953: 162).

30 Miałeś czapkę / Hat with Peacock Feathers

Sung by Bernice Bartosz, Stevens Point, Wisconsin, August 11, 1941.
Recorded by Helene Stratman-Thomas and Robert Draves.
Transcription and translation by Paulina Michalewicz, 2010.

4976 B3

Miałeś chłopie złoty róg.	You had a golden horn, peasant.
Miałeś czapkę z pawich piór.	You had a hat with peacock feathers, peasant.
Czapke wiatr po lesie,	The wind in the woods took the hat,
Na rozwoli niesie.	It is freely floating about.
Ostał ci sie jeno,	You were left with,
Ostał ci sie jeno sznur.	You were left with only a string.
Trzymaj chłopie złoty róg,	Peasant, hold on to the golden horn,
Trzymaj czapke z pawich piór.	Hold onto the hat with the peacock feathers.
Słyszysz wiatr po lesie,	Hear the wind through the forest,
Echo rogu niesie.	It brings the echo of the horn.
Uwiąż mocno złoty,	Tie up the golden,
Uwiąż mocno złoty sznur.	Tie up the golden string well.
Szukaj chłopie w lesie, idz	Look peasant, go in the forest,
Może znadziesz czapkę gdzieś.	Maybe you'll find your hat somewhere.
Zagnij róg swój złoty	Play the golden horn
Ze szczerej ochoty	From honest desire.
Wiatr ci twoją cazpkę,	The wind will let go of your hat,
Wiatr ci twoja czapke zniesł.	The wind will let go of your hat.

In 1947, when Bernice Bartosz was asked by Stratman-Thomas to provide the original lyrics and translation of this song, her husband responded with just one verse, a slightly different rendering of the first his wife had sung six years earlier.

Miałeś, chamie, złoty róg.	You had, peasant, a golden horn.
Miałeś, chamie, czapkę z piór.	You had, peasant, a cap of feathers.
Róg huka po lesie,	The horn howls over the forest,
Wicher czapkę niesie,	The wind carries your cap,
Został ci się jeno sznur.	Only a rope remains.

Adam Bartosz added, "There are various stanzas to the last song. I don't know which you have, but one should be enough." Yet there is much more to examine and ponder.

The lone verse provided by Bartosz was from a three-verse song composed by Stanisław Wyspiański (1869–1928) for his play *Wesele*, first performed in 1901 (Got

1977; Wyspiański [1901] 1990). Wyspiański was born and lived most of his life in the ancient southern Polish city of Kraków, formerly the nation's capital but then part of the Austrian partition of Poland. Raised in a family of artists and intellectuals, Wyspiański was attracted nonetheless to Polish folk culture, particularly that of the peasants in southern Poland's villages. His career coincided with both the development of folksong scholarship in Poland and the veneration of southern Poland's mountainous Podhale region as exemplary of unspoiled folk culture (Cooley 2005; Czekanowska 1990: 55–60, 84–87). Wyspiański relied on folk culture for its wealth of poetic and national symbols that might fuse and advance political and aesthetic ends.

The single verse that Adam Bartosz extracted for Stratman-Thomas from the three-verse song in Wyspiański's *Wesele* makes critical use of the respective symbolism of a feathered hat and a golden horn. The former is a four-cornered men's hat adorned with peacock feathers. Originating in and characteristic of the Kraków region, this hat came to be regarded in the nineteenth century as part of Poland's national dress. The latter resonates with a continuous Kraków tradition, which had been established by the fourteenth century, involving a trumpeter playing a melody from a church tower, at dawn and dusk in each of the four cardinal directions, to signal the opening and closing of the old city's gates. Played likewise to alarm the populace when fires or invaders threatened, Kraków's golden trumpet became linked with national self-determination from the late eighteenth through the early twentieth centuries, when Poland was partitioned by Austria, Germany, and Russia (Dobrzycki 1983). Focusing on the village wedding of an intellectual from Kraków to a peasant bride, Wyspiański's *Wesele* featured traditional peasant clothing, a peasant orchestra, and familiar folksongs and tunes. His verse about a peacock hat and a golden horn borrows the tune of a well-known folksong "Od Krakówa czarny las" ("A Black Forest Near Kraków") (Kapolka in Wyspiański 1990: 202, note 45). Although too complex to sketch here, *Wesele*'s plot raises the hope that Polish intellectuals and peasants might collectively advance the cause of national self-determination. Hope fails, however, when a peasant dispatched to the four corners of Poland loses not only his feathered hat but also a golden horn essential to sounding revolt. Hence, the verse that Adam Bartosz conveyed verbatim to Stratman-Thomas has been best known by Poles and Polish Americans for its despairing opening line, "Miałeś, chamie, złoty róg" (You had, cham, a golden horn). Although referring to a peasant, *cham* is an especially derogatory term akin to "nigger" in American context. Adam Bartosz defined cham as "a person without honor or courtesy."

Sometimes translating *cham* as "yokel," "boor," or "lout," two bilingually published Polish American versions of this song invoke yet depart intriguingly from Wyspiański's original three verses. A Detroit rendition, transcribed from oral tradition in the 1940s, combines three verses of "Od Krakówa czarny las" with Wyspiański's "Miałeś, chamie" as its fourth and final verse, transforming the song into a spat between lovers that eliminates nationalist implications (Pawlowska 1983: 208–209, 225). A similar lovers' quarrel version set down by Poles in Minneapolis in the 1940s fuses two verses from "Od Krakówa czarny las" with a pair of Wyspiański's verses to the same tune (Contoski 1953: 97). Strikingly, Bernice Bartosz's performance for Stratman-Thomas sustains the tune but draws no verses from "Od Krakówa czarny las." Concerned like Wyspiański with Polish self-determination and sung at a historical moment when Nazi invaders ruled Poland, her version nonetheless replaced the playwright's highly derogatory *cham* in the final verse with *chłopie*, a far less pejorative term for "peasant," thus countering his tone of angry despair with the hopeful sentiment that Poles acting from "honest desire" might yet reclaim what they had lost.

31 Zajumiały bory / The Forests Roared

Sung by Adam Bartosz, Stevens Point, Wisconsin, August 11, 1941.
Recorded by Helene Stratman-Thomas and Robert Draves.
Transcription and translation by Adam Bartosz, 1947, with editorial corrections by Paulina Michalewicz, 2010, and Max Statkiewicz, 2013.
5005 A1

Zaszumiały bory, zahuczały lasy—
Gdeśta se podzeli, gdeśta se podzeli,
Moje młode czasy?

Prendzy młeński kamień we łzy se obracy,
Ale moja młodość, ale moja młodość
Już se nie nawracy.

The woods hummed, the forests roared—
Where are you hiding, where are you hiding,
My youthful times?

A millstone might turn in a teardrop,
But my youth, but my youth
Will never return.

Adam Bartosz (1894–1981) was born in the tiny village of Gora Ropczycka, part of the Austrian partition in the Rzeszow region of southeastern Poland. "My father was a shoemaker. . . . There were seven of us and we all learned to read and write in his shoemaker's shop" since the village lacked a school. The elder Bartosz also organized a cooperative library. "I spent most of my time in the library. . . . That's how I got my education, most of it." After immigrating to Baltimore in 1913, Adam Bartosz worked days and attended school at night, eventually earning a law degree from the University of Baltimore. Following his marriage to Bernice Dombrowski in 1929, Bartosz practiced law part-time in Baltimore. He also worked as an editor for the local Polish newspaper *Jednosc-Polonia* (Unity Polonia), leading to his recruitment in 1937 by the Worzalla family of Stevens Point, prominent printers and publishers of the largest Polish-language weekly newspaper in the United States (*Stevens Point Daily Journal*, July 28, 1973).

Stratman-Thomas's notes indicate that Bartosz's repertoire went beyond his home region to include Kashubian songs from along the Baltic Sea, as well as Ukrainian songs. The former he likely acquired in his travels, or perhaps in Stevens Point, where the Poles were overwhelmingly Kashubes; the latter he may have learned while growing up. The Austrian partition of Poland, in which he was raised, included the western extent of present-day Ukraine, and his home village in extreme southeastern Poland was a border area. "Zaszumiały bory" has definite Ukrainian elements, particularly (as noted by Maciej Statkiewicz) the Ukrainian use of *prendzy*, *obracy*, and *nawracy* instead of the Polish *predzej*, *obroci*, and *nawroci*. Perhaps the song circulated in Polish, Ukrainian, and mixed-language versions. The first verse is much the same as the opening verse of "Młodość miniona" (Departed Youth) by the poet Kazimierz Brodziński (1791–1835). Born in Galicia of peasant parentage, he served as an artillery officer in the Polish army. Captivated by Romanticism, Brodziński was an early chronicler of Polish folk dance who also regarded the songs of peasants as both intrinsically valuable and the basis for a national poetry. He published a collection from southern Poland, *Pieśni rolników polskich* (The Songs of Polish Farmers), in 1811 and drew on folksongs for several of his own compositions (Witkowska 1968).

32 A witajże / Oh Hello

Sung and spoken by Stasia Pokora, Milwaukee, Wisconsin, August 29, 1946. Recorded by Helene Stratman-Thomas and Aubrey Snyder. Transcription and translation by Paulina Michalowicz, 2010.

8453 B2

"A witajże, jak się miewasz Kasiu jedyna.

Czy ty sobie przypominasz
   swego Marcina, hej,

"Hello and welcome, how are
   you my only Katie,

Are you remembering your Martin, hey,

Swego Marcina?
Co to z tobą raz na wiencu, w
    karczmie wywijoł.
I od rana do wieczora twe zdrowie spijoł, hej,

Twe zdrowie spijoł."

"I ja ciebie także witam, miły Marcinie
I o twe sie zdrowie pytam, tylko jedynie, hej,

Tylko jedynie.
Bo jakiem sie z tobą luby roztać musiała,
Tom od rana do wieczora
    rzewnie płakała, hej,
Rzewnie płakała.

Bo matula mnie swataja; ze
    starym Borowym,
A tatuś mnie tez. wciąż łajoł
    ciężkiemy słowy, hej,
Ciężkiemy słowy.
A ja biedna, nieszczęśliwa, nie moja wina
Że nie mogę słuchać Stacha,
    jeno Marcina, hej,
Jeno Marcina."

"Jeno mi nie becz dziewucho,
    jeno mi nie becz.
Utrzyj oczka, uśmiechnijsie, rzuć
    frasunek precz, hej,
Rzuć frasunek precz."
Bo tu zaraz w ojców chacie
    rzucim sie śmiele.
"Dom nam ojcu, dom nam matce
    będzie wesele, hej,
Bedzie wesele."

your Martin?
Once he danced with you at the bar

And from morning to night he
    drank to your health, hey,
He drank to your health."

"And I welcome you too, Martin
And ask after your health,
    your only health, hey,
Your only health.
And when your lover had to part with you
Then from morning to night
    heavily you cried, hey,
Heavily you cried.

My mother promised me to the old forester,

And my father hailed me constantly
    with heavy words, hey,
With heavy words.
And poor me, unhappy me, it's not my fault
That I can't listen to Stan,
    only to Martin, hey,
Only to Martin."

"Only don't weep girl, only don't weep.

Wipe your eyes, put on a smile, and
    toss aside your cares, hey,
Toss aside your cares."
Here at your parents' hut he came boldly.

"Father, mother, there will be a wedding, hey,

There will be a wedding."

Stasia Felixa Pokora (1895–1979) was the youngest of seven children whose parents—Felix Pokora (b. 1855) and Anastasia Mlynarek Pokora (b. 1858)—came from German Poland to Milwaukee in 1886. Raised in an immigrant neighborhood on the city's south side, Pokora immersed herself in Polish American musical activities. In 1937 she had a lead role in *Children Be Good*, an "original musical comedy" by Milwaukeean Conrad

Stasia Pokora in front of her American Relief for Poland office, Milwaukee, Wisconsin, 1946. (Wisconsin Historical Society, WHi-25392)

A. Saskowski, which was produced at the South Side Armory by the Polish Fine Arts Club (*Milwaukee Journal*, May 9, 1937). In October 1939 she sang in *Polonaise*, another Saskowski creation that premiered "with a complete cast of Milwaukee artists" to a sold-out audience at the Pabst Theater. The following August a performance at the Blatz Temple of Music drew thirty-five hundred (*Stevens Point Daily Journal*, October 21, 1939; *Milwaukee Sentinel,* August 16, 1940).

Pokora also sang on the *Polish Radio Hour*, founded by Stanislaus Nastal on Milwaukee's WEMP in 1936 but subsequently airing on WFOX. A former captain in the Polish army, following World War I Nastal (1899–1947) introduced Polish films to the United States, whereupon he met his wife, Halina Leonarski, and settled in her home town. In the 1940s, while Poland suffered from Nazi occupation, Nastal was vice president of American Relief for Poland, with Stasia Pokora serving as the executive secretary of the organization's Milwaukee office (*Nowiny Polskie*, Milwaukee, September, 8, 1947; translation by Peter J. Obst, 2011). One of her accomplishments was the translation of "original Polish recipes" for a fund-raising publication: *Polish Cook Book: Traditional Polish Christmas and Easter Dishes* (1945). Her papers are in the Milwaukee Area Research Center of the Wisconsin Historical Society.

Contacted by Stratman-Thomas in July 1946, Pokora responded on August 2: "If necessary I would do the recording of Polish folk songs, Miss Thomas, but that would have to be some time after the 11th of August because up to that time I shall be so busy that it would be absolutely impossible for me to do anything like that. My work here as the executive secretary of the American Relief for Poland keeps me really 'hopping.'" As Stratman-Thomas tells us in her notes for August 29, the recording session occurred while "Miss Stasia Pokora" was on the job: "We found her in the Polish Relief headquarters, surrounded by boxes and bundles which were ready to be shipped to Poland. We set up the recording equipment with these as a background, and Miss Pokora sang one Polish song after another. She told us that she had learned a great many of her songs from Polish immigrants who roomed at her home when she was a little girl."

Although Pokora's refined vocalizing strays from the probable Old Country village style of the boarders from whom she learned, "A witajże" is a well-known folksong in Poland and Polish America, as is the theme of conflict between a poor young suitor and a wealthy older rival. The Library of Polish Song in Kraków registers the song's appearance in a workers' song book from 1919 and in a twenty-first century regional anthology,

Poznański spiewnik (Poznan Songbook) (published in Gdańsk 2001: 113; http://www.bibliotekapiosenki.pl/Oj_witajze, accessed January 13, 2013). Across the Atlantic an unknown singer, possibly Alexandri N. Panasiewicz, recorded a version in 1915 for Columbia (E2498), and the Worzalla Brothers of Stevens Point included the song in *Lutnia polska* (The Polish Lute) (Bracia Worzałłowie 1917: 274–275).

LITHUANIAN

Lithuania was part of the Russian empire in the late nineteenth century when peasants, pushed by an agricultural depression and the prospect of conscription into the czar's army, sought work in American mines and mills. Many immigrants were young men who left wives and sweethearts in hopes of returning with wealth or earning enough to send for loved ones. By 1900 there were substantial Lithuanian settlements in Cleveland and Chicago and smaller but active enclaves in industrial cities along the Wisconsin shore of Lake Michigan: Kenosha, Racine, Milwaukee, and Sheboygan, the self-proclaimed Furniture Capital of the World. Folksongs flourished in homes, amid ethnic organizations, and at church events, especially during and in the aftermath of World War II, as Lithuania was ravaged and occupied in turn by the German and Russian armies.

33 Subatos vakarėli / Saturday Night I Saddled My Black Horse

Sung by the Lithuanian Group from the Church of the Immaculate Conception (John Abromaitis, John Aldakauskas, Lucia Aldakauskas, Mary Aldakauskas, Ruth Baranoucky, Ann Belekevich, Edward Girdaukas, Alexander F. Skeris, Stella Skeris, Agnes Zupancich), Sheboygan, Wisconsin, August 30, 1946. Recorded by Helene Stratman-Thomas and Aubrey Snyder. Transcription and translation for verses 1–3 and 7 from the files of Helene Stratman-Thomas, 1947; verses 4–6 transcribed and translated by Tom DuBois, 2009.

8456 B2

Subatos vakarėlį	Saturday night
Balnojau juodbėrėlį.	I saddled my black horse.
Oi lylia lylia lylia.	Oi lylia lylia lylia.
Balnojau juodbėrėlį	I saddled my black horse.

Juodbėrėlį balnojau,	Black horse saddled,
Pas mergelę nujojau.	To a I girl I rode.
Oi lylia lylia lylia.	Oi lylia lylia lylia.
Pas mergelę nujojau.	To a girl I rode.
Nujojau šimtą mylių,	I rode a hundred miles,
Prijojau žulią girią.	And I came to a green forest.
Oi lylia lylia lylia.	Oi lylia lylia lylia.
Prijojau žulią girią.	And I came to a green forest.
Toji žalioj girelej	In that green forest
Kukuoj raiba gegele.	Cuckooed something like a cuckoo.
Oi lylia lylia lylia.	Oi lylia lylia lylia.
Kukuoj raiba gegele.	Cuckooed something like a cuckoo.
Gegutele raiboji.	The cuckoo sang.
Ko taip gailiai kukoji?	Why so sadly did it cuckoo?
Oi lylia lylia lylia.	Oi lylia lylia lylia.
Ko taip gailiai kukoji?	Why so sadly did it cuckoo?
Atsake gegutele?	What did the cuckoo sing?
Kad mire mergužele.	That a young girl has died.
Oi lylia lylia lylia.	Oi lylia lylia lylia.
Kad mire mergužele.	That a young girl has died.
Mire mano mieliausia	My love died and
Kitos tokios negausiu.	I won't get another like her.
Oi lylia lylia lylia.	Oi lylia lylia lylia.
Kitos tokios negausiu.	I won't get another like her.

Mary Aldakauskas (1908–1998) was the leader of Sheboygan's Lithuanian singers. Her father, John Yochis (1867–1953), was born in Lithuania's Suvalkija region. Arriving in Sheboygan in 1891, he worked in succession for the Phoenix Chair Company and Dillingham Manufacturing, a producer of cabinets and woodenware. Yochis was also a founder of Immaculate Conception Catholic Church, a center of Lithuanian activities in Sheboygan. A mature, established single man, Yochis wed Mary Bobinas in 1905, the year she emigrated from Simnas, a village in the Alytus region of Lithuania. Steeped in a repertoire of peasant songs, Mary Bobinas Yochis (1883–1966) was a strong influence on her daughter, Mary Yochis Aldakauskas. *The Sheboygan Press* edition of May 11, 1948, reported on "an interesting program Sunday evening in the newly remodeled Immaculate Conception parish hall," including not only Lithuanian folk dances "brought to America by Lithuanian immigrants," but also "Mrs. Mary Aldakauskas" performing a medley, "Songs My Mother Taught Me," dedicated to "the mothers in the audience." Mary Aldakauskas was the program chair for this and similar Sheboygan events featuring Lithuanian folk culture. In the late 1940s she served as chair and secretary of the Wisconsin District of the Lithuanian Roman Catholic Alliance of America and organized a Lithuanian Day program recognizing the recent arrival of displaced Lithuanians.

> The Lithuanian element of Sheboygan's population had cause for both joy and sorrow on Sunday as they staged a Lithuanian Day observance at Lakeview Shooting Park. In a well-planned, smoothly-moving program the Sheboyganites of Lithuanian ancestry celebrated the day and gave heartfelt thanks for the freedom, peace, and prosperity they have enjoyed in this country. They paused, however, in their dancing and singing to pledge their aid to fellow countrymen who still are in Lithuania suffering under Russian domination. . . . The program opened shortly after 2:30 p.m. with the Sheboygan Lithuanian chorus, directed by Marie Posewitz, singing the "Star-Spangled Banner" and the Lithuanian anthem. The Rev. Father James J. Shilkas, pastor of the Immaculate Conception church, acted as chairman. . . . The Sheboygan chorus presented a number of folk songs in the native tongue and a group of Milwaukeeans, including several displaced persons who have been in the country for brief periods, staged a number of dances. They were attired in the colorful costumes of their native land. The entire program brought back many vivid memories for the hard-working citizens of Sheboygan who still can recall their homeland. Many of the older folks joined in the Lithuanian anthem and folk songs with a feeling of joy and sorrow. Included in the local group which took part in the dancing and singing during the program were: Julia Hidde, Ann Belekevich, Lucia Aldakauskas, Lalma Sematis, Mary Aldakauskas, Donna Bobulis, Eugenia Skeris, Walter Daugird, Walter Jocis, William Schloskey, George Aldakauskas, Peter Adamavich, Alex Skeris, Charles Schultz, and Ignace Mardosas . . . a DP who is working in Sheboygan. (*Sheboygan Press*, July 5, 1949; July 8, 1949)

Four years later, when Sheboygan celebrated its centennial, Mary Aldakauskas organized and taught a Lithuanian chorus and dancers for an All Nation's Day program that included "Holland Dutch" from Cedar Grove, Greek, Irish, Lithuanian, Croatian,

English, Norwegian, German, and Slovenian performers from Sheboygan, and Israelis from Milwaukee (*Sheboygan Press*, August 8, 1953). Sometimes accompanied by organist and choir director Agnes Zupancich, Aldakauskas sang for church services and weddings into the 1970s (*Sheboygan Press*, November 9, 1971).

In her field notes for August 30, 1946, Stratman-Thomas wrote:

> When Mrs. Robert Karner of Sheboygan heard one of my lectures on folk music in Wisconsin, she became enthusiastic about the wealth of folk music which was available in Sheboygan. The recording of folk music of a Wisconsin city such as Sheboygan should be a continuous municipal project. Our limited time made it necessary to select only one of the many nationalities represented there.
>
> In the evening Mrs. Karner opened her home for the recording of a group of Lithuanian young people, who were members of the choir of the Church of the Immaculate Conception. We were told that the Lithuanians came to Sheboygan about 1890 and that Lithuanian was one of the world's oldest original languages. The names of the singers were fascinating: Ruth Baranoucky, Stella and Alexander F. Skeris, Ann Belekevich, Edward Girdaukas, Mary, Lucia, and John (Jr.) Aldakauskas, Agnes Zupancich, and John Abromaitis.
>
> The Lithuanian folk hymns were especially beautiful. . . ."Subatos Vakareli" (Saturday Night I Saddled My Black Horse) told of the heartbroken lover who rode through the forest to see his sweetheart only to hear the sad singing of the bird which told him that his girl had died.

Folksong collectors in early nineteenth-century Lithuania encountered "Subatos vakareli." The refugee Lithuanian folklorist, Jonas Balys, recorded a version in Cleveland in 1949 from Jonas Alekna (b. 1886), who had immigrated in 1906. Balys gives this summary: "Saturday evening a boy saddled his steed and rode to see his girl. . . . Riding horse in Lithuanian songs is always called *žirgas*/steed to differentiate from a working horse—*arklys*" (1977: 4, 292, 326). In 1930 Antanas Vanagaitis and Juozas Olsauskas recorded a 78 rpm version in Chicago (Columbia, 16205-F), and folklorist Elena Bradunas found it widely sung in the 1970s by post–World War II refugees and their children in Pennsylvania (Leary 1987: 58).

FINNISH

Finns settled in northern Wisconsin from the late nineteenth through the early twentieth centuries, establishing small farms on logged-off acres and toiling in the mines, mills, and ports along the shores of Lake Superior in Iron, Ashland, Bayfield, and Douglas Counties. With their counterparts in adjacent areas of Michigan and Minnesota, Wisconsin's Finns created cooperatives, built workers' and temperance halls, sustained Old World songs and tunes, and formed bands and choirs.

34 Tula tullallaa, posket pullalla / Cheeks Full of Pulla

Sung by Jalmar Nukala and played on piano by Mamie Wirtanen Nukala, Superior, Wisconsin, September 3, 1940. Recorded by Helene Stratman-Thomas and Robert Draves. Transcription and translation by Tom DuBois, 2009.

4185 A1

Tula tullallaa	Tula tullallaa
Posket pullalla	Cheeks full of pulla
Ja on sillä pojan kullalla	And that's what that boy's darling has
Tralalallalaa, tralalallalaa,	Tralalallalaa, Tralalallalaa,
Ja on sillä pojan kullalla.	And that's what that boy's darling has.
Tule ovesta,	Come from the doorway
Älä nurkista	Not from the corner
Ja älä sinä nurkista kurkista	And don't peer at me from the corner.
Tralalallalaa, tralalallalaa,	Tralalallalaa, tralalallalaa,
Ja älä sinä nurkista kurkista	And don't peer at me from the corner.
Tule illalla,	Come in the evening
Olet tallella	You're nice and safe
Saat maata mun käsivarrella.	You can lie down [i.e., rest your head] on my arm.
Tralalallalaa, tralalallalaa,	Tralalallalaa, tralalallalaa,
Saat maata mun käsivarrella.	You can lie down on my arm.

Gust Jalmar Nukala (1899–1971) was born and raised in Ishpeming, Michigan, the child of Finnish immigrants Gust Nukala (b. 1862) and Sanna Koski (b. 1878). We know little about his early life beyond his registration for the World War I draft in

Clatsop County, Oregon, where Astoria's Finns supported socialist cooperatives and a substantial hall featuring plays, dances, and concerts. In 1926 Nukala was a produce buyer for the People's Co-operative Society in Superior, Wisconsin, before becoming the manager in 1928 (Anonymous 1940). He married a fellow Finnish American, Mamie Wirtanen (1903–1983), about that time. The Nukalas were active performers in the Duluth and Superior Finnish workers' combined chorus, with Jalmar contributing solos and acting in plays (Anonymous 1940, 1949; Wastasjerna 1957; Niemela 1996). Jalmar occasionally ventured east to Michigan, where in 1933 he is mentioned as part of "a group of entertainers from Superior" who sang in Finnish and English at Ironwood's Walo Hall. Nukala sang "Saarejarvin lissa" as a solo, teamed with the erstwhile comic singer Frank Meriuso for "Oh Susanna," and also joined Meriuso, George Lee, and Bill Hill in a pair of quartet selections: "Nause laulu" and "Kumous laulu" (*Ironwood Daily Globe*, January 31, 1933). In their later years, the Nukalas ventured to Florida's Finnish American stronghold in the Lake Worth–Lantana area, where Jalmar sometimes sang for programs at the community hall with music "furnished by the Lundstedt and Orqvist orchestra" (*Palm Beach Post*, April 20, 1962).

Unlike Sidney Robertson and Alan Lomax, each of whom recorded a wide range of Finnish performers in Minnesota and Michigan, Helene Stratman-Thomas devoted but one recording session in Superior to Wisconsin's Finns. In her field notes for September 3, 1940, she wrote: "We found some of the loveliest of folk melodies in the Finnish songs which we recorded in Superior. These were sung by Mrs. Martha Leppanenn Hayes and Jalmar Nukala. Mr. Nukala included 'Tuoll'on mun kultani,' a beautiful love song which says, 'My heart will break if my sweetheart does not soon return.' The melody was familiar to me for it has been used by F. Melius Christiansen as the theme of his sacred choral work, 'Lost in the Night.'"

Nukala's booming voice, trilling elocution, and dramatic, assured delivery testify to his familiarity with the stage; and perhaps his performance was influenced by the Finnish opera singer Toivo Louko (1884–1944), who recorded "Tula tullallaa" in 1929 (Odeon 228070). Addressed to a small boy chomping *pulla*, the quintessential Finnish sweet bread, the song is an old traditional lullaby that a parent might sing in a far less theatrical fashion.

SWEDISH

In the post–Civil War era, rural Swedes flocked to Minneapolis and to the nearby Minnesota-Wisconsin borderland, where they dominated both sides of the St. Croix River valley, farming, logging, and contributing to the region's persistent Swedish identity. In the 1940s, Swedes constituted more than 75 percent of the "foreign born" in northwestern Wisconsin's Burnett and Polk Counties (Holmes 1944: 240–241). Using the stage name Olle i Skratthult (Ole from Laughtersville), the immigrant Swedish vaudevillian Hjalmar Peterson (1886–1960) regularly toured the St. Croix River valley with his troupe of actors, singers, and musicians from 1910 through the early 1930s. He was especially popular in the Grantsburg area, where his brother, David, had a photography business (Kanne 1994: 140). And in the 1940s the celebrated Swedish novelist Vilhelm Moberg (1898–1973) spent an extended time in the region preparatory to publishing *The Emigrants* quartet of novels from 1949 to 1959.

35 Flickan på Bellmansro / The Girl at Bellmansro

Sung by Abel Jotblad, Grantsburg, Wisconsin, August 11, 1946.
Recorded by Helene Stratman-Thomas and Aubrey Snyder.
Transcription and translation by Paul F. Anderson, 2009.

8405 B1

På Djurgårdsslätten, en sommarkväll	One summer evening I chanced to meet
Ja' mötte honom, han va' så snäll.	In Djurgård's meadow a boy so sweet.
Ty mitt på slätten han knöt min sko,	He kindly offered to tie my shoe,
Å vi fick sällskap till Bellmansro.	And then we walked along to Bellmansro.
Där uti gräset vi slog oss ned	Out on the grass there we sat us down
Allt intill roten utav ett träd,	Beneath a tree with a leafy crown,
På samma ställe där Bellman stod	The very same spot where long ago
När han sjöng visor på Bellmansro.	The poet Bellman sang at Bellmansro.

Abel Ninian Jotblad (1896–1954) lived his life in the Burnett County town of West Marshland, east of Grantsburg. His parents, Anders Jotblad and Mathilda Anderson, were among the area's many Swedish immigrants. In 1946 Jotblad, his wife, Mildred, and the youngest of their six children were farming. Two years later this poignant

> Abel Jotblad *(left)* and unknown man, possibly Orrin Olson, Grantsburg, Wisconsin, 1946. (Wisconsin Historical Society, WHi-25299)

advertisement was published in regional newspapers: "WISCONSIN FARM 123 under cult. 9 rm house Water in barn and room for 30 cows Silo large good granary mach. sheds Ill Health Must Sell $6700 ABEL JOTBLAD Rte. 4 Grantsburg, Wis." (*Moulton [Iowa] Weekly Tribune*, August 19, 1948; *Elma [Iowa] New Era*, September 9, 1948).

Jotblad's recording was serendipitous. Helene Stratman-Thomas had traveled to Grantsburg expecting to record a Swedish singer recommended by the immigrant doctor Charles O. Lindberg. When sudden illness prevented that fellow from recording, she prevailed on Lindberg to contact other singers and to spread the word about an open recording session at the Eat and Sleep Inn.

> The recording was a novelty to all who stopped at the inn. One man was particularly interested. He said repeatedly, "I wish I knew the name of the man I heard singing in the tavern a few weeks ago. He had one of the sweetest voices I ever heard and he sang song after song." Finally, towards the middle of the afternoon, one of the patrons was able to identify the singer as someone he had known for years. He said the man was Abel Jotblad, who lived about twenty-five miles from Grantsburg on a farm near Webster. He too was enthusiastic about his friend's voice and decided that he would drive up to Webster and try to persuade Mr. Jotblad to come back with him and sing.
>
> Mr. Jotblad, of course, was taken by surprise and he wasn't sure whether he wanted to make recordings or not, but, as he said, he reasoned with himself, "Well, I sing all the time whether anybody wants me to or not. Now somebody really wants me to sing, so I guess I better do it!" Mr. Jotblad was a second generation Swede who had learned songs from his parents. In an unusually lovely tenor voice, he filled several records with "I sommar kyabl" [*sic*; "en sommarkväll"] (one summer evening), "En visa vil jag sjunga" (A song I will sing), "Jänta å ja" (The girl and I), and other songs.

Perhaps Jotblad acquired "Flickan på Bellmansro" from his parents, but he may also have learned it from Olle i Skratthult. The song was composed by Kalle Nämdeman, the stage name of Karl Gustafsson (1883–1945), a Swedish performer from the *bondkomiker*, or rural comedian, tradition that begat Olle i Skratthult. In 1926 Skratthult recorded "Flickan på Bellmansro" for Victor's Swedish series (Victor 79278). Incorporating the

< Olle i Skratthult (Hjalmer Peterson) takes a break from a performance at the first *Svensk Hyllningsfest*, a biennial tribute to Swedish immigrants, Lindsborg, Kansas, 1941. (courtesy of McPherson County Old Mill Museum and Archives)

song into his Upper Midwestern shows, he also published it in several songbooks, including *Most Popular Songs and Radio Hits* (H. Peterson ca. 1930: 29). Jotblad's lyrics exactly match the first two of the seven verses in Skratthult's songster. Perhaps they were all he knew?

Set in Djurgård, an island park in Stockholm that included the popular restaurant Bellmansro, the song also invokes Carl Michael Bellman (1740–1795), a Swedish poet, songwriter, and performer celebrated for drinking songs suffused with humor, satire, and romance. Jotblad's truncated rendition signals romance, while the unsung verses spin a comic tale of deception.

Beyond five Swedish songs, Jotblad sang two in English (Lull 2013). "Now Folks, I'll Sing You a Funny Little Song" and "That Silver-Haired Daddy of Mine" testify to the influence of Chicago's WLS *National Barn Dance* in the culturally diverse Upper Midwestern hinterlands. The former was recorded as "Bib-a-lollie-boo" by the hillbilly banjoist and comedian Chubby Parker in 1927, two years after he had joined *Barn Dance*. In 1932 the latter was the first million-selling hit for cowboy crooner Gene Autry before he left Chicago for Hollywood.

36 Luffarevisa / Hobo Song

Sung by Charles O. Lindberg, Grantsburg, Wisconsin, August 11, 1946.
Recorded by Helene Stratman-Thomas and Aubrey Snyder.
Transcription, translation, and annotation by Susan Brantly, 2010.

8403 A2

Att gå ut på luffan,[1] det är så roligt	To be a hobo, it is such fun
Ja allra helst när det är varmt och soligt	Especially when it is warm and sunny.
En dag så log jag där i solen varm	One day I lay in the sun so warm
Jag drömde att jag log på flickans arm.	I dreamed that I lay in my girl's arms
För Julia vi gå, att glada nöjen få[2]	For Julia we wander, to enjoy ourselves a lot
För Julia sjung hoppfalarej	For Julia we sing "hoppfalarej"
För Julia vi gå[3]	For Julia we wander.

1. *Att gå ut på luffan* means "to be a hobo" or, literally, "to go out on the tramp."
2. *Att glada nöjen få* literally means "to receive happy pleasures," or in English, "to enjoy ourselves a lot"; *gå* means simply "go," but specifically "walk."
3. Perhaps the second verse offers a motive for becoming a hobo, and that is echoed by the use of *gå*. In other words, "För Julia vi gå (ut på luffan)" (For Julia we go [out on the tramp]).

Dr. Charles O. Lindberg (*left*) and Alf Olson, Grantsburg, Wisconsin, 1946. (Wisconsin Historical Society, WHi-25300)

Charles O. Lindberg (1891–1963) was born and raised in Gävle, Sweden, in the province of Norrland on the Gulf of Bothnia. A medical student in Sweden, he enrolled at the University of Oklahoma in 1920 to finish his degree (D. Montgomery 1921: 12). Sometime in the 1920s, the young doctor found his way to Grantsburg. Lindberg was featured in a chapter of *Old World Wisconsin: Around Europe in the Badger State*, by Madison-based journalist Fred Holmes, that illuminated Swedish life in the Grantsburg area. Holmes was particularly struck by a visit to Lindberg's home: "The doctor took me into his back yard to show me a rock garden in the construction of which he had spent years. It is a microcosm of the [Gävle] community in Sweden where he was born and confirmed and where he grew to manhood. The Swedish countryside for five miles around has been landscaped to exact scale—the birthplace, church, blacksmith shop, railroad tunnel, and all the unusual features in the terrain. 'When I grow tired I come out here,' observed the doctor. . . . 'It makes me feel young to vision familiar scenes where many of my people and friends still dwell'" (Holmes 1944: 246).

Stratman-Thomas was familiar with Holmes's account, and her field notes for August 10–11, 1946, reveal that she contacted Lindberg in advance.

> Our next stop was Grantsburg, where Dr. Charles O. Lindberg had offered to help us locate Swedish singers. . . . When we introduced ourselves to Dr. Lindberg, he greeted us sorrowfully because the elderly man whose songs Dr. Lindberg hoped to have recorded had suffered a stroke a few days earlier. Dr. Lindberg was so disappointed that at first it seemed he couldn't think of another Swedish singer in Grantsburg. During the course of our conversation it became evident that Dr. Lindberg himself was a singer. After some persuading, he consented to make some recordings. This was about midnight so we asked what time in the morning he wished us to come to his home. He replied that we'd better go over to the house and start recording right then because in the morning there would probably be another baby coming and he wouldn't be available.
>
> Several of the friends at the inn came with us to Dr. Lindberg's home where we recorded until two in the morning. About ten o'clock next morning Dr. Lindberg called and took us to the hospital to meet the old man who could no longer sing his Swedish songs. We returned to Dr. Lindberg's home to see his unique rock garden, which is a miniature replica of a Swedish village with its quaint houses, white church, and mill.

Perhaps Lindberg knew that Joe Hill—the Swedish immigrant songwriter for the Industrial Workers of the World who was framed then murdered by a firing squad in Utah in 1915—was also born in Gävle, in 1879. An itinerant worker and frequent hobo, Hill would have appreciated Lindberg's "Hobo Song." The source of the first verse is elusive, but the second is a slight alteration of a well-known Swedish folksong, "Kom Julia vi gå," which is still sung in Gävle both at midsummer while dancing around a garlanded pole and at Christmas while encircling a decorated tree (Karlsson 2010).

37 Julen är inne / Christmas Is Here

Sung by Ruth Johnson Olson and Alice Johnson Carlson, Grantsburg, Wisconsin, August 11, 1946. Recorded by Helene Stratman-Thomas and Aubrey Snyder. Translations of verses 1 and 2 by Alice Carlson, 1947; translation of verse 3 by Paul F. Anderson, 2010.

8402 B2

Julen är inne,	Christmas is here,
Fröjdas, vart sinne,	Bringing us cheer,
Frälsaren kommen är.	For Christ has come.
Se, huru ljusen	See how the lights
Brinna i husen,	Burn within the homes,
Prisande vännen kär.	Praising our friend so dear.
Gamla och unga,	Old and young,
Låtom oss sjunga:	Let us sing:
Ära ske Jehova!	Glory be to God!
Ljude de orden	Sound forth the words
Vitt över jorden,	Over all the earth,
Amen, halleluja!	Amen, hallelujah!
Driv ur mitt hjärta	Drive from my heart
Oro och smärta,	Unrest and pain,
Jesus, ack, bliv hos mig!	Jesus, oh, stay with me!
Världen må fara,	The world may go away,
Din vill jag vara	Yours will I be
Nu och evinnerlig.	Now and for eternity.

The sisters Alice Johnson Carlson (1906–1992) and Ruth Johnson Olson (1907–1999) grew up in an extended family near Falun, a hamlet east of Grantsburg named for the capital of Dalarna in rural central Sweden. Their parents, Carl E. and Charlotta Johnson,

were born in Wisconsin and Sweden, respectively, while their paternal grandparents, Carl M. and Brita L. Johnson, had emigrated from Sweden in 1869.

"Julen är inne" is the best-known Christmas carol in Swedish America's Covenant Church (Anderson 2010). The Johnson sisters likely attended the Calvary Covenant Church, which was near their Falun home. Yet the sequence of their three verses—corresponding with the first, then fifth, then fourth verse of the published version—and their assured duet performance indicate the song's vibrant circulation in oral tradition. "Julen är inne" was composed by Nils Frykman (1842–1911), a native of Värmland. A schoolteacher caught up in the "free church" revival of 1875, Frykman was inspired to compose hymns and serve as a lay preacher. At odds with the Lutheran state church, he was welcomed in 1888 as a Covenant Church pastor, serving briefly in Chicago and then in Minnesota for the rest of his career. In 1906 he compiled the Covenant Church's first hymnal, which was published in 1908, three years before his death in Minneapolis where, like fellow Värmlander Olle i Skratthult, he is buried in Lakewood Cemetery (Anderson 2010; Erickson 1976).

DANISH

The oldest Danish Lutheran church in North America was founded in Racine in 1851. A port and an industrial center in southeastern Wisconsin, Racine attracted Danes, especially in the late nineteenth century, when jobs were plentiful with such companies as J. I. Case, the heavy equipment manufacturer, and S. C. Johnson, producer of chemical and cleaning products. By the early twentieth century, Racine's citizens asserted that their city was "the most Danish" in America. Danish farmers also settled in northwestern Wisconsin, notably alongside Swedes in the Polk County hamlet of West Denmark, where followers of the influential Lutheran bishop N. F. S. Grundtvig (1783–1872) established a short-lived folk school in 1884. Known as "happy" Danes, as opposed to pietistic "gloomy" Danes, Grundtvigian Lutherans valued rural life as expressed through Danish folk cultural traditions. Mindful of "the tradition of Danish folk schools," the West Denmark Lutheran Church held its thirty-sixth annual Family Camp in summer 2013, featuring Danish foodways, handwork, and folk dancing and singing.

< Ruth Olson and Alice Carlson, Grantsburg, Wisconsin, 1946. (Wisconsin Historical Society, WHi-25303)

38 Fra fjerne lande kom hun dronning Dagmar /
From Far Lands Came Queen Dagmar

Sung by Kamma Grumstrup, West Denmark, Wisconsin, August 10,
1946. Recorded by Helene Stratman-Thomas and Aubrey Snyder.
Danish lyrics provided by Kamma Grumstrup, 1947; translation by
William Banks, 2010.

8399 B1

Fra fjerne lande kom hun dronning Dagmar.
Hun var så ung, så favr og fin,
Talte med hver Mand mildt,
Med Ridder og med bonde,
Med ringesta Gangerpilt.

From far lands came Queen Dagmar.
She was so young, so fair and fine,
She spoke with every man gently,
With knight and with peasant,
With the humblest page.

Fra fjerne lande kom hun dronning Dagmar.
Så vandt de op de Silkesejl
Højt i den gyldne Rå,
Så fik de Bør så blide
Og lode til Danmark stå.

From far lands came Queen Dagmar.
Then they wound up the silken sail,
High in the golden yardarm,
Then up came a tailwind so mild
And they set course for Denmark.

Fra fjerne lande kom hun dronning Dagmar
Og kongen hende gik igen,
Der hun i land blev sat,
Og Bonden stod på Strande
Og viftede med sin Hat.

From far lands came Queen Dagmar
And the King met her there,
Where she was put ashore,
And the peasant stood on the beach
And waved with his hat.

Fra fjerne lande kom hun dronning Dagmar.

From far lands came Queen Dagmar.

Karen Margrethe Jorgensen Grumstrup (1888–1989) was born in Denmark and died at the age of one hundred in Polk County, Wisconsin. Nicknamed Kamma, she was the fourth of Kjerstina and Jens Jorgensen's eight children. The entire family immigrated in the early twentieth century to West Denmark, where Jens Jorgensen served as the Lutheran pastor. As "happy" Danes committed to Grundtvigian Lutheranism, the Jorgensens were not only immersed in the folk-school movement but also in frequent contact with like-minded immigrant communities in the Midwest, including Kimballton, Iowa, which was founded by Danes in 1883. In 1913 Kamma Jorgensen married Aage "Augie" Grumstrup of Kimballton, and the couple had four children, two

> Helene Stratman-Thomas, Kamma Grumstrup, and possibly Berit Sanford, West Denmark, Wisconsin, 1946. (Wisconsin Historical Society, WHi-25302)

of whom also sang for Helene Stratman-Thomas in August 1946: "In the rural community of West Denmark we recorded Danish songs by Mrs. Kamma Grumstrup and her daughters, Alma and Mrs. Esther Utoft. One of Mrs. Grumstrup's songs, 'Fra fjerne lande kom hun dronning Dagmar,' told of the beloved Danish queen who had come from the far land of Bohemia. Again we found that folk art and folk music are often preserved together, as Mrs. Grumstrup graciously showed us her Danish folk needlework."

The daughter of Bohemian royalty, who came to Denmark in 1205 and became the much beloved queen of King Valdemar prior to her death in 1212, Dagmar was the subject of a lengthy late-medieval Danish ballad that circulated for centuries in oral tradition and in print (Olrik 1939: 37–41; Jonsson et al. 1978: 63–64). But the three lyrical verses Grumstrup sang were exactly those composed by the Danish playwright and poet Henrik Hertz (1797–1870). Introduced in the opening act of his 1841 play, *Svanhammen*, "Fra fjerne lande kom hun dronning Dagmar," as well as the older folk ballad, were subsequently published in folk-school songbooks in Denmark and Danish America. *Den dansk-amerikanske Höjskolesangbog* (The Danish-American High School Songbook), for example, includes a twelve-verse rendition of "Dronning Dagmar," preceded by Hertz's shorter poem (Knudsen et al. 1907: 494–496). In her field notes, Stratman-Thomas mentions Grumstrup's reliance on *Fællesdansk Folketone* (Common Danish Folk Songs), a songbook "used in the local Danish folk school." No such songbook turns up in libraries, however, and in a September 5, 1947, letter to Stratman-Thomas, Grumstrup's daughter Esther attributes this particular song to Frederik Lange Grundtvig's *Sangbog for det danske Folk I Amerika* (Songbook for the Danish Folk in America), first published in 1888 and then in many subsequent editions.

NORWEGIAN

Wisconsin was the primary destination for Norwegian immigrants from the late 1830s through the early 1860s, with settlers establishing farms and dominating small towns throughout southern and western Wisconsin, especially in Dane and Vernon Counties. A second wave of Norwegian "newcomers" flocked to these communities in the late nineteenth century, as well as to northwestern Wisconsin's St. Croix and Chippewa River valleys, where woods work and cutover farms beckoned. Their rich vocal and instrumental traditions not only evolved in Wisconsin but often influenced their ethnically diverse neighbors.

39 Fannitullen / Devil on the Wine Keg

Played on Hardanger fiddle by Otto
Rindlisbacher, Rice Lake, Wisconsin, August
15, 1941. Recorded by Helene Stratman-
Thomas and Robert Draves.

5016 A1

Otto Rindlisbacher with Hardanger
fiddle, Rice Lake, Wisconsin, early
1970s. (author's collection, courtesy
of the *Rice Lake Chronotype*)

Born into a musical Swiss immigrant family but
raised alongside Ojibwes, Czechs, French Canadians,
Germans, Irish, and especially Norwegians, Otto
Rindlisbacher absorbed an astonishing range of
musical styles on fiddle and accordion from performers who included Thorstein Skarning. Hailing
from Drammen, Norway, Skarning (1888–1939)
was a virtuoso on the chromatic button accordion
who, having recorded and toured in Europe, sought his fortune in America's Upper
Midwest. Arriving in summer 1909 in Rice Lake, where he had relatives, Skarning lived
subsequently in Chicago and Minneapolis, recorded for Victor and Columbia in 1918,
and played for concerts and dances throughout Norwegian communities in Wisconsin,
Minnesota, North Dakota, and Iowa until his death. In 1973 Rindlisbacher told inter-
viewers for the Barron County Historical Society that he had performed for a decade "all
over the U.S." with Thorstein Skarning (Rindlisbacher 1973). *The Rice Lake Chronotype*'s
edition of September 3, 1924, announces "SKARNING COMING with Larger
Company and Better Program than Ever Before," including "THE RINDLISBACHERS
Famous Swiss-Italian Alp Players." About that time, while a farm boy one hundred miles
to the south near Mondovi, Wisconsin, the noted Norwegian American fiddler Leonard
Finseth (1911–1993) recalled that "Otto was dressed up just like a good Norwegian" for
one such program. There was a formal concert in which Skarning dazzled, playing classical pieces by Grieg, but when it came to the subsequent dance, Otto Rindlisbacher "carried the load" (Finseth 1988). Rindlisbacher's musical world also included the Helland
Brothers, Knut (c. 1880–1920) and Gunnar (1889–1976), Norwegian immigrants from
Bø, Telemark. Third-generation Hardanger-fiddle makers, the brothers lived in nearby
Cameron, where they not only had a workshop but also hosted the annual *kappleik*, or
contest, of the region's Hardanger Violin Association in 1913.

The walls of Rindlisbacher's Buckhorn tavern, which Stratman-Thomas visited on August 15, 1941, were festooned with musical instruments, including a Hardanger fiddle of his own making: "We drove on to Rice Lake and there we found two versatile musicians, Mr. and Mrs. Otto Rindlisbacher. Mr. Rindlisbacher had an unusual collection of folk instruments, including the Norwegian Hardanger violin and *psalmodikon*. . . . Mr. Rindlisbacher played a number of tunes on the Hardanger violin."

The devil has been traditionally associated with the fiddle and fiddle tunes both in Scandinavia and the Upper Midwest (L. Larson 1975: chap. 4). Otto Rindlisbacher not only cited the renowned Telemark hardanger fiddler Targjei Augundsson (1801–1872)—best known as *Myllarguten* (Miller Boy)—as his source for "Fannitullen" (Devil on the Wine Keg), but also praised Augundsson in a pair of essays, "The Hardanger Violin" and "Miller Boy," that he published in the music educator's magazine, *The Etude*, in 1938 and 1939. Stratman-Thomas's notes offer Rindlisbacher's version of an associated legend: "At the wedding dance the fiddler was so good the guests thought he was possessed by the devil, so they murdered him. They were pretty well drunk but decided to go downstairs and get the rest of the wine. There sat the devil on the keg playing this tune. The broken chord is the devil kicking his heels against the keg." Norwegian folklorist Jørgen Moe (1813–1882) published a famous poem, "Fannitullen," with another version of the legend. Two Hallingdal men were fighting at a wedding, so the fiddler went to the cellar for some beer. The devil sat on the keg playing music that sounded like the devil's word, a steel ax, and a fist hitting the table. The music stopped only when one of the fighters fell dead (Moe 1914).

40 Kom kjyra / Come Cows

Sung by Alice Everson, Blair, Wisconsin, August 16, 1946. Recorded by Helene Stratman-Thomas and Aubrey Snyder. Transcription by Alice Everson, 1947; translation by Anna Rue, 2010.

8414 B2

Kom kjyra, kom kjyra!
Her kommer et dyr aa tar dig.
Aa nei, da. Aa nei, da.
Ho mamma passer nok mig da.

"Come cows, come cows!
An animal is coming to take you."
"Oh no. Oh no.
My mother will surely watch over me."

Alice Everson (1891–1983) was born near Blair, which is in a heavily Norwegian area of rural Trempealeau County that had been settled prior to the Civil War. Her parents, Ebert S. Everson (b. 1858) and Anna Everson (b. 1862), were both children of Norwegian immigrants. Alice was a teacher in the nearby Oak Ridge country school, lived with and cared for her elderly parents, and was especially active with community organizations. From snippets in the *La Crosse Tribune and Leader-Press*, we know that in 1937 she became the secretary for Trempealeau County's twenty 4-H clubs (Thursday, May 27, 1937). Two years later, at the local county fair, she sang in a chorus and served as a reader for the Trempealeau County Homemakers Clubs' concert and pageant—*What the Nations Have Done for Wisconsin and What Wisconsin Is Doing for the Nation*—saluting the contributions of immigrants to her home state (August 15, 1939). And in 1948 one of her students, Jean Onsrud, became "the grand winner of the farm safety essay contest promoted in the Arcadia community by the Arcadia chapter of Future Farmers" (January 26, 1948).

Alice Everson was prompted by newspaper articles to write Helene Stratman-Thomas on June 29, 1946: "I'm just an ordinary person with a very ordinary voice, but I know quite a number of Norwegian folksongs taught me by my parents." In Norway the care of cattle fell to women who spent summers with their livestock in mountain pastures, making cheese, doing handwork, and relying on such calls as "Kom kjyra"—sometimes sung, sometimes played on a birchbark trumpet, or *lur*—to summon and warn the cattle (Plantenga 2004: 100, 102). This tradition persisted in the Upper Midwest: "Before creameries appeared in Trempealeau in the 1890s, women were responsible for the entire process of dairying, from milking the animals to churning the butter and making the cheese, as they had been in Norway" (J. Peterson 1992: 167). Indeed, the average milk cow per farm in the county was only 3.1 in 1880 and 5.6 in 1900, milking was by hand, and Norwegians in hilly western Wisconsin typically sustained the Old World custom of giving cattle endearing names associated with their physical features or human owners (J. Peterson 1992: 170; Haugen 1969: 216–219). Very likely Alice Everson, her mother, and her grandmother all sang this song to their cows. In July 1968, amid a revitalization of Norwegian folk music, Reverend George Ulvilden of Decorah, Iowa, played "Kom kjyra" on the lur for a packed house gathered for the Vesterheim Museum's Norwegian American Folk Music Festival (*That Old Norwegian Song and Dance* 2009).

Alice Everson, Blair, Wisconsin, 1941. (Helene Stratman-Thomas Collection, Mills Music Library, University of Wisconsin–Madison)

41 Her er det land / This Is the Land

Sung and spoken by Britha Lothe; sung by Hannah Haug, Milltown,
Wisconsin, August 10, 1946. Recorded by Helene Stratman-Thomas and
Aubrey Snyder. Transcription and translation by Britha Lothe, 1947.
8397 A2

Lothe and Haug sing the first and third verse, with Lothe reciting the second.

Her er det land som hugar meg best
Og hid hev eg langta lange
Her var det stødt som hugar var fest
Og gjekk i sit gamla gjenge.
Vida hav eg flutt og faret ikring,
Aldrig såg eg slike hyggjelege ting.
Ja mykje hav eg set og meir hev eg frett,
Men her hev eg set det besta.

Her er vel jordi hugleg å sjå
Og yndeleg på alle tider,
Helst når ho heve sumars-ploggi på
Og blømer til dei øvste lider,
Aldrig vild eg bytt i nokon handa skatt,
Denne vår sæle sumarsljose natt
Då jordi ligg i skrud og søv sa ei brud
Og dagen vakar trutt om Landet.

Her hev alt ein vonare lit
Han gjerer meg so godt i hjarta.
Her er da liksom alt hadde vit
Og kunde både læ og graata [garta].
Folket og eg er like som eitt,
All kva dei segjer skynar eg so greiti [greidt]
Og aldrig er det ord på al den vida jord.

Som ganga me so til hjarta.

Here is the most delightful land
And here I have longed for long.
Here it was always wishes came true
And everything old delightful.
Wide have I traveled and seen many things,
Never I saw such delightful things.
Yes much I have tried and much I have seen,
But here I have seen the best.

Here is nature wonderful to see
And beautiful at all occasions,
Most when she has her summer-dresses on
And blooms near the mountains.
Never would I change anything I saw,
Our night lights and the midnight sun
When earth slips in shroud like a bride
And daylight washes over the country.

Here everything has a wonderful color
That gives a delight to my heart.
Here it looks like everything is smart
And could both leap and cry.
People and me are just like one,
All that they say I know so well
And never is there a word in
all the wide earth
That goes so deep to my heart.

[Note: The words in brackets in the prior verse seem to be what is sung despite Lothe setting down other words in her transcription. Lothe sent Stratman-Thomas a fourth verse that was not sung.]

Her kan eg kjenna bygder og bol	Here I know the valleys and hills
Og berg is so ymsa rader,	And mountains in different lines,
Fjøra og fjell og himmel og sol	Shores and mountains and heavens and sun
Er kjendar end andre stader.	I know better than other places.
Saart hev eg sakna heimen ei tid,	Sadly have I missed my home awhile,
Difyr er han no so kjær og so blid.	That's why it's so dear to me now.
Lat koma kva som kan, eg	Let come what may, I'll meet like a man
møter som ein man	
Og aldrig fer eg ut or lande.	And never will I leave my country.

Britha Lothe (1871–1954) was born in Norway and immigrated to Wisconsin in 1896 with her husband, Nels Lothe. Based on her sung and spoken dialect, as well as photographic evidence of her traditional clothing and weavings, Lothe was "likely a Hardanger native" (Steiner 2013: 4). She and her husband joined other Scandinavian newcomers in the St. Croix Valley, operating a small Polk County farm on cutover land where they raised four children. In her mid-seventies in 1946, Lothe was esteemed locally for her handwork skills and sustenance of Old World customs. Her younger neighbor and fellow singer, Hannah Haug (1885–1972), had likewise come from Norway, in 1902.

On June 25, 1946, inspired by a newspaper article regarding the quest for folksongs in Wisconsin, Berit Sanford of Balsam Lake, whose husband Earle managed the Polk County Dairy Cooperative, wrote to Stratman-Thomas championing Lothe as a worthy singer who also "used to help us out at local affairs with spinning, weaving, and carding displays. She and several of her old friends have their original national costumes to wear." Stratman-Thomas soon wrote to Lothe, resulting in an enthusiastic response: "Received your very interesting letter, and will be very glad to assist you in any way I can. I have been living here in Wisconsin for nearly fifty years and worked plenty hard most of the time, but those folk tunes from Norway have brightened my days many a time when we were working hard in clearing land and building a home in this blessed land of opportunity. I have a neighbor lady that is willing to assist me, so we are awaiting further notice from you."

Stratman-Thomas described the visit in her field notes for August 10, 1946: "Mrs. Lothe and her neighbor, Mrs. Hannah Haug, sang 'Her er det Land' . . . and many others. Mrs. Lothe's only regret was that she became so hoarse and couldn't sing more. Her

> Brithe Lothe, wearing her Norwegian *bunad* and holding a *tine* box, poses with Hannah Haug (Lothe's Norwegian weavings are arrayed behind), Milltown, Wisconsin, 1946. (Wisconsin Historical Society, WHi-25409)

fine collection of Norwegian weaving and folk art was a counterpart to her interest in Norwegian folk music. Throughout the afternoon Mrs. Lothe's daughter kept watch over the *rommegrot*, a wonderful Norwegian cream pudding which must cook slowly for hours."

The prevailing songs in Lothe's repertoire were created by participants in nineteenth-century Norway's national-romantic movement and as such circulated in schools and songbooks (Steiner 2013). Two of her songs, "Dei vil altid klaga og kyta" (They Will Always Whine and Complain) and "Her er det land," were composed by the linguist, poet, and playwright Ivar Andreas Aasen (1813–1896). Raised on a small farm along the west coast of Norway in the Sunnmøre district, Aasen was an avid reader appreciative of his home region's cultural traditions. Like his contemporaries Jørgen Engebretsen Moe (1813–1882) and Peter Christian Asbjørnsen (1812–1885)—best known for their celebrated collections of Norwegian folktales—Aasen was inspired by Germany's Grimm Brothers, and in 1843 he published a collection of folksongs in local dialect, followed by a grammar and dictionary of Norwegian dialects. Aasen's best known play, *Ervingen* (The Heir, 1855), a drama concerning conflicts prompting emigration, features "Her et det land, som hugar meg best" as the song of a returned emigrant (Haugen 1937: 199).

Well-known in America, the song was recorded by August Werner for Victor in 1920 (73408), and it was published, along with a rhymed translation, in the first bilingual edition of the *Sons of Norway Songbook* (Hansen and Wick 1948: 134). Lothe, whose English was imperfect, informed Stratman-Thomas that she relied on a bilingual songbook to furnish a translation (September 3, 1947). She must also have been familiar with the play's performance, as Aasen's stage directions required that the second verse be recited, not sung (Steiner 2013). Aasen's "Her er det land" was so familiar to Norwegians that the teacher, playwright, and songwriter Margrethe Aabel Munthe (1860–1931) borrowed its folk tune and verse structure for what has become the traditional Norwegian happy birthday song, "Hurra for deg som fyller år" (Hurray for You for Celebrating Your Birthday).

42 Gamle mor / Old Mother

Sung by Hans Waag, Stevens Point, Wisconsin, August 11, 1941.
Recorded by Helene Stratman-Thomas and Robert Draves. Lyrics and
free translation from Hansen and Wick, *Sons of Norway Song Book*
(1948: 90–91).

8416 A

Du gamle Mor! du sliter arm,
So Sveitten er som Blod,
Men enddå i dit Hjarta varm,
Og du meg gav min sterke Arm
Og dette ville Mod.

Du turka Tårer af mit Kinn
So mang ein Herrens Gong,
Og kyste meg som Guten din
Og bles meg uti Barmen in
Min sigerfulle Song.

Og gamle du, du gav til meg
Mi mjuke Hjarterot,
Og difor må eg elska deg,
Kvar helst eg vankar på min Veg,
Om so på villan Fot.

My dear old mother, poor thou art,
And toilest day and toilest night,
But ever warm remains my heart,
'Twas thou my courage did'st impart.
My arm of sturdy might.

Thou'st wip'd away each childish tear,
When I was sore distrest,
And kiss'd thy little laddie dear,
And taught him songs that banish fear
From ev'ry manly breast.

And more than all thou'st given me,
A humble true and tender heart;
So dear old mother, I'll love thee
Where e'er my foot may wander free,
Till death our lives shall part.

Hans M. Waag (1877–1956) was born in Norway and arrived in the United States in 1902. He attended the Lutheran Normal School at Madison, Minnesota, which had been established in 1892 as a coeducational institution for training parochial school teachers. Waag taught subsequently in the Iola-Scandinavia area of western Waupaca County, Wisconsin, just east of Stevens Point, where Norwegians had settled prior to the Civil War. There he met his wife, Florence Ambroson (1886–1978), a third-generation Norwegian American whose father, Ambrose Gregorson, was born in Waupaca County in 1856. The Waags lived subsequently in Ferryville, on the Mississippi River, before settling in Stevens Point in the late 1930s, and they are buried in the Hitterdahl Lutheran Church cemetery near Iola.

We do not know how Helene Stratman-Thomas happened on Waag, but he was recorded on the same day as the Polish singers Adam and Bernice Bartosz. "Gamle mor" is a *nynorsk*, or dialect, poem composed in 1859 by Aasmund Olavsson Vinje (1818–1870).

Raised in a poor family in Vinje, Telemark, A. O. Vinje was a voracious reader like his fellow dialect poet Ivar Aasen. He eventually became an attorney, travel writer, journalist, and poet. This particular poem was set to music in the 1870s, along with other Vinje poems, by the prominent Norwegian composer Edvard Grieg (1843–1907). A son's meditation on his beloved mother, the song also personifies Norway as humble, steadfast, and maternal.

"Gamle mor" was well known in Norwegian America, thanks to Carsten Woll (1885–1962). Born in Oslo, Woll was an accomplished singer and teacher before immigrating to the Upper Midwest in 1913, where he was a music professor at several institutions, including St. Olaf College in Northfield, Minnesota. Woll made nearly two hundred 78 rpm recordings, including two performances of "Du gamle mor": in Chicago for Columbia (E2491) in 1915 and in New York City for Vocalion (14422) in 1922. In 1926 he included the song in his influential *Sangbog for Sönner af Norge* (Songbook for the Sons of Norway). Hans Waag's flawless verbatim rendering of "Gamle mor" bespeaks his familiarity with published versions, while his melodious emotional performance not only echoes Woll but reminds us that the Nazis had occupied Norway since the previous April. The "singable" English translation offered here is from a bilingual adaptation of Woll's 1926 songbook.

43 Yderst mod norden / Far in the North

Played by the Psalmodikon Quartet (Elsie Thompson, Emily Thompson Flugstad, Nora Thompson Brickson, and Bertha Larson), McFarland, Wisconsin, May 16, 1941. Recorded by Helene Stratman-Thomas and Robert Draves.

4957 B1

Else "Elsie" Vick Thompson, the moving force in the Psalmodikon Quartet, was joined for this recording by her daughters Emily Flugstad and Nora Brickson, along with a niece, Bertha Larson. Thompson was born on a Wisconsin farm near Lake Waubesa in 1864, the first child of Norwegian immigrant parents, Thorbjorn and Bergit Vick. Her father, who was born in 1842 and immigrated in 1862, eventually served as the choir director for the local Norwegian church. In 1882 Else Vick married Stener Thompson (1855–1929), a farmer, overseer for local road construction, and sometime constable. The couple had twelve children. Both Thorbjorn Vick and Stener Thompson hailed from

Psalmodikon Quartet dressed in Norwegian *bunads: (left to right)* Bertha Larson, Nora Brickson, Charlotte Sullivan (replacing her sister, Emily Flugstad), and Elsie Thompson, McFarland, Wisconsin, ca. 1940. (Helene Stratman-Thomas Collection, Mills Music Library, University of Wisconsin–Madison)

Telemark and were accomplished woodworkers. Either or both might have made the family's psalmodikons.

The psalmodikon—*salmodikon* in the Swedish spelling—was adapted from the ancient monochord in 1828 by Johannes Dillner, a Swedish Lutheran pastor in the Stockholm area. The state church had introduced a new hymnal in 1819. Since most rural parishes lacked organs and musical literacy was not widespread, hymn singing declined. Dillner's solution was a simple, inexpensive instrument accompanied by a book of psalm melodies set down in a rudimentary numerical system of musical notation (*sifferskrift*). Dillner's instrument was soon used widely throughout Sweden as well as in Finland and Estonia. Meanwhile Lars Roverud, a Norwegian, modified the instrument and made changes in the notation.

Swedes and Norwegians alike brought psalmodikons to America or made them here. In the twentieth century the psalmodikon, abandoned by church choirs, asserted ethnic heritage through a repertoire that went beyond hymns to include folksongs, classical compositions, and patriotic anthems for a range of Norwegian American events. An exclusively solo instrument no more, it figured in ensembles paralleling the tamburitza orchestras of Croatians and Serbs. As Else Thompson explained in a letter to Stratman-Thomas: "Our group uses four instruments, a different cello string on each, so that we can play four part music" (September 3, 1947). Carl J. B. Felland of Stoughton constructed at least six psalmodikons for his Norwegian neighbors around 1900, while his wife taught local women to play in two- and three-part arrangements. The Harmonium Ladies of Stoughton played publicly in 1929. Nearby Verona included Alma Tenjum and Pearl Lillesand, who played psalmodikon duets, and even in a quartet, for church and school programs in the mid-1940s; and Alma Tenjum continued to give programs into the 1980s (Melloh 1981). Else Thompson's McFarland group was especially active in the 1930s and 1940s as they entertained both Norwegian American and mainstream audiences.

In 1934 the June 4 edition of *The Wisconsin State Journal* reported their presence at a picnic held in DeForest by descendants from Norway's Sogn district. The lineup included: a sermon by Rev. Olin Reigstad; duet singing by the sisters Evelyn and Sylvia Kvalheim; "droll stories" from Ben Bergum; a "humorous reading" by "Mrs. Ben Bergum . . . dressed as a *Sognakjarring*" (an old woman from Sogn); "the Ladies Aid Chorus of Spring Prairie, directed by Mrs. C. G. Naeseth," performing "Se Norges Blomsterdal" and "Det var slik en vakker Solskinnsdag"; and, as "a feature of the program," the McFarland Psalmodikon Quartet, joined by Mrs. Elsie Felland of Stoughton—all garbed "in full Norse costumes of a century ago"—performed Ole Bull's "Saeterjenten's Sondag," "Island," "Aftensolen Smiler," and "Vingede Skarer." The McFarland group played at the Wisconsin State Fair in 1935 and "at the National Folk Festival in Chicago in 1937 and in Washington, DC, in 1940 and 1941" (R. Larson 1991: 36–37; Holmes 1944: 91–92).

"Yderst mod Norden," sometimes spelled "Ytterst mot Norden" but also known as "Island" (Iceland), is a folksong celebrating the Norsemen who settled that island in the ninth century. Like other songs in the Psalmodikon Quartet's repertoire, it was performed without vocals. Yet the Norwegians in their audiences would have recognized this piece, since it and the others they played were favorites from the influential *Sons of Norway* songbooks.

ICELANDIC

Washington Island, situated off the tip of Wisconsin's Door County peninsula as it juts into Lake Michigan, attracted fishermen from the south coast of Iceland in the 1870s. Iceland was ruled by Denmark at the time, and in the late 1860s, "An Icelandic gentleman and the Danish consul in Milwaukee had married sisters. And so it came that the Icelander went to visit his kinsman in Milwaukee. He wrote back to Iceland and this is what he said: 'All the gold in the mountains of California cannot equal the wealth that is to be found in the waters of Lake Michigan.' He meant fish" (Holmes 1944: 220).

Like many letters from the New World, this one was published and read aloud. Its audience included Gudmund Gudmunder: "I was thirty years old, a fisherman and a netmaker, and I had my own fishing boat." Fishing first from Milwaukee's Jones Island, alongside Kashubes, Gudmunder soon found the fishing even better off Washington Island and settled there. His letters to Icelandic friends attracted more immigrants, who soon established a flourishing fishing community (Holmes 1944: 220–221).

44 Ólafur reið með björgum fram / Olafur Rode Beneath the Cliffs

Sung by Sigurline Bjarnarson and Christine Gudmundsen, Washington Island, Wisconsin, August 23, 1940. Recorded by Helene Stratman-Thomas and Robert Draves. Transcription, translation, and annotation by Dick Ringler, February 2010.

4164 B

Ólafur reið með björgum fram	Ólafur rode beneath the cliffs[1]
—villir hann, stillir hann—	—villir hann, stillir hann—[2]
Hann var ekki Kristi kær	He was not dear to Christ[3]
—þar rauður loginn brann—	—where the red fire burned—[4]

Blíðan lagði byrinn undan björgunum,
Blíðan lagði byrinn undan björgunum fram.

Þar kom út ein álfamær
—villir hann, stillir hann—
Hún var ekki Kristi kær
—þar rauður loginn brann—
Blíðan lagði byrinn undan björgunum,
Blíðan lagði byrinn undan björgunum fram.

Þar came[5] út ein önnur
—villir hann, stillir hann—
Hún hélt á silfur í könnu
—þar rauður loginn brann—
Blíðan lagði byrinn undan björgunum,
Blíðan lagði byrinn undan björgunum fram.

Þar came út in þriðja
—villir hann, stillir hann—
Með gullband um sig miðja
—þar rauður loginn brann—
Blíðan lagði byrinn undan björgunum,
Blíðan lagði byrinn undan björgunum fram.

Þar came út in fjórða
—villir hann, stillir hann—
Hún tók svo til orða
—þar rauður loginn brann—
Blíðan lagði byrinn undan björgunum,
Blíðan lagði byrinn undan björgunum fram.

"Velkominn Ólafur liljurós"
—villir hann, stillir hann—
"Gakkt'í björg og bú með oss"
—þar rauður loginn brann—
Blíðan lagði byrinn undan björgunum,
Blíðan lagði byrinn undan björgunum fram.

"Ekki vil ég með álfum búa"
—villir hann, stillir hann—
"Heldur vil ég á Krist minn trúa"
—rauður loginn brann—
Blíðan lagði byrinn undan björgunum.
Blíðan lagði byrinn undan björgunum fram.

The breeze blew gently beneath the cliffs,
The breeze blew gently beneath the cliffs.

There came out an elf maiden
—villir hann, stillir hann—
She was not dear to Christ
—where the red fire burned—
The breeze blew gently beneath the cliffs,
The breeze blew gently beneath the cliffs.

There came out a second one
—villir hann, stillir hann—
She was holding silver in a beaker
—where the red fire burned—
The breeze blew gently beneath the cliffs,
The breeze blew gently beneath the cliffs.

There came out the third one
—villir hann, stillir hann—
With a golden belt around her waist
—where the red fire burned—
The breeze blew gently beneath the cliffs,
The breeze blew gently beneath the cliffs.

There came out the fourth one
—villir hann, stillir hann—
She spoke thus to Ólafur
—where the red fire burned—
The breeze blew gently beneath the cliffs,
The breeze blew gently beneath the cliffs.

"Welcome, Ólafur liljurós,"
—villir hann, stillir hann—
"Come into the cliff and live with us"
—where the red fire burned—
The breeze blew gently beneath the cliffs,
The breeze blew gently beneath the cliffs.

"I do not want to live with elves"
—villir hann, stillir hann—
"I prefer to have faith in my Christ"
—the red fire burned—
The breeze blew gently beneath the cliffs,
The breeze blew gently beneath the cliffs.

---

1. In Iceland the cliffs are widely understood to be the dwelling place of the elves.
2. Although not easily translatable, this ominous refrain means roughly "he is lost (astray), he is still."
3. The performers likely intended to sing "she" rather than "he," since Olafur, as evident in the final verse, is a steadfast Christian.
4. Red fire here may connote hellfire.
5. The singers clearly use the English "came" rather than the Icelandic "kom" in this verse and the two that follow.

Stratman-Thomas's notes reveal only the incomplete names of her Icelandic singers, "Mrs. Karl Bjarnarson and her daughter, Mrs. Christine Gudmundsen (Mrs. H. A. Gudmundsen)." Census records reveal that Mrs. Bjarnarson's given name was Sigurline. Known as Lena to her Wisconsin neighbors, she lived from 1878 to 1961 and was born in Iceland, as was her daughter Christine (1899–1975). Twelve years older than his wife, Karl Bjarnarson (1866–1945) ventured to Washington Island as early as 1890, with the entire family following sometime between Christine's birth and their appearance in the 1910 census. Notably, both women dropped the continuous Icelandic tradition of gendered patronymics that would have given Christine, for example, the surname of Bjarnarsdottir. She married Halldor Gudmundsen—the son of one of the original settlers, Arni Gudmundsen—in 1920 (Holmes 1944: 220).

On August 23, 1940, Stratman-Thomas and her sound engineer, Robert Draves, traveled by ferry to Washington Island. Lacking leads, they called on Ben Johnson at his Washington Hotel. Having lived on the island since 1887, Johnson "was not only a proprietor but also a very fine cook and an excellent guide to the people on Washington Island who knew Icelandic." Johnson directed them to Mrs. Mary Richter, daughter of an early Icelandic settler. As Stratman-Thomas sets down in her field notes: "She decided she could sing better if she could have some more ladies sing with her. Therefore we asked Mrs. Christine Gudmundsen to join us, and she suggested that we all drive on to the home of her mother, Mrs. Karl Bjarnarson. Among the Icelandic songs recorded was the ballad of Olafur, the Christian knight who tried in vain to resist the charms of the pagan elfin maidens, the *hulda* [hidden] folk." Sigurline Bjarnarson led the singing, with Christine chiming in more hesitantly, and the two were eventually joined by their canary.

Intrigued by the song's supernatural elements, Stratman-Thomas soon discovered its relationship to "Clerk Colvill," number 42 in Francis James Child's monumental collection *The English and Scottish Popular Ballads* (1882–1898). Listed as type A63,

"Elveskud"—glossed "Elf maid causes man's sickness and death"—in the standard index *The Types of the Medieval Scandinavian Ballad: A Descriptive Catalogue* (Jonsson et al. 1978: 42), this song has been performed in many versions throughout the Scandinavian countries, including Iceland, where, according to the ballad scholar Vésteinn Ólason, it was "still sung" well into the twentieth century, with "both the text and the melody . . . widely available in printed form" (Ólason 1982: 112). Indeed, the song remains very well known in contemporary Iceland, where it is sung vigorously to accompany a *vikivaki*, or chain dance, during the mid-winter festival, *Þorrablót*. Stratman-Thomas had no inkling of vikivaki and Þorrablót connections; nor did Sidney Robertson who, in May 1938, recorded a version from Icelandic immigrants in San Francisco.

SOURCES

Aim, Robert. 1983. "Ray Calkins." In *History of Rusk County*, by the people of Rusk County, 123. Ladysmith, Wisconsin: Rusk County Historical Society.

Alanen, Arnold A. 2005. Email to James P. Leary, June 29.

Albrecht, Lois Rindlisbacher. 1990. Tape-recorded interview by James P. Leary. Cameron, Wisconsin, January 23.

Anderson, Paul F. 2010. Email to James P. Leary, April 20.

Anonymous. 1940. "Twenty-five Years of Co-operation in Superior, Wisconsin." http://www.genealogia.fi/emi/art/article296e.htm (accessed January 13, 2013).

_____. 1949. *Who's Who of Finnish Extraction in America 1949*. Fitchburg, Massachusetts: Raivaaja Publishing Company.

Asplund, Anneli. 1994. *Balladeja ja arkkiveisuja: Suomalaisia kertomalauluja / Ballads and Broadsides: Finnish Narrative Popular Songs*. Helsinki: Finnish Literature Society.

Averill, Gage. 2011. *Alan Lomax in Haiti: Recordings for the Library of Congress, 1936–1937*. San Francisco: Harte Recordings.

Bachmann-Geiser, Brigitte. 1996. *Traditional Swiss Musical Instruments*. CD and booklet 50-9621. Thun, Switzerland: Claves Records.

Bailey, William Francis. 1914. *History of Eau Claire County, Wisconsin*. Chicago: C. F. Cooper.

Bakk-Hansen, Heidi. 2012. "Scotland's Isle of Lewis Helped Shape Duluth." *Zenith City Online*, June 8. http://zenithcity.com/scotlands-isle-of-lewis-helped-shape-duluth/ (accessed July 10, 2013).

Balys, Jonas. 1977. *Lietuvių Dainos Amerikoje / Lithuanian Folksongs in America*. Silver Spring, Maryland: Lietuvių Tautosakos Leidykla.

Barfuss, Gerald. 1983. *David Stone in Sunset Valley: The Story of the KSTP Barn Dance*. Minneapolis: James D. Thueson.

Barrett, William Alexander. 1890. *English Folk-Songs*. London: Novello, Ewer & Co.

Bartlett, William W. 1929. *History, Tradition, and Adventure in the Chippewa Valley*. Chippewa Falls, Wisconsin: Chippewa Printery.

Bayard, Samuel Preston. 1945. *Hill Country Tunes: Instrumental Folk Music of Southwestern Pennsylvania*. Philadelphia: American Folklore Society.

_____. 1982. *Dance to the Fiddle, March to the Fife: Instrumental Folk Tunes in Pennsylvania*. University Park: Pennsylvania State University Press.

Beck, Earl C. 1942. *Songs of the Michigan Lumberjacks*. Ann Arbor: University of Michigan Press.

_____. 1948. *Lore of the Lumber Camps*. Ann Arbor: University of Michigan Press.

_____. 1960. *Songs of the Michigan Lumberjacks*. LP AAFS L56. Washington, D.C.: Library of Congress.

Bercovici, Konrad. 1925. *On New Shores*. New York: Century Company.

Berry, Chad. 2008. *The Hayloft Gang: The Story of the National Barn Dance*. Urbana: University of Illinois Press.

Bianco, Carla. 1974. *The Two Rosetos*. Bloomington: Indiana University Press.

Bohlman, Philip V. 2002. "World Music at the 'End of History.'" *Ethnomusicology* 46(1): 1–32.

Boyer, Walter E., Albert F. Buffington, and Don Yoder. 1964. *Songs Along the Mahantongo: Pennsylvania Dutch Folksongs*. Hatboro, Pennsylvania: Folklore Associates.

Bracia Worzałłowie [Worzalla Brothers]. 1917. *Lutnia polska: czyli, Śpiewnik, największy ze wszystkich wydanych dotychczas*. Stevens Point, Wisconsin: Worzalla Press.

Braithwaite, Phillip C. 1998. *Yuba: A History of a Wisconsin Czech Community*. Richland Center, Wisconsin: Hynek Printing.

Brantly, Susan. 2014. Email to James P. Leary, January 31.

Brendle, Thomas R., and William S. Troxell. 1949. "Pennsylvania German Songs." In *Pennsylvania Songs and Legends*, 72–77. Philadelphia: University of Pennsylvania Press, 1949.

Brink, Carol Ryrie. 1936. *Caddie Woodlawn*. New York: Macmillan Company.

Burdett, James S. 1884. *Burdett's Dutch Dialect Recitations and Humorous Readings*. New York: Excelsior Publishing House.

Burnett, Richard D. ca. 1913. *Songs Sung by R. D. Burnett, the Blind Man*. Monticello, Kentucky: Self-published.

Cadeau, John, Ed Cadeau Jr., and Rosemary Vizina Jestila. 1991. Tape-recorded interview by James P. Leary. Baraga, Michigan, July 25.

Calkins, Ray. 1988. Tape-recorded interview by James P. Leary. Chetek, Wisconsin, May 25.

Campisi, Jack, and Laurence Hauptman. 1981. "Talking Back: The Oneida Language and Folklore Project." *Proceedings of the American Philosophical Society* 125(6): 441–448.

Cardinal, Charles. 1981. Tape-recorded interview by Judy Woodward for Wisconsin Public Radio, March 3. Blotz Special Collection, Mills Music Library, University of Wisconsin–Madison.

Cassidy, Frederic, and Joan Houston Hall. 1996. *Dictionary of American Regional English*. Vol. 3. Cambridge, Massachusetts: Harvard University Press.

Clark, William Leslie, and Walker D. Wyman. 1973. *Charles Round Low Cloud, Voice of the Winnebago*. River Falls, Wisconsin: University of River Falls Press.

Cohen, Ronald D. 2011. *Alan Lomax, Assistant in Charge: The Library of Congress Letters, 1935–1945*. Jackson: University Press of Mississippi.

Contoski, Josepha K. 1953. *Treasured Polish Songs with English Translations*. Minneapolis, Minnesota: Polanie Publishing Company.

Cooley, Timothy J. 2005. *Making Music in the Polish Tatras: Tourists, Ethnographers, and Mountain Musicians*. Bloomington: Indiana University Press.

————. 2012. Email to James P. Leary, July 3.

Cooper, Zachary. 1977. *Black Settlers in Rural Wisconsin*. Madison: State Historical Society of Wisconsin.

Cotone, Henry, and Mary Cotone. 1974. "Italian History." In *The History of the City of Cumberland*, compiled by Cumberland Women's Club, chap. 8. Cumberland, Wisconsin: Cumberland Advocate.

Cowell, Sidney Robertson. 1956. *Wolf River Songs*. LP record and booklet, P 1001. New York: Folkways Records.

Cray, Ed. 1999. *The Erotic Muse: American Bawdy Songs*. 2nd ed. Urbana: University of Illinois Press.

Crichton, Mrs. David. 1946. Letter to Helene Stratman-Thomas regarding Lillie Greene Richmond, July 15. Stratman-Thomas Papers, Mills Music Library, University of Wisconsin–Madison.

Curtiss-Wedge, Franklin. 1922. *History of Barron County*. H. C. Cooper Jr. & Co.

Czekanowska, Anna. 1990. *Polish Folk Music: Slavonic Heritage—Polish Tradition—Contemporary Trends*. Cambridge: Cambridge University Press.

Davies, Phillips G. 2006. *Welsh in Wisconsin*. Madison: Wisconsin Historical Society Press.

Deane, Tony, and Tony Shaw. 1975. *The Folklore of Cornwall*. Totowa, New Jersey: Rowman and Littlefield.

De Haan, I. 1881. *Klein, klein, kleutertje en anderen: Hollandsche kindereuntjes*. No.1. Haarlem: Emrik & Binger.

Densmore, Frances. 1928. "Music of the Winnebago Indians." In *Explorations and Field-work of the Smithsonian Institution in 1927*, 183–188. Washington, D.C.: Smithsonian Institution.

———. 1929. "Music of the Winnebago and Menominee Indians of Wisconsin." In *Explorations and Field-work of the Smithsonian Institution in 1928*, 189–198. Washington, D.C.: Smithsonian Institution.

———. 1930. "Music of the Winnebago, Chippewa, and Pueblo Indians." In *Explorations and Field-work of the Smithsonian Institution in 1930*, 217–224. Washington, D.C.: Smithsonian Institution.

———. 1940. "Winnebago Music." Unpublished manuscript. Washington, D.C.: Smithsonian Institution.

Dobrzycki, Jerzy. 1983. *Hejnał Krakowski*. Kraków: PWM.

Doerflinger, William Main. 1972. *Songs of the Sailor and Lumberman*. New York: Macmillan Company.

Dorson, Richard M. 1947. "Folk Traditions of the Upper Peninsula." *Michigan History* 31(1): 48–65.

———. 1948. "Dialect Stories of the Upper Peninsula: A New Form of American Folklore." *Journal of American Folklore* 61: 240.

———. (1952) 2008. *Bloodstoppers and Bearwalkers: Folk Traditions of Michigan's Upper Peninsula*, 3rd ed. Madison: University of Wisconsin Press.

———. 1975. *Folktales Told around the World*. Chicago: University of Chicago Press.

Dziewanowska, Ada. 1997. *Polish Folk Dances and Songs: A Step-by-Step Guide*. New York: Hippocrene Books.

Earle, Harry. 1894. "I'd Rather Be a Nigger than a Poor White Man." New York: M. Witmark and Sons.

Ebert, Isabel J. (1940s) 1998. "The Wanigan Song Book." In *Wisconsin Folklore*, ed. James P. Leary, 200–218. Madison: University of Wisconsin Press.

Eckstrom, Fanny Hardy. 1935. "The Twelve Apostles." *Bulletin of the Folk Song Society of the Northeast* 9: 8–9.

Edgar, Marjorie. 1934. "Finnish Charms from Minnesota." *Journal of American Folklore* 47(186): 381–383.

———. 1935. "Finnish Folksongs in Minnesota." *Minnesota History* 16(3): 319–321.

———. 1936. "Finnish Charms and Folksongs in Minnesota." *Minnesota History* 17(4): 406–410.

———. ca. 1940. Untitled manuscript on Duluth's Lewis Society. William C. Edgar and Family Papers, Box 6, Marjorie Edgar manuscripts. St. Paul: Minnesota Historical Society.

———. ca. 1950. "Songs from Metsola." Unpublished manuscript. William C. Edgar and Family Papers, Box 6, Marjorie Edgar manuscripts. St. Paul: Minnesota Historical Society.

Ellis-Fermor, Una. 1939. *The Irish Dramatic Movement*. London: Methuen.

Erickson, J. Irving. 1976. *Twice-Born Hymns*. Chicago: Covenant Press.

Federal Writers Project of the Works Progress Administration of Wisconsin. 1935–1937. Correspondence records of the Wisconsin Folklore project of the WPA Federal Writers Project. Madison: Wisconsin Historical Society Archives.

Filene, Benjamin. 2000. *Romancing the Folk: Public Memory and American Roots Music.* Chapel Hill: University of North Carolina Press.

Finseth, Leonard. 1988. Tape-recorded interview by James P. Leary. Mondovi, Wisconsin, May 23.

Floriani, James V. 2013. Email to James P. Leary, March 25.

Fowke, Edith. 1965. *Traditional Singers and Songs from Ontario.* Hatboro, Pennsylvania: Folklore Associates.

———. 1970. *Lumbering Songs from the Northern Woods.* Austin: University of Texas Press.

Frandy, Tim. 2010. "Lust, Labor, and Lawlessness: The Bad Finn in Finnish American Folksong." *Journal of Finnish Studies* 14(1): 29–45.

Frederick, Dennis. 1998. *O-De-Jit-Wa-Win-Ning, or The Memoirs of Elizabeth T. Baird.* Green Bay: Heritage Hill Foundation.

Fredrickson, Corey. 2013. Emails to James P. Leary, November 7 and 8.

Funmaker, Ken, Sr. 1995. Tape-recorded interview by James P. Leary. Mauston, Wisconsin, March 24.

Gard, Robert E., and L. G. Sorden. 1962. *Wisconsin Lore.* New York: Duell, Sloan, and Pearce.

Geiser, Brigitte. ca. 1970. *Musical Instruments in the Swiss Folk Tradition.* Zurich: Pro Helvetia.

Gifford, Paul. 2007. Email to James P. Leary, August 22.

———. 2010. Email to James P. Leary, August 5.

———. 2011. Email to James P. Leary, February 2.

Goertzen, Chris. 1997. *Fiddling for Norway: Revival and Identity.* Chicago: University of Chicago Press.

Got, Jerzy. 1977. *Stanisław Wyspiański Wesele, tekst I inscenizacja z roku 1901.* Warsaw, Poland: Państwowy Instytut Wydawniczy.

Gray, Judith, and Dorothy Sara Lee. 1985. *The Federal Cylinder Project: A Guide to Field Cylinder Collections in Federal Agencies.* Vol. 2. Washington, D.C.: American Folklife Center, Library of Congress.

Grazulis, Marius K. 2009. *Lithuanians in Michigan.* East Lansing: Michigan State University Press.

Gromada, Thaddeus V. 2012. *Tatra Highlander Folk Culture in Poland and America: Collected Essays from "The Tatra Eagle."* Hasbrouck Heights, New Jersey: Tatra Eagle Press.

Hakala, Joyce. 1997. *Memento of Finland: A Musical Legacy.* St. Paul, Minnesota: Pike Bone Music.

———. 2007. *The Rowan Tree: The Lifework of Marjorie Edgar, Girl Scout Pioneer and Folklorist. With Her Finnish Folk Song Collection, Songs from Metsola.* St. Paul, Minnesota: Pikebone Music.

Hall, Wade. 1996. *Hell Bent for Music: The Life of Pee Wee King.* Lexington: University Press of Kentucky.

Hansen, Carl G. O., and Frederick Wick. 1948. *Sons of Norway Song Book.* Minneapolis: Supreme Lodge of the Sons of Norway.

Harvey, Todd. 2013. *Michigan-I-O: Alan Lomax and the 1938 Library of Congress Folk-Song Expedition.* Atlanta: Dust-to-Digital, in cooperation with the Library of Congress.

Haugen, Einar. 1937. Review of *Norwegian Emigrant Songs and Ballads,* by Theodore Blegen and Martin Ruud. *Minnesota History* 18(2): 198–201.

———. 1969. *The Norwegian Language in the New World.* Bloomington: Indiana University Press.

Hickerson, Joseph C. 1982. "Early Field Recordings of Ethnic Music." In *Ethnic Recordings in America: A Neglected Heritage,* 67–83. Washington, D.C.: United States Government Printing Office.

Hildebrant, Marie. 1915. *Moeder de Gans. Baker- en kinderrijmpjes.* Amsterdam: Van Holkema & Warendorf.

Hoelscher, Stephen D. 2008. *Picturing Indians: Photographic Encounters and Tourist Fantasies in H. H. Bennett's Wisconsin Dells*. Madison: University of Wisconsin Press.

Hofmann, Charles. 1947. "American Indian Music in Wisconsin." *Journal of American Folklore* 60(237): 289–293.

Hokkanen, Laura. 1976. *Pioneers of Green: A Collection of Contributed Historical Data*. Ontonagon, Michigan: Ontonagon Herald.

Holmberg, Leo. 2013. Email to Hilary Virtanen, June.

Holmes, Fred L. 1944. *Old World Wisconsin: Around Europe in the Badger State*. Eau Claire, Wisconsin: E. M. Hale.

Holmquist, June D., Joseph Stipanovich, and Kenneth B. Moss. 1981. "The South Slavs: Bulgarians, Croatians, Montenegrins, Serbs, and Slovenes." In *They Chose Minnesota: A Survey of the State's Ethnic Groups*, edited by June D. Holmquist, 381–404. St. Paul: Minnesota Historical Society Press.

Howe, Elias. 1863. *Musicians Omnibus Complete*. Boston: Elias Howe.

Hugill, Stan. 1961. *Shanties from the Seven Seas: Shipboard Work-Songs and Songs Used as Work-Songs from the Great Days of Sail*. London: Routledge & Kegan Paul.

———. 1977. *Songs of the Sea: The Tales and Tunes of Sailors and Sailing Ships*. Maidenhead, England: McGraw-Hill.

Humphrey, Ron. 2010. "Orben Sime." Personal communication to James P. Leary, August 30.

Ives, Edward D. 1964. *Larry Gorman: The Man Who Made the Songs*. Bloomington: Indiana University Press.

Jääskeläinen, Pasi. 1908. *Lauluja*. Fitchburg, Massachusetts: Raivaajan Kirjpainossa ja Kustannuksella.

Jabbour, Alan., ed. 1971. *American Fiddle Tunes*. LP record and booklet, AFS L62. Washington, D.C.: Archive of Folk Culture, Library of Congress.

Johnson, J. H., Jerry Sheridan, and Ruth Lawrence, eds. 1936. *The Laughter Library*. Indianapolis: Maxwell Droke.

Jones, Hugh P. 1965. Tape-recorded interview by Robert W. Sherman for the Wisconsin Historical Society. Redgranite History Project. Redgranite, Wisconsin, December 8.

Jones, Tom, Michael Schmudlach, Matthew Daniel Mason, Amy Lonetree, and George A. Greendeer. 2011. *People of the Big Voice: Photographs of Ho-Chunk Families by Charles Van Schaick, 1879–1942*. Madison: Wisconsin Historical Society Press.

Jonsson, Bengt R., Svale Solheim, and Eva Danielson, in collaboration with Mortan Nolsøe and W. Edson Richmond, eds. 1978. *The Types of the Medieval Scandinavian Ballad: A Descriptive Catalogue*. Oslo: Universitetsforlaget.

Kania, Edward. 1989. Interviews by James P. Leary. Posen, Michigan, March 29 and August 24.

Kanne, Eunice. 1994. *Were They Really the Good Old Days?* Grantsburg, Wisconsin: Grantsburg Area Historical Society.

Karamanski, Theodore J. 1989. *Deep Woods Frontier: A History of Logging in Northern Michigan*. Detroit: Wayne State University Press.

Karlsson, Owe. 2010. Email (from Gävle, Sweden) to Paul F. Anderson, forwarded James P. Leary, April 20.

Karttunen, Douglas D. 2002. "Green, Michigan, and the Kaukas Connection." *Finnish American Reporter*, February.

———. 2012. Email to James P. Leary, May 24.

————. 2013. Email to James P. Leary, November 6.

Kerst, Catherine Hiebert. 1997. "The Ethnographic Experience: Sidney Robertson Cowell in Northern California." In *California Gold: Northern California Folk Music from the Thirties, American Memory*. Washington, D.C.: Library of Congress. http://memory.loc.gov/ammem/afcchtml/cowhome.html (accessed April 13, 2014).

————. 1998. "Outsinging the Gas Tank: Sidney Robertson and the California Music Project." *Folklife Center News* 20(1): 6–12.

————. 2007. "A 'Government Song Lady' in Pursuit of Folksong: Sidney Robertson's New Deal Field Documentation for the Resettlement Administration." Paper presented at the American Folklore Society meeting, Quebec, Canada, October 8.

Kilar, Jeremy W. 2002. *Germans in Michigan*. East Lansing: Michigan State University Press.

King, Esther Maki. 1991. Letter to James P. Leary. Baraga, Michigan, July.

Kinzie, Juliet. (1866) 1930. *Wau-bun*. Menasha, Wisconsin: George Banta.

Knortz, Karl. 1902. *Streifzüge auf dem Gebiete amerikanischer Volkskunde: Altes und Neues*. Leipzig: E. Wartigs Verlag E. Hoppe.

Knudsen, Thorvald, B. Nordentoft, H. C. Strandskov, and Kristjan Østergaard. 1907. *Den dansk-amerikanske Höjskolesangbog*. Cedar Falls, Iowa: Dansk Boghandels Forlag.

Kolberg, Oskar. (1880) 1961. *Dzieła Wszystkie*. Vol. 13. Poznan, Poland: Polskie Towarzystwo Ludoznawcze.

Kozma, LuAnne Gaykowski. 1991. "E. C. Beck: Collector of Michigan Lumberback Lore." In *1991 Festival of Michigan Folklife*, edited by Ruth D. Fitzgerald and Yvonne R. Lockwood, 30–34. East Lansing: Michigan State University Museum.

Krogsæter, Johan. 1968. *Folk Dancing in Norway*. Oslo: Tanum-Norli.

Kuitunen, Cecilia. 1974. Interview by Adrian Niemi, Ely, Minnesota, November 16. Finnish Folklore and Social Change in the Great Lakes Mining Region Oral History Collection, Finnish American Historical Archive and Museum, Finlandia University.

Kuntz, Andrew. 2012. *The Fiddler's Companion: A Descriptive Index of North American, British Isles and Irish Music for Folk Violin and Other Instruments*. http://www.ibiblio.org/fiddlers/index.html (accessed July 7, 2013).

Kurtti, James. 2007. Email to Hilary Virtanen, August 10.

Landon, Melville D., ed. 1883. "How Sockery Set a Hen." In *Wit and Humor of the Age*, 540–541. Chicago: Star Publishing Company.

Larner, Sam. 1961. *Now Is the Time for Fishing*. TSCD 511. London: Topic Records.

Larson, LeRoy. 1975. "Scandinavian-American Folk Dance Music of the Norwegians in Minnesota." PhD diss., University of Minnesota.

Larson, Ron. 1991. *McFarland's Norwegian Heritage*. McFarland, Wisconsin: McFarland Historical Society.

Laws, G. Malcolm. 1957. *American Balladry from British Broadsides: A Guide for Students and Collectors of Traditional Song*. Philadelphia: American Folklore Society.

————. 1964. *Native American Balladry: A Descriptive Study and a Bibliographical Syllabus*. Philadelphia: American Folklore Society.

Leary, James P. 1987. *The Wisconsin Patchwork: A Commentary on Recordings from the Helene Stratman-Thomas Collection of Wisconsin Folk Music.* Includes bibliography, discography, and 13 half-hour Wisconsin Public Radio programs on cassette. Madison: University of Wisconsin Department of Continuing Education in the Arts.

———. 1988. "The *Legacy of Viola Turpeinen*." *Finnish Americana* 8: 6–11.

———. 1991. *Yodeling in Dairyland: A History of Swiss Music in Wisconsin.* Mount Horeb: Wisconsin Folk Museum.

———. 1992. "Sawdust and Devils: Indian Fiddling in the Western Great Lakes Region." In *Medicine Fiddle,* edited by James P. Leary, 30–35. Bismarck: North Dakota Humanities Council.

———. 1998. *Wisconsin Folklore.* Madison: University of Wisconsin Press.

———. 2001a. "The Discovery of Finnish American Folksong." *Scandinavian Studies* 73(1): 475–492.

———. 2001b. *So Ole Says to Lena: Folk Humor of the Upper Midwest.* Madison: University of Wisconsin Press.

———. 2001c. "Fieldwork Forgotten, or Alan Lomax Goes North." *Midwestern Folklore* 27(2): 5–20.

———. 2006. *Polkabilly: How the Goose Island Ramblers Redefined American Folk Music.* New York: Oxford University Press.

———. 2007. "Woods Men, Shanty Boys, Bawdy Songs, and Folklorists in America's Upper Midwest." *The Folklore Historian* 42: 41–63.

———. 2008. "'The Irish and the Dutch, They Don't Amount to Much': Germans and Irish in Wisconsin's Folk Humor." In *Die deutsche Präsenz in den USA / The German Presence in the USA,* edited by Josef Raab and Jan Wirrer, 331–355. Berlin: Lit Verlag.

———. 2011. "Songcatchers in the Midwest." In *The Ballad Collectors of North America: How Gathering Folksongs Transformed Academic Thought and American Identity,* edited by Scott B. Spencer, 85–103. Lanham, Maryland: Scarecrow Press.

———. 2014. "Czech Polka Music in Wisconsin." In *America's Musical Diversity,* edited by Kip Lornell and Anne Rasmussen. Jackson: University Press of Mississippi.

Leary, James P., and Richard March. 1993. "Farm, Forest, and Factory: Songs of Midwestern Labor." In *Songs about Work: Essays in Occupational Culture for Richard A. Reuss,* edited by Archie Green, 253–286. Bloomington, Indiana: Folklore Institute.

———. 1996. *Down Home Dairyland: A Listener's Guide.* Madison: University of Wisconsin Extension.

Lempereur, Francoise. 1981. *Les Wallons d'Amerique (Wisconsin).* LP recording and booklet, FM 33010. Namur, Belgium: Centre d'Action Culturelle de la Coummunauté d'Expression Française.

Lempereur, Francoise, and Xavier Itasse. 2011. *Les Wallons du Wisconsin / The Walloons in Wisconsin.* Bilingual book and DVD. Malmedy, Belgium: Syndicat d'Initiative de Jambes & Environs.

Linna, Jukka. 2009. Email to Corey Fredrickson, April 19.

Lipson-Walker, Carolyn. 1976. *American Folklore Films and Videotapes: An Index.* Memphis: Center for Southern Folklore.

Lloyd, Timothy. 1997. "Whole Work, Whole Play, Whole People: Folklore and Social Therapeutics in 1920s and 1930s America." *Journal of American Folklore* 110(437): 239–259.

Logsdon, Guy. 1989. *"The Whorehouse Bells Were Ringing" and Other Songs Cowboys Sing.* Urbana: University of Illinois Press.

Lomax, Alan. 1938. Correspondence, field notes. Michigan 1938 section, Alan Lomax Collection. Washington, D.C.: American Folklife Center, Library of Congress.

———. 1939. "Archive of American Folksong: Report of the Assistant in Charge." *Annual Report of the Librarian of Congress, 1939*, 218–225. Washington, D.C.: United States Government Printing Office.

Lomax, John A. 1910. *Cowboy Songs and Other Frontier Ballads*. New York: Sturgis & Walton.

Lomax, John A., and Alan Lomax. 1934. *American Ballads and Folk Songs*. New York: Macmillan.

Lord, Albert. 1960. *The Singer of Tales*. Cambridge, Massachusetts: Harvard University Press.

Lull, Kenny. 2013. "The Swedish Folksongs of Abel Jotblad." Paper for Scandinavian American Folklore, taught by James P. Leary, fall semester, University of Wisconsin–Madison.

Lurie, Nancy Oestreich. 1961. *Mountain Wolf Woman, Sister of Crashing Thunder.* Ann Arbor: University of Michigan Press.

Maas, Josina M. van der. 2007. *Pappa's Papers: Memories of a Dutch Childhood*. Philadelphia: Xlibris Corp.

MacColl, Ewan. 1963. *Fourpence a Day: British Industrial Folk Songs*. LP liner notes, Stinson SLP 79.

MacKenzie, Laura. 2012. Email to James P. Leary, September 9.

Mahoski, Henry, Jr. 2008. Email to Hilary Virtanen, forwarded to James P. Leary, January 28.

Maier, C. F. 1982. "French Canadians of Baraga County since 1870." In *Baraga County Ethnic Pageant Book*, by Aino Hill, 15–21. Baraga, Michigan: Baraga County Historical Society.

March, Richard. 1983. "The Tamburitza Tradition." PhD diss., Indiana University.

———. 2012. Email to James P. Leary, June 14.

———. 2013. *The Tamburitza Tradition in America*. Madison: University of Wisconsin Press.

McIntosh, Waters. 1938. Interviewed by Samuel S. Taylor, Little Rock, Arkansas, for the Federal Writers Project. http://www.gutenberg.org/files/11544/11544-h/11544-h.htm (accessed January 10, 2013).

Meade, Guthrie T., with Dick Spottswood and Douglas S. Meade. 2002. *Country Music Sources: A Biblio-Discography of Commercially Recorded Traditional Music*. Chapel Hill: Southern Folklife Collection, University of North Carolina at Chapel Hill Libraries.

Melloh, Ardith K. 1981. "Grandfather's Songbooks, or the Psalmodikon in America." *Swedish Pioneer Historical Quarterly* 32(4): 265–288.

Mills, Alan. 1960. "Michaud Est Tombé." Side 1, track 6, Folkways FC 7208. *French Folksongs for Children*. New York: Folkways Records.

Miner, Horace. 1939. *St. Denis: A French Canadian Parish*. Chicago: University of Chicago Press.

Moe, Jørgen. 1914. "Fannitullen." In *Samlede Skrifter Hundredaarsudgave*. Oslo: H. Aschehoug & Co.

Moen, Bill, and Doug Davis. 2008. *Badger Bars and Tavern Tales: An Illustrated History of Wisconsin Saloons*. Woodruff, Wisconsin: Guest Cottage.

Montgomery, Dove. 1921. "These Americans' English! Their Grammar!" *University of Oklahoma Magazine* 10(1): 12.

Montgomery, L. M., Wendy Elizabeth Barry, Margaret Anne Doody, and Mary Doody Jones. 1997. *The Annotated Anne of Green Gables*. New York: Oxford University Press.

Mueller, Albert. 1987. Tape-recorded interview by James P. Leary, September 25, Milwaukee, Wisconsin. Wisconsin German Music Project.

Musgrove, Alan. 2011. Emails to James P. Leary, January 28 and February 1.

Newall, William Wells. 1891. "The Carol of the Twelve Numbers." *Journal of American Folklore* 4(14): 215–220.

Newlin, O. A. 1911. "Sockery's Day Off." In *A Bad Case*. Findlay, Ohio: Findlay College Press.

Ní Chonghaile, Deirdre. 2013. "In Search of America: Sidney Robertson Cowell in Ireland in 1955–1956." *Journal of American Folklore* 126(500): 174–200.

Niemela, Juha. 1996. "Dictionary of Finnish American Musicians." Unpublished manuscript.

Niemisto, Paul. 2013. *Cornets and Pickaxes: Finnish Brass on the Iron Range*. Northfield, Minnesota: Ameriikan Poijat.

Nupen, Dagfinn. 1999. *Eldre Folkemusikkinstrument*. Ørsta, Norway: Self-published.

O'Grady, Terence J. 1991. "The Singing Societies of Oneida." *American Music* 9(1): 67–91.

Ólason, Vésteinn. 1982. *The Traditional Ballads of Iceland: Historical Studies*. Reykjavík: Stofnun Árna Magnússonar.

Olrik, Axel. 1939. *A Book of Danish Ballads*. New York: American Scandinavian Foundation.

Opacich, Milan. 2005. *Tamburitza America*. Tucson, Arizona: Black Mountain Publishers.

Owens, William A. 1983. *Tell Me a Story, Sing Me a Song*. Austin: University of Texas Press.

Palos, Dwayne. 2010. Email to Hilary Virtanen, forwarded to James P. Leary, April 20.

Palosaari, Evelyn. 2008. Email to Hilary Virtanen, forwarded to James P. Leary, April 30.

Paton, Sandy. (1977) 1995. *Brave Boys: New England Traditions in Folk Music*. CD and booklet 80239-2. New World Records.

Pawlowska, Harriet. 1983. *Merrily We Sing: 105 Polish Folksongs*. Detroit: Wayne State University Press.

Pelto, Jeanine Bellaire. 1991. Letter to James P. Leary. Baraga, Michigan, September 22.

Peltonen, Eila. 1984. *Minun onneni minttumaa*. Helsinki: Self-published.

Peterson, Hjalmar. ca. 1930. *Most Popular Songs and Radio Hits*. Minneapolis: Self-published.

Peterson, Jane Marie. 1992. *Between Memory and Reality: Family and Community in Rural Wisconsin, 1870–1970*. Madison: University of Wisconsin Press.

Pike, Robert E. 1935. "Folk Songs from Pittsburg, New Hampshire." *Journal of American Folklore* 48(190): 337–351.

Pitkänen, Silja, and Ville-Juhani Sutinen. 2011. *Värssyjä Sieltä ja Täältä: Hiski Salomaan Elämä ja Laulut*. Helsinki: Kustannususakeyhtiü Teos.

Plantenga, Bart. 2004. *Yodel-ay-ee-oooo: The Secret History of Yodeling Around the World*. London: Routledge.

Poppy, C. Harry. 1997. *Crandon Is My Hometown*. Hailey, Idaho: James H. Poppy.

Porter, Grace Cleveland. 1914. *Negro Folk Singing-Games and Folk Games of the Habitants*. London: J. Curwen & Sons.

Posen Centennial Committee. 1970. *Posen Centennial*. Posen, Michigan.

Post, Jennifer C. 2004. *Music in Rural New England Family and Community Life, 1870–1940*. Lebanon: University of New Hampshire Press.

Protheroe, Daniel, ed. 1918. *Cân a Mawl: Llyfr Hymnau A Thonau Methodistiaid Calfinaidd Unol Dalaethau Yr America / Song and Praise: The Hymnal of the Calvinistic Methodist Church of the United States of America*. Chicago: General Assembly of the Calvinistic Methodist Church of the United States of America.

Radin, Paul. 1923. "The Winnebago Tribe." In *Thirty-seventh Annual Report of the United States Bureau of American Ethnology*, 335–550. Washington, D.C.: Smithsonian Institution. Reprint, Lincoln: University of Nebraska Press, 1990.

———. 1926. *Crashing Thunder: The Autobiography of an American Indian*. New York and London: Appleton and Company.

Randolph, Vance. 1980. *Ozark Folksongs*. 4 vols. Columbia: University of Missouri Press.

———. 1992a. *Roll Me in Your Arms*. Vol. 1 of *"Unprintable" Ozark Folksongs and Folklore*, edited by Gershon Legman. Fayetteville: University of Arkansas Press.

———. 1992b. *Blow the Candle Out*. Vol. 2 of *"Unprintable" Ozark Folksongs and Folklore*, edited by Gershon Legman. Fayetteville: University of Arkansas Press.

Reeves, James. 1958. *The Idiom of the People*. New York: Norton Library.

Richards, Henry Brinley. 1873. *The Songs of Wales*. London: Boosey and Company.

Rickaby, Franz. 1926. *Ballads and Songs of the Shanty-Boy*. Cambridge, Massachusetts: Harvard University Press.

Riippa, Timo. 1981. "The Finns and Swede-Finns." In *They Chose Minnesota: A Survey of the State's Ethnic Groups*, edited by June D. Holmquist, 296–322. St. Paul: Minnesota Historical Society Press.

Riley, Jocelyne. 1990. *Mountain Wolf Woman: 1884–1960*. Madison, Wisconsin: Her Own Words Productions. Videocassette.

Rindlisbacher, Otto. 1931. *20 Original Jigs, Reels, and Hornpipes*. Rice Lake: Rice Lake Chronotype.

———. 1938. "The Hardanger Violin." *Etude* 56 (June): 408.

———. 1939. "Miller Boy." *Etude* 57 (November): 747.

———. 1973. Tape-recorded interview by Katharine Leary Antenne and Minda Hugdahl, Rice Lake, Wisconsin. Barron County Historical Society Oral History Project.

Robertson, Sidney. 1936–1938. Correspondence, field notes. Resettlement Administration section, Sidney Robertson Cowell Collection. Washington, D.C.: Music Division, Library of Congress.

Romel, Sylvester. 1989. Interview by James P. Leary. Posen, Michigan, August 24.

Ross, Edward A. 1914. *The Old World in the New: The Significance of Past and Present Immigration to the American People*. New York: Century Company.

Rubinstein, Sarah P. 1981. "The British: English, Scots, Welsh, and British Canadians." In *They Chose Minnesota: A Survey of the State's Ethnic Groups*, edited by June D. Holmquist, 111–128. St. Paul: Minnesota Historical Society Press.

Rudalevičiūtė, Rasa. 2008. "Našliai ir Našlaičiai Lietuvių Liaudies Daionose ir Raudose" (Widows and Orphans in Lithuanian Folksongs and Laments). MA thesis, Vytautas Magnus University, Kaunas, Lithuania.

Saylor, Nicole. 2004. *Folk Music of Wisconsin 1937*. http://csumc.wisc.edu/src/story.htm (accessed April 13, 2014).

Scarborough, Dorothy. 1925. *On the Trail of Negro Folksongs*. Cambridge, Massachusetts: Harvard University Press.

Schafer, William J., and Johannes Riedel. 1973. "Indian Intermezzi." *Journal of American Folklore* 86: 382–387.

Schamschula, Eleanore. 1996. *A Pioneer of American Folklore: Karl Knortz and His Collections*. Moscow: University of Idaho Press.

Sebastian, Oliver. 1987. Interview by James P. Leary and Michael Loukinen. Sault Ste. Marie, Michigan, August.

Sharp, Cecil. 1932. *English Folk Songs from the Southern Appalachians*, edited by Maud Karpeles. London: Oxford University Press.

Shaw, Bradford. 1926. "Scandihoovian Dialect Song / #2101." In *Gordon Manuscripts: American Folk-Song Collection*. Vol. 8, *Letters 1871–2400 (1921–1930)*. Washington, D.C.: American Folklife Center, Library of Congress.

Sickles, Abraham W. 1855. *A Collection of Hymns, in the Oneida Language: For the Use of Native Christians*. Toronto: Wesleyan Missionary Society.

Smith, Christina. 2007. "Crooked as the Road to Branch: Asymmetry in Newfoundland Dance Music." *Newfoundland and Labrador Studies* 22(1): 139–164.

Sommers, Laurie Kay. 1996. *Beaver Island House Party*. East Lansing: Michigan State University Press.

Sorden, L. G. 1969. *Lumberjack Lingo*. Spring Green, Wisconsin: Wisconsin House.

Spaeth, Sigmund. 1927. *Weep Some More, My Lady*. New York: Doubleday, Page & Company.

Spottswood, Richard K. 1990. *Ethnic Music on Records. A Discography of Ethnic Recordings Produced in the United States, 1893–1942*. Vol. 3, *Eastern Europe*. Urbana: University of Illinois Press.

Starr, Mary Agnes. 1981. *Pea Soup and Johnny Cake*. Madison: Red Mountain Publishing House.

Steiner, Sallie. 2013. "Brithe Lothe and Hannah Haug: A Brief Anthology of Two Wisconsin Tradition-Bearers." Paper for Scandinavian American Folklore, taught by James P. Leary, fall semester, University of Wisconsin–Madison.

Stief, Wiegand (Deutsches Volksliedarchiv). 1984. Letter to Judy Woodward, Wisconsin Public Radio, March 3.

Stone, Peter. 2009. "Sidney and Henry Cowell." New York: Association for Cultural Equity. http://www.culturalequity.org/alanlomax/ce_alanlomax_profile_cowells.php (accessed January 3, 2014).

Stratman-Thomas, Helene. 1940–1960. Correspondence, field notes, song and tune notes. Helene Stratman-Thomas Collection. Madison: Mills Music Library, University of Wisconsin.

_____. 1960. *Folk Music from Wisconsin*. LP recording and booklet AFS L55. Washington, D.C.: Library of Congress.

_____. 2001. *Folk Music from Wisconsin*. CD recording and booklet Rounder 1521. Cambridge, Massachusetts: Rounder Records.

Strzelecki, Jacob. 1989. Interview by James P. Leary. Hawks, Michigan, March 30.

Strzelecki, Joseph. 1989. Interview by James P. Leary. Posen, Michigan, March 30.

Stuttgen, Joanne Raetz. 1991. "Kentucky Folksong in Northern Wisconsin: Evolution of the Folksong Tradition in Four Generations of Jacobs Women." *Southern Folklore* 48: 275–289.

Swadesh, Morris, Floyd Lounsbury, and Oscar Archiquette. 1941. *Onayoda'agá Deyelihwahgwáta*. Oneida, Wisconsin: Works Progress Administration.

Sweeney, John, William Kirkpatrick, and John J. Lowe. 1889. *Redemption Songs*. Philadelphia: John J. Hood.

Szwed, John. 2010. *Alan Lomax: The Man Who Recorded the World*. New York: Viking Penguin.

Tahtinen, Priscilla Bellaire. 1991. Letter to James P. Leary. Baraga, Michigan, August 27.

Talley, Thomas Washington. 1922. *Negro Folk Rhymes: Wise and Otherwise with a Study*. New York: J. J. Little & Ives.

Taylor, Bayard. 1852. *At Home and Abroad*. New York: G. P. Putnam.

Taylor, Donna S. 1976. *Leland G. Sorden: An Interview*. Oral History Program, University Archives, University of Wisconsin–Madison.

That Old Norwegian Song and Dance. 2009. Compact disc and booklet accompanying *Vesterheim* 7:2.

Theut, Betty. 2009. Email to Hilary Virtanen, forwarded to James P. Leary, October 2.

Toyras, Helmer. 1981. "Finnish Medley." Field recording by James P. Leary in Aura, Michigan, March. Issued on *Accordions in the Cutover: Field Recordings of Ethnic Music from Lake Superior's South Shore*, 1986. Ashland, Wisconsin: Northland College.

Treat, Asher. 1939. "Kentucky Folksong in Northern Wisconsin." *Journal of American Folklore* 52(203): 1–50.

Uchytil, James. 2013. Conversation with James P. Leary. Rice Lake, Wisconsin, August 3.

Verret, Jules. 1975. *La Famille Verret / The Verret Family*. LP record and booklet. Vol. 1. Philo 2007. North Ferrisburg, Vermont: Philo Records.

Virtanen, Hilary. 2010. "What Official History Forgets Lives on in Song: On a Finnish-American Parody of 'It's a Long Way to Tipperary.'" *Journal of Finnish Studies* 14(1): 46–52.

Virtanen, Leea, and Thomas DuBois. 2000. *Finnish Folklore*. Helsinki and Seattle: Finnish Literature Society in cooperation with University of Washington Press.

Wasastjerna, Hans R. 1957. *History of the Finns in Minnesota*. Translated from the original Finnish by Toivo Rosvall. Duluth: Finnish-American Historical Society.

White, Newman I. 1928. *American Negro Folk Rhymes*. Cambridge, Massachusetts: Harvard University Press.

White Eagle, Winslow. (1958) 1996. "Winnebago Tribal Songs." *The Original American Indian Soundchiefs*. American Indian Soundchiefs CD, SC 117.

Williams, Michael Ann. 2006. *Staging Tradition: John Lair and Sarah Gertrude Knott*. Urbana: University of Illinois Press.

Williams, Vivian, ed. 2008. *The Peter Beemer Manuscript: Dance Music Collected in the Gold Mining Camp of Warren's Diggins, Idaho in the 1860s*. Seattle: Voyager Recordings & Publications.

Williams, William H. A. 1996. *'Twas Only an Irishman's Dream: The Image of Ireland and the Irish in American Popular Song Lyrics, 1800–1920*. Urbana: University of Illinois Press.

Wilson, Joe. 1988. "The National Folk Festival: 1934–1936." In *50th National Folk Festival*, 6–15. Washington, D.C.: National Council for the Traditional Arts.

Winton, Ward. 1976. *Washburn County Historical Collections*. Shell Lake, Wisconsin: Washburn County Historical Society.

Witkowska, Alina. 1968. *Kazimierz Brodzinski*. Warszawa: Panstwowy Instytut Wydawniczy.

Wolford, Leah Jackson. (1917) 1959. *The Play-Party in Indiana*. Indianapolis: Indianapolis Historical Society.

Woll, Carsten. 1926. *Sangbog for Sönner af Norge*. Minneapolis: Sönner af Norge.

Wyspiański, Stanisław. (1901) 1990. *The Wedding* [*Wesele*]. Translated and annotated by Gerard T. Kapolka. Ann Arbor, Michigan: Ardis Publishers.

INDEX OF RECITATIONS, SONGS, AND TUNES

GENERAL INDEX

Brodziński, Kazimierz, 360
Broemer, Anna Store, 205
Broemer, Wesley, 205
Brown, Charles E., 12, 76, 267
Brown, Frank C., 6
Brown, Noble, 281–283, 297–299
Brunet, David, xx
Brunet, Maria, xx
Brusoe, Leizime, 16, 21–25, 88, 224–225
Bulatović, Mitar, 52
Bull, Ole, 94, 394
Bundy, Jack, 91
Bunyan, Paul, 83, 187, 285
Burkhalter, Rudy, 313
Buzzard, Jim, 259–260

Cadeau, Adolphus, 112
Cadeau, Anne, 19
Cadeau, Delima, 111
Cadeau, Ed, Jr., 114, 195
Cadeau, Ed, Sr., 110, 114
Cadeau, Jean Baptiste, 111
Cadeau, John, xx, 18, 110–112, 114, 195
Cadeau, Madeline, 198
Cadeau, Mathilde (Matilda), 112, 198
Calkins, Albert, 83
Calkins, Ray, xvii, 78, 79–80, 83, 87–89, 91, 95–96, 187–188
Calkins, Reuben, 83
Campbell, Booth, 278
Capone, Al, xiv
Capra, Frank, 187
Cardinal, Charles, 228–230
Cardinal, Felix, 229
Carlascio, Angelina, 331
Carley, Sam, 219
Carlson, Alice Johnson, 377–379
Carlson, Ruth Bolo, 205
Carlson, Soley, 205
Carrière, Dolphis, 117
Carrière, Fred, 115–117, 119–121
Carrière, Jean Baptiste, 117
Carrington, Virginia Cloud, xx, 102
Carson, Fiddlin' John, 257
Caruso, Enrico, 335
Casey, Jeanette, xviii
Caw, Tom, xviii
Centala, Boleslaw, 148

Charles, David, 244
Cherney, Mrs., 341
Child, Francis James, 34, 270, 397–398
choirs: Duluth and Superior Finnish Workers Combined Chorus, 369; Dutch Reformed choir, 327; Finnish American Mixed Choir, 69; Ladies Aid Chorus of Spring Prairie, 394; Lithuanian, 364–367; Madison Civic Chorus, 14; Madison Swiss Chorus, 313; male quartet, 341; Monroe Yodel Club, 90; New Glarus Yodelers, 313; Norwegian church choir, 392; Oneida, 221; Trempealeau County Homemakers Club chorus, 385; University of Wisconsin, 14; Welsh, 242, 251–255
Christian, Bessie, 292
Christian, Father William, 221
Christian, John, 287, 291–292
Christiansen, F. Melius, 369
Christofferson, Andrea, xix
churches: Baptist, 242, 247; Catholic, 117, 148, 238, 329, 350, 364–367; Congregationalist, 242; Covenant (Swedish), 379; Dutch Reformed, 320, 325–327; Episcopal, 220–222; Lutheran, 52; Lutheran (Danish), 219, 379–380; Lutheran (Finnish/Suomi Synod), 158, 178–179, 183, 219; Lutheran (Finnish Apostolic Lutheran/Laestadian), 159, 199–202; Lutheran (German), 219, 311; Lutheran (Norwegian), 219, 391–392; Lutheran (Swedish), 219, 379, 393; Methodist, 14, 220–222, 242, 244–245, 251, 256; Methodist (Primitive Methodist), 14; Native American Church, 214, 216; Presbyterian, 14, 41, 242
Ciezczak, John, 350–354
Clark, "Honest" John, 12
Clark, Jenny, 83
Clifford, Billy S., 35

Cloud, Clarence, 102–103, 105
Cloud, George, 102
Cloud, Harriet, 102–103
Cloud, Joe, 12, 101–105
Cole, Nat "King," 158
Connor, Phyllis Crandall, 218
Conroy, Kevin, xxi, 281
Cooley, Tim, xxi, 353–354
Coon, Leland, 12, 16, 287
Cortot, Alfred, 4
Cosby, Matthew, xix
cowboys, 3, 5, 8, 22, 23, 125, 167, 295, 374
Cowell, Henry, 4, 127
Crandall, George, 217–218
Crashing Thunder. See Blowsnake, Jasper
Creedon, Jerry, 285
Crichton, Ida, 280
Crosby, Fanny, 256
Crosshaul, Chris, 76
Crow, Jim, 259–260
Crusell, Bernhard Henrik, 181
Cywinski, Gail, xx

Dacre, Harry, 328
Daley, Joseph M., 97
dance forms: bandit's dance, 350–351; buzzard lope, 260; *bygdedans*, 97; Fish Dance, 218; galop, 163, 343; *gammaldans*, 97; Green Corn Dance, 218; *halling*, 97; Highland fling, 24; hornpipe, 21, 24; Horse Dance, 218–219; jig (step dance), 11, 23, 77, 80, 82, 95, 97, 102, 104, 114, 135, 159, 187–188, 198, 280; *ländler*, 91, 312, 315, 317; march, 47, 91, 148–149, 169, 312, 343–344; mazurka, 149, 162; *oberek*, 149, 154; polka, 97, 149, 152, 158–159, 162, 164, 340–341, 344; polka (hop waltz), 154; quadrille, 24, 25, 137, 239, 299; reel, 23, 24, 44; reinlander, 97–98; ring/circle dance, 161, 167–168; schottische, 24, 82, 97–98, 137, 162, 164, 207; *schuhplattler*, 91; *springar*, 97–98; square dance, 24, 25, 114, 136–137,

ABOUT THE AUTHOR

JAMES P. LEARY is an emeritus professor of folklore and Scandinavian studies and a founder of the Center for the Study of Upper Midwestern Cultures at the University of Wisconsin–Madison.

Born in Rice Lake, Wisconsin, in 1950, Leary grew up fascinated by the dialects, stories, music, and customs of his culturally diverse neighbors, and through part-time work on farms, logging, in a warehouse and a foundry, and as a "printer's devil," he learned to appreciate the school of hard knocks. Leary has done research since the 1970s on the cultural traditions of workers, Native peoples, European Americans, and new immigrants in the Upper Midwest, contributing to numerous folklife festivals, museum exhibits, films, public radio programs, documentary sound recordings, and accessible archival collections.

Besides *Folksongs of Another America*, his other documentary recordings and films include *Accordions in the Cutover; Ach Ya! Traditional German-American Music from Wisconsin* (with Philip Martin); *Midwest Ramblin': The Goose Island Ramblers; Downhome Dairyland* (with Richard March); and *The Art of Ironworking*.

His books include *Wisconsin Folklore; So Ole Says to Lena: Folk Humor of the Upper Midwest; Polkabilly: How the Goose Island Ramblers Redefined American Folk Music* (winner of the Chicago Folklore Prize); *Yodeling in Dairyland: A History of Swiss Music in Wisconsin*; and an updated edition of Richard Dorson's *Bloodstoppers and Bearwalkers: Folk Traditions of Michigan's Upper Peninsula*; and *Pinery Boys: Songs and Songcatching in the Lumberjack Era*, with Franz Rickaby and Gretchen Dykstra.

Leary is a Fellow of the American Folklore Society and a recipient of its Benjamin Botkin Prize for significant achievement in public folklore, its Chicago Folklore Prize for best book in folklore, and its Kenneth Goldstein Award for lifetime academic leadership. In Wisconsin, he has been inducted as a Fellow of the Wisconsin Academy of Sciences, Arts and Letters and received the Governor's Award for Excellence in Public Humanities Scholarship and the Chancellor's Award for Excellence in Teaching at the University of Wisconsin–Madison.

CREDITS

COMPILED AND ANNOTATED BY
James P. Leary

PRODUCED BY
James P. Leary and Steven Lance Ledbetter

PRODUCTION COORDINATION
April G. Ledbetter, Nathan Salsburg, Terry Emmrich,
Sheila Leary, and Adam Mehring

IMAGES
Jerome Bartosz, Maria Aukee Brunet, Corey Fredrickson, Joyce Hakala, Leo
Holmberg, Doug Karttunen, Isabella Leary, James P. Leary, Library of Congress,
McPherson County Old Mill Museum and Historical Archives, April Miller, Mills
Music Library at the University of Wisconsin–Madison, Hilary Virtanen, and
Wisconsin Historical Society

ART DIRECTION AND DESIGN
Debbie Berne Design

AUDIO TRANSFERS
Brad McCoy, Library of Congress

AUDIO RESTORATION AND MASTERING
Michael Graves, Osiris Studio

FILM TRANSFERS
Guha Shankar, Library of Congress

DVD MASTERING
Brandon Duerst, Instructional Communication Systems,
University of Wisconsin–Extension

AUDIO AND VIDEO PRESERVATION AND HOSTING
University of Wisconsin Digital Collections Center